MW00852093

The Editor

MICHAEL NORTH is a professor of English at the University of California, Los Angeles. He is the author of *The Dialect of Modernism: Race, Language, and Twentieth-Century Literature*; *Reading 1922: A Return to the Scene of the Modern*; *Camera Works*; and *Novelty: A History of the New*, as well as other books and articles on various aspects of twentieth-century literature, art, and culture.

NORTON CRITICAL EDITIONS
Modernist & Contemporary Eras

For a complete list of Norton Critical Editions, visit
wwnorton.com/nortoncriticals

A NORTON CRITICAL EDITION

T. S. Eliot
THE WASTE LAND AND OTHER POEMS

AUTHORITATIVE TEXTS
CONTEXTS
CRITICISM

SECOND EDITION

Edited by

MICHAEL NORTH
UNIVERSITY OF CALIFORNIA, LOS ANGELES

W. W. NORTON & COMPANY
Independent Publishers Since 1923

W. W. Norton & Company has been independent since its founding in 1923, when William Warder Norton and Mary D. Herter Norton first published lectures delivered at the People's Institute, the adult education division of New York City's Cooper Union. The firm soon expanded its program beyond the Institute, publishing books by celebrated academics from America and abroad. By midcentury, the two major pillars of Norton's publishing program—trade books and college texts—were firmly established. In the 1950s, the Norton family transferred control of the company to its employees, and today—with a staff of five hundred and hundreds of trade, college, and professional titles published each year—W. W. Norton & Company stands as the largest and oldest publishing house owned wholly by its employees.

Manufacturing by Maple Press
Book design by Antonina Krass
Production manager: Brenda Manzanedo

Library of Congress Cataloging-in-Publication Data

Names: Eliot, T. S. (Thomas Stearns), 1888–1965, author. | North, Michael, 1951– editor.
Title: The waste land and other poems : an authoritative text, contexts, criticism / T. S. Eliot ; edited by Michael North.
Description: Second edition. | New York : W. W. Norton & Company, [2022] | Series: A Norton critical edition | Includes bibliographical references.
Identifiers: LCCN 2021035158 | ISBN 9780393679434 (paperback) | ISBN 9780393887921 (epub)
Subjects: LCSH: Eliot, T. S. (Thomas Stearns), 1888–1965. Waste land.
Classification: LCC PS3509.L43 W3 2022 | DDC 821/.912—dc23
LC record available at https://lccn.loc.gov/2021035158

W. W. Norton & Company, Inc., 500 Fifth Avenue, New York, N.Y. 10110
www.wwnorton.com
W. W. Norton & Company Ltd., 15 Carlisle Street, London W1D 3BS

1 2 3 4 5 6 7 8 9 0

Contents

Contents

Criticism   171

Preface

The publication of a new version of this Norton Critical Edition has made possible a great many corrections, changes, and additions. The most significant change is the inclusion of the poems Eliot published before *The Waste Land*. This edition now includes all the poems in Eliot's first collection, *Prufrock and Other Observations*, issued by Egoist Press in 1917, and all the poems in the American version of his second collection, published as *Poems* by Knopf in 1920, with the exception of four poems originally written in French. These last were omitted on the assumption that they are unlikely to be approached as originally written in any classroom situation. To include a verse translation is well beyond the competence of this editor, and including a prose translation threatens to reduce the poems to their paraphrasable content. With these exceptions, though, this edition contains everything Eliot published within hard covers from "The Love Song of J. Alfred Prufrock" to *The Waste Land*.

Of course, a great deal has changed in the critical landscape since the first edition appeared in 2001. All of Eliot's poems, including many never intended for public consumption, have been published and relentlessly annotated in the grand scholarly variorum edited by Christopher Ricks and Jim McCue. All of Eliot's prose works, including many pieces previously lost to view, have been included in the ongoing, online compendium edited by Ronald Schuchard and several others. Robert Crawford's biography, *Young Eliot: From St. Louis to* The Waste Land, has made available significant new details about Eliot's schooling in St. Louis, Cambridge, and Oxford. New scholarly investigations by Lawrence Rainey have made it possible for the first time to date the *Waste Land* manuscripts with some precision. The letters Eliot sent between 1930 and 1956 to American drama teacher Emily Hale (1891–1969), during the long continuation of their earlier relationship in Boston, were finally made available to the public in 2020. Scholarly opinion on Eliot has shifted so that the once rather outrageous suggestion that Eliot was actually a willing participant in the general culture of his time has now become the preoccupation of Eliot studies. In short, a great deal more is now known about Eliot and his work, and this new information has helped to fuel an increase in what was already a high level of interest.

The accumulated study of the last two decades has made it necessary and possible to reflect on and reconsider the contents of the first edition. Minor corrections and changes have been made to many texts in this volume, and the critical readings have been substantially rearranged and updated. The inclusion of the earlier poems has made it necessary to represent critical opinion about those poems, which has been done with a selection of readings from Virginia Woolf's originally anonymous review, "Is This Poetry?" to some recent essays on "Prufrock" and "Gerontion." In all, there are eight essays, new in this edition, on Eliot's early poetry. Eliot's own criticism, already represented by a selection of classic essays, has been augmented by the inclusion of two early pieces reflecting his theories about contemporary poetry. The critical history of *The Waste Land* has also been updated so that there is now less emphasis on the New Criticism and on academic reactions from the 1970s and 1980s, and this change has made possible an entirely new section of critical work from the twenty-first century.

Unchanged from the first edition is the substantial collection of background material on *The Waste Land*. This includes a set of excerpts from the sources that stand behind many of the allusions and references that make up the poem. The general aim of this section is still that of the first edition, to make available crucial passages from texts such as Jessie L. Weston's *From Ritual to Romance* so as to allow readers to at least sample the works from which Eliot drew and to which he alluded. The inclusion of such material also makes it possible to streamline the editor's notes to the poem, which frequently direct readers to items in the Sources section. Instead of reducing a complex text such as Weston's to an interpretive summary small enough to be squeezed into a footnote, this edition refers readers to excerpts from the work. In part, the aim of this practice is to reduce the amount of editorial intervention usual in editions of this kind by including enough information to allow readers to come to their own conclusions. It is still difficult to do this when it comes to the many sources Eliot drew from in languages other than English. As before, the expedient in these cases has been to use, whenever feasible, translations that would have been available to Eliot's first readers.

Finally, this edition includes a general introduction, not present in the first. One aim of this introduction is to link together the events of Eliot's life up through the publication of *The Waste Land*, which are also available in summary form in the Chronology. Thus the introduction tries to give the reader a biographical context for the poems in this collection. But it also tries to show, in as brief a way as possible, how Eliot's poetic practice grew and developed in these years as he made his way from the hesitant equivocations of "Prufrock" to the stunning innovations of *The Waste Land*.

For their help with the first edition, I would like to thank Erin Templeton and the staffs of the Clark Library at UCLA and the Beinecke Rare Book and Manuscript Library at Yale University.

A Note on the Texts

Since the first edition of this book appeared, a good deal of scholarly work has been done on the texts of Eliot's poems. The fullest representation of this work is the massive two-volume *Poems of T. S. Eliot: Collected and Uncollected Poems*, edited by Christopher Ricks and Jim McCue. It is clear from the very full textual history included in this publication that Eliot's poems have always existed in several different versions, varying by time, place, and publisher. Eliot cared deeply about the texts of his works and often took pains to correct proofs and even to amend printings owned by friends. Unfortunately, he did not always do this consistently, nor were his wishes always observed by his publishers, even when that publisher was Faber and Faber, of which he was a director. Thus many differences remain among the various editions of Eliot's poems, and it is often impossible to determine which variant should have priority. Fortunately, most of those differences are minor matters of punctuation, spelling, or spacing, though even these can, in certain cases, affect the meaning of the poem. From among the many less-than-ideal solutions to this problem, this Norton Critical Edition bases its texts on the earliest version of each poem to appear in a book, with precedence given to the American *Poems* of 1920 over its nearly simultaneous British counterpart, *Ara Vos Prec* (London: Ovid Press, 1920). Thus the texts of this edition are based on *Prufrock and Other Observations* (London: Egoist Press, 1917), *Poems* (New York: Knopf, 1920), and *The Waste Land* (New York: Boni & Liveright, 1922) with the following exceptions.

"The Love Song of J. Alfred Prufrock"

   l. 3: Egoist reads "etherized."

"Rhapsody on a Windy Night"

   l. 7: Egoist ends this line with a comma instead of a period.

   ll. 48–49: Egoist has a space between these lines.

   l. 58: Egoist reads "old Cologne."

   l. 61: Egoist has close quotes at l. 68 instead of here.

   l. 74: Egoist ends this line with a comma instead of a period.

"Mr. Apollinax"

> Epigraph: does not appear in Egoist.
>
> ll. 12–13: Egoist has no space between these lines.

"La Figlia Che Piange"

> Epigraph: does not appear in Egoist.

"Gerontion"

> l. 8: *Poems* reads "jew."
>
> l. 17: *Poems* reads "'We would see a sign':"
>
> l. 60: *Poems* has "it" instead of "them."

"Burbank with a Baedeker: Bleistein with a Cigar"

> l. 23: *Poems* reads "jew."

"Sweeney Erect"

> l. 10: *Poems* has a comma instead of a period.

"A Cooking Egg"

> l. 16: *Poems* has no period after "five per cent."
>
> l. 24: *Poems* ends the line with an ellipsis instead of a period.
>
> l. 33: *Poems* has no period at the end of the line and includes an explanatory note. See this edition, p. 33.

"Whispers of Immortality"

> l. 10: *Poems* ends the line with a colon instead of a comma.
>
> l. 11: *Poems* ends the line with a comma instead of a semicolon.

"Mr. Eliot's Sunday Morning Service"

> Epigraph: *Poems* reads "religions" instead of "religious" and omits the article from the title of the play.
>
> l. 27: *Poems* reads "pistilate."

"Sweeney Among the Nightingales"

> l. 8: *Poems* reads "horned," without the accent.

The Waste Land

> dedication: added by Eliot to editions after 1925.
>
> l. 32: B&L has no comma.

l. 42: B&L reads "Od' und leer das Meer" and omits the space between ll. 41 and 42.

l. 69: B&L has a comma instead of a colon before the quotation.

l. 111: B&L reads "My nerves are bad tonight." It is the only edition to omit the hyphen.

l. 112: B&L reads "Why do you never speak." It is the only one of the four first editions to omit the question mark.

l. 131: B&L reads "'What shall I do now? What shall I do?'" The close quote is clearly a misprint.

ll. 149, 153: B&L omits the apostrophe from "don't" in both lines, though other contractions are formed correctly. Apparently a misprint.

l. 161: B&L reads "The chemist said it would be alright."

l. 259: B&L reads "O City city." The version adopted appears in the *Dial* and Hogarth versions and was inserted by Eliot into proofs of the 1936 *Collected Poems*.

l. 278: B&L omits the space after this line.

l. 291: B&L omits the space after this line.

l. 299: B&L omits the space after this line.

l. 415: B&L reads "aetherial."

l. 428: B&L reads "Quando fiam ceu chelidon."

note to l. 125: B&L misnumbers as 126 and also cites l. 37 instead of l. 39.

note to l. 137: B&L misnumbers as 138.

notes to ll. 196, 197: These are reversed in B&L.

Introduction

Today, after a hundred years of reading and study, the poetry of
T. S. Eliot retains much of its original mystery. Since the first edition of this book appeared, a great deal of new material has been
unearthed and published—letters, articles, lectures—and yet Eliot
is as much of an enigma as he was when his friend the poet Ezra
Pound nicknamed him the Possum. How did the timid, naive St. Louis
boy for whom Boston was the furthest outpost of modern freedom
and recklessness become the author of the most outrageous English-
language poem of the early twentieth century? How did that
avant-garde poet then reveal himself just half a dozen years later as
"classicist in literature, royalist in politics, and anglo-catholic in
religion"?[1] And how are we to take the poems he wrote before that
declaration, which are alternately tender, snide, fretful, presump-
tuous, painfully open, and coldly ironic?

The mystery may begin with the fact that Eliot was something of
a puzzle to himself. In 1915, living in England but teetering on the
edge of returning to the U.S., he wrote to his Harvard friend Con-
rad Aiken, "The great need is to know one's own mind, and I don't
know that."[2] Making decisions seemed only to intensify this chronic
indecision, until it became a state of "*aboulie* and emotional derange-
ment" requiring treatment.[3] There were many reasons for this situ-
ation, but one of the more obvious, especially in the crisis year of
1915, was the tension between the conservative narrowness of his
American upbringing and the cosmopolitan world he discovered as
a student in Europe.

Eliot grew up in St. Louis because his grandfather, William
Greenleaf Eliot, had brought Unitarianism to the wilds of the Middle
West in the 1830s, and the memory of the great man, a revered min-
ister and educator, still presided over the family when Tom was
born in 1888. Eliot later described the atmosphere of his childhood

---

1. T. S. Eliot, "Preface," *For Lancelot Andrewes* (Garden City, NY: Doubleday, Doran, 1929), p. vii.
2. *The Letters of T. S. Eliot, Vol 1: 1898–1922*, ed. Valerie Eliot and Hugh Haughton (New Haven: Yale University Press, 2011), p. 95.
3. Ibid., p. 602.

as one of "Unitarian piety and strict Puritanism,"[4] and it is easy to caricature a family in which the father could have written, as Eliot's did, "I hope that a cure for Syphilis will never be discovered. It is God's punishment for nastiness."[5] No matter how far he moved from his family, Eliot always preserved his own version of this physical and moral fastidiousness. At the same time, he recoiled from the life his background had prepared for him, the life he trained for as an undergraduate and graduate student at Harvard, where he seemed destined to remain as a professor of philosophy.

Part of that training involved study abroad, which Eliot commenced in 1910, when he sailed to France and enrolled as a foreign student at the Sorbonne. For someone who had been studying French symbolist poetry, the Paris Eliot came to in 1910 must have seemed the very source of literary vitality and innovation. Studying French with Henri-Alban Fournier, who was soon to become famous as Alain-Fournier, the author of the now-classic novel *Le Grandes Meaulnes* (1913), Eliot came in contact with a cultural milieu that included avant-garde fiction and poetry, the Ballets Russes, and the first exhibitions of cubism. Modernism was well under way in all the arts when Eliot came to Europe, and if he was attracted to it as a relief from mere conformity, he was also drawn by the different kind of seriousness it represented, one in which art was not a diversion but part of a revolution in sensibility, perception, and even morality. After a brief exposure to this revolution, Eliot returned to the U.S. to pursue his PhD in philosophy, and when he traveled abroad again, in 1914, it was to pursue his studies at Oxford, which seemed a dull and pedantic place to him in comparison to Paris or even London. Thus he began to dread the prospect of an academic life and to fecklessly imagine an alternative.

For Eliot, though, there was no natural route from the past he brought with him to the future he could imagine for himself as an innovative poet. Since these were antithetical and not just different, one required the renunciation of the other. In practical terms, he was faced in 1915 with a decision between going back to the U.S. to complete his degree work in philosophy and staying in England to become a poet, but this strict geographical separation also represented a classic modern dilemma between a purely repetitive past and an unknown future, a situation in which safety and freedom are incompatible alternatives. The only way across a divide like this is to leap, which is what Eliot did in June of that year, when he decided quite suddenly to marry, stay in England, and dedicate himself to

---

4. Unpublished address to the All Soul's Club, June 1, 1960, qtd. in *The Poems of T. S. Eliot*, ed. Christopher Ricks and Jim McCue (New York: Farrar, Straus and Giroux, 2015), 1:535.
5. *Letters*, p. 41.

poetry. What seems a wildly impulsive commitment to a young Englishwoman, Vivien Haigh-Wood, he had known only for a few months, happened to coincide, that same June, with the first publication of "The Love Song of J. Alfred Prufrock." On the slender promise of this single poem, which is, of course, about the terror of commitment, Eliot took the step that utterly changed his life. Later, when the marriage, at least, seemed a mistake, he looked back at his leap into the unknown with fatalistic regret: "The awful daring of a moment's surrender / Which an age of prudence can never retract" (*The Waste Land*, ll. 403–04). And yet this remained for Eliot, through *The Waste Land* at least, the only possible formula for change, the only escape from an ossified past to a daunting future.

Eliot felt a similar gap between the verse that Americans most revered and the modern poetry produced in Europe. For many American readers, and not just for Eliot, the years between 1900 and 1914 seemed "a complete blank" as far as poetry was concerned. The great American poets of the nineteenth century were dead, and one of them, Emily Dickinson, was just starting to be read. By the time Eliot began looking for models, no one new had appeared: "I cannot remember the name of a single poet of that period whose work I read." The situation in England was not much better: "Certainly I cannot remember any English poet then alive who contributed to my own education."[6] Where is the new to come from when the current of history has simply petered out? For Eliot, as for many modernists before and after him, moving forward meant first swerving through another tradition, in his case through the French poetry beginning with Charles Baudelaire. This was the poetry, discovered in what he called "the dead year of 1908," that became for him the source of "all English poetry that matters."[7]

Throughout his career Eliot developed as a poet not by a process of gradual growth but rather in discontinuous stages, shedding the skin of each successive style as he moved on. As he put it himself in 1917, "I feel that the best promise of continuing is to be able to forget, in a way, what one has written already; to be able to detach it completely from one's present self and begin quite afresh, with only the technical experience preserved."[8] Thus the poetry that Eliot wrote between the dead year of 1908 and *The Waste Land* in 1922 falls intro three distinct groups. The first of these, running from "The Love Song of J. Alfred Prufrock," parts of which date to 1909, to "La Figlia Che Piange," written in 1911, is composed of poems

6. T. S. Eliot, "Ezra Pound," *Poetry* 68 (September 1946): 326.
7. T. S. Eliot, Review of Peter Quennell, *Baudelaire and the Symbolists, Criterion* 9 (January 1930): 11–14.
8. *Letters*, p. 211.

Eliot wrote when he had no notion of poetry as a profession. He did not write these poems for publication, and if he had not shared them with one person, Conrad Aiken, himself a poet, they might have disappeared forever and his poetic career along with them. Writing only for his own notebook certainly gave Eliot the necessary leeway to produce poems that were recognized later as utterly unlike anything written before.

Still, it is hard to think of these as inaugural poems, since everything in them is over before it can begin. The epigraph to "Prufrock," taken from Dante's *Inferno*, addresses the reader as if from beyond the grave, and the persona assumed by the twenty-one-year-old poet looks back on his life as something already finished: "I grow old . . . I grow old . . . / I shall wear the bottoms of my trousers rolled" (ll. 119–20). There is a distinct temporal gap between the poems of antediluvian indoor ritual such as "Prufrock" and "Portrait of a Lady" and those in which a modern urban scene imposes itself on an unwilling consciousness. The beer and sawdust of "Preludes" are a rude shock after the "wax candles in the darkened room" of "Portrait of a Lady," and this difference expresses Eliot's sense of this particular time in history and his own life, stalled between a constant dying on one hand and a sordid vitality on the other. Eliot finds his way in this situation by rhyming. The markedly excessive rhyme in these poems marks the poet's mocking distance from the past, a self-ironizing distance, to be sure, but apparently the only one possible. Turning himself into a "dull tom-tom" ("Portrait of a Lady," I.32), Eliot establishes the bases of a new poetry by exaggerating the foibles of the old.

Between 1911 and 1915, Eliot produced nothing that he wanted to preserve. He was in fact convinced that "Prufrock" was what it looked like, a swan song and not the first successful poem of a new career. But he changed his mind in 1914 upon meeting Ezra Pound, who had already established a prominent, if controversial, position for himself as poet and impresario in the London literary world. Pound used his many contacts to produce a series of publications that revived Eliot's confidence and led to a set of new poems. Four of these—"The *Boston Evening Transcript*," "Aunt Helen," "Cousin Nancy," and "Mr. Apollinax"—introduce a new tone, distant and even smug where the earlier poems had been diffident. Eviscerating fictional relatives, trampling the pieties of traditional Boston, mocking the dullness of fictional academics such as Professor Cheetah, Eliot seems intent on announcing a newfound independence from the past. These are very short poems, where "Prufrock" and "Portrait of a Lady" had been long, even languid, and they have a nasty bite where the earlier poems had swooned away with a "dying fall" ("Portrait of a Lady," III.39). They are also remarkably free of rhyme, apart from the rhymes on "street" (which include rhyming it with itself) that Eliot had used so many times they have already come to seem obsessive. Where the earlier poems had been composed privately and were published only by a kind of accident, these were self-consciously set before a public, to whom Eliot apparently wished to appear as an acidulous wit.

Though these poems were published more or less immediately in magazines such as *Poetry*, there followed another short gap in Eliot's poetic output. One reason for this pause was that his marriage had produced instant anxiety and unhappiness. Needing to support a wife who was almost constantly unwell, Eliot threw himself into a series of efforts, from teaching to lecturing, meant to scratch a living from his excellent education. He had also begun to write reviews and articles for scholarly journals and literary magazines, which increased his visibility as a writer and often paid a small sum. By 1917, though, when *Prufrock and Other Observations* appeared, including all the presentable poetry he had written to date, it was clearly necessary to sustain the reputation he and Pound had developed. In the next two years, then, amid almost constant anxiety about his wife's health and his own, Eliot wrote the dozen poems, from "A Cooking Egg" to "Gerontion," that would help fill out his second collection.

By then, Eliot had taken a position at Lloyds Bank that was to give him a fair degree of financial security in return for the better part of his time. His reputation as a writer of critical prose had also made him something of a presence in the literary scene. Through the philosopher Bertrand Russell he met literary lions such as Ottoline Morrell and writers such as Virginia and Leonard Woolf, who were to become his British publishers. The poems written under these circumstances—anxiety and want mixed inconsistently with heady success—took the brittle, disillusioned wit of poems such as "Mr. Apollinax" and threw it into overdrive. These poems, written in regular quatrains, are overtly, even aggressively rhymed, in tune with Eliot's sense, shared with Pound, that free verse had run its course. The sheer sound of these poems thus has a kind of lashing authority, as Eliot hacks his victims into line-sized bits.

Quite new to these poems is a network of allusion so dense as sometimes to become almost opaque. "Burbank with a Baedeker: Bleistein with a Cigar," for example, is a tissue of references centered on Venice. Nowadays, the poem threatens to disappear into its footnotes, but when it was first published it must have read like something between a challenge and an affront. There is also a purposely exclusionary tone to a poem such as "Mr. Eliot's Sunday Morning Service," whose first line consists of the word "polyphilo-progenitive." The wry self-reference in the title may suggest that the whole thing is a joke, but if so it is a particularly sour joke, with more than an edge of hostile anger.

Much of this anger is focused on the fictional Sweeney, who figures in several of these poems as the epitome of cheap thrills and easy virtue. But a helping of vicious wit is also measured out for his opposite, the rootless cosmopolitans that Eliot tagged with what he may have thought were funny names. The gap between past and present thus returns as the contrast between these "epicene" ("Mr. Eliot's Sunday Morning Service," l. 28) aristocrats and hairy slum-dwellers such as Sweeney. This is Eliot's version of the Eloi and the Morlocks, H. G. Wells's expression in his novel *The Time Machine* of the late Victorian fear that society will break down into mutually exclusive cohorts of effeminate aesthetes and brutish workers, as history disintegrates into the opposing tendencies of decadence and atavism. Virginia Woolf once described Eliot as "sardonic, guarded, precise, & slightly malevolent,"[9] but in these poems at least the superficial precision of the ornate diction is always at odds with the crudity of the social anger, especially when it is focused on the Jewish characters, who are made to represent both Eloi and Morlock at once. The casually dismissive way in which Jewish figures are introduced into poems such as "Burbank" and "Gerontion" may seem an instance of a prejudice common at the time, but even early readers such as Laura Riding and Robert Graves were offended, and these figures now stand as early evidence of a tendency that was to emerge more explicitly in *After Strange Gods*, a lecture collection first published in 1934 and then withheld.

Almost as if he needed to sum up everything he had done before he could move on, Eliot wrote "Gerontion" in 1919 as a conscious prelude to *The Waste Land*. The poet, now past thirty, returns to the old pose of "Prufrock," but his persona is no longer inexperienced and disillusioned but simply disillusioned. The gerontology in this case, though, is more than personal, and the fault seems to lie with history, which always gives "too late" or "too soon." Time simply does not advance in the way it is supposed to, so that everything is always either stale or unripe. As in "Portrait of a Lady," the staleness is represented by aristocratic women in candlelit rooms, and as in the quatrain poems the untimeliness of a pushy future is represented by "the Jew," by Mr. Silvero and Hakagawa, whose very names are supposed to tell us why they have no rightful place "among the Titians." Fearing the new as a devouring monster, the old man simply protracts a life that he is equally unwilling to change or to end. It is not too hard to imagine him, nodding off in his "sleepy

9. *The Diary of Virginia Woolf*, ed. Anne Olivier Bell (New York: Harcourt Brace Jovanovich, 1977), 2:187.

corner" at the end of "Gerontion," as the corpse who is forced awake in the first lines of *The Waste Land*.

In the few years between those poems, though, Eliot packed in a great deal of misery. Having finally convinced his widowed mother to cross the Atlantic for a visit, he added anxiety about her disapproval of his remaining in England to anxiety about his wife's health and weariness from chronic overwork, having built a busy career as reviewer and essayist while also advancing at the bank. He was humiliated by Pound's public attempts to raise subscription funds to free him from the bank and fearful that these attempts would jeopardize his only really secure source of money. His father-in-law collapsed and was seriously ill for months. A possible patron appeared for a new literary magazine to be founded and edited by Eliot, but this good news started a seemingly endless series of quibbling negotiations.

Through all this, he was somehow able to write at least some of the new poem he had mentioned to his mother late in 1920, but he could not bring it together. In fact, his mental health deteriorated to such an extent that toward the end of 1921 he was forced to ask for leave from the bank. Anxieties about his life and about his future as a poet combined to produce a state of tense mental paralysis. The "lifelong affliction" of indecisive, obsessional thought had flared up, to such an extent that nothing less than a complete break could clear his head.[1] In the course of these months at the end of 1921, at a hotel in Margate, England, and later at a sanitarium in Lausanne, Switzerland, Eliot settled his nerves and simultaneously brought the scattered drafts of his poem together and wrote a conclusion to what became *The Waste Land*.

Much of the personal misery of these years appears in the poem, which Eliot once dismissed as "the relief of a personal and wholly insignificant grouse against life."[2] Aspects of Eliot's personal life do peek out from among the literary and historical allusions. His marriage is the source of the pointless squabble at the center of "A Game of Chess," and his nervous breakdown is reflected in what seems almost a self-quotation in "The Fire Sermon": "On Margate Sands. / I can connect / Nothing with nothing" (ll. 300–02). One of the many achievements of *The Waste Land*, though, is the way it inserts literal renderings of personal experiences such as marital squabbles into a context that makes them part of a general social calamity. The contest between men and women that is at the heart of "A Game of Chess" is just an instance, it appears, of a pervasive social process

1. *Letters*, p. 95.
2. See below, p. 135.

in which people are forced closer and closer together while simultaneously being deprived of any genuine means of connection.

Before it could appear in print, the poem was put through the wringer at Pound's apartment in Paris, where Eliot stopped on his way home from Lausanne. Not only did Pound not try to make the poem sound like his own work, but he also saved it from sounding too much like Eliot's recent verse. Cutting out long passages in snarling quatrains, Pound helped keep the poem from becoming mere satire. Leaving gaps where these passages had been, Pound increased the already fragmentary quality that was the poem's most striking innovation. Pound also had the good sense to leave untouched the final section, which Eliot had written in Lausanne almost exactly as it finally appears.

For Pound, whose literary training and interests were very close to Eliot's, the poem did not need any notes. In fact, many of the apparently recondite references in *The Waste Land* are actually schoolroom chestnuts familiar to Eliot from his days at Smith Academy.[3] The Fire Sermon, a discourse from the Pali Canon, was an undergraduate reading assignment at Harvard, and the edition of the Upanishads that Eliot used in a 1912 class has a helpful note translating "Da da da" into *"damyata datta dayadhvam."*[4] In other words, the celebrated Harvard elective system allowed Eliot to accumulate a miscellaneous fund of knowledge that then appeared like a sort of code to anyone who had not taken the same set of classes. It did not add up to a coherent whole for Eliot any more than it did for his readers, but the parts, such as the dirge from John Webster's tragedy *The White Devil*, first read at school in Palgrave's Golden Treasury and then taken for the conclusion of "Burial of the Dead," had an awful familiarity for him. Somehow, when he flung those lines—"Oh keep the Dog far hence, that's friend to men / Or with his nails he'll dig it up again!"—at his "hypocrite lecteur" (ll. 74–76), the private meaning had a general impact without becoming less mysterious.

Thus *The Waste Land* became well-known without being very thoroughly known. The general sense of waste was clear from the beginning, and though critics busied themselves with constructing an elaborate alter ego for the poem, based more or less on the medievalist and folklorist Jessie L. Weston's *From Ritual to Romance*, it should have been obvious that when a poem presents itself as "a heap of broken images" (l. 22) what matters is the heap, not any particular image. The past, as presented in the poem, does not add up, and

3. Robert Crawford, *Young Eliot: From St. Louis to* The Waste Land (New York: Farrar, Straus and Giroux, 2015), p. 62.
4. Ibid., p. 169.

tradition fails to accomplish its defining task of handing on when it comes to the present with nothing more than "a handful of dust" (l. 30). The agonizing gap between the past and the future, which was the defining problem of Eliot's private life in these years, is dramatized in *The Waste Land* as the "shadow at morning striding behind you" and "the shadow at evening rising to meet you" (ll. 28–29), and it is generalized in the crowds for whom memory and desire conspire to empty out the present.

In *The Waste Land* as in Eliot's private life, the only way across this gap is to leap, but in this case it is not so much a leap of faith as a leap of doubt. The last section of the poem is all about wandering in the desert without hope of rain, which is, among other things, a spatial figure for a temporal stasis, a suspension as the past refuses to yield any future. Thunder is looked to in this situation as a kind of prophecy, almost a promise, but what it delivers is more a question than an answer. DA is a riddle, and the passage from the Upanishads that Eliot adapts here concerns the various ways in which that riddle can be misinterpreted. On one level, Eliot must be miming the inevitable fate of his poem in the hands of its readers. But perhaps he is also offering these words as a different kind of sacred text, one to be blundered through in a cloud of unknowing. Waiting for certainty, in other words, is sure to end in stasis. To the seekers in "Gerontion" who declare "We would see a sign!" (l. 17) *The Waste Land* offers a single gnomic syllable, the meaning of which is wrapped up somewhere inside, like the hooded figure "wrapt in a brown mantle" (l. 363), who turns out to be Jesus, inexplicably risen from the dead.

Even the hostile reactions to *The Waste Land*, the sarcastic reviews that declared it nothing more than a waste of paper, helped make Eliot famous. *The Waste Land* became an inescapable point of reference, even for those who disliked it. For a general readership, it came to epitomize the modern movement in poetry, and all its characteristics—its obscurity, its skepticism, its resistant relationship to traditional forms, its own dispersed and inconclusive form—were taken to be the hallmarks of modernism in general. In the years when modernism was favored by the academy, this meant that *The Waste Land* was something like the master text for all literary study, and yet a great deal of this study seemed bent on working away the poem's most salient characteristics, showing that it was indeed coherent, clear, and positive in its beliefs. When postmodernism made its big splash in the 1970s, it liked to present itself as the opposite of this *Waste Land*, one that was associated with the literary authority Eliot had accumulated since the 1920s. As time went on and the differences between modernism and postmodernism came to matter less and less, many of the characteristics that had defined the postmodern, particularly its tensely parodic relationship to popular culture, were discovered in *The Waste Land* as well. At the same time, much of the burden of defining modernism was lifted from the poem, as Eliot's method came to seem just one of the many modernisms possible in an expanded and pluralized field. With its authority diminished and its centrality questioned, the poem is more likely to be read for its own peculiar virtues. Now, a hundred years after its first publication, having survived all attempts to explain it, *The Waste Land* retains the shocking power that made it popular and disconcerting in equal measure.

The Texts of
THE WASTE LAND AND OTHER POEMS

Prufrock and Other Observations

TO
JEAN VERDENAL[1]
1889–1915

1. French student and medical officer, who befriended Eliot during his 1910 stay in Paris. Died attending wounded soldiers at Battle of Gallipoli.

The Love Song of J. Alfred Prufrock

S'io credesse che mia risposta fosse
A persona che mai tornasse al mondo,
Questa fiamma staria senza piu scosse.
Ma perciocche giammai di questo fondo
Non torno vivo alcun, s'i'odo il vero,
Senza tema d'infamia ti rispondo.[1]

Let us go then, you and I,
When the evening is spread out against the sky
Like a patient etherised upon a table;
Let us go, through certain half-deserted streets,
The muttering retreats   5
Of restless nights in one-night cheap hotels
And sawdust restaurants with oyster-shells:
Streets that follow like a tedious argument
Of insidious intent
To lead you to an overwhelming question. . . .   10

Oh, do not ask, "What is it?"
Let us go and make our visit.

In the room the women come and go
Talking of Michelangelo.

The yellow fog that rubs its back upon the window-panes,   15
The yellow smoke that rubs its muzzle on the window-panes,
Licked its tongue into the corners of the evening,
Lingered upon the pools that stand in drains,
Let fall upon its back the soot that falls from chimneys,
Slipped by the terrace, made a sudden leap,   20
And seeing that it was a soft October night,
Curled once about the house, and fell asleep.

And indeed there will be time
For the yellow smoke that slides along the street,
Rubbing its back upon the window-panes;   25
There will be time, there will be time
To prepare a face to meet the faces that you meet;
There will be time to murder and create,

---

1. Dante, *Inferno* 27: 61–66. Addressed to Dante by Guido da Montefeltro (1223–1298), whose false counsel and insufficient repentance has condemned him to Hell. Guido feels safe in speaking freely to Dante because he believes that no one could leave Hell to tell his story elsewhere.

And time for all the works and days of hands[2]
That lift and drop a question on your plate;   30
Time for you and time for me,
And time yet for a hundred indecisions,
And for a hundred visions and revisions,
Before the taking of a toast and tea.

In the room the women come and go   35
Talking of Michelangelo.

And indeed there will be time
To wonder, "Do I dare?" and, "Do I dare?"
Time to turn back and descend the stair,
With a bald spot in the middle of my hair—   40
(They will say: "How his hair is growing thin!")
My morning coat, my collar mounting firmly to the chin,
My necktie rich and modest, but asserted by a simple pin—
(They will say: "But how his arms and legs are thin!")
Do I dare   45
Disturb the universe?
In a minute there is time
For decisions and revisions which a minute will reverse.

For I have known them all already, known them all:
Have known the evenings, mornings, afternoons,   50
I have measured out my life with coffee spoons;
I know the voices dying with a dying fall
Beneath the music from a farther room.
    So how should I presume?

And I have known the eyes already, known them all—   55
The eyes that fix you in a formulated phrase,
And when I am formulated, sprawling on a pin,
When I am pinned and wriggling on the wall,
Then how should I begin
To spit out all the butt-ends of my days and ways?   60
    And how should I presume?

And I have known the arms already, known them all—
Arms that are braceleted and white and bare
(But in the lamplight, downed with light brown hair!)
Is it perfume from a dress   65

2. Reference to *Works and Days*, by Hesiod (ca. 700 BCE), a poem that mixes practical
advice with fable and myth.

That makes me so digress?
Arms that lie along a table, or wrap about a shawl.
  And should I then presume?
  And how should I begin?

                •   •   •   •

Shall I say, I have gone at dusk through narrow streets   70
And watched the smoke that rises from the pipes
Of lonely men in shirt-sleeves, leaning out of windows? . . .

I should have been a pair of ragged claws
Scuttling across the floors of silent seas.

                •   •   •   •

And the afternoon, the evening, sleeps so peacefully!   75
Smoothed by long fingers,
Asleep . . . tired . . . or it malingers,
Stretched on the floor, here beside you and me.
Should I, after tea and cakes and ices,
Have the strength to force the moment to its crisis?   80
But though I have wept and fasted, wept and prayed,
Though I have seen my head (grown slightly bald)
     brought in upon a platter,[3]
I am no prophet—and here's no great matter;
I have seen the moment of my greatness flicker,
And I have seen the eternal Footman hold my coat, and snicker,   85
And in short, I was afraid.

And would it have been worth it, after all,
After the cups, the marmalade, the tea,
Among the porcelain, among some talk of you and me,
Would it have been worth while,   90
To have bitten off the matter with a smile,
To have squeezed the universe into a ball[4]
To roll it toward some overwhelming question,
To say: "I am Lazarus, come from the dead,[5]
Come back to tell you all, I shall tell you all"—   95
If one, settling a pillow by her head,
     Should say: "That is not what I meant at all;
     That is not it, at all."

3. According to the accounts in Matthew 14:8 and Mark 6:25, the head of John the Bap-
   tist was delivered to Salome on a platter.
4. "Let us roll all our strength and all / Our sweetness up into one ball" ("To His Coy
   Mistress," Andrew Marvell [1621–1678]).
5. The story of Jesus raising Lazarus from the dead is told in John 11:1–44.

And would it have been worth it, after all,
Would it have been worth while,   100
After the sunsets and the dooryards and the sprinkled streets,
After the novels, after the teacups, after the skirts that trail
        along the floor—
And this, and so much more?—
It is impossible to say just what I mean!
But as if a magic lantern threw the nerves in patterns on
        a screen: 105
Would it have been worth while
If one, settling a pillow or throwing off a shawl,
And turning toward the window, should say:
        "That is not it at all,
        That is not what I meant, at all."   110

·   ·   ·   ·

No! I am not Prince Hamlet, nor was meant to be;
Am an attendant lord, one that will do
To swell a progress, start a scene or two,
Advise the prince; no doubt, an easy tool,
Deferential, glad to be of use,   115
Politic, cautious, and meticulous;
Full of high sentence, but a bit obtuse;[6]
At times, indeed, almost ridiculous—
Almost, at times, the Fool.

I grow old . . . I grow old . . .   120
I shall wear the bottoms of my trousers rolled.

Shall I part my hair behind? Do I dare to eat a peach?
I shall wear white flannel trousers, and walk upon the beach.
I have heard the mermaids singing, each to each.

I do not think that they will sing to me.   125

I have seen them riding seaward on the waves
Combing the white hair of the waves blown back
When the wind blows the water white and black.

We have lingered in the chambers of the sea
By sea-girls wreathed with seaweed red and brown   130
Till human voices wake us, and we drown.

6. Reference perhaps to Polonius, a minor character who gives some fatuous advice in
Hamlet.

Portrait of a Lady

Thou hast committed—
Fornication: but that was in another country,
And besides, the wench is dead.
THE JEW OF MALTA[1]

I

Among the smoke and fog of a December afternoon
You have the scene arrange itself—as it will seem to do—
With "I have saved this afternoon for you";
And four wax candles in the darkened room,
Four rings of light upon the ceiling overhead,   5
An atmosphere of Juliet's tomb[2]
Prepared for all the things to be said, or left unsaid.
We have been, let us say, to hear the latest Pole
Transmit the Preludes, through his hair and fingertips.[3]
"So intimate, this Chopin, that I think his soul   10
Should be resurrected only among friends
Some two or three, who will not touch the bloom
That is rubbed and questioned in the concert room."
—And so the conversation slips
Among velleities and carefully caught regrets   15
Through attenuated tones of violins
Mingled with remote cornets
And begins.

"You do not know how much they mean to me,
   my friends,
And how, how rare and strange it is, to find   20
In a life composed so much, so much of odds and ends,
(For indeed I do not love it . . . you knew? you are
   not blind!
How keen you are!)

---

1. A play generally attributed in whole or part to Christopher Marlowe (1564–1593), first performed in 1592. In the first scene of Act 4, Barabas, a Jewish moneylender who has poisoned most of the other characters in the play, pretends to confess to two friars. In the epigraph, the words before the colon are an accusation and those after it are Barabas's retort. The epigraph to "Mr. Eliot's Sunday Morning Service" (see below, p. 38) is taken from the same scene.
2. In *Romeo and Juliet* 5.3, Romeo drinks poison and dies at the family tomb where Juliet has been interred. A sarcophagus in the vaults of the Abbey of San Francesco, in Verona, Italy, is known as Juliet's Tomb and has been a popular tourist attraction since at least the early 19th century.
3. Artur Rubinstein (1887–1982) followed his Polish compatriot Ignacy Paderewski (1860–1941) in fame as a pianist. Both were particularly known for their performances of pieces by Fréderic Chopin (1810–1849).

To find a friend who has these qualities,
Who has, and gives   25
Those qualities upon which friendship lives.
How much it means that I say this to you—
Without these friendships—life, what *cauchemar!*"[4]
Among the windings of the violins
And the ariettes   30
Of cracked cornets
Inside my brain a dull tom-tom begins
Absurdly hammering a prelude of its own,
Capricious monotone
That is at least one definite "false note."   35
—Let us take the air, in a tobacco trance,
Admire the monuments
Discuss the late events,
Correct our watches by the public clocks.
Then sit for half an hour and drink our bocks.   40

II

Now that lilacs are in bloom
She has a bowl of lilacs in her room
And twists one in her fingers while she talks.
"Ah, my friend, you do not know, you do not know
What life is, you who hold it in your hands";   5
(Slowly twisting the lilac stalks)
"You let it flow from you, you let it flow,
And youth is cruel, and has no remorse
And smiles at situations which it cannot see."
I smile, of course,   10
And go on drinking tea.
"Yet with these April sunsets, that somehow recall
My buried life,[5] and Paris in the Spring,
I feel immeasurably at peace, and find the world
To be wonderful and youthful, after all."   15

The voice returns like the insistent out-of-tune
Of a broken violin on an August afternoon:
"I am always sure that you understand
My feelings, always sure that you feel,
Sure that across the gulf you reach your hand.   20

4. Nightmare (French).
5. Matthew Arnold's poem "The Buried Life" (1852) laments the way "the unregarded
river of our life" pursues its way within "the deep recesses of our breast."

You are invulnerable, you have no Achilles' heel.
You will go on, and when you have prevailed
You can say: at this point many a one has failed.

But what have I, but what have I, my friend,
To give you, what can you receive from me?   25
Only the friendship and the sympathy
Of one about to reach her journey's end.

I shall sit here, serving tea to friends. . . ."

I take my hat: how can I make a cowardly amends
For what she has said to me?   30
You will see me any morning in the park
Reading the comics and the sporting page.
Particularly I remark
An English countess goes upon the stage.
A Greek was murdered at a Polish dance,   35
Another bank defaulter has confessed.
I keep my countenance,
I remain self-possessed
Except when a street piano, mechanical and tired
Reiterates some worn-out common song   40
With the smell of hyacinths across the garden
Recalling things that other people have desired.
Are these ideas right or wrong?

III

The October night comes down; returning as before
Except for a slight sensation of being ill at ease
I mount the stairs and turn the handle of the door
And feel as if I had mounted on my hands and knees.

"And so you are going abroad; and when do you return?   5
But that's a useless question.
You hardly know when you are coming back,
You will find so much to learn."
My smile falls heavily among the bric-à-brac.

"Perhaps you can write to me."   10
My self-possession flares up for a second;
This is as I had reckoned.
"I have been wondering frequently of late
(But our beginnings never know our ends!)

Why we have not developed into friends."   15
I feel like one who smiles, and turning shall remark
Suddenly, his expression in a glass.
My self-possession gutters; we are really in the dark.

"For everybody said so, all our friends,
They all were sure our feelings would relate   20
So closely! I myself can hardly understand.
We must leave it now to fate.
You will write, at any rate.
Perhaps it is not too late.
I shall sit here, serving tea to friends."   25

And I must borrow every changing shape
To find expression . . . dance, dance
Like a dancing bear,
Cry like a parrot, chatter like an ape.
Let us take the air, in a tobacco trance—   30

Well! and what if she should die some afternoon,
Afternoon grey and smoky, evening yellow and rose;
Should die and leave me sitting pen in hand
With the smoke coming down above the housetops;
Doubtful, for quite a while   35
Not knowing what to feel or if I understand
Or whether wise or foolish, tardy or too soon . . .
Would she not have the advantage, after all?
This music is successful with a "dying fall"[6]
Now that we talk of dying—   40
And should I have the right to smile?

---

6. From Duke Orsino's famous speech about the power of music at the beginning of
   Shakespeare's *Twelfth Night*. Note "The Love Song of J. Alfred Prufrock," l. 52.

Preludes

I

The winter evening settles down
With smell of steaks in passageways.
Six o'clock.
The burnt-out ends of smoky days.
And now a gusty shower wraps   5
The grimy scraps
Of withered leaves about your feet
And newspapers from vacant lots;
The showers beat
On broken blinds and chimney-pots,   10
And at the corner of the street
A lonely cab-horse steams and stamps.
And then the lighting of the lamps.

II

The morning comes to consciousness
Of faint stale smells of beer
From the sawdust-trampled street
With all its muddy feet that press
To early coffee-stands.   5

With the other masquerades
That time resumes,
One thinks of all the hands
That are raising dingy shades
In a thousand furnished rooms.   10

III

You tossed a blanket from the bed,
You lay upon your back, and waited;
You dozed, and watched the night revealing
The thousand sordid images
Of which your soul was constituted;   5
They flickered against the ceiling.
And when all the world came back
And the light crept up between the shutters,
And you heard the sparrows in the gutters,
You had such a vision of the street   10
As the street hardly understands;

Sitting along the bed's edge, where
You curled the papers from your hair,
Or clasped the yellow soles of feet
In the palms of both soiled hands.   15

IV

His soul stretched tight across the skies
That fade behind a city block,
Or trampled by insistent feet
At four and five and six o'clock;
And short square fingers stuffing pipes,   5
And evening newspapers, and eyes
Assured of certain certainties,
The conscience of a blackened street
Impatient to assume the world.

I am moved by fancies that are curled   10
Around these images, and cling:
The notion of some infinitely gentle
Infinitely suffering thing.

Wipe your hand across your mouth, and laugh;
The worlds revolve like ancient women   15
Gathering fuel in vacant lots.

Rhapsody on a Windy Night

Twelve o'clock.
Along the reaches of the street
Held in a lunar synthesis,
Whispering lunar incantations
Dissolve the floors of the memory   5
And all its clear relations,
Its divisions and precisions.
Every street lamp that I pass
Beats like a fatalistic drum,
And through the spaces of the dark   10
Midnight shakes the memory
As a madman shakes a dead geranium.

Half-past one,
The street lamp sputtered,
The street lamp muttered,   15
The street lamp said, "Regard that woman
Who hesitates toward you in the light of the door
Which opens on her like a grin.
You see the border of her dress
Is torn and stained with sand,   20
And you see the corner of her eye
Twists like a crooked pin."

The memory throws up high and dry
A crowd of twisted things;
A twisted branch upon the beach   25
Eaten smooth, and polished
As if the world gave up
The secret of its skeleton,
Stiff and white.
A broken spring in a factory yard,   30
Rust that clings to the form that the strength has left
Hard and curled and ready to snap.

Half-past two,
The street lamp said,
"Remark the cat which flattens itself in the gutter,   35
Slips out its tongue
And devours a morsel of rancid butter."
So the hand of a child, automatic,
Slipped out and pocketed a toy that was running along the quay.

I could see nothing behind that child's eye.   40
I have seen eyes in the street
Trying to peer through lighted shutters,
And a crab one afternoon in a pool,
An old crab with barnacles on his back,
Gripped the end of a stick which I held him.   45

Half-past three,
The lamp sputtered,
The lamp muttered in the dark.
The lamp hummed:
"Regard the moon,   50
La lune ne garde aucune rancune,¹
She winks a feeble eye,
She smiles into corners.
She smoothes the hair of the grass.
The moon has lost her memory.   55
A washed-out smallpox cracks her face,
Her hand twists a paper rose,
That smells of dust and eau de Cologne,
She is alone
With all the old nocturnal smells   60
That cross and cross across her brain."
The reminiscence comes
Of sunless dry geraniums
And dust in crevices,
Smells of chestnuts in the streets,   65
And female smells in shuttered rooms,
And cigarettes in corridors
And cocktail smells in bars.

The lamp said,
"Four o'clock,   70
Here is the number on the door.
Memory!
You have the key,
The little lamp spreads a ring on the stair.
Mount.   75
The bed is open; the tooth-brush hangs on the wall,
Put your shoes at the door, sleep, prepare for life."

The last twist of the knife.

---

1. The moon does not hold a grudge (French).

Morning at the Window

They are rattling breakfast plates in basement kitchens,
And along the trampled edges of the street
I am aware of the damp souls of housemaids
Sprouting despondently at area gates.

The brown waves of fog toss up to me   5
Twisted faces from the bottom of the street,
And tear from a passer-by with muddy skirts
An aimless smile that hovers in the air
And vanishes along the level of the roofs.

The *Boston Evening Transcript*

The readers of the *Boston Evening Transcript*[1]
Sway in the wind like a field of ripe corn.

When evening quickens faintly in the street,
Wakening the appetites of life in some
And to others bringing the *Boston Evening Transcript*,   5
I mount the steps and ring the bell, turning
Wearily, as one would turn to nod good-bye to
    Rochefoucauld,[2]
If the street were time and he at the end of the street,
And I say, "Cousin Harriet, here is the *Boston Evening
    Transcript*."

1. A newspaper published from 1830 to 1941. In 1910, it printed one of Eliot's college poems.
2. François VI, Duc de la Rochefoucauld (1613–1680), author of *Maximes* (1665), short, pithy observations on life, frequently quoted by later authors.

Aunt Helen

Miss Helen Slingsby was my maiden aunt,
And lived in a small house near a fashionable square
Cared for by servants to the number of four.
Now when she died there was silence in heaven
And silence at her end of the street.   5
The shutters were drawn and the undertaker wiped his feet—
He was aware that this sort of thing had occurred before.
The dogs were handsomely provided for,
But shortly afterwards the parrot died too.
The Dresden clock continued ticking on the mantelpiece,   10
And the footman sat upon the dining-table
Holding the second housemaid on his knees—
Who had always been so careful while her mistress lived.

Cousin Nancy

Miss Nancy Ellicott
Strode across the hills and broke them,
Rode across the hills and broke them—
The barren New England hills—
Riding to hounds   5
Over the cow-pasture.

Miss Nancy Ellicott smoked
And danced all the modern dances;
And her aunts were not quite sure how they felt about it,
But they knew that it was modern.   10

Upon the glazen shelves kept watch
Matthew and Waldo,[1] guardians of the faith,
The army of unalterable law.

---

1. Matthew Arnold (1822–1888) and Ralph Waldo Emerson (1803–1882), authoritative poets and essayists. The final line of the poem is quoted from the sonnet "Lucifer in Starlight" (1883), by George Meredith (1828–1909).

Mr. Apollinax

Ω τῆς καινότητος. Ἡράκλεις, τῆς παραδοξολογιας. εὐμήχανος
ἂνθρωπος.

LUCIAN[1]

When Mr. Apollinax visited the United States[2]
His laughter tinkled among the teacups.
I thought of Fragilion,[3] that shy figure among the
    birch-trees,
And of Priapus[4] in the shrubbery
Gaping at the lady in the swing.   5
In the palace of Mrs. Phlaccus, at Professor
    Channing-Cheetah's
He laughed like an irresponsible fœtus.
His laughter was submarine and profound
Like the old man of the sea's
Hidden under coral islands   10
Where worried bodies of drowned men drift down
    in the green silence,
Dropping from fingers of surf.

I looked for the head of Mr. Apollinax rolling under
    a chair,
Or grinning over a screen
With seaweed in its hair.   15
I heard the beat of centaurs' hoofs over the hard turf
As his dry and passionate talk devoured the afternoon.
"He is a charming man"—"But after all what did he
    mean?"—
"His pointed ears . . . he must be unbalanced,"—
"There was something he said that I might have
    challenged."   20
Of dowager Mrs. Phlaccus, and Professor and Mrs. Cheetah
I remember a slice of lemon, and a bitten macaroon.

---

1. The Greek epigraph is a series of exclamatory phrases praising the eloquence and wit
   of the poet Lucian (ca. 125–180), quoted ironically by Lucian as evidence of the low
   standards of his audience.
2. The title character is generally held to have been based on Bertrand Russell (1872–
   1970), English philosopher and pacifist, who in 1914 visited the U.S., where he met
   Eliot at Harvard.
3. The poem includes a number of fanciful names, invented by Eliot and meant to sound
   ludicrous.
4. Greek and Roman god of fertility, conventionally represented with a gigantic phallus.

Hysteria

As she laughed I was aware of becoming involved in her laughter and being part of it, until her teeth were only accidental stars with a talent for squad-drill. I was drawn in by short gasps, inhaled at each momentary recovery, lost finally in the dark caverns of her throat, bruised by the ripple of unseen muscles. An elderly waiter with trembling hands was hurriedly spreading a pink and white checked cloth over the rusty green iron table, saying: "If the lady and gentleman wish to take their tea in the garden, if the lady and gentleman wish to take their tea in the garden . . ." I decided that if the shaking of her breasts could be stopped, some of the fragments of the afternoon might be collected, and I concentrated my attention with careful subtlety to this end.

Conversation Galante

I observe: "Our sentimental friend the moon!
Or possibly (fantastic, I confess)
It may be Prester John's balloon[1]
Or an old battered lantern hung aloft
To light poor travellers to their distress."   5
    She then: "How you digress!"

And I then: "Some one frames upon the keys
That exquisite nocturne, with which we explain
The night and moonshine; music which we seize
To body forth our own vacuity."   10
    She then: "Does this refer to me?"
    "Oh no, it is I who am inane."

"You, madam, are the eternal humorist,
The eternal enemy of the absolute,
Giving our vagrant moods the slightest twist!   15
With your air indifferent and imperious
At a stroke our mad poetics to confute—"
    And—"Are we then so serious?"

---

1. Reference to a legendary Christian patriarch, monarch of a lost realm and focus of a number of fanciful tales in the 12th to 17th centuries. In one of these tales, he is represented as using a balloon to send a bird to London from Africa.

La Figlia Che Piange[1]

O quam te memorem virgo . . .[2]

Stand on the highest pavement of the stair—
Lean on a garden urn—
Weave, weave the sunlight in your hair—
Clasp your flowers to you with a pained surprise—
Fling them to the ground and turn   5
With a fugitive resentment in your eyes:
But weave, weave the sunlight in your hair.

So I would have had him leave,
So I would have had her stand and grieve,
So he would have left   10
As the soul leaves the body torn and bruised,
As the mind deserts the body it has used.
I should find
Some way incomparably light and deft,
Some way we both should understand,   15
Simple and faithless as a smile and shake of the hand.

She turned away, but with the autumn weather
Compelled my imagination many days,
Many days and many hours:
Her hair over her arms and her arms full of flowers.   20
And I wonder how they should have been together!
I should have lost a gesture and a pose.
Sometimes these cogitations still amaze
The troubled midnight and the noon's repose.

1. The girl who weeps (Italian).
2. What shall I call you, maiden? (Latin, from *Aeneid* 1.327).

From Poems (1920)

Gerontion[1]

Thou hast nor youth nor age
But as it were an after dinner sleep
Dreaming of both.[2]

Here I am, an old man in a dry month,
Being read to by a boy, waiting for rain.[3]
I was neither at the hot gates
Nor fought in the warm rain
Nor knee deep in the salt marsh, heaving a cutlass,   5
Bitten by flies, fought.
My house is a decayed house,
And the Jew squats on the window sill, the owner,
Spawned in some estaminet[4] of Antwerp,
Blistered in Brussels, patched and peeled in London.   10
The goat coughs at night in the field overhead;
Rocks, moss, stonecrop, iron, merds.[5]
The woman keeps the kitchen, makes tea,
Sneezes at evening, poking the peevish gutter.

                    I an old man,   15
A dull head among windy spaces.

---

1. Little old man (Greek). Perhaps an allusion to Gerontius, Roman general who failed to oppose the Goths at Thermopylae in 396 CE. "Hot gates" (l. 3) is a literal English translation of the name of that famous pass.
2. From Shakespeare's *Measure for Measure* (3.2.). Eliot has slightly misquoted these sentiments on the brevity of life, delivered by Duke Vincentio (disguised as a friar) to reconcile Claudio to his coming execution.
3. Ll. 1–2 are adapted from A. C. Benson's 1905 biography of the English translator Edward FitzGerald (1809–1883), who, having strained his eyes, was read to by an assistant. Ll. 13–14 also bear strong resemblance to details in Benson's book.
4. A small café or bar (French, but more common in French-speaking parts of Belgium).
5. Pieces of excrement (French, but borrowed as an English term from the 15th to 17th centuries). "Stonecrop": common name for plants of the genus *Sedum*.

Signs are taken for wonders.[6] "We would see a sign!"
The word within a word, unable to speak a word,
Swaddled with darkness. In the juvescence[7] of the year
Came Christ the tiger   20

In depraved May,[8] dogwood and chestnut, flowering judas,
To be eaten, to be divided, to be drunk
Among whispers; by Mr. Silvero[9]
With caressing hands, at Limoges[1]
Who walked all night in the next room;   25
By Hakagawa, bowing among the Titians;[2]
By Madame de Tornquist, in the dark room
Shifting the candles; Fraulein von Kulp
Who turned in the hall, one hand on the door. Vacant
     shuttles
Weave the wind. I have no ghosts,   30
An old man in a draughty house
Under a windy knob.

After such knowledge, what forgiveness? Think now
History has many cunning passages, contrived corridors
And issues, deceives with whispering ambitions,   35
Guides us by vanities. Think now
She gives when our attention is distracted
And what she gives, gives with such supple confusions
That the giving famishes the craving. Gives too late
What's not believed in, or if still believed,   40
In memory only, reconsidered passion. Gives too soon
Into weak hands, what's thought can be dispensed with
Till the refusal propagates a fear. Think
Neither fear nor courage saves us. Unnatural vices
Are fathered by our heroism. Virtues   45
Are forced upon us by our impudent crimes.
These tears are shaken from the wrath-bearing tree.

---

6. From a Christmas sermon delivered in 1618 by the English bishop and scholar Lance-lot Andrewes (1555–1626) on the episode recounted in Matthew 12:38–39, in which Christ is asked for and refuses to give a sign of his divinity. The next two lines also paraphrase this sermon, which explores the paradox created when the Logos, or Christ as word of God, was born as an infant.
7. The process of becoming youthful (apparently Eliot's coinage, on the model of *senescence* as the process of becoming old).
8. In Chapter 18 of his essayistic autobiography, the American historian Henry Adams (1838–1918) refers to "the passionate depravity that marked the Maryland May."
9. Eliot populated this poem with a number of characters with fanciful names, the macabre comedy of which was apparently related, for him, to their international derivation.
1. A city in central France, known for its porcelain.
2. Paintings by the Venetian artist Tiziano Vicelli (1488–1577).

The tiger springs in the new year. Us he devours. Think
   at last
We have not reached conclusion, when I
Stiffen in a rented house. Think at last   50
I have not made this show purposelessly
And it is not by any concitation[3]
Of the backward devils.
I would meet you upon this honestly.
I that was near your heart was removed therefrom   55
To lose beauty in terror, terror in inquisition.
I have lost my passion: why should I need to keep it
Since what is kept must be adulterated?
I have lost my sight, smell, hearing, taste and touch:
How should I use them for your closer contact?   60

These with a thousand small deliberations
Protract the profit of their chilled delirium,
Excite the membrane, when the sense has cooled,
With pungent sauces, multiply variety
In a wilderness of mirrors. What will the spider do,   65
Suspend its operations, will the weevil
Delay? De Bailhache, Fresca, Mrs. Cammel, whirled
Beyond the circuit of the shuddering Bear[4]
In fractured atoms. Gull against the wind, in the windy
   straits
Of Belle Isle, or running on the Horn,[5]   70
White feathers in the snow, the Gulf claims,
And an old man driven by the Trades[6]
To a a sleepy corner.

            Tenants of the house,
Thoughts of a dry brain in a dry season.   75

---

3. Inciting or provoking to action (archaic).
4. The Arctic Circle, from the northern circumpolar constellation Ursa Major or Great
   Bear (*arktos* in Greek). Perhaps an allusion to a passage from George Chapman's play
   Bussy d'Ambois (1607) that Eliot admired: "Beneath the chariot of the snowy Bear"
   (5.4).
5. Belle Isle, off the coast of Labrador, Canada, and Cape Horn, at the southern tip of
   South America, mark narrow straits. The gulf in the next line is probably not specific.
6. East to west equatorial winds that facilitated global trade in the days before steam-
   ships.

Burbank with a Baedeker:
Bleistein with a Cigar[1]

Tra-la-la-la-la-la-laire—nil nisi divinum stabile est; caetera fumus—the gondola stopped, the old palace was there, how charming its grey and pink—goats and monkeys, with such hair too!—so the countess passed on until she came through the little park, where Niobe presented her with a cabinet, and so departed.[2]

Burbank crossed a little bridge
  Descending at a small hotel;
Princess Volupine[3] arrived,
  They were together, and he fell.

Defunctive music[4] under sea
  Passed seaward with the passing bell[5]
Slowly: the God Hercules[6]
  Had left him, that had loved him well.

The horses, under the axletree
  Beat up the dawn from Istria[7]
With even feet. Her shuttered barge
  Burned on the water all the day.

But this or such was Bleistein's way:
  A saggy bending of the knees

5

10

1. Though there was a famous Burbank, the plant scientist Luther Burbank (1849–1926), and a relatively well-known Bleistein, a fur merchant in London in the early 20th century, the names are probably not meant to designate real people. Baedekers were travel handbooks, published by Germany's Karl Baedeker company from the 1830s until the 1970s.
2. A tissue of oblique references to Venice, where the poem is supposed to take place: the cry of a gondolier, as given in Théophile Gautier's poem "Sur les lagunes" (1884); a Latin motto from a painting of St. Sebastian by Andrea Mantegna (1480); a quotation from Henry James's novella *The Aspern Papers* (1888); a quotation from Shakespeare's *Othello* (4.1) combined with a phrase from Robert Browning's poem *A Toccata of Galuppi's* (1855); a quotation from a masque by John Marston performed in 1607.
3. The name may be meant to suggest voluptuousness, but its oddity, like that of the other names in the poem, is primarily meant to establish the characters as denizens of a deracinated demimonde. The next line is an adaptation of a line from Alfred, Lord Tennyson's poem "The Sisters" (1832): "They were together and she fell" (l. 4).
4. Shakespeare's poem "The Phoenix and the Turtle," l. 14. "Defunctive": dying.
5. Church bells rung to signify a recent death.
6. Divine hero in Greek and Roman mythology. The stanza is apparently meant to evoke an episode in Shakespeare's *Antony and Cleopatra* 4.3, in which the passage of mysterious music through the streets of Alexandria signifies the abandonment of Mark Antony by Hercules, his favorite and model among the gods. The barge in l. 11 is a reference to the one Cleopatra uses in the same play (2.2).
7. Both "horses" and "axletree" are references to the chariot of Phoebus, ancient mythological representation of the sun, which arrives in Venice from the direction of Istria, a peninsula to the east.

And elbows, with the palms turned out, 15
    Chicago Semite Viennese.

A lustreless protrusive eye
    Stares from the protozoic slime
At a perspective of Canaletto.[8]
    The smoky candle end of time 20

Declines. On the Rialto[9] once.
    The rats are underneath the piles.
The Jew is underneath the lot.
    Money in furs. The boatman smiles,

Princess Volupine extends 25
    A meagre, blue-nailed, phthisic[1] hand
To climb the waterstair. Lights, lights,
    She entertains Sir Ferdinand

Klein. Who clipped the lion's wings
    And flea'd his rump and pared his claws?[2] 30
Thought Burbank, meditating on
    Time's ruins, and the seven laws.[3]

---

8. Giovanni Antonio Canal (1697–1768), Italian painter known for city views, especially of Venice.
9. Central area of Venice.
1. Affected by a lung disease, such as tuberculosis.
2. To "clip the lion's claws" is a proverbial metaphor for the taming of a great power. The symbol of St. Mark, evangelist and legendary founder of the city of Venice, is a winged lion holding a Bible.
3. In *The Stones of Venice* (2.4:30–47), the English essayist and art critic John Ruskin (1819–1900) lists seven laws, or customs, derived from the natural conditions of Venice, that describe the necessary forms of its architecture.

Sweeney Erect

> *And the trees about me,*
> *Let them be dry and leafless; let the rocks*
> *Groan with continual surges; and behind me*
> *Make all a desolation. Look, look, wenches![1]*

Paint me a cavernous waste shore
  Cast in the unstilled Cyclades,[2]
Paint me the bold anfractuous[3] rocks
  Faced by the snarled and yelping seas.

Display me Aeolus[4] above   5
  Reviewing the insurgent gales
Which tangle Ariadne's hair
  And swell with haste the perjured sails.[5]

Morning stirs the feet and hands
  (Nausicaa and Polypheme).[6]   10
Gesture of orang-outang
  Rises from the sheets in steam.

This withered root of knots of hair
  Slitted below and gashed with eyes,
This oval O cropped out with teeth: 15
  The sickle motion from the thighs

Jackknifes upward at the knees
  Then straightens out from heel to hip
Pushing the framework of the bed
  And clawing at the pillow slip.   20

1. From *The Maid's Tragedy* 2.2 (1610), by Francis Beaumont and John Fletcher. Aspatia, abandoned by her lover, criticizes her maid's needlework portrayal of Ariadne abandoned by Theseus as not being sufficiently desolate. Aspatia offers herself as a more appropriate model.
2. A group of islands forming a circle around the island of Delos, in the Aegean Sea.
3. Craggy.
4. Greek god of wind. He appears as a character in the masque presented in the first act of *The Maid's Tragedy* and often as a decorative device on maps.
5. In Greek mythology, Ariadne is the daughter of King Minos of Crete. She gives Theseus the thread that enables him to find his way through the labyrinth and defeat the Minotaur. After abandoning Ariadne on Naxos, one of the Cyclades, Theseus returns to Athens. Because he forgets to change his black sails to white ones signifying victory, his father commits suicide as the ship approaches.
6. Two characters in Homer's *Odyssey*: the young girl who discovers Odysseus in Book 6 and the Cyclops who captures him in Book 9.

Sweeney[7] addressed full length to shave
   Broadbottomed, pink from nape to base,
Knows the female temperament
   And wipes the suds around his face.

(The lengthened shadow of a man   25
   Is history, said Emerson[8]
Who had not seen the silhouette
   Of Sweeney straddled in the sun).

Tests the razor on his leg
   Waiting until the shriek subsides.   30
The epileptic on the bed
   Curves backward, clutching at her sides.

The ladies of the corridor
   Find themselves involved, disgraced,
Call witness to their principles   35
   And deprecate the lack of taste

Observing that hysteria
   Might easily be misunderstood;
Mrs. Turner intimates
   It does the house no sort of good.   40

But Doris, towelled from the bath,
   Enters padding on broad feet,
Bringing sal volatile[9]
   And a glass of brandy neat.

7. Originally *Suibhne* (Gaelic), meaning pleasant or well-disposed and associated with Clan Sweeney of Scotland. Also the name of an Irish legendary hero, who wanders Ireland after having been driven mad in the course of battle. Of the many possible sources for this particular namesake, one is Sweeney Todd, the murdering barber who was a fixture of Victorian melodrama.
8. In the essay "Self-Reliance" (1841), Ralph Waldo Emerson (1803–1882) uses this metaphor to maintain that all history is really biography.
9. Smelling salts.

A Cooking Egg[1]

En l'an trentiesme de mon aage
Que toutes mes hontes j'ay beues . . .[2]

Pipit[3] sate upright in her chair
　Some distance from where I was sitting;
Views of the Oxford Colleges[4]
　Lay on the table, with the knitting.

Daguerreotypes and silhouettes,   5
　Her grandfather and great great aunts,
Supported on the mantelpiece
　An *Invitation to the Dance.*[5]

· · · · · ·

I shall not want Honour in Heaven
　For I shall meet Sir Philip Sidney[6]   10
And have talk with Coriolanus
　And other heroes of that kidney.

I shall not want Capital in Heaven
　For I shall meet Sir Alfred Mond:[7]
We two shall lie together, lapt   15
　In a five per cent. Exchequer Bond.

I shall not want Society in Heaven,
　Lucretia Borgia[8] shall be my Bride;

1. A term, somewhat old-fashioned even in 1920, for an egg that is not fresh enough to eat by itself but is good enough for cooking. It appears in the chapter on eggs in editions of Fannie Merritt Farmer's *Boston Cooking-School Cookbook* (1896) up through 1922 but is gone by 1946.
2. "In the thirtieth year of my life / Having drunk up all my shame . . ." (French). The opening lines of *Grand Testament* (1461), by the French poet François Villon (ca. 1431–1463), in which Villon takes stock of the life that has landed him in prison.
3. Perhaps an infantile nickname, given to or adopted by a female of indeterminate age. Eliot later complained about the confusion caused by this name but did little to clear it up. He also insisted on the archaic spelling of the verb in this line.
4. No such book has been identified.
5. Either an actual invitation or a picture evoking a musical piece with a title of that nature, such as Carl Maria von Weber's *Aufforderung zum Tanz* (1819).
6. English courtier poet and soldier (1554–1586). The other hero mentioned in this stanza is the Roman general Gaius Marcus Coriolanus, said to have distinguished himself at the battle for Corioli in the 5th century BCE.
7. British industrialist and politician (1868–1930), first commissioner of works in the cabinet of Prime Minister Lloyd George at the time the poem was written. As a financier, he is associated here with British government securities bearing 5 percent interest.
8. Italian noblewoman (1480–1519), daughter of Pope Alexander VI; member of the influential house of Borgia; wife, successively, to three European nobles; and governor of

Her anecdotes will be more amusing
  Than Pipit's experience could provide.   20

I shall not want Pipit in Heaven:
  Madame Blavatsky[9] will instruct me
In the Seven Sacred Trances;
  Piccarda de Donati[1] will conduct me.

     •   •   •   •   •   •

But where is the penny world I bought   25
  To eat with Pipit behind the screen?
The red-eyed scavengers are creeping
  From Kentish Town and Golder's Green;[2]

Where are the eagles[3] and the trumpets?

Buried beneath some snow-deep Alps.   30
Over buttered scones and crumpets
  Weeping, weeping multitudes
Droop in a hundred A.B.C.'s.[4]

the Italian regions of Spoleto and Ferrara. The many rumors attached to her included incest and poisoning.

9. Helena Blavatsky (1831–1891), founder of the Theosophical Society, an occult group that included the Irish writer W. B. Yeats (1865–1939) and promised the adept access to trance states under the influence of the Seven Rays of the Sun, a concept common to several ancient religions.

1. An Italian noblewoman and nun, encountered by Dante at the beginning of his journey through Paradise in the third book of the *Divine Comedy*. She is at the very lowest level of Heaven because she acquiesced to her removal from the convent and marriage to a political ally of her brother's.

2. Once-rural districts that had become suburbs of London by the late 19th century.

3. Military insignia. This line and the next one evoke famous invasions of Italy through the Alps, such as that of the Carthaginian general Hannibal in 218 BCE. They also echo the most famous line from Villon: "Où sont les neiges d'antan?" (Where are the snows of yesteryear?).

4. *Poems* (1920) includes a note for American readers: "*i.e.* an endemic teashop, found in all parts of London. The initials signify: Aerated Bread Company, Limited."

The Hippopotamus

Similiter et omnes revereantur Diaconos, ut mandatum Jesu Christi; et Episcopum, ut Jesum Christum, existentem filium Patris; Presbyteros autem, ut concilium Dei et conjunctionem Apostolorum. Sine his Ecclesia non vocatur; de quibus suadeo vos sic habeo.

S. IGNATII AD TRALLIANOS.[1]

And when this epistle is read among you, cause that it be read also in the church of the Laodiceans.[2]

The broad-backed hippopotamus
Rests on his belly in the mud;
Although he seems so firm to us
He is merely flesh and blood.

Flesh-and-blood is weak and frail,   5
Susceptible to nervous shock;
While the True Church can never fail
For it is based upon a rock.[3]

The hippo's feeble steps may err
In compassing material ends,   10
While the True Church need never stir
To gather in its dividends.

The 'potamus can never reach
The mango on the mango-tree;
But fruits of pomegranate and peach   15
Refresh the Church from over sea.

At mating time the hippo's voice
Betrays inflexions hoarse and odd,
But every week we hear rejoice
The Church, at being one with God.   20

1. Likewise let all reverence the deacons, as Jesus Christ commanded, and also the bishop, as Jesus Christ, living son of the Father, and the presbyters as the council of God and the band of the Apostles. Without these there is no church deserving of the name. Concerning these matters, I am convinced you are so disposed (Latin). Letter from Ignatius (d. ca. 140 CE), bishop of Antioch, to the congregation in Tralles, in western Asia Minor. This is a 17th-century translation with some differences from the Greek original.
2. Colossians 4:16. Laodicea was about ten miles from Colossae, in western Asia Minor, and both were sites of early Christian congregations. Because of a disputable reading of Revelation 3:15–16, the Laodiceans were traditionally thought of as lukewarm in their devotion.
3. "And I tell you, you are Peter, and on this rock I will build my church" (Matthew 16:18). A pun on Peter's name, which in Aramaic, Greek, and Latin means *rock*. Peter is traditionally considered the founder of the churches of Antioch and Rome.

The hippopotamus's day
Is passed in sleep; at night he hunts;
God works in a mysterious way—[4]
The Church can sleep and feed at once.

I saw the 'potamus take wing   25
Ascending from the damp savannas,
And quiring angels round him sing
The praise of God, in loud hosannas.

Blood of the Lamb shall wash him clean[5]
And him shall heavenly arms enfold,   30
Among the saints he shall be seen
Performing on a harp of gold.

He shall be washed as white as snow,
By all the martyr'd virgins kist,
While the True Church remains below   35
Wrapt in the old miasmal mist.

4. Now virtually proverbial, but originally from William Cowper's poem "Light Shining
   out of Darkness" (1773), later a popular hymn.
5. Revelation 7:14.

Whispers of Immortality

Webster[1] was much possessed by death
And saw the skull beneath the skin;
And breastless creatures under ground
Leaned backward with a lipless grin.

Daffodil bulbs instead of balls　　　　　　　　5
Stared from the sockets of the eyes!
He knew that thought clings round dead limbs
Tightening its lusts and luxuries.

Donne,[2] I suppose, was such another
Who found no substitute for sense,　　　　　　10
To seize and clutch and penetrate;
Expert beyond experience,

He knew the anguish of the marrow
The ague of the skeleton;
No contact possible to flesh　　　　　　　　　15
Allayed the fever of the bone.

•　•　•　•　•　•　•

Grishkin[3] is nice: her Russian eye
Is underlined for emphasis;
Uncorseted, her friendly bust
Gives promise of pneumatic bliss.　　　　　　20

The couched Brazilian jaguar
Compels the scampering marmoset
With subtle effluence of cat;
Grishkin has a maisonette;[4]

The sleek Brazilian jaguar　　　　　　　　　25
Does not in its arboreal gloom
Distil so rank a feline smell
As Grishkin in a drawing-room.

1. John Webster (ca. 1580–ca. 1632), English dramatist, author of *The Duchess of Malfi* and other tragedies.
2. John Donne (1572–1631), English metaphysical poet.
3. Based, according to Eliot's friend and fellow poet Ezra Pound (1885–1972), on the Russian ballerina Serafina Astieva (1876–1934), who performed with the Ballets Russes.
4. Part of a house, rented separately and with its own entrance, usually with more than one floor.

And even the Abstract Entities[5]
Circumambulate her charm;   30
But our lot crawls between dry ribs
To keep our metaphysics warm.

5. Concepts such as roundness or number, derived from concrete experience but
   immaterial.

Mr. Eliot's Sunday Morning Service[1]

Look, look, master, here comes two religious caterpillars.
THE JEW OF MALTA.[2]

> Polyphiloprogenitive[3]
> The sapient sutlers[4] of the Lord
> Drift across the window-panes.
> In the beginning was the Word.[5]
>
> In the beginning was the Word.   5
> Superfetation of τὸ ἔν,[6]
> And at the mensual[7] turn of time
> Produced enervate Origen.[8]
>
> A painter of the Umbrian school[9]
> Designed upon a gesso ground   10
> The nimbus of the Baptized God.
> The wilderness is cracked and browned
>
> But through the water pale and thin
> Still shine the unoffending feet
> And there above the painter set   15
> The Father and the Paraclete.[1]

·   ·   ·   ·   ·   ·

1. There were a number of clergymen among Eliot's family and forebears, including his grandfather, William Greenleaf Eliot (1811–1887).
2. Ithamore to his master, Barabas, in Act 4, Scene 1 of *The Jew of Malta* (1592), attributed to Christopher Marlowe. Having just poisoned an entire convent, the two encounter a pair of friars. The epigraph to "Portrait of a Lady" (see above, p. 9) is taken from the same scene.
3. A coinage of Eliot's, now rather dryly defined by most dictionaries as "very prolific" but certainly meant to evoke early Christian attempts to define, in Greek, the attributes of God, in this case an all-encompassing love of creation.
4. Wise attendants. Perhaps to be associated with the "presbyters" of l. 17.
5. John 1:1.
6. "Superfetation": the addition of a secondary fetus to a pregnancy in progress. The Greek, pronounced *ta-hen*, means "the one" and is used in Greek philosophy to designate the ineffable unity that precedes, subtends, or transcends all categories. Thus the line suggests the mystery by which the Word, described in John 1:1, is both added to and inseparable from the unity of God.
7. Monthly.
8. Early Church father (185–254 CE), described here as "enervate," or weak, perhaps because he was purported to have castrated himself. Among his many works of biblical exegesis was a massive commentary on the Gospel of John, meant in part to help establish the oneness of the three persons of the Trinity (Father, Son, and Holy Spirit).
9. Renaissance painters from the province of Umbria, in central Italy. The painting described in the next few lines, started with a layer of "gesso," a kind of primer, is of the baptism of Christ, who is conventionally represented with a halo, or "nimbus."
1. In many versions of this scene, such as the one by Pietro Perugino (1446/52–1523), the Holy Spirit, or "Paraclete," is represented as a dove hovering over the head of Christ, while God the Father looks down from a circular enclosure supported by angels.

The sable presbyters approach
The avenue of penitence;
The young are red and pustular
Clutching piaculative pence.[2]   20

Under the penitential gates
Sustained by staring Seraphim[3]
Where the souls of the devout
Burn invisible and dim.

Along the garden-wall the bees   25
With hairy bellies pass between
The staminate and pistillate,
Blest office of the epicene.[4]

Sweeney[5] shifts from ham to ham
Stirring the water in his bath.   30
The masters of the subtle schools
Are controversial, polymath.[6]

2. Offerings that are meant to expiate a sin.
3. Highest order of angels, closest to the throne of God.
4. Neither of one sex or another. Applied to the bees in this case because they pass
   between the pollen-bearing stamens and the seed-bearing pistils.
5. See "Sweeney Erect," note 8.
6. Of wide learning in many subjects.

Sweeney Among the Nightingales

ὤμοι, πέπληγμαι καιρίαν πληγὴν ἔσω.[1]

Apeneck Sweeney[2] spreads his knees
Letting his arms hang down to laugh,
The zebra stripes along his jaw
Swelling to maculate[3] giraffe.

The circles of the stormy moon   5
Slide westward toward the River Plate,[4]
Death and the Raven drift above
And Sweeney guards the hornèd gate.[5]

Gloomy Orion and the Dog
Are veiled; and hushed the shrunken seas;   10
The person in the Spanish cape
Tries to sit on Sweeney's knees

Slips and pulls the table cloth
Overturns a coffee-cup,
Reorganized upon the floor   15
She yawns and draws a stocking up;

The silent man in mocha brown
Sprawls at the window-sill and gapes;
The waiter brings in oranges
Bananas figs and hothouse grapes;   20

The silent vertebrate in brown
Contracts and concentrates, withdraws;
Rachel *née* Rabinovitch
Tears at the grapes with murderous paws;

She and the lady in the cape   25
Are suspect, thought to be in league;

1. Alas, I am struck deep with a mortal blow (Greek; Aeschylus, *Agamemnon*, ca. 458 BCE). Spoken by Agamemnon as he is killed in his bath by his wife, Clytemnestra. Thus l. 38.
2. See "Sweeney Erect," note 8.
3. Spotted or stained, an implied antithesis to *immaculate*.
4. Río de la Plata, between Argentina and Uruguay. "The Raven" (Corvus), in l. 7, is a southern constellation. The constellations mentioned in l. 9 are visible in both hemispheres.
5. In Homer's *Odyssey* (19.560–69), Penelope distinguishes between true dreams, guarded by gates of horn, and deceptive ones, guarded by gates of ivory. This distinction became traditional in later literature. Also possibly a reference to Cape Horn, at the tip of South America.

Therefore the man with heavy eyes
Declines the gambit, shows fatigue,

Leaves the room and reappears
Outside the window, leaning in,   30
Branches of wistaria
Circumscribe a golden grin;

The host with someone indistinct
Converses at the door apart,
The nightingales are singing near   35
The Convent of the Sacred Heart,

And sang within the bloody wood[6]
When Agamemnon cried aloud,
And let their liquid droppings fall
To stain the stiff dishonoured shroud.   40

---

6. Eliot apparently transfers the murder of Agamemnon to a wood, complete with nightingales. There are none in *Agamemnon*, though Cassandra, his daughter, compares her own coming death unfavorably to that of Procne, transformed into a nightingale.

The Waste Land

"Nam Sibyllam quidem Cumis ego ipse oculis meis vidi in ampulla pendere, et cum illi pueri dicerent: Σίβυλλα τί θέλεις; respondebat ila: ἀποθανεῖν θέλω."[1]

For Ezra Pound
il miglior fabbro.[2]

---

1. For I once saw with my own eyes the Cumean Sibyl hanging in a jar, and when the boys asked her, "Sibyl, what do you want?" she answered, "I want to die" (Greek). Quoted from the *Satyricon* of Petronius Arbiter, a noted libertine of the 1st century CE. It is one of many empty boasts and tall stories delivered at the banquet of Trimalchio, a freedman. The Sibyl, one of a number of prophetic figures so named in ancient times, is confined to a jar because her body threatens to deliquesce. Granted a wish by Apollo, she had asked for as many years of life as there are grains in a handful of sand, but she forgot to ask for eternal youth as well.
2. The better craftsman (Italian). Eliot's tribute to his friend and fellow poet Ezra Pound (1885–1972), whose poetic craftsmanship was invaluable in editing the *Waste Land* manuscript. The phrase echoes the tribute offered by Dante to 12th-century Provençal poet Arnaut Daniel in Canto 26 of Dante's *Purgatorio*, a section from which Eliot also borrows for l. 427.

I. The Burial of the Dead[3]

April is the cruellest month, breeding
Lilacs out of the dead land, mixing
Memory and desire, stirring
Dull roots with spring rain.
Winter kept us warm, covering   5
Earth in forgetful snow, feeding
A little life with dried tubers.
Summer surprised us, coming over the Starnbergersee[4]
With a shower of rain; we stopped in the colonnade,
And went on in sunlight, into the Hofgarten,   10
And drank coffee, and talked for an hour.
Bin gar keine Russin, stamm' aus Litauen, echt deutsch.[5]
And when we were children, staying at the arch-duke's,
My cousin's, he took me out on a sled,
And I was frightened. He said, Marie,   15
Marie, hold on tight. And down we went.[6]
In the mountains, there you feel free.
I read, much of the night, and go south in the winter.

What are the roots that clutch, what branches grow
Out of this stony rubbish? Son of man,[7]   20
You cannot say, or guess, for you know only
A heap of broken images, where the sun beats,
And the dead tree gives no shelter, the cricket no relief,[8]
And the dry stone no sound of water. Only
There is shadow under this red rock,   25
(Come in under the shadow of this red rock),
And I will show you something different from either
Your shadow at morning striding behind you

---

3. The title given to the burial service in the Anglican Book of Common Prayer.
4. A lake near Munich, Germany; the Hofgarten (l. 10) is a park in the same city.
5. I'm not Russian at all; I come from Lithuania, a true German (German).
6. According to Valerie Eliot's notes to the published manuscript of *The Waste Land*, Eliot based this sledding incident on a conversation he had with the Countess Marie Larisch, who published her reminiscences of the Austrian nobility in *My Past* (1913).
7. In his own note, Eliot cites Ezekiel 2:1: "And he said unto me, Son of man, stand upon thy feet, and I will speak unto thee." Thereafter, God addresses the prophet by this phrase: "Son of man, I have made thee a watchman unto the house of Israel" (3:17).
8. Eliot cites Ecclesiastes 12:5: "Also when they shall be afraid of that which is high, and fears shall be in the way, and the almond tree shall flourish, and the grasshopper shall be a burden, and desire shall fail: because man goeth to his long home, and the mourners go about the streets." The chapter, is devoted to the sorrow of old age and decline, when it is discovered that "all is vanity" (12:8).

Or your shadow at evening rising to meet you;[9]
I will show you fear in a handful of dust.   30

> Frisch weht der Wind
> Der Heimat zu,
> Mein Irisch Kind,
> Wo weilest du?[1]

"You gave me hyacinths[2] first a year ago;   35
"They called me the hyacinth girl."
—Yet when we came back, late, from the Hyacinth garden,
Your arms full, and your hair wet, I could not
Speak, and my eyes failed, I was neither
Living nor dead, and I knew nothing,   40
Looking into the heart of light, the silence.

Oed' und leer das Meer.[3]

Madame Sosostris, famous clairvoyante,[4]
Had a bad cold, nevertheless
Is known to be the wisest woman in Europe,   45
With a wicked pack of cards.[5] Here, said she,
Is your card, the drowned Phoenician Sailor,
(Those are pearls that were his eyes. Look!)[6]
Here is Belladonna, the Lady of the Rocks,[7]

---

9. Eliot salvaged ll. 26–29 from "The Death of St. Narcissus," which he completed in 1915 but never published.
1. Fresh blows the wind / To the homeland / My Irish child / Where do you wait? (German). The first of two quotations from Richard Wagner's *Tristan und Isolde* (first performed in 1865). This one, which occurs at the beginning of the opera, is part of a song overheard by Isolde, who is being taken by Tristan to Ireland, where she is to marry King Mark. The original story, put into German verse in the Middle Ages by Gottfried von Strassburg (Wagner's source), gradually became part of Arthurian literature and thus came to be associated with the Grail legend Eliot refers to elsewhere in the poem.
2. The flower now referred to by this name is not the one so named by the Greeks, who saw the letters "AI," spelling out a cry of woe, in its petals. The story told about this flower makes it a memorial to a young man loved and accidentally killed by Apollo.
3. Desolate and empty is the sea (German). The second quotation from Wagner's *Tristan und Isolde*. This one, taken from the third act of the opera, occurs as the dying Tristan waits for news of Isolde, arriving by sea.
4. Eliot may have taken the name from Aldous Huxley's novel *Crome Yellow* (1921). See below, pp. 81–82.
5. As Eliot's note slyly admits, this passage has only a very loose connection with the Tarot pack used by fortune tellers to probe the past and predict the future. But there is a discussion of the Tarot in Jessie L. Weston's *From Ritual to Romance*, which connects the pack to the Grail legend and fertility rituals. See "[The Tarot Pack]," below, pp. 77–78.
6. One of a number of borrowings from Shakespeare's *The Tempest*, 1.2. This line is from the song the spirit Ariel sings to Ferdinand of his father's supposed drowning. See also l. 125.
7. The literal meaning of the name is "beautiful lady." She is frequently associated by commentators with Leonardo da Vinci's *Madonna of the Rocks* and with his *Mona Lisa*, who is famously described in Walter Pater's *The Renaissance* (1893) as "older than the rocks among which she sits." There is no such card in the Tarot pack.

The lady of situations.   50
Here is the man with three staves, and here the Wheel,[8]
And here is the one-eyed merchant, and this card,
Which is blank, is something he carries on his back,
Which I am forbidden to see. I do not find
The Hanged Man. Fear death by water.   55
I see crowds of people, walking round in a ring.
Thank you. If you see dear Mrs. Equitone,
Tell her I bring the horoscope myself:
One must be so careful these days.

Unreal City,[9]   60
Under the brown fog of a winter dawn,
A crowd flowed over London Bridge, so many,
I had not thought death had undone so many.[1]
Sighs, short and infrequent, were exhaled,
And each man fixed his eyes before his feet.   65
Flowed up the hill and down King William Street,
To where Saint Mary Woolnoth[2] kept the hours
With a dead sound on the final stroke of nine.
There I saw one I knew, and stopped him, crying: "Stetson!
"You who were with me in the ships at Mylae![3]   70
"That corpse you planted last year in your garden,
"Has it begun to sprout? Will it bloom this year?
"Or has the sudden frost disturbed its bed?
"Oh keep the Dog far hence, that's friend to men,[4]
"Or with his nails he'll dig it up again!   75
"You! hypocrite lecteur!—mon semblable,—mon frère!"[5]

---

8. The man with the three staves and the wheel are authentic Tarot cards, but the one-eyed merchant is a mystery of Eliot's devising.
9. As Eliot notes, this is his adaptation of Charles Baudelaire's "Fourmillante cité" from his poem "Le sept vieillards" (in *Les Fleurs du Mal*, 1857). See "The Seven Old Men," below, pp. 84–85.
1. In his note, Eliot refers the reader to two passages from Dante's *Inferno*. The first is from Canto 3, which takes place just inside the Gates of Hell, in a vestibule to which are consigned those who are equally without blame and without praise. Looking at this great company, Dante delivers the exclamation Eliot translates in l. 63. The next line is taken from Canto 4, in which Dante descends into the first circle of Hell, or Limbo, where those who died without baptism languish, sighing impotently, for there is nothing that can be done about their condition.
2. A church at the corner of Lombard and King William streets in the City (or financial district) of London. The last part of its name refers to Wulfnoth, who may have founded the medieval church that was demolished in the 18th century and completely rebuilt in 1727. Bank Station nearby was a frequent stop on Eliot's commute to work.
3. A battle (260 BCE) in the First Punic War between Rome and Carthage.
4. Eliot's adaptation of some lines from a dirge in John Webster's *The White Devil* (1612), sung by Cornelia as she prepares her son's body for burial. See "[Cornelia's Dirge]," below, p. 86.
5. "Hypocrite reader!—my likeness,—my brother!" (French). Eliot's version of the final line of Baudelaire's "Au Lecteur," the introductory poem in *Les Fleurs du Mal*. See "To the Reader," below, pp. 83–84.

II. A Game of Chess[6]

The Chair she sat in, like a burnished throne,[7]
Glowed on the marble, where the glass
Held up by standards wrought with fruited vines
From which a golden Cupidon peeped out   80
(Another hid his eyes behind his wing)
Doubled the flames of sevenbranched candelabra
Reflecting light upon the table as
The glitter of her jewels rose to meet it,
From satin cases poured in rich profusion;   85
In vials of ivory and coloured glass
Unstoppered, lurked her strange synthetic perfumes,
Unguent, powdered, or liquid—troubled, confused
And drowned the sense in odours; stirred by the air
That freshened from the window, these ascended   90
In fattening the prolonged candle-flames,
Flung their smoke into the laquearia,[8]
Stirring the pattern on the coffered ceiling.
Huge sea-wood fed with copper
Burned green and orange, framed by the coloured stone,   95
In which sad light a carvèd dolphin swam.
Above the antique mantel was displayed
As though a window gave upon the sylvan scene[9]
The change of Philomel, by the barbarous king
So rudely forced;[1] yet there the nightingale   100
Filled all the desert with inviolable voice
And still she cried, and still the world pursues,
"Jug Jug"[2] to dirty ears.
And other withered stumps of time
Were told upon the walls; staring forms   105

6. Eliot takes the title of this section from a satirical play of the same name by Thomas
   Middleton (1570?–1627). First produced in 1624, *A Game of Chess* was suppressed
   because it bitingly allegorized English conflict with Spain as a chess match. The title
   also alludes to Middleton's *Women Beware Women* (published in 1657), in which a
   young wife is seduced while her unwitting mother-in-law plays chess.
7. In his note, Eliot cites Shakespeare's *Antony and Cleopatra* 2.2.190. In this passage,
   Enobarbus describes to Agrippa how Cleopatra looked on her first meeting with Mark
   Antony: "The barge she sat in, like a burnished throne, / Burned on the water: the poop
   was beaten gold."
8. The panels of a coffered ceiling. In his note, Eliot cites a passage from Virgil's *Aeneid*:
   "Burning torches hang from the gold-panelled ceiling, / And vanquish the night with
   their flames" (Latin).
9. Eliot cites a passage from Milton's *Paradise Lost*, Book 4, in which Satan, approaching Eden,
   sees it as a "delicious Paradise" and a "Sylvan Scene" overgrown with trees and bushes.
1. Eliot refers in his note to the story of Tereus and Philomela as told in Ovid's *Metamor-
   phoses* (ca. 8 CE). See "[The Story of Tereus and Philomela]," below, pp. 87–91.
2. Conventional literary onomatopoeia for the sound a nightingale supposedly makes.

Leaned out, leaning, hushing the room enclosed.
Footsteps shuffled on the stair.
Under the firelight, under the brush, her hair
Spread out in fiery points
Glowed into words, then would be savagely still.   110

"My nerves are bad to-night. Yes, bad. Stay with me.
"Speak to me. Why do you never speak? Speak.
"What are you thinking of? What thinking? What?
"I never know what you are thinking. Think."

I think we are in rats' alley   115
Where the dead men lost their bones.

"What is that noise?"
                    The wind under the door.
"What is that noise now? What is the wind doing?"
                    Nothing again nothing.   120
                                        "Do
"You know nothing? Do you see nothing? Do you remember
"Nothing?"
                    I remember
Those are pearls that were his eyes.[3]   125
"Are you alive, or not? Is there nothing in your head?"
                                        But

O O O O that Shakespeherian Rag[4]—
It's so elegant
So intelligent   130

"What shall I do now? What shall I do?"
"I shall rush out as I am, and walk the street
"With my hair down, so. What shall we do tomorrow?
"What shall we ever do?"
                    The hot water at ten.   135
And if it rains, a closed car at four.
And we shall play a game of chess,
Pressing lidless eyes and waiting for a knock upon
    the door.

---

3. A reference to the line from Ariel's song in *The Tempest* quoted above, l. 48.
4. Eliot's syncopated version of a popular song, published in 1912, with lyrics by Gene
   Buck and Herman Ruby and music by Dave Stamper. See "That Shakespearian Rag,"
   below, pp. 92–95.

When Lil's husband got demobbed,⁵ I said—
I didn't mince my words, I said to her myself,   140
HURRY UP PLEASE ITS TIME⁶
Now Albert's coming back, make yourself a bit smart.
He'll want to know what you done with that money he
    gave you
To get yourself some teeth. He did, I was there.
You have them all out, Lil, and get a nice set,   145
He said, I swear, I can't bear to look at you.
And no more can't I, I said, and think of poor Albert,
He's been in the army four years, he wants a good time,
And if you don't give it him, there's others will, I said.
Oh is there, she said. Something o' that, I said.   150
Then I'll know who to thank, she said, and give me a straight
    look.
HURRY UP PLEASE ITS TIME
If you don't like it you can get on with it, I said.
Others can pick and choose if you can't.
But if Albert makes off, it won't be for lack of telling.   155
You ought to be ashamed, I said, to look so antique.
(And her only thirty-one.)
I can't help it, she said, pulling a long face,
It's them pills I took, to bring it off, she said.
(She's had five already, and nearly died of young George.)   160
The chemist⁷ said it would be all right, but I've never been
    the same.
You *are* a proper fool, I said.
Well, if Albert won't leave you alone, there it is, I said,
What you get married for if you don't want children?
HURRY UP PLEASE ITS TIME   165
Well, that Sunday Albert was home, they had a
    hot gammon,⁸
And they asked me in to dinner, to get the beauty of
    it hot—
HURRY UP PLEASE ITS TIME
HURRY UP PLEASE ITS TIME
Goonight Bill. Goonight Lou. Goonight May. Goonight.   170
Ta ta. Goonight. Goonight.

5. Demobilized, or released from the armed services after World War I. According to
Valerie Eliot's notes to the *Waste Land* manuscript, this final passage was based on
gossip recounted to the Eliots by Ellen Kellond, their maid.
6. Closing time, as announced at a pub.
7. Pharmacist.
8. Ham.

Good night, ladies, good night, sweet ladies, good night, good
    night.⁹

III. The Fire Sermon¹

The river's tent is broken: the last fingers of leaf
Clutch and sink into the wet bank. The wind
Crosses the brown land, unheard. The nymphs are
    departed.   175
Sweet Thames, run softly, till I end my song.²
The river bears no empty bottles, sandwich papers,
Silk handkerchiefs, cardboard boxes, cigarette ends
Or other testimony of summer nights. The nymphs are
    departed.
And their friends, the loitering heirs of city directors;   180
Departed, have left no addresses.
By the waters of Leman I sat down and wept³ . . .
Sweet Thames, run softly till I end my song,
Sweet Thames, run softly, for I speak not loud or long.
But at my back in a cold blast I hear⁴   185
The rattle of the bones, and chuckle spread from ear to ear.

A rat crept softly through the vegetation
Dragging its slimy belly on the bank
While I was fishing in the dull canal
On a winter evening round behind the gashouse   190
Musing upon the king my brother's wreck
And on the king my father's death before him.⁵
White bodies naked on the low damp ground
And bones cast in a little low dry garret,
Rattled by the rat's foot only, year to year.   195

9. In *Hamlet* 4.5.71–72, the mad Ophelia's parting words to Queen Gertrude and King
   Claudius before her death.
1. The title of this section is taken from a sermon preached by Buddha against the things
   of this world, all figured as consuming fires. See "The Fire-Sermon," below, pp. 96–97.
2. The refrain from "Prothalamion" (1596), by Edmund Spenser (1552 or 1553–1599).
   See "*From* Prothalamion," below, pp. 97–98.
3. An adaptation of Psalm 137, which begins, "By the rivers of Babylon, there we sat
   down, yea, we wept, when we remembered Zion." In the original, the people of Israel,
   in Babylonian exile, remember the city of Jerusalem. Eliot substitutes "Leman," the
   French name for Lake Geneva, where he spent several weeks in 1921 on a rest cure
   while working on *The Waste Land*.
4. The first of two references to Andrew Marvell's poem "To His Coy Mistress," first pub-
   lished in 1681, three years after the poet's death. Eliot adapts the lines, "But at my back
   I always hear / Time's wingèd chariot hurrying near," with which the speaker turns
   from his leisurely catalog of his lady's physical charms to the urgent carpe diem theme
   that has made the poem famous. See also l. 196.
5. Another reference to *The Tempest* 1.2. Just before hearing Ariel's song (see l. 48), Ferdinand
   describes himself as "Sitting on a bank, / Weeping again the King my father's wrack."

But at my back from time to time I hear
The sound of horns and motors, which shall bring
Sweeney to Mrs. Porter in the spring.[6]
O the moon shone bright on Mrs. Porter
And on her daughter   200
They wash their feet in soda water
Et O ces voix d'enfants, chantant dans la coupole![7]

Twit twit twit
Jug jug jug jug jug jug
So rudely forc'd.   205
Tereu[8]

Unreal City
Under the brown fog of a winter noon
Mr. Eugenides, the Smyrna[9] merchant
Unshaven, with a pocket full of currants   210
C.i.f. London: documents at sight,
Asked me in demotic[1] French
To luncheon at the Cannon Street Hotel[2]
Followed by a weekend at the Metropole.[3]

---

6. Eliot apparently had in mind for these lines an elaborate parallel to a story told in, among other places, the allegorical masque *The Parliament of Bees* (1607), by John Day (1574–1640), which is cited in his notes. Sweeney, who seems from his actions in other of Eliot's poems ("Sweeney Erect" and "Sweeney Among the Nightingales"; see above, pp. 30 and 40), to have been his idea of an urban lout, approaches Mrs. Porter as Actaeon approaches Diana in the story referred to by Day. Actaeon surprises Diana (goddess of chastity as well as the hunt) while she is bathing, is turned into a stag by her, and is subsequently hunted to death by his own hounds.

7. The last line of French poet Paul Verlaine's sonnet "Parsifal," which first appeared in 1886 and was subsequently included in *Amour* (1888). The original line reads, "—Et, ô ces voix d'enfants chantant dans la coupole!" It can be translated as "And oh those children's voices singing in the dome!" In Verlaine's poem, Parsifal resists the temptations of female flesh, vanquishes Hell, restores the ailing king, and kneels to adore the Holy Grail, having become its priest. In general, the sonnet paraphrases its source, Richard Wagner's opera *Parsifal* (1877), in which Parsifal resists the wiles of Kundry, seizes the spear that had originally wounded King Amfortas, and heals him with it. The line Eliot quotes refers to the end of the opera, in which the dome of the Grail Castle fills with unearthly voices as Parsifal unwraps and raises the Grail. Many commentators have noticed as well that in the opera (though not in Verlaine's poem) Parsifal receives a ritual footbath before his final approach to the Grail Castle.

8. Noises made by the protagonists in the story of Tereus and Philomela, all of whom were turned into birds. "Tereu" is the vocative form of the name of Tereus, indicating that he is being addressed. In at least one Elizabethan source, *Alexander and Campaspe* (attributed to John Lyly), the ravished Philomela, turned into a nightingale, accuses Tereus in her song: "Jug, jug, jug, jug, tereu!" See "The Story of Tereus and Philomela," below, pp. 87–91.

9. A city in Anatolia, now the Turkish city of Izmir. After World War I, Smyrna was the focus of a calamitous war between Greece and Turkey, which was much in the news while Eliot composed his poem. Greece's loss of Smyrna resulted in a military coup in that country, while Britain's role became a factor in the fall of the Lloyd George government in 1922.

1. Colloquial (of the people), as opposed to scholarly.

2. A commercial hotel in the City of London.

3. A fashionable hotel in Brighton, a popular resort.

At the violet hour, when the eyes and back   215
Turn upward from the desk, when the human engine waits
Like a taxi throbbing waiting,
I Tiresias, though blind, throbbing between two lives,
Old man with wrinkled female breasts,[4] can see
At the violet hour, the evening hour that strives   220
Homeward, and brings the sailor home from sea,[5]
The typist home at teatime, clears her breakfast, lights
Her stove, and lays out food in tins.
Out of the window perilously spread
Her drying combinations[6] touched by the sun's last rays,   225
On the divan are piled (at night her bed)
Stockings, slippers, camisoles, and stays.
I Tiresias, old man with wrinkled dugs
Perceived the scene, and foretold the rest—
I too awaited the expected guest.   230
He, the young man carbuncular,[7] arrives,
A small house agent's clerk, with one bold stare,
One of the low on whom assurance sits
As a silk hat on a Bradford millionaire.[8]
The time is now propitious, as he guesses,   235
The meal is ended, she is bored and tired,
Endeavours to engage her in caresses
Which still are unreproved, if undesired.
Flushed and decided, he assaults at once;
Exploring hands encounter no defence;   240
His vanity requires no response,
And makes a welcome of indifference.
(And I Tiresias have foresuffered all
Enacted on this same divan or bed;
I who have sat by Thebes below the wall   245
And walked among the lowest of the dead.)[9]
Bestows one final patronising kiss,
And gropes his way, finding the stairs unlit . . .

4. The mythological figure Tiresias, who had once been turned into a woman and thus
   had lived "two lives," was blinded in a dispute between Juno and Jove. For the story, see
   "[The Blinding of Tiresias]," below, p. 86.
5. In his note, Eliot refers to a poem by Sappho (630–ca. 570 BCE), Fragment 149, a prayer
   to the Evening Star.
6. One-piece undergarments.
7. A carbuncle is an infected boil.
8. Bradford is a manufacturing town in the north of England. A millionaire from that
   town would have made his money in trade or manufacturing. Hence, nouveau riche.
9. Ll. 245–46 draw on other classical references to the story of Tiresias, particularly his
   role (as a Theban seer) in *Antigone* and *Oedipus Rex* by Sophocles (496–406 BCE), and
   in Homer's *Odyssey*, where he appears in the underworld to advise Odysseus.

She turns and looks a moment in the glass,
Hardly aware of her departed lover;   250
Her brain allows one half-formed thought to pass:
"Well now that's done: and I'm glad it's over."
When lovely woman stoops to folly[1] and
Paces about her room again, alone,
She smoothes her hair with automatic hand,   255
And puts a record on the gramophone.

"This music crept by me upon the waters"[2]
And along the Strand, up Queen Victoria Street.[3]
O City City, I can sometimes hear
Beside a public bar in Lower Thames Street,[4]   260
The pleasant whining of a mandoline
And a clatter and a chatter from within
Where fishmen lounge at noon: where the walls
Of Magnus Martyr[5] hold
Inexplicable splendour of Ionian white and gold.   265

The river sweats
Oil and tar
The barges drift
With the turning tide
Red sails   270
Wide
To leeward, swing on the heavy spar.
The barges wash
Drifting logs
Down Greenwich reach[6]   275
Past the Isle of Dogs.
                    Weialala leia
                    Wallala leialala[7]

---

1. In his note, Eliot refers to Oliver Goldsmith's novel *The Vicar of Wakefield* (1762). See
   "[Olivia's Song]," below, p. 98.
2. As Eliot points out in his note, another reference to Ariel's Song in *The Tempest*. See
   also ll. 48 and 125.
3. Streets in the City of London, running more or less parallel to the River Thames.
4. A street in the City of London, running parallel to the Thames near London Bridge.
   The Church of St. Magnus Martyr is on Lower Thames Street.
5. A church on this site, dedicated to the Norse martyr St. Magnus, is mentioned as far
   back as William the Conqueror. Rebuilt (1671–76) after the Great Fire by the English
   architect Sir Christopher Wren, the present church is on Lower Thames Street at the
   foot of London Bridge, in a district traditionally associated with fishmongers. The col-
   umns dividing the nave from the side aisles are Ionic.
6. The Thames at Greenwich, downstream from London. The Isle of Dogs is the name
   given to the riverbank opposite Greenwich.
7. The lament of the Rhine-maidens in Richard Wagner's *Die Götterdämmerung*, the last
   of the four operas that comprise *Der Ring des Nibelungen* (first performed as a whole
   in 1876). In *Das Rheingold*, the first opera in the series, the maidens lose the gold

Elizabeth and Leicester[8]
Beating oars   280
The stern was formed
A gilded shell
Red and gold
The brisk swell
Rippled both shores   285
Southwest wind
Carried down stream
The peal of bells
White towers
        Weialala leia   290
        Wallala leialala

"Trams and dusty trees.
Highbury bore me. Richmond and Kew[9]
Undid me. By Richmond I raised my knees
Supine on the floor of a narrow canoe."   295

"My feet are at Moorgate,[1] and my heart
Under my feet. After the event
He wept. He promised 'a new start.'
I made no comment. What should I resent?"

"On Margate Sands.[2]   300
I can connect
Nothing with nothing.
The broken fingernails of dirty hands.
My people humble people who expect
Nothing."   305
        la la

---

deposited in their river. It is this gold, forged into a ring, that sets in motion the events of the four operas.

8. Eliot's note quotes a passage from James Anthony Froude's *History of England*. For the context, see "[Elizabeth and Leicester]," below, p. 99.

9. Eliot's note suggests a parallel between this scene and a passage in Canto 5 of Dante's *Purgatorio*, in which Dante is addressed in turn by three spirits, the last of whom identifies herself as La Pia, born in Siena and murdered by her husband in Maremma. The formula is common in epitaphs, as, for example, in Virgil's as given by Suetonius: "Mantua me genuit, Calabri rapuere" (Mantua gave me light; Calabria slew me [Latin]). But Eliot adapts it in this case to a seduction; Highbury is the London suburb in which the victim was born, Richmond and Kew two riverside districts west of London where her virtue was "undone."

1. An area in east London.

2. Eliot spent three weeks in October 1921 at the Albemarle Hotel, Cliftonville, Margate, a seaside resort in the Thames estuary. This was the first part of a three-month rest cure during which he composed the bulk of *The Waste Land*. His hotel bill has survived, attached to the manuscript of "The Fire Sermon."

To Carthage then I came[3]

Burning burning burning burning[4]
O Lord Thou pluckest me out
O Lord Thou pluckest   310

burning

IV. Death by Water

Phlebas the Phoenician, a fortnight dead,
Forgot the cry of gulls, and the deep sea swell
And the profit and loss.
                          A current under sea   315
Picked his bones in whispers. As he rose and fell
He passed the stages of his age and youth
Entering the whirlpool.
                          Gentile or Jew
O you who turn the wheel and look to windward,   320
Consider Phlebas, who was once handsome and tall as you.

V. What the Thunder Said

After the torchlight red on sweaty faces
After the frosty silence in the gardens
After the agony in stony places
The shouting and the crying   325
Prison and palace and reverberation
Of thunder of spring over distant mountains[5]
He who was living is now dead
We who were living are now dying
With a little patience   330

Here is no water but only rock
Rock and no water and the sandy road
The road winding above among the mountains

3. Eliot's note refers to a passage in Augustine (354–430 CE), *Confessions*, in which he describes the sensual temptations of his youth. For the context of the passage, see "From *Confessions*," below, p. 99.
4. Eliot's drastic redaction from Buddha's Fire Sermon. For the text to which he refers in his note, see "The Fire-Sermon," below, pp. 96–97.
5. Eliot's headnote to this section helps us see these lines as a description of the betrayal, arrest, interrogation, and crucifixion of Christ, with the earthquake that follows in Matthew 27.

Which are mountains of rock without water
If there were water we should stop and drink   335
Amongst the rock one cannot stop or think
Sweat is dry and feet are in the sand
If there were only water amongst the rock
Dead mountain mouth of carious teeth that cannot spit
Here one can neither stand nor lie nor sit   340
There is not even silence in the mountains
But dry sterile thunder without rain
There is not even solitude in the mountains
But red sullen faces sneer and snarl
From doors of mudcracked houses   345
                          If there were water
   And no rock
   If there were rock
   And also water
   And water
   A spring   350
   A pool among the rock
   If there were the sound of water only
   Not the cicada
   And dry grass singing
   But sound of water over a rock   355
   Where the hermit-thrush sings in the pine trees
   Drip drop drip drop drop drop drop
   But there is no water

Who is the third who walks always beside you?[6]
When I count, there are only you and I together   360
But when I look ahead up the white road
There is always another one walking beside you
Gliding wrapt in a brown mantle, hooded
I do not know whether a man or a woman
—But who is that on the other side of you?   365

What is that sound high in the air[7]
Murmur of maternal lamentation

---

6. According to Eliot's note, he adapted this passage from an episode in Sir Ernest Shackleton's *South* in which three Antarctic explorers fancy that there is a fourth man with them. The passage also bears a strong resemblance to the story told in Luke 24 of the two men on the road to Emmaus who do not recognize the risen Christ. See "[The Road to Emmaus]," below, pp. 100–01, and "[The Extra Man]," below, p. 101.

7. As a source for the next ten lines, Eliot cites in his note German author Hermann Hesse's *Blick ins Chaos* (1922), translated, at Eliot's urging, as *In Sight of Chaos*. For a translation of the excerpt quoted in Eliot's note and the relevant context, see "[The Downfall of Europe]," below, pp. 102–04.

Who are those hooded hordes swarming
Over endless plains, stumbling in cracked earth
Ringed by the flat horizon only   370
What is the city over the mountains
Cracks and reforms and bursts in the violet air
Falling towers
Jerusalem Athens Alexandria
Vienna London   375
Unreal

A woman drew her long black hair out tight
And fiddled whisper music on those strings
And bats with baby faces in the violet light
Whistled, and beat their wings   380
And crawled head downward down a blackened wall
And upside down in air were towers
Tolling reminiscent bells, that kept the hours
And voices singing out of empty cisterns and exhausted wells.

In this decayed hole among the mountains   385
In the faint moonlight, the grass is singing
Over the tumbled graves, about the chapel
There is the empty chapel, only the wind's home.[8]
It has no windows, and the door swings,
Dry bones can harm no one.   390
Only a cock stood on the rooftree
Co co rico co co rico
In a flash of lightning. Then a damp gust
Bringing rain

Ganga[9] was sunken, and the limp leaves   395
Waited for rain, while the black clouds
Gathered far distant, over Himavant.[1]
The jungle crouched, humped in silence.
Then spoke the thunder
DA   400
Datta: what have we given?[2]

8. According to the headnote to this section, Eliot has in mind the Chapel Perilous as
   described in Jessie L. Weston's *From Ritual to Romance*. See "[The Perilous Chapel],"
   below, p. 79.
9. The Ganges, sacred river of India. Ganga is a colloquial version of its name.
1. More commonly Himavat or Himavan. Sanskrit adjective meaning snowy, usually
   applied to the mountains known as the Himalayas, especially when personified as the
   father of the Ganges, among other deities.
2. As Eliot reveals in his note, this part of the poem is based on a section of the
   Brihadāranyaka Upanishad in which God presents three sets of disciples with the enig-
   matic syllable DA, challenging each group to understand it. Each group is supposed to

My friend, blood shaking my heart
The awful daring of a moment's surrender
Which an age of prudence can never retract[3]
By this, and this only, we have existed   405
Which is not to be found in our obituaries
Or in memories draped by the beneficent spider[4]
Or under seals broken by the lean solicitor
In our empty rooms
Da   410
Dayadhvam: I have heard the key
Turn in the door once and turn once only[5]
We think of the key, each in his prison
Thinking of the key, each confirms a prison
Only at nightfall, aethereal rumours   415
Revive for a moment a broken Coriolanus[6]
Da
Damyata: The boat responded
Gaily, to the hand expert with sail and oar
The sea was calm, your heart would have responded   420
Gaily, when invited, beating obedient
To controlling hands

                    I sat upon the shore[7]
Fishing, with the arid plain behind me
Shall I at least set my lands in order?[8]   425

---

understand the syllable as the root of a different imperative: "damyata" (control) for
the gods, who are naturally unruly; "datta" (give) to men, who are avaricious; "dayadh-
vam" (compassion) to the demons, who are cruel. For the full passage, see "The Three
Great Disciplines," below, pp. 104–05.

3. Behind this line lies the lament of Francesca da Rimini, whom Dante encounters in the
   second circle of Hell, where she is being punished eternally for having committed adul-
   tery with her brother-in-law Paolo Malatesta. As she tells the story in Canto 5 of the
   Inferno, the two fell in love while reading a romance about Lancelot: "ma solo un punto
   fu quel che ci vinse" (but one moment alone it was that overcame us [Italian]).
4. As Eliot says in his note, he found the model for this love-denying spider in Webster's
   The White Devil.
5. According to Eliot's note, these lines combine two references. The first is to the story
   of Count Ugolino, whom Dante encounters in Canto 33 of the *Inferno.* Accused of
   treason, the count was shut up in a tower, where he starved to death. The second refer-
   ence is to the philosophy of F. H. Bradley (1846–1924), on whom Eliot had written his
   doctoral thesis, which insists on and then tries to overcome the radical privacy of all
   experience.
6. Another image of isolation. Coriolanus was a Roman war hero who defied public opin-
   ion and ended his life leading a foreign army against Rome. He is the subject of a play
   by Shakespeare, *Coriolanus* (1607–08), and of a poem by Eliot, "Coriolan" (1931).
7. In his note, Eliot refers the reader to Chapter 9 of Weston's *From Ritual to Romance.*
   For an excerpt, see "The Fisher King," below, p. 78.
8. The prophet Isaiah challenges King Hezekiah: "Thus saith the Lord, Set thine house
   in order; for thou shalt die and not live" (Isaiah 38:1).

London Bridge is falling down falling down falling down[9]
Poi s'ascose nel foco che gli affina[1]
Quando fiam uti chelidon[2]—O swallow swallow
Le Prince d'Aquitaine à la tour abolie[3]
These fragments I have shored against my ruins   430
Why then Ile fit you. Hieronymo's mad againe.[4]
Datta. Dayadhvam. Damyata.

      Shantih   shantih   shantih

---

9. A children's nursery rhyme, made somewhat more pertinent by the fact that most of
the London place names in *The Waste Land* are in the vicinity of London Bridge.
1. Then he hid himself in the fire that refines them (Italian). This is the last line of Canto
26 of Dante's *Purgatorio*, in which Dante meets the poet Arnaut Daniel, who warns
him in his own language, "Sovegna vos a temps de ma dolor" (In due time be heedful of
my pain [Provençal]). This was a passage of extraordinary importance to Eliot, as evi-
denced by the fact that he borrowed the term applied to Daniel, "miglior fabbro," for
his dedicatory line to Ezra Pound.
2. When shall I be like the swallow? (Latin). A line from the anonymous poem *Pervigil-
ium Veneris*, which ends with a reference to the Philomela story Eliot had already used
elsewhere in *The Waste Land*. For the context, see below, pp. 105–06.
3. The Prince of Aquitaine of the ruined tower (French). The second line of "El Desdi-
chado" (The Dispossessed) (1854), a sonnet by Gerard de Nerval (1808–1855).
4. Eliot's note refers to Thomas Kyd's *The Spanish Tragedie* (1592), the subtitle of which
is *Hieronymo Is Mad Againe*. In Act 4 of the play, Hieronymo, driven mad by the mur-
der of his son, stages a play in which he convinces the murderers to act a part. In the
course of the play, Heironymo actually kills the murderers and then himself. For the
scene in Act 4 in which Hieronymo convinces his adversaries to take part, see "From
The Spanish Tragedie," below, pp. 106–10.

Notes[1]

Not only the title, but the plan and a good deal of the incidental symbolism of the poem were suggested by Miss Jessie L. Weston's book on the Grail legend: *From Ritual to Romance* (Cambridge). Indeed, so deeply am I indebted, Miss Weston's book will elucidate the difficulties of the poem much better than my notes can do; and I recommend it (apart from the great interest of the book itself) to any who think such elucidation of the poem worth the trouble.[2] To another work of anthropology I am indebted in general, one which has influenced our generation profoundly; I mean *The Golden Bough*; I have used especially the two volumes *Adonis, Attis, Osiris*.[3] Anyone who is acquainted with these works will immediately recognise in the poem certain references to vegetation ceremonies.

I. THE BURIAL OF THE DEAD

Line 20. Cf. Ezekiel II, i.
23. Cf. Ecclesiastes XII, v.
31. V. Tristan und Isolde, I, verses 5–8.
42. Id. III, verse 24.

1. There are a number of different accounts of the genesis and purpose of these notes, which were first included in the Boni & Liveright edition. Late in his life, Eliot tended to disparage the notes, suggesting in his *On Poetry and Poets* (1957) that they were little more than "bogus scholarship" designed to bulk out a poem that was too short to fill a volume by itself (see "[On the *Waste Land* Notes]," below, p. 136). However, it is clear from the correspondence of Gilbert Seldes and James Sibley Watson of *The Dial* that the notes existed well before the poem was published there, so they cannot have been a mere afterthought. Clive Bell suggested in reminiscences put down in the 1950s that the Bloomsbury art critic Roger Fry first suggested to Eliot that he add notes to the poem, a suggestion to which Eliot rather vaguely agreed when asked by Daniel Woodward in the 1960s. The notes are notoriously evasive, and they are the source of some of the most intractable controversies attending the poem. No attempt will be made in the editorial footnotes here to adjudicate those controversies, which are well represented in the critical selections. Quotations from original sources in languages other than English will be translated here only if they have not been translated in the notes to the poem or in the Sources section.
2. *From Ritual to Romance* (1920), by folklorist Jessie L. Weston, traces medieval stories about the Holy Grail, supposed to be the chalice used at the Last Supper, to much older fertility rituals. The exact extent to which *The Waste Land* depends on Weston's text is one of the central issues addressed by critics. For selections, see below, pp. 75–80.
3. Sir James George Frazer (1854–1941) was perhaps the best known and most influential anthropologist of his era. He worked exclusively from documents, not from field study, and derived his conclusions from the exhaustive comparison of classical texts and modern practices. His work *The Golden Bough*, first published in 1890, expanded to the twelve-volume edition cited here by Eliot in 1911–15 and then abridged in 1922, affected Eliot primarily by suggesting parallels between ancient and modern beliefs. In particular, Frazer's analysis of ancient rituals having to do with the sacrificial death of an old king and beliefs associating the new king's potency with the fertility of the land left its impression on *The Waste Land*. For selections, see below, pp. 69–75.

46. I am not familiar with the exact constitution of the Tarot pack
of cards, from which I have obviously departed to suit my own con-
venience. The Hanged Man, a member of the traditional pack, fits
my purpose in two ways: because he is associated in my mind with
the Hanged God of Frazer, and because I associate him with the
hooded figure in the passage of the disciples to Emmaus in Part V. The
Phoenician Sailor and the Merchant appear later; also the "crowds
of people," and Death by Water is executed in Part IV. The Man with
Three Staves (an authentic member of the Tarot pack) I associate,
quite arbitrarily, with the Fisher King himself.

60. Cf. Baudelaire:

> "Fourmillante cité, cité pleine de rêves,
> "Où le spectre en plein jour raccroche le passant."[4]

63. Cf. Inferno III, 55–57:

> "si lunga tratta
> di gente, ch'io non avrei mai creduto
> che morte tanta n'avesse disfatta."[5]

64. Cf. Inferno IV, 25–27:

> "Quivi, secondo che per ascoltare,
> "non avea pianto, ma' che di sospiri,
> "che l'aura eterna facevan tremare."[6]

68. A phenomenon which I have often noticed.
74. Cf. the Dirge in Webster's *White Devil*.
76. V. Baudelaire, Preface to *Fleurs du Mal*.

II. A GAME OF CHESS

77. Cf. *Antony and Cleopatra*, II, ii, l. 190.
92. Laquearia. V. *Aeneid*, I, 726:

dependent lychni laquearibus aureis incensi, et noctem
flammis funalia vincunt.

98. Sylvan scene. V. Milton, *Paradise Lost*, IV, 140.
99. V. Ovid, *Metamorphoses*, VI, Philomela.
100. Cf. Part III, l. 204.
115. Cf. Part III, l. 195.

---

4. For an English version of the poem from which these lines are taken, see "The Seven
   Old Men," below, pp. 84–85.
5. "So long a train / of people, that I should not have believed / that death had undone so
   many" (Italian).
6. "Here, there was to be heard / no complaint but the sighs, / which caused the eternal
   air to tremble" (Italian).

118. Cf. Webster: "Is the wind in that door still?"[7]
125. Cf. Part I, l. 39, 48.
137. Cf. The game of chess in Middleton's *Women beware Women*.

III. THE FIRE SERMON

176. V. Spenser, *Prothalamion*.
192. Cf. *The Tempest*, I, ii.
196. Cf. Marvell, *To His Coy Mistress*.
197. Cf. Day, *Parliament of Bees*:

> "When of the sudden, listening, you shall hear,
> "A noise of horns and hunting, which shall bring
> "Actaeon to Diana in the spring,
> "Where all shall see her naked skin . . ."

199. I do not know the origin of the ballad from which these lines are taken: it was reported to me from Sydney, Australia.[8]
202. V. Verlaine, *Parsifal*.
210. The currants were quoted at a price "carriage and insurance free to London"; and the Bill of Lading etc. were to be handed to the buyer upon payment of the sight draft.[9]
218. Tiresias, although a mere spectator and not indeed a "character," is yet the most important personage in the poem, uniting all the rest. Just as the one-eyed merchant, seller of currants, melts into the Phoenician Sailor, and the latter is not wholly distinct from Ferdinand Prince of Naples, so all the women are one woman, and the two sexes meet in Tiresias. What Tiresias *sees*, in fact, is the substance of the poem. The whole passage from Ovid is of great anthropological interest:

> '. . . Cum Iunone iocos et maior vestra profecto est
> Quam, quae contingit maribus,' dixisse, 'voluptas.'

---

7. Eliot's reference is to John Webster's play *The Devil's Law-Case* (1623). In Act 3, Scene 2 of the play, two surgeons, caring for Lord Contarino, whose case they assume to be hopeless, are surprised to hear him groan. To the first surgeon's question, "Did he not groane?" the second replies, "Is the wind in that doore still?" The note implies a metaphorical reading of the line, in which the wind would be the dying breath of the patient, and this would give an eery resonance to l. 118 of *The Waste Land*. But according to F. L. Lucas, whose edition of Webster's plays Eliot read and reviewed in 1928, the line is merely idiomatic slang meaning something like "Is that the way the wind blows still?" and the second surgeon is not making any metaphorical reference but merely wondering that Contarino is still alive. Eliot later admitted as much and denied the relationship between this line and *The Devil's Law-Case*.
8. According to Clive Bell, Eliot reported to dinner-party guests shortly after the poem appeared that Mrs. Porter and her daughter "are known only from an Ayrian camp-fire song of which one other line has been preserved: *And so they oughter*." Ayr is a town in Queensland, Australia, named after the seaport town in Scotland, and so this may corroborate Eliot's rather vague claim about the origin of these lines.
9. An alternate possibility for the initials "C.i.f." has been suggested: "cost, insurance, freight."

Illa negat; placuit quae sit sententia docti
Quaerere Tiresiae: venus huic erat utraque nota.
Nam duo magnorum viridi coeuntia silva
Corpora serpentum baculi violaverat ictu
Deque viro factus, mirabile, femina septem
Egerat autumnos; octavo rursus eosdem
Vidit et 'est vestrae si tanta potentia plagae,'
Dixit 'ut auctoris sortem in contraria mutet,
Nunc quoque vos feriam!' percussis anguibus isdem
Forma prior rediit genetivaque venit imago.
Arbiter hic igitur sumptus de lite iocosa
Dicta Iovis firmat; gravius Saturnia iusto
Nec pro materia fertur doluisse suique
Iudicis aeterna damnavit lumina nocte,
At pater omnipotens (neque enim licet inrita cuiquam
Facta dei fecisse deo) pro lumine adempto
Scire futura dedit poenamque levavit honore.[1]

221. This may not appear as exact as Sappho's lines, but I had in mind the "longshore" or "dory" fisherman, who returns at nightfall.

253. V. Goldsmith, the song in *The Vicar of Wakefield.*

257. V. *The Tempest,* as above.

264. The interior of St. Magnus Martyr is to my mind one of the finest among Wren's interiors. See *The Proposed Demolition of Nineteen City Churches*: (P.S. King & Son, Ltd.).[2]

266. The Song of the (three) Thames-daughters begins here. From line 292 to 306 inclusive they speak in turn. V. *Götterdämmerung,* III, i: the Rhine-daughters.

279. V. Froude, *Elizabeth,* Vol. I, ch. iv, letter of De Quadra to Philip of Spain: "In the afternoon we were in a barge, watching the games on the river. (The queen) was alone with Lord Robert and myself on the poop, when they began to talk nonsense, and went so far that Lord Robert at last said, as I was on the spot there was no reason why they should not be married if the queen pleased."

293. Cf. *Purgatorio,* V, 133:

"Ricorditi di me, che son la Pia;
"Siena mi fe', disfecemi Maremma."

---

1. For an English prose version of this passage, see "[The Blinding of Tiresias]," below, p. 86.
2. In 1920 a commission appointed by the Bishop of London recommended the consolidation of the parishes in the City of London and the "removal" of nineteen churches, some of them dating, in earlier forms, to before the Norman conquest. Both St. Magnus Martyr and St. Mary Woolnoth were slated for demolition, but the plan was voted down by the House of Lords in 1926.

307. V. St. Augustine's *Confessions:* "to Carthage then I came, where a cauldron of unholy loves sang all about mine ears."

308. The complete text of the Buddha's Fire Sermon (which corresponds in importance to the Sermon on the Mount) from which these words are taken, will be found translated in the late Henry Clarke Warren's *Buddhism in Translation* (Harvard Oriental Series). Mr. Warren was one of the great pioneers of Buddhist studies in the Occident.

312. From St. Augustine's *Confessions* again. The collocation of these two representatives of eastern and western asceticism, as the culmination of this part of the poem, is not an accident.

V. WHAT THE THUNDER SAID

In the first part of Part V three themes are employed: the journey to Emmaus, the approach to the Chapel Perilous (see Miss Weston's book) and the present decay of eastern Europe.

357. This is *Turdus aonalaschkae pallasii,* the hermit-thrush which I have heard in Quebec County. Chapman[3] says (*Handbook of Birds of Eastern North America*) "it is most at home in secluded woodland and thickety retreats. . . . Its notes are not remarkable for variety or volume, but in purity and sweetness of tone and exquisite modulation they are unequalled." Its "water-dripping song" is justly celebrated.

360. The following lines were stimulated by the account of one of the Antarctic expeditions (I forget which, but I think one of Shackleton's): it was related that the party of explorers, at the extremity of their strength, had the constant delusion that there *was one more member* than could actually be counted.

366–76. Cf. Hermann Hesse, *Blick ins Chaos:*

> "Schon ist halb Europa, schon ist zumindest der halbe Osten Europas auf dem Wege zum Chaos, fährt betrunken im heiligem Wahn am Abgrund entlang und singt dazu, singt betrunken und hymnisch wie Dmitri Karamasoff sang. Ueber diese Lieder lacht der Bürger beleidigt, der Heilige und Seher hört sie mit Tränen."

401. "Datta, dayadhvam, damyata" (Give, sympathise, control). The fable of the meaning of the Thunder is found in the *Brihadaranyaka—Upanishad,* 5, 1. A translation is found in Deussen's *Sechsig Upanishads des Veda,* p. 489.

407. Cf. Webster, *The White Devil,* V, vi:

---

3. Frank M. Chapman (1864–1945). His *Handbook* was first published in 1895. The account of the thrush that captivated Eliot was contributed by Eugene P. Bicknell (1859–1925), American botanist and ornithologist.

"... they'll remarry
Ere the worm pierce your winding-sheet, ere the spider
Make a thin curtain for your epitaphs."

411. Cf. *Inferno*, XXXIII, 46:

"ed io sentii chiavar l'uscio di sotto
all'orribile torre."[4]

Also F. H. Bradley, *Appearance and Reality*, p. 346.

"My external sensations are no less private to myself than are
my thoughts or my feelings. In either case my experience falls
within my own circle, a circle closed on the outside; and, with
all its elements alike, every sphere is opaque to the others which
surround it. . . . In brief, regarded as an existence which appears
in a soul, the whole world for each is peculiar and private to
that soul."

424. V. Weston: *From Ritual to Romance*; chapter on the Fisher
King.

427. V. *Purgatorio*, XXVI, 148.

"'Ara vos prec, per aquella valor
'que vos guida al som de l'escalina,
'sovegna vos a temps de ma dolor.'
Poi s'ascose nel foco che gli affina."[5]

428. V. *Pervigilium Veneris*. Cf. Philomela in Parts II and III.
429. V. Gerard de Nerval, Sonnet *El Desdichado*.
431. V. Kyd's *Spanish Tragedy*.
433. Shantih. Repeated as here, a formal ending to an
Upanishad.

"The Peace which passeth understanding" is a feeble translation
of the content of this word.

---

4. "And below I heard them nailing shut the door / Of the horrible tower" (Italian).
5. "'Now I pray you, by that power / that guides you to the top of the stair, / be heedful in
time of my pain!' / Then he hid himself in the refining fire" (Italian and Provençal).

CONTEXTS

Sources of *The Waste Land*

SIR JAMES G. FRAZER[†]

The King of the Wood

In antiquity this sylvan landscape was the scene of a strange and recurring tragedy. On the northern shore of the lake, right under the precipitous cliffs on which the modern city of Nemi[1] is perched, stood the sacred grove and sanctuary of Diana Nemorensis, or Diana of the Wood. * * * In this sacred grove there grew a certain tree round which at any time of the day, and probably far into the night, a grim figure might be seen to prowl. In his hand he carried a drawn sword, and he kept peering warily about him as if at every instant he expected to be set upon by an enemy. He was a priest and a murderer; and the man for whom he looked was sooner or later to murder him and hold the priesthood in his stead. Such was the rule of the sanctuary. A candidate for the priesthood could only succeed to office by slaying the priest, and having slain him, he retained office till he was himself slain by a stronger or a craftier.

*   *   *

The strange rule of this priesthood has no parallel in classical antiquity, and cannot be explained from it. To find an explanation we must go farther afield. No one will probably deny that such a custom savours of a barbarous age, and, surviving into imperial times, stands out in striking isolation from the polished Italian society of the day, like a primaeval rock rising from a smooth-shaven lawn. It is the very rudeness and barbarity of the custom which allow us a hope of explaining it. For recent researches into the early history of man have revealed the essential similarity with which, under many

---

[†] From *The Golden Bough: A Study in Magic and Religion,* abr. ed. (London: Macmillan, 1922), pp. 1–2, 135–36, 139–40, 324–25, 345–46. Notes are by the editor of this Norton Critical Edition.
1. In the Alban Hills of central Italy, Nemi was the site of the principal shrine of the woodland goddess, Diana. Possession of a bough from one of the trees in the sacred grove there was part of the office of the priest-king whose curious role Frazer tries to explain in *The Golden Bough.*

superficial differences, the human mind has elaborated its first crude philosophy of life.[2] Accordingly, if we can show that a barbarous custom, like that of the priesthood of Nemi, has existed elsewhere; if we can detect the motives which led to its institution; if we can prove that these motives have operated widely, perhaps universally, in human society, producing in varied circumstances a variety of institutions specifically different but generically alike; if we can show, lastly, that these very motives, with some of their derivative institutions, were actually at work in classical antiquity; then we may fairly infer that at a remoter age the same motives gave birth to the priesthood of Nemi.

The Influence of the Sexes on Vegetation

From the preceding examination of the spring and summer festivals of Europe[1] we may infer that our rude forefathers personified the powers of vegetation as male and female and attempted, on the principle of homeopathic or imitative magic,[2] to quicken the growth of trees and plants by representing the marriage of the sylvan deities in the persons of a King and Queen of May, a Whitsun Bridegroom and Bride, and so forth. Such representations were accordingly no mere symbolic or allegorical dramas, pastoral plays designed to amuse or instruct a rustic audience. They were charms intended to make the woods to grow green, the fresh grass to sprout, the corn to shoot, and the flowers to blow. And it was natural to suppose that the more closely the mock marriage of the leaf-clad or flower-decked mummers aped the real marriage of the woodland sprites, the more effective would be the charm. Accordingly we may assume with a high degree of probability that the profligacy which notoriously attended these ceremonies was at one time not an accidental excess but an essential part of the rites, and that in the opinion of those who performed them the marriage of trees and plants could not be fertile without the real union of the human sexes. At the present day it might perhaps be vain to look in civilised Europe for customs of this sort observed for the explicit purpose of promoting the growth of vegetation. But ruder races in other parts of the world have consciously employed the intercourse of the sexes as a means to ensure

2. For Eliot's repetition of this idea, see "[*The Rite of Spring* and *The Golden Bough*]," below, pp. 169–70.
1. May Day, St. George's Day, St. Brides' Day, and other festivals celebrating the coming of spring, which seem to Frazer to carry ancient nature worship into medieval times.
2. The principle that "like produces like, or that an effect resembles its cause," which was, according to Frazer, at the heart of many ancient rituals and magical practices.

the fruitfulness of the earth; and some rites which are still, or were till lately, kept up in Europe can be reasonably explained only as stunted relics of a similar practice.

*   *   *

We have seen that according to a widespread belief, which is not without a foundation in fact, plants reproduce their kinds through the sexual union of male and female elements, and that on the principle of homeopathic magic this reproduction is supposed to be stimulated by the real or mock marriage of men and women, who masquerade for the time being as spirits of vegetation. Such magical dramas have played a great part in the popular festivals of Europe, and based as they are on a very crude conception of natural law, it is clear that they must have been handed down from a remote antiquity. We shall hardly, therefore, err in assuming that they date from a time when the fore fathers of the civilised nations of Europe were still barbarians, herding their cattle and cultivating patches of corn in the clearings of the vast forests, which then covered the greater part of the continent, from the Mediterranean to the Arctic Ocean. But if these old spells and enchantments for the growth of leaves and blossoms, of grass and flowers and fruit, have lingered down to our own time in the shape of pastoral plays and popular merrymakings, is it not reasonable to suppose that they survived in less attenuated forms some two thousand years ago among the civilised peoples of antiquity? Or, to put it otherwise, is it not likely that in certain festivals of the ancients we may be able to detect the equivalents of our May Day, Whitsuntide, and Midsummer celebrations, with this difference, that in those days the ceremonies had not yet dwindled into mere shows and pageants, but were still religious or magical rites, in which the actors consciously supported the high parts of gods and goddesses? Now in the first chapter of this book we found reason to believe that the priest who bore the title of King of the Wood at Nemi had for his mate the goddess of the grove, Diana herself. May not he and she, as King and Queen of the Wood, have been serious counterparts of the merry mummers who play the King and Queen of May, the Whitsuntide Bridegroom and Bride in modern Europe? and may not their union have been yearly celebrated in a *theogony* or divine marriage? Such dramatic weddings of gods and goddesses, as we shall see presently, were carried out as solemn religious rites in many parts of the ancient world; hence there is no intrinsic improbability in the supposition that the sacred grove at Nemi may have been the scene of an annual ceremony of this sort. Direct evidence that it was so there is none, but analogy pleads in favour of the view. * * *

The Killing of the Divine King

If the high gods, who dwell remote from the fret and fever of this earthly life, are yet believed to die at last, it is not to be expected that a god who lodges in a frail tabernacle of flesh should escape the same fate, though we hear of African kings who have imagined themselves immortal by virtue of their sorceries. Now primitive peoples, as we have seen, sometimes believe that their safety and even that of the world is bound up with the life of one of these god-men or human incarnations of the divinity. Naturally, therefore, they take the utmost care of his life, out of a regard for their own. But no amount of care and precaution will prevent the man-god from grow- ing old and feeble and at last dying. His worshippers have to lay their account with this sad necessity and to meet it as best they can. The danger is a formidable one; for if the course of nature is depen- dent on the man-god's life, what catastrophes may not be expected from the gradual enfeeblement of his powers and their final extinc- tion in death? There is only one way of averting these dangers. The man-god must be killed as soon as he shows symptoms that his pow- ers are beginning to fail, and his soul must be transferred to a vig- orous successor before it has been seriously impaired by the threatened decay. The advantages of thus putting the man-god to death instead of allowing him to die of old age and disease are, to the savage, obvious enough. For if the man-god dies what we call a natu- ral death, it means, according to the savage, that his soul has either voluntarily departed from his body and refuses to return, or more commonly, that it has been extracted, or at least detained in its wanderings, by a demon or sorcerer. In any of these cases the soul of the man-god is lost to his worshippers, and with it their prosper- ity is gone and their very existence endangered. Even if they could arrange to catch the soul of the dying god as it left his lips or his nostrils and so transfer it to a successor, this would not effect their purpose; for dying of disease, his soul would necessarily leave his body in the last stage of weakness and exhaustion, and so enfee- bled it would continue to drag out a languid, inert existence in any body to which it might be transferred. Whereas by slaying him his worshippers could, in the first place, make sure of catching his soul as it escaped and transferring it to a suitable successor; and, in the second place, by putting him to death before his natural force was abated, they would secure that the world should not fall into decay with the decay of the man-god. Every purpose, therefore, was answered, and all dangers averted by thus killing the man- god and transferring his soul, while yet at its prime, to a vigorous successor.

[Adonis and Christ]

The spectacle of the great changes which annually pass over the face of the earth has powerfully impressed the minds of men in all ages, and stirred them to meditate on the causes of transformations so vast and wonderful. Their curiosity has not been purely disinterested; for even the savage cannot fail to perceive how intimately his own life is bound up with the life of nature, and how the same processes which freeze the stream and strip the earth of vegetation menace him with extinction. At a certain stage of development men seem to have imagined that the means of averting the threatened calamity were in their own hands, and that they could hasten or retard the flight of the seasons by magic art. Accordingly they performed ceremonies and recited spells to make the rain to fall, the sun to shine, animals to multiply, and the fruits of earth to grow. In course of time, the slow advance of knowledge, which has dispelled so many cherished illusions, convinced at least the more thoughtful portion of mankind that the alternations of summer and winter, of spring and autumn, were not merely the result of their own magical rites, but that some deeper cause, some mightier power, was at work behind the shifting scenes of nature. They now pictured to themselves the growth and decay of vegetation, the birth and death of living creatures, as effects of the waxing and waning strength of divine beings, of gods and goddesses, who were born and died, who married and begot children, on the pattern of human life.

Thus the old magical theory of the seasons was displaced, or rather supplemented, by a religious theory. For although men now attributed the annual cycle of change primarily to corresponding changes in their deities, they still thought that by performing certain magical rites they could aid the god, who was the principle of life, in his struggle with the opposing principal of death. They imagined that they could recruit his failing energies and even raise him from the dead. The ceremonies which they observed for this purpose were in substance a dramatic representation of the natural processes which they wished to facilitate; for it is a familiar tenet of magic that you can produce any desired effect by merely imitating it. And as they now explained the fluctuations of growth and decay, of reproduction and dissolution, by the marriage, the death, and the rebirth or revival of the gods, their religious or rather magical dramas turned in great measure on these themes. They set forth the fruitful union of the powers of fertility, the sad death of one at least of the divine partners, and this joyful resurrection. Thus a religious theory was blended with a magical practice. The combination is familiar in history. Indeed, few religions have

ever succeeded in wholly extricating themselves from the old tram-
mels of magic.

*   *   *

Nowhere, apparently, have these rites been more widely and sol-
emnly celebrated than in the lands which border the eastern Mediter-
ranean. Under the names of Osiris, Tammuz, Adonis, and Attis, the
peoples of Egypt and Western Asia represented the yearly decay
and revival of life, especially of vegetable life, which they personi-
fied as a god who annually died and rose again from the dead. In
name and detail the rites varied from place to place: in substance
they were the same. * * *

*   *   *

When we reflect how often the Church has skilfully contrived to
plant the seeds of the new faith on the old stock of paganism, we
may surmise that the Easter celebration of the dead and risen Christ
was grafted upon a similar celebration of the dead and risen Adonis,[1]
which * * * was celebrated in Syria at the same season. The type, cre-
ated by Greek artists, of the sorrowful goddess with her dying lover
in her arms, resembles and may have been the model of the *Pietà* of
Christian art, the Virgin with the dead body of her divine Son in her
lap, of which the most celebrated example is the one by Michael
Angelo in St. Peter's. That noble group, in which the living sorrow of
the mother contrasts so wonderfully with the languor of death in the
son, is one of the finest compositions in marble. Ancient Greek art
has bequeathed to us few works so beautiful, and none so pathetic.

In this connexion a well-known statement of Jerome[2] may not be
without significance. He tells us that Bethlehem, the traditionary
birthplace of the Lord, was shaded by a grove of that still older Syr-
ian Lord, Adonis, and that where the infant Jesus had wept, the lover
of Venus was bewailed. Though he does not expressly say so, Jerome
seems to have thought that the grove of Adonis had been planted by
the heathen after the birth of Christ for the purpose of defiling the
sacred spot. In this he may have been mistaken. If Adonis was
indeed, as I have argued, the spirit of the corn, a more suitable name
for his dwelling-place could hardly be found than Bethlehem, "the

---

1. Adonis, lover of the goddess Aphrodite, is killed by a boar. But Frazer is more inter-
ested in an earlier part of his story, in which Aphrodite hides the infant Adonis in a
chest and entrusts it to the goddess Persephone in the underworld. When Persephone
refuses to return Adonis to Aphrodite, Aphrodite must descend to the underworld to
ransom him. The dispute is finally settled only when Zeus rules that Adonis will live
half the year with Persephone and half with Aphrodite. Adonis is thus a version of the
fallen and risen god, of which the Babylonian Tammuz may be the prototype.
2. Pilgrim, scholar, and Christian saint, born in Dalmatia (Slovenia) in 347, died in
419/420 in the monastery he had established in Bethlehem.

House of Bread," and he may well have been worshipped there at his House of Bread long ages before the birth of Him who said, "I am the bread of life." Even on the hypothesis that Adonis followed rather than preceded Christ at Bethlehem, the choice of his sad figure to divert the allegiance of Christians from their Lord cannot but strike us as eminently appropriate when we remember the similarity of the rites which commemorated the death and resurrection of the two.

JESSIE L. WESTON[†]

[The Grail Legend]

The main difficulty of our research lies in the fact that the Grail legend[1] consists of a congeries of widely differing elements—elements which at first sight appear hopelessly incongruous, if not completely contradictory, yet at the same time are present to an extent, and in a form, which no honest critic can afford to ignore.

* * *

A prototype, containing the main features of the Grail story—the Waste Land, the Fisher King, the Hidden Castle with its solemn Feast, and mysterious Feeding Vessel, the Bleeding Lance and Cup—does not, so far as we know, exist. None of the great collections of Folk-tales * * * has preserved specimens of such a type; it is not such a story as, *e.g., The Three Days Tournament*, examples of which are found all over the world.

* * *

Some years ago, when fresh from the study of Sir J. G. Frazer's epoch-making work, *The Golden Bough*, I was struck by the resemblance between certain features of the Grail story, and characteristic details of the Nature Cults described. The more closely I analysed the tale, the more striking became the resemblance, and I finally asked myself whether it were not possible that in this mysterious legend—mysterious alike in its character, its sudden appearance, the importance apparently assigned to it, followed by as sudden and

---

† From *From Ritual to Romance* (Cambridge: Cambridge University Press, 1920), pp. 2–4, 19, 21, 74–76, 108, 117–19, 165, 176–77. Notes are by the editor of this Norton Critical Edition.
1. The Holy Grail is the chalice supposed to have been used by Jesus at the Last Supper and then by Joseph of Arimathea to catch the blood flowing from Jesus's wounds on the cross. The search for this precious relic is the focus of a number of medieval stories, poems, and legends, which are, as Weston says, quite miscellaneous.

complete a disappearance—we might not have the confused record
of a ritual, once popular, later surviving under conditions of strict
secrecy? This would fully account for the atmosphere of awe and
reverence which even under distinctly non-Christian conditions
never fails to surround the Grail * * *; and also for the presence in
the tale of distinctly popular, and folk-lore, elements.

*   *   *

It has taken me some nine or ten years longer to complete the evi-
dence, but the chain is at last linked up, and we can now prove by
printed texts the parallels existing between each and every feature
of the Grail story and the recorded symbolism of the Mystery cults.
Further, we can show that between these Mystery cults and Chris-
tianity there existed at one time a close and intimate union, such a
union as of itself involved the practical assimilation of the central
rite, in each case a 'Eucharistic' Feast, in which the worshippers par-
took of the Food of Life from the sacred vessels.

[The Grail Quest]

(a) There is a general consensus of evidence to the effect that the
main object of the Quest is the restoration to health and vigour of a
King suffering from infirmity caused by wounds, sickness, or old age;

(b) and whose infirmity, for some mysterious and unexplained rea-
son, reacts disastrously upon his kingdom, either by depriving it of
vegetation, or exposing it to the ravages of war.

(c) In two cases it is definitely stated that the King will be restored
to youthful vigour and beauty.

(d) In both cases where we find Gawain[1] as the hero of the story,
and in one connected with Perceval, the misfortune which has fallen
upon the country is that of a prolonged drought, which has destroyed
vegetation, and left the land Waste; the effect of the hero's question
is to restore the waters to their channel, and render the land once
more fertile.

*   *   *

(e) But this much seems certain, the aim of the grail Quest is two-
fold; it is to benefit (a) the King, (b) the land. The first of these two

---

1. A key figure in Arthurian legend and romance, Gawain is usually represented as the
nephew of King Arthur. His character varies a great deal from story to story, so that in
some instances he is a model of courtly virtue and in others weak or even cruel. In
some versions of the Grail story, particularly that set down by Chrétien de Troyes in the
12th century, Perceval sees the chalice in the castle of a wounded king, and he is chal-
lenged to ask the question that will restore the kingdom and heal the king.

is the more important, as it is the infirmity of the King which entails misfortune on his land, the condition of the one reacts, for good or ill, upon the other; how, or why, we are left to discover for ourselves.

✻ ✻ ✻

(*f*) To sum up the result of the analysis, I hold that we have solid grounds for the belief that the story postulates a close connection between the vitality of a certain King, and the prosperity of his kingdom; the forces of the ruler being weakened or destroyed, by wound, sickness, old age, or death, the land becomes Waste, and the task of the hero is that of restoration.

[The Tarot Pack]

Students of the Grail texts, whose attention is mainly occupied with Medieval Literature, may not be familiar with the word Tarot, or aware of its meaning. It is the name given to a pack of cards, seventy-eight in number, of which twenty-two are designated as the 'Keys.'

These cards are divided into four suits, which correspond with those of the ordinary cards; they are:

> Cup (Chalice, or Goblet)—Hearts.
> Lance (Wand, or Sceptre)—Diamonds.
> Sword—Spades.
> Dish (Circles, or Pentangles, the form varies)—Clubs.

To-day the Tarot has fallen somewhat into disrepute, being principally used for purposes of divination, but its origin, and precise relation to our present playing-cards, are questions of considerable antiquarian interest. Were these cards the direct parents of our modern pack, or are they entirely distinct therefrom?

Some writers are disposed to assign a very high antiquity to the Tarot. Traditionally, it is said to have been brought from Egypt; there is no doubt that parallel designs and combinations are to be found in the surviving decorations of Egyptian temples, notably in the astronomic designs on the ceiling of one of the halls of the palace of Medinet Abou, which is supported on twenty-two columns (a number corresponding to the 'keys' of the Tarot), and also repeated in a calendar sculptured on the southern façade of the same building, under a sovereign of the XXIII dynasty. This calendar is supposed to have been connected with the periodic rise and fall of the waters of the Nile.

The Tarot has also been connected with an ancient Chinese monument, traditionally erected in commemoration of the drying up of the waters of the Deluge by Yao. The face of this monument is divided up into small sections corresponding in size and number with the cards of the Tarot, and bearing characters which have, so far, not been deciphered.

What is certain is that these cards are used to-day by the Gipsies for purposes of divination, and the opinion of those who have studied the subject is that there is some real ground for the popular tradition that they were introduced into Europe by this mysterious people.

*   *   *

But if the connection with the Egyptian and Chinese monuments, referred to above, is genuine, the original use of the 'Tarot' would seem to have been, not to foretell the future in general, but to predict the rise and fall of the waters which brought fertility to the land.

Such use would bring the 'Suits' into line with the analogous symbols of the Grail castle * * * connected with the embodiment of the reproductive forces of Nature.

The Fisher King

* * * [T]he personality of the King, the nature of the disability under which he is suffering, and the reflex effect exercised upon his folk and his land, correspond, in a most striking manner, to the intimate relation at one time held to exist between the ruler and his land; a relation mainly dependent upon the identification of the King with the Divine principle of Life and Fertility. * * * But what about his title, why should he be called the Fisher King?[1] * * * In my opinion the key to the puzzle is to be found in the rightful understanding of the Fish-Fisher symbolism. Students of the Grail literature have been too prone to treat the question on the Christian basis alone, oblivious of the fact that Christianity did no more than take over, and adapt to its own use, a symbolism already endowed with a deeply rooted prestige and importance. * * * So far as the present state of our knowledge goes we can affirm with certainty that the Fish is a Life symbol of immemorial antiquity, and that the title of Fisher has, from the earliest ages, been associated with Deities who

---

1. In versions of the Grail legend centered on Perceval, the wounded king, whom Perceval is supposed to restore, is usually referred to as the Fisher King. In some versions, those of Chrétien de Troyes and Wolfram von Eschenbach, for example, the king is in fact a fisherman. In one of the versions discussed by Weston, however, a fish is caught as part of a eucharistic ceremony, a reenactment of the Last Supper, in which the fish provides the food and the Grail the wine. The Fisher King is then the hereditary possessor of the Grail and, if not a fisherman himself, a descendant of those who performed the original fishing ritual.

were held to be specially connected with the origin and preservation of life. * * * There is thus little reason to doubt that, if we regard the Fish as a Divine Life symbol, of immemorial antiquity, we shall not go very far astray.

[The Perilous Chapel]

Students of the Grail romances will remember that in many of the versions the hero—sometimes it is a heroine—meets with a strange and terrifying adventure in a mysterious Chapel, an adventure which, we are given to understand, is fraught with extreme peril to life. The details vary: sometimes there is a Dead Body laid on the altar; sometimes a Black Hand extinguishes the tapers; there are strange and threatening voices, and the general impression is that this is an adventure in which supernatural, and evil, forces are engaged.

Such an adventure befalls Gawain on his way to the Grail Castle. He is overtaken by a terrible storm, and coming to a Chapel, standing at a crossways in the middle of a forest, enters for shelter. The altar is bare, with no cloth, or covering, nothing is thereon but a great golden candlestick with a tall taper burning within it. Behind the altar is a window, and as Gawain looks a Hand, black and hideous, comes through the window, and extinguishes the taper, while a voice makes lamentations loud and dire, beneath which the very building rocks. Gawain's horse shies for terror, and the knight, making the sign of the Cross, rides out of the Chapel, to find the storm abated, and the great wind fallen. Thereafter the night was calm and clear.

[Conclusion]

The Grail romances repose eventually, not upon a poet's imagination, but upon the ruins of an august and ancient ritual, a ritual which once claimed to be the accredited guardian of the deepest secrets of Life. Driven from its high estate by the relentless force of religious evolution—for after all Adonis, Attis,[1] and their congeners, were but the 'half gods' who must needs yield place when 'the God's themselves arrive—it yet lingered on; openly, in Folk practice, in Fast and Feast, whereby the well-being of the land might be

---

1. According to Frazer, Attis was the Phrygian version of Adonis and both were vegetation gods whose death and resurrection were celebrated in the spring. They are thus, by Weston's argument, prototypes of the Fisher King. For the story of Adonis, see p. 73 above.

assured; secretly, in cave or mountain-fastness, or island isolation, where those who craved for a more sensible (not necessarily sensuous) contact with the unseen Spiritual forces of Life than the orthodox development of Christianity afforded, might, and did, find satisfaction.

Were the Templars[2] such? Had they, when in the East, come into touch with a survival of the Naassene, or some kindred sect? It seems exceedingly probable. If it were so we could understand at once the puzzling connection of the Order with the Knights of the Grail, and the doom which fell upon them. That they were held to be Heretics is very generally admitted, but in what their Heresy consisted no one really knows; little credence can be attached to the stories of idol worship often repeated. If their Heresy, however, were such as indicated above, a Creed which struck at the very root and vitals of Christianity, we can understand at once the reason for punishment, and the necessity for secrecy. In the same way we can now understand why the Church knows nothing of the Grail; why that Vessel, surrounded as it is with an atmosphere of reverence and awe, equated with the central Sacrament of the Christian Faith,[3] yet appears in no Legendary, is figured in no picture, comes on the scene in no Passion Play. The Church of the eleventh and twelfth centuries knew well what the Grail was, and we, when we realize its genesis and true lineage, need no longer wonder why a theme, for some short space so famous and so fruitful a source of literary inspiration, vanished utterly and completely from the world of literature.

Were Grail romances forbidden? Or were they merely discouraged? Probably we shall never know, but of this one thing we may be sure, the Grail is a living force, it will never die; it may indeed sink out of sight, and, for centuries even, disappear from the field of literature, but it will rise to the surface again, and become once more a theme of vital inspiration even as, after slumbering from the days of Malory, it woke to new life in the nineteenth century, making its fresh appeal through the genius of Tennyson and Wagner.[4]

2. A religious order of knights, established during the Crusades and quartered in Jerusalem in the area once occupied by the Temple of Solomon, from which they derived their name. After they were displaced from the Holy Land by the Muslim victory of 1291, the Templars fell under suspicion as heretics and were widely persecuted in Europe.
3. I.e., Holy Communion.
4. Sir Thomas Malory's *Le Morte Darthur* (1485) is the first English prose version of the Arthurian romances. Alfred, Lord Tennyson (1809–1892) published his verse treatment of the same material as *Idylls of the King* in 1859, with a revised and extended version in 1885. Richard Wagner (1813–1883) used the stories centered on Perceval for his opera *Parsifal* (1882).

ALDOUS HUXLEY

[Madame Sosostris]†

Mr. Scogan[1] had been accommodated in a little canvas hut. Dressed in a black skirt and a red bodice, with a yellow-and-red bandanna handkerchief tied round his black wig, he looked—sharp-nosed, brown, and wrinkled—like the Bohemian Hag of Frith's Derby Day.[2] A placard pinned to the curtain of the doorway announced the presence within the tent of "Sesostris, the Sorceress of Ecbatana."[3] Seated at a table, Mr. Scogan received his clients in mysterious silence, indicating with a movement of the finger that they were to sit down opposite him and to extend their hands for his inspection. He then examined the palm that was presented him, using a magnifying glass and a pair of horned spectacles. He had a terrifying way of shaking his head, frowning and clicking with his tongue as he looked at the lines. Sometimes he would whisper, as though to himself, "Terrible, terrible!" or "God preserve us!" sketching out the sign of the cross as he uttered the words. The clients who came in laughing grew suddenly grave; they began to take the witch seriously. She was a formidable-looking woman; could it be, was it possible, that there was something in this sort of thing after all? After all, they thought, as the hag shook her head over their hands, after all . . . And they waited, with an uncomfortably beating heart, for the oracle to speak. After a long and silent inspection, Mr. Scogan would suddenly look up and ask, in a hoarse whisper, some horrifying question, such as, "Have you ever been hit on the head with a hammer by a young man with red hair?" When the answer was in the negative, which it could hardly fail to be, Mr. Scogan would nod several times, saying, "I was afraid so. Everything is still to come, still to come, though it can't be very far off now." Sometimes, after a long examination, he would just whisper, "Where ignorance is bliss, 'tis folly to be wise," and refuse to divulge any details of

† From *Crome Yellow* (London: Chatto & Windus, 1921), pp. 132–34. Notes are by the editor of this Norton Critical Edition.
1. A middle-aged academic modeled in part on British philosopher Bertrand Russell (1872–1970), a friend of both Huxley and Eliot. He is telling fortunes at an annual charity fair.
2. William Powell Frith's *Derby Day* (1858) depicts the crush when the general public is admitted to the racecourse at Epsom on Derby Day, traditionally the first Wednesday in June. It epitomizes a certain kind of busy representational painting very popular in the Victorian period. The Hag referred to is one of a number of beggars and fortune-tellers mixing with the crowd.
3. The ancient capital of the Medes, now the city of Hamadan in Iran. "Sesotris": the name of several ancient kings of ancient Egypt, the first of whom ruled almost two thousand years before the birth of Jesus. The name became well known in Europe through the Histories of Herodotus.

a future too appalling to be envisaged without despair. Sesostris had a success of horror. People stood in a queue outside the witch's booth waiting for the privilege of hearing sentence pronounced upon them.

*   *   *

"Is there going to be another war?" asked the old lady to whom he had predicted this end.

"Very soon," said Mr. Scogan, with an air of quiet confidence.

The old lady was succeeded by a girl dressed in white muslin, garnished with pink ribbons. She was wearing a broad hat, so that Denis[4] could not see her face; but from her figure and the roundness of her bare arms he judged her young and pleasing. Mr. Scogan looked at her hand, then whispered, "You are still virtuous."

The young lady giggled and exclaimed, "Oh, lor'!"

"But you will not remain so for long," added Mr. Scogan sepulchrally. The young lady giggled again. "Destiny, which interests itself in small things no less than in great, has announced the fact upon your hand." Mr. Scogan took up the magnifying glass and began once more to examine the white palm. "Very interesting," he said, as though to himself—"very interesting. It's as clear as day." He was silent.

"What's clear?" asked the girl.

"I don't think I ought to tell you." Mr. Scogan shook his head; the pendulous brass earrings which he had screwed on to his ears tinkled.

"Please, please!" she implored.

The witch seemed to ignore her remark. "Afterwards, it's not at all clear. The fates don't say whether you will settle down to married life and have four children or whether you will try to go on the cinema and have none."

*   *   *

"Is it really true?" asked white muslin.

The witch gave a shrug of the shoulders. "I merely tell you what I read in your hand. Good afternoon. That will be six-pence. Yes, I have change. Thank you. Good afternoon."

---

4. Denis Stone, a young poet and protagonist of the novel.

CHARLES BAUDELAIRE

To the Reader[†]

Au Lecteur

Ignorance, error, cupidity, and sin
Possess our souls and exercise our flesh;
Habitually we cultivate remorse
As beggars entertain and nurse their lice.

Our sins are stubborn. Cowards when contrite   5
We overpay confession with our pains,
And when we're back again in human mire
Vile tears, we think, will wash away our stains.

Thrice-potent Satan in our cursèd bed
Lulls us to sleep, our spirit overkissed,   10
Until the precious metal of our will
Is vaporized—that cunning alchemist!

Who but the Devil pulls our waking-strings!
Abominations lure us to their side;
Each day we take another step to hell,   15
Descending through the stench, unhorrified.

Like an exhausted rake who mouths and chews
The martyrized breast of an old withered whore
We steal, in passing, whatever joys we can,
Squeezing the driest orange all the more.   20

Packed in our brains incestuous as worms
Our demons celebrate in drunken gangs,
And when we breathe, that hollow rasp is Death
Sliding invisibly down into our lungs.

If the dull canvas of our wretched life   25
Is unembellished with such pretty ware
As knives or poison, pyromania, rape,
It is because our soul's too weak to dare!

† Translated by Stanley Kunitz. From *The Poems of Stanley Kunitz 1928–1978* by Stanley Kunitz (New York: Norton, 1979), p. 119. Copyright © 1958, 2000 by Stanley Kunitz. Used by permission of W. W. Norton & Company, Inc.

But in this den of jackals, monkeys, curs,
Scorpions, buzzards, snakes . . . this paradise   30
Of filthy beasts that screech, howl, grovel, grunt—
In this menagerie of mankind's vice

There's one supremely hideous and impure!
Soft-spoken, not the type to cause a scene,
He'd willingly make rubble of the earth   35
And swallow up creation in a yawn.

I mean *Ennui!* who in his hookah-dreams
Produces hangmen and real tears together.
How well you know this fastidious monster, reader,
—Hypocrite reader, you!—my double! my brother!   40

The Seven Old Men[†]

Les Sept vieillards

TO VICTOR HUGO[1]

Teeming city, full of dreams, where in broad
Daylight the specter grips the passer-by!
Mystery flows everywhere like sap
In the ducts of the mighty colossus.

One morning when mist in the gloomy street   5
Made the houses seem taller, like the two
Quays of a swollen river; when—décor
In harmony with the state of my soul—

A foul, yellow fog inundated space,
I went, steeling my nerves like a hero,   10
Disputing with my Soul, already weary,
Along the faubourg jarred by heavy carts.

Suddenly I saw an old man, in rags
Of the same yellow as the rainy sky,
Whose aspect would have made alms rain down   15
Except for the wicked gleam in his eye.

† Translated by Barbara Gibbs. From *An Anthology of French Poetry from Nerval to Valery in English Translation*, ed. Angel Flores (New York: Doubleday Anchor 1958), pp. 34–35. Copyright © 1958 and renewed 1986 by Angel Flores. Reprinted with the permission of The Permissions Company, LLC on behalf of The Estate of Angel Flores, LLC, www.permissionscompany.com. Notes are by the editor of this Norton Critical Edition. This English title translates the French, in italics below.
1. French poet, novelist, and dramatist (1802–1885).

You might have thought the pupils of his eyes
Were soaked in bile; his gaze sharpened the sleet,
And his beard of long hairs, stiff as a sword,
Jutted forward like the beard of Judas.   20

He was not bowed, but broken, for his spine
Made a perfect right angle with his leg,
So that his staff, completing his presence,
Gave him the bearing and the clumsy gait

Of a crippled dog or three-legged Jew.   25
He stumbled over the snow and mud as though
He were grinding the dead under his shoes,
Hostile to life, more than indifferent.

His like followed him; beard, eye, back, staff, rags,
Nothing distinguished, come from the same hell,   30
This centenarian twin, and these specters
Walked with the same step towards an unknown goal.

Of what infamous scheme was I the butt
Or what ill chance humiliated me?
Full seven times, from minute to minute,   35
I saw this old man multiply himself!

Let him who laughs at my disquietude
And is not seized by a fraternal chill
Ponder that, for all their decrepitude,
These seven monsters appeared eternal!   40

Would I, and lived, have beheld the eighth
Counterpart, ironical and fatal,
Vile Phoenix, father and son of himself?
—I turned my back on the procession.

Enraged as a drunk man who sees double,   45
I went inside and closed my door, frightened,
Sick and chilled, my mind feverish and turbid,
Offended by the senseless mystery!

In vain my reason tried to take the helm;
The tempest rollicking led it astray,   50
And my soul danced, danced, like an old lighter
Without masts, on a monstrous, shoreless sea!

JOHN WEBSTER

[Cornelia's Dirge from *The White Devil*]†

"Call for the robin-red breast and the wren,
Since o'er shady groves they hover,
And with leaves and flowers do cover
The friendless bodies of unburied men.[1]
Call unto his funeral dole   5
The ant, the field-mouse, and the mole,
To rear him hillocks that shall keep him warm,
And (when gay tombs are robbed) sustain no harm;
But keep the wolf far thence, that's foe to men,
For with his nails he'll dig them up again."[2]   10
They would not bury him 'cause he died in a quarrel:
But I have an answer for them:
"Let holy church receive him duly,
Since he paid the church-tithes truly."
His wealth is summed, and this is all his store,   15
This poor men get, and great men get no more.
Now the wares are gone, we may shut up shop.
Bless you all, good people.

OVID

[The Blinding of Tiresias]‡

Now while these things were happening on the earth by the
decrees of fate, when the cradle of Bacchus, twice born, was safe, it
chanced that Jove (as the story goes), while warmed with wine, put
care aside and bandied good-humoured jests with Juno in an idle
hour. "I maintain," said he, "that your pleasure in love is greater than
that which we enjoy." She held the opposite view. And so they decided

† From *Webster & Tourneur*, ed. John Addington Symonds (London: Vizetelly, 1888),
  pp. 110–11. Notes are by the editor of this Norton Critical Edition.
1. Cornelia is preparing the body of her son, Marcello, for burial.
2. Symonds quotes this comment from English essayist and poet Charles Lamb (1775–
   1834): "I never saw anything like this dirge, except the ditty which reminds Ferdinand
   of his drowned father in the Tempest. As that is of the water, watery; so this is of the
   earth, earthy. Both have that intenseness of feeling, which seems to resolve itself into
   the elements which it contemplates." Eliot, of course, quotes the "ditty" from *The Tem-
   pest* as he does this line from Cornelia's dirge.
‡ From *Metamorphoses*, Vol. III, trans. Frank Justus Miller, rev. G. P. Gould (Cambridge,
  MA: Harvard University Press, 1916; rpt. 1977). Notes are by the editor of this Norton
  Critical Edition.

to ask the judgment of wise Tiresias. He knew both sides of love. For once, with a blow of his staff he had outraged two huge serpents mating in the green forest; and, wonderful to relate, from man he was changed into a woman, and in that form spent seven years. In the eighth year he saw the same serpents again and said: "Since in striking you there is such magic power as to change the nature of the giver of the blow, now will I strike you once again." So saying, he struck the serpents and his former state was restored and he became as he had been born. He therefore, being asked to arbitrate the playful dispute of the gods, took sides with Jove. Saturnia,[1] they say, grieved more deeply than she should and than the issue warranted, and condemned the arbitrator to perpetual blindness. But the Almighty Father[2] (for no god may undo what another god has done) in return for his loss of sight gave Tiresias the power to know the future, lightening the penalty by the honour.

[The Story of Tereus and Philomela]

Now Tereus of Thrace had put these[1] to flight with his relieving troops, and by the victory had a great name. And since he was strong in wealth and in men * * * Pandion, King of Athens, allied him to himself by wedding him to Procne. But neither Juno, bridal goddess, nor Hymen, nor the Graces were present at that wedding. The Furies[2] lighted them with torches stolen from a funeral; the Furies spread the couch; and the uncanny screech-owl brooded and sat on the roof of their chamber. Under this omen were Procne and Tereus wedded; under this omen was their child conceived. Thrace, indeed, rejoiced with them, and they themselves gave thanks to the gods; both the day on which Pandion's daughter[3] was married to their illustrious king, and that day on which Itys was born, they made a festival: even so is our true advantage hidden.

Now Titan[4] through five autumnal seasons had brought round the revolving years, when Procne coaxingly to her husband said: "If I have found any favour in your sight, either send me to visit my sister or let my sister come to me. You will promise my father that after a brief stay she shall return. If you give me a chance to see my sister you will confer on me a precious boon." Tereus accordingly bade them launch his ship, and plying oar and sail, he entered the

---

1. I.e., Juno.
2. I.e., Jove.
1. Enemies threatening Athens.
2. Goddesses of vengeance. Hymen is the god of marriage, and the Graces are goddesses of fertility.
3. I.e., Procne.
4. I.e., Cronos, most powerful of the Titans, children of Uranus (Heaven) and Gaia (Earth). He is associated with the harvest.

Cecropian[5] harbour and came to land on the shore of Piraeus.[6] As soon as he came into the presence of his father-in-law they joined right hands, and the talk began with good wishes for their health. He had begun to tell of his wife's request, which was the cause of his coming, and to promise a speedy return should the sister be sent home with him, when lo! Philomela entered, attired in rich apparel, but richer still in beauty; such as we are wont to hear the naiads described, and dryads when they move about in the deep woods, if only one should give to them refinement and apparel like hers. The moment he saw the maiden Tereus was inflamed with love, quick as if one should set fire to ripe grain, or dry leaves, or hay stored away in the mow. Her beauty, indeed, was worth it; but in his case his passionate nature pricked him on, and, besides, the men of his clime are quick to love: his own fire and his nation's burnt in him. His impulse was to corrupt her attendants' care and her nurse's faithfulness, and even by rich gifts to tempt the girl herself, even at the cost of all his kingdom; or else to ravish her and to defend his act by bloody war. There was nothing which he would not do or dare, smitten by this mad passion. His heart could scarce contain the fires that burnt in it. Now, impatient of delay, he eagerly repeated Procne's request, pleading his own cause under her name. * * * Ay, more— Philomela herself has the same wish; winding her arms about her father's neck, she coaxes him to let her visit her sister; by her own welfare (yes, and against it, too) she urges her prayer. Tereus gazes at her, and as he looks feels her already in his arms; as he sees her kisses and her arms about her father's neck, all this goads him on, food and fuel for his passion. * * * The father yields to the prayers of both. The girl is filled with joy; she thanks her father and, poor unhappy wretch, she deems that success for both sisters which is to prove a woeful happening for them both.

*   *   *

And now they were at the end of their journey, now, leaving the travel-worn ship, they had landed on their own shores; when the king dragged off Pandion's daughter to a hut deep hidden in the ancient woods; and there, pale and trembling and all fear, begging with tears to know where her sister was, he shut her up. Then, openly confessing his horrid purpose, he violated her, just a weak girl and all alone, vainly calling, often on her father, often on her sister, but most of all upon the great gods. * * * Soon, when her senses came back, she dragged at her loosened hair, and like one in mourning, beating and tearing her arms, with outstretched hands she cried: "Oh, what a

5. Reference to Cecrops, mythological first king of Athens.
6. A town that has served since about the 5th century as the seaport of Athens.

horrible thing you have done, barbarous, cruel wretch! Do you care nothing for my father's injunctions, his affectionate tears, my sister's love, my own virginity, the bonds of wedlock? * * * If those who dwell on high see these things, nay, if there are any gods at all, if all things have not perished with me, sooner or later you shall pay dearly for this deed. I will myself cast all shame aside and proclaim what you have done. If I should have the chance, I would go where people throng and tell it; if I am kept shut up in these woods, I will fill the woods with my story and move the very rocks to pity." * * *

The savage tyrant's wrath was aroused by these words, and his fear no less. Pricked on by both these spurs, he drew his sword which was hanging by his side in its sheath, caught her by the hair, and twisting her arms behind her back, he bound them fast. At sight of the sword, Philomela gladly offered her throat to the stroke, filled with the eager hope of death. But he seized her tongue with pincers, as it protested against the outrage, calling ever on the name of her father and struggling to speak, and cut it off with his merciless blade. * * *

With such crimes upon his soul he had the face to return to Procne's presence. She on seeing him at once asked where her sister was. He groaned in pretended grief and told a made-up story of death; his tears gave credence to the tale. Then Procne tore from her shoulders the robe gleaming with a broad golden border and put on black weeds; she built also a cenotaph in honour of her sister, brought pious offerings to her imagined spirit, and mourned her sister's fate, not meet to be so mourned.

Now through the twelve signs, a whole year's journey, has the sungod passed. And what shall Philomela do? A guard prevents her flight; stout walls of solid stone fence in the hut; speechless lips can give no token of her wrongs. But grief has sharp wits, and in trouble cunning comes. She hangs a Thracian web on her loom, and skilfully weaving purple signs on a white background, she thus tells the story of her wrongs. This web, when completed, she gives to her one attendant and begs her with gestures to carry it to the queen. The old woman, as she was bid, takes the web to Procne, not knowing what she bears in it. The savage tyrant's wife unrolls the cloth, reads the pitiable tale of her misfortune, and (a miracle that she could!) says not a word. Grief chokes the words that rise to her lips, and her questing tongue can find no words strong enough to express her outraged feelings. Here is no room for tears, but she hurries on to confound right and wrong, her whole soul bent on the thought of vengeance.

It was the time when the Thracian matrons were wont to celebrate the biennial festival of Bacchus.[7] * * * [S]o by night the queen

---

7. God of wine. Bacchantes, below, are female participants in his festival, the Bacchanalia, characterized by frenzied dancing. "Euhoe" is a transcription of their traditional cry.

goes forth from her house, equips herself for the rites of the god and dons the array of frenzy. * * * She comes to the secluded lodge at last, shrieks aloud and cries "Euhoe!" breaks down the doors, seizes her sister, arrays her in the trappings of a Bacchante, hides her face with ivy-leaves, and, dragging her along in amazement, leads her within her own walls.

When Philomela perceived that she had entered that accursed house the poor girl shook with horror and grew pale as death. Procne found a place, and took off the trappings of the Bacchic rites and, uncovering the shame-blanched face of her wretched sister, folded her in her arms. But Philomela could not lift her eyes to her sister, feeling herself to have wronged her. And, with her face turned to the ground, longing to swear and call all the gods to witness that that shame had been forced upon her, she made her hand serve for voice. But Procne was all on fire, she could not contain her own wrath, and chiding her sister's weeping, she said: "This is no time for tears, but for the sword, for something stronger than the sword, if you have such a thing. I am prepared for any crime, my sister; * * * I am prepared for some great deed; but what it shall be I am still in doubt."

While Procne was thus speaking, Itys came into his mother's presence. His coming suggested what she could do, and regarding him with pitiless eyes, she said: "Ah, how like your father you are!" Saying no more, she began to plan a terrible deed and boiled with inward rage. But when the boy came up to her and greeted his mother, put his little arms around her neck and kissed her in his winsome, boyish way, her mother-heart was touched, her wrath fell away, and her eyes, though all unwilling, were wet with tears that flowed in spite of her. But when she perceived that her purpose was wavering through excess of mother-love, she turned again from her son to her sister; and gazing at both in turn, she said: "Why is one able to make soft, pretty speeches, while her ravished tongue dooms the other to silence? * * *" Without more words she dragged Itys away, as a tigress drags a suckling fawn through the dark woods on Ganges' banks. And when they reached a remote part of the great house, while the boy stretched out pleading hands as he saw his fate, and screamed, "Mother! mother!" and sought to throw his arms around her neck, Procne smote him with a knife between breast and side—and with no change of face. This one stroke sufficed to slay the lad; but Philomela cut the throat also, and they cut up the body still warm and quivering with life. * * *

This is the feast to which the wife invites Tereus, little knowing what it is. She pretends that it is a sacred feast after their ancestral fashion, of which only a husband may partake, and removes all attendants and slaves. So Tereus, sitting alone in his high ancestral banquet-chair, begins the feast and gorges himself with flesh of his own flesh. And in the utter blindness of his understanding he cries: "Go, call me Itys hither!" Procne cannot hide her cruel joy, and eager to be the messenger of her bloody news, she says: "You have, within, him whom you want." He looks about and asks where the boy is. And then, as he asks and calls again for his son, just as she was, with streaming hair, and all stained with her mad deed of blood, Philomela springs forward and hurls the gory head of Itys straight into his father's face; nor was there ever any time when she longed more to be able to speak, and to express her joy in fitting words. Then the Thracian king overturns the table with a great cry * * * then with drawn sword he pursues the two daughters of Pandion. As they fly from him you would think that the bodies of the two Athenians were poised on wings: they were poised on wings! One flies to the woods, the other rises to the roof. And even now their breasts have not lost the marks of their murderous deed, their feathers are stained with blood. Tereus, swift in pursuit because of his grief and eager desire for vengeance, is himself changed into a bird. Upon his head a stiff crest appears, and a huge beak stands forth instead of his long sword. His is the hoopoe, with the look of one armed for war.

GENE BUCK AND HERMAN RUBY

That Shakespearian Rag[†]

Words by
GENE BUCK and HERMAN RUBY

Music by
DAVID STAMPER

[†] "That Shakespearian Rag" (New York: Joseph W. Stern & Co., 1912).

Bill Shakespeare nev-er knew Of rag-time in his days,____ But the
"As you like it" Bru-tus, We'll play a rag to-day.____ Then old

high browed rhymes, Of his syn-co-pat-ed lines, You'll ad-mit, sure-ly fit, an-y
Shy - lock danced, And the Moor, O-thel-lo pranced, Feel-ing gay, he would say, as he

song that's now a hit, So this rag, I sub-mit.____
start-ed in to sway, "Bring the rag, right a - way."____

CHORUS. Not fast

That Shakes - pea-ri-an rag,____ Most in-tel-li-gent, ve-ry

el - e-gant,   That   old   clas-sic-al drag, Has the proper stuff,   the line Lay

on Macduff,"   Des - de - mon - a was the col - ored   pet,__

Ro - me - o____ loved his Ju - li - et____   And they were some

lov-ers, you can bet,_____   and yet,_____   I   know__

GOTAMA BUDDHA

The Fire-Sermon[†]

All things, O priests, are on fire. And what, O priests, are all these things which are on fire?

The eye, O priests, is on fire; forms are on fire; eye-consciousness is on fire; impressions received by the eye are on fire; and whatever sensation, pleasant, unpleasant, or indifferent, originates in dependence on impressions received by the eye, that also is on fire.

And with what are these on fire?

With the fire of passion, say I, with the fire of hatred, with the fire of infatuation; with birth, old age, death, sorrow, lamentation, misery, grief, and despair are they on fire.

The ear is on fire; sounds are on fire; * * * the nose is on fire; odors are on fire; * * * the tongue is on fire; tastes are on fire; * * * the body is on fire; things tangible are on fire; * * * the mind is on fire; ideas are on fire; * * * mind-consciousness is on fire; impressions received by the mind are on fire; and whatever sensation, pleasant, unpleasant, or indifferent, originates in dependence on impressions received by the mind, that also is on fire.

* * *

Perceiving this, O priests, the learned and noble disciple conceives an aversion for the eye, conceives an aversion for forms, conceives an aversion for eye-consciousness, conceives an aversion for the impressions received by the eye; and whatever sensation, pleasant, unpleasant, or indifferent, originates in dependence on impressions received by the eye, for that also he conceives an aversion. Conceives an aversion for the ear, conceives an aversion for sounds, * * * conceives an aversion for the nose, conceives an aversion for odors, * * * conceives an aversion for the tongue, conceives an aversion for tastes, * * * conceives an aversion for the body, conceives an aversion for things tangible, * * * conceives an aversion for the mind, conceives an aversion for ideas, conceives an aversion for mind-consciousness, conceives an aversion for the impressions received by the mind; and whatever sensation, unpleasant, or indifferent, originates in dependence on impressions received by the mind, for this also he conceives an aversion. And in conceiving this aversion, he becomes divested of passion, and by the absence of passion he becomes free, and when he is free he becomes aware

---

[†] From Henry Clarke Warren, *Buddhism in Translations* (Cambridge, MA: Harvard University Press, 1922), pp. 350–51.

that he is free; and he knows that re-birth is exhausted, that he has lived the holy life, that he has done what it behooved him to do, and that he is no more for this world.

EDMUND SPENSER

From Prothalamion[†]

Calme was the day, and through the trembling ayre,
Sweete breathing *Zephyrus*[1] did softly play
A gentle spirit, that lightly did delay
Hot *Titans* beames, which then did glyster[2] fayre:
When I whom sullein care,   5
Through discontent of my long fruitlesse stay
In Princes Court, and expectation vayne
Of idle hopes, which still doe fly away,
Like empty shaddowes, did aflict my brayne,
Walkt forth to ease my payne   10
Along the shoare of silver streaming *Themmes,*
Whose rutty Bancke, the which his River hemmes,
Was paynted all with variable[3] flowers,
And all the meades[4] adornd with daintie gemmes,
Fit to decke maydens bowres,   15
And crowne their Paramours,
Against the Brydale day, which is not long:[5]
     Sweete *Themmes* runne softly, till I end my Song.

There, in a Meadow, by the Rivers side,
A Flocke of *Nymphes* I chaunced to espy,   20
All lovely Daughters of the Flood thereby,
With goodly greenish locks all loose untyde,
As[6] each had bene a Bryde,
And each one had a little wicker basket,

[†] From *The Poetical Works of Edmund Spenser,* ed. J. C. Smith and E. De Selincourt (London: Oxford University Press, 1912), p. 601. Notes are by the editor of this Norton Critical Edition. The full title of Spenser's poem, first printed in 1596, is "Prothalamion, Or, A Spousall Verse made by Edm. Spenser In Honour of the Double mariage of the two Honorable & vertuous Ladies, the Ladie Elizabeth and the Ladie Katherine Somerset, Daughters to the Right Honourable the Earle of Worcester and espoused to the two worthie Gentlemen M. Henry Gilford, and M. William Peter Esquyers." "Prothalamion" literally means "before the marriage."
1. The west wind. The Titan referenced below is Helios, also god of the sun.
2. Glisten.
3. Of various different colors.
4. Meadows.
5. Not far off.
6. As if.

Made of fine twigs entrayled curiously,[7]   25
In which they gathered flowers to fill their flasket:[8]
And with fine Fingers, cropt full feateously[9]
The tender stalks on hye.
Of every sort, which in that Meadow grew,
They gathered some; the Violet pallid blew,   30
The little Dazie, that at evening closes,
The virgin Lillie, and the Primrose trew,
With store of vermeil[1] Roses,
To decke their Bridegromes posies,
Against the Brydale day, which was not long: 35
      Sweete *Themmes* runne softly, till I end my Song.

❊   ❊   ❊

OLIVER GOLDSMITH

[Olivia's Song from *The Vicar of Wakefield*][†]

The next morning the sun arose with peculiar warmth for the season; so that we agreed to breakfast together at the honeysuckle bank; where, while we sat, my youngest daughter, at my request, joined her voice with the concert on the trees about us. It was here my poor Olivia first met her seducer, and every object seemed to recal her sadness.[1] But that melancholy which was excited by objects of pleasure, or inspired by sounds of harmony, soothes the heart instead of corroding it. Her mother, too, upon this occasion, felt a pleasing distress, and wept, and loved her daughter as before. "Do, my pretty Olivia," cried she, "let us have that little melancholy air your Papa was so fond of; your sister Sophy has already obliged us. Do child; it will please your old father." She complied in a manner so exquisitely pathetic as moved me.

    When lovely woman stoops to folly,
        And finds too late that men betray,
   What charm can soothe her melancholy,
    What art can wash her guilt away?

---

7. Woven carefully.
8. Wicker basket.
9. Picked skillfully.
1. Vermilion.
† From *The Vicar of Wakefield* (London: Alnwick Davison, 1812), p. 148. Notes are by the editor of this Norton Critical Edition.
1. Olivia, deceived by Mr. Thornhill, entered into a bigamous union with him, and she has just been restored to her family.

The only art her guilt to cover,
  To hide her shame from every eye,
To give repentance to her lover,
  And wring his bosom,—is to die.

JAMES ANTHONY FROUDE

[Elizabeth and Leicester]†

The Queen invited me[1] to a party given by Lord Robert[2] on
St. John's day.

* * *

In the afternoon we were in a barge, watching the games on the
river. She was alone with the Lord Robert and myself on the poop,
when they began to talk nonsense, and went so far that Lord Robert
at last said, as I was on the spot there was no reason why they should
not be married if the Queen pleased. She said that perhaps I did
not understand sufficient English. I let them trifle in this way for a
time, and then I said gravely to them both, that if they would be
guided by me they would shake off the tyranny of those men who
were oppressing the realm and them; they would restore religion[3]
and good order; and they could then marry when they pleased—and
gladly would I be the priest to unite them.

ST. AUGUSTINE

From Confessions‡

I sank away from Thee, and I wandered, O my God, too much
astray from Thee my stay, in these days of my youth, and I became
to myself a barren land.

To Carthage I came, where there sang all around me in my ears a
cauldron of unholy loves. I loved not yet, yet I loved to love, and out

† From *History of England from the Fall of Wolsey to the Death of Elizabeth*, 12 vols. (New
  York: Scribner, 1865–73), 7:356–57. Notes are by the editor of this Norton Critical Edition.
1. Alvarez de Quadra, bishop of Aquila and Spanish ambassador to the court of Queen
  Elizabeth I (d. 1564), from whose letters to King Philip II of Spain (1527–1598) Froude
  is quoting.
2. Lord Robert Dudley, Earl of Leicester (1532–1588), who is considered by de Quadra
  and others likely to marry the queen, whose prospects in marriage constitute the main
  subject of correspondence between de Quadra and King Philip, as well as the main
  subject of intrigue in the English court.
3. The Catholic Church, replaced as the official religion of England by Elizabeth in 1559.
‡ From *The Confessions of St. Augustine*, tr. E. B. Pusey (London: Dent, 1907), pp. 31–32.
  Notes are by the editor of this Norton Critical Edition.

of a deep-seated want, I hated myself for wanting not. I sought what I might love, in love with loving, and safety I hated, and a way without snares. For within me was a famine of that inward food, Thyself, my God; yet, through that famine I was not hungered; but was without all longing for incorruptible sustenance, not because filled therewith, but the more empty, the more I loathed it. For this cause my soul was sickly and full of sores, it miserably cast itself forth, desiring to be scraped by the touch of objects of sense. * * * I defiled, therefore, the spring of friendship with the filth of concupiscence, and I beclouded its brightness with the hell of lustfulness; and thus foul and unseemly, I would fain, through exceeding vanity, be fine and courtly. I fell headlong into the love, wherein I longed to be ensnared. My God, my Mercy, with how much gall didst thou out of thy great goodness besprinkle for me that sweetness? For I was both beloved, and secretly arrived at the bond of enjoying; and was with joy fettered with sorrow-bringing bonds, that I might be scourged with the iron burning rods of jealousy, and suspicions, and fears, and angers, and quarrels.

FROM THE KING JAMES BIBLE

[The Road to Emmaus]†

And, behold, two of them went that same day to a village called Emmaus, which was from Jerusalem about three score furlongs.

And they talked together of all these things which had happened.

And it came to pass, that, while they communed together and reasoned, Jesus himself drew near, and went with them.

But their eyes were holden that they should not know him.

And he said unto them, What manner of communication are these that ye have one to another, as ye walk, and are sad?

And the one of them, whose name was Cleopas, answering said unto him, Art thou only a stranger in Jerusalem, and hast not known the things which are come to pass there in these days?

And he said unto them, What things? And they said unto him, Concerning Jesus of Nazareth, which was a prophet mighty in deed and word before God and all the people:

And how the chief priests and our rulers delivered him to be condemned to death, and have crucified him.

But we trusted that it had been he which should have redeemed Israel: and beside all this, to day is the third day since these things were done.

† Luke 24:13–32.

Yea, and certain women also of our company made us astonished, which were early at the sepulchre;

And when they found not his body, they came, saying, that they had also seen a vision of angels, which said that he was alive.

And certain of them which were with us went to the sepulchre, and found it even so as the women had said: but him they saw not.

Then he said unto them, O fools, and slow of heart to believe all that the prophets have spoken:

Ought not Christ to have suffered these things, and to enter into his glory?

And beginning at Moses and all the prophets, he expounded unto them in all the scriptures the things concerning himself.

And they drew nigh unto the village, whither they went; and he made as though he would have gone further.

But they constrained him, saying, Abide with us: for it is toward evening, and the day is far spent. And he went in to tarry with them.

And it came to pass, as he sat at meat with them, he took bread, and blessed it, and brake, and gave to them.

And their eyes were opened, and they knew him; and he vanished out of their sight.

And they said to one another, Did not our heart burn within us, while he talked with us by the way, and while he opened to us the scriptures?

SIR ERNEST SHACKLETON

[The Extra Man][†]

When I look back at those days I have no doubt that Providence guided us, not only across those snow-fields, but across the storm-white sea that separated Elephant Island from our landing-place on South Georgia. I know that during that long and racking march of thirty-six hours over the unnamed mountains and glaciers of South Georgia it seemed to me often that we were four, not three. I said nothing to my companions on the point, but afterwards Worsley said to me, "Boss, I had a curious feeling on the march that there was another person with us." Crean confessed to the same idea. One

---

† From *South: The Story of Shackleton's Last Expedition 1914–1917* (New York: Macmillan, 1920), p. 211. Notes are by the editor of this Norton Critical Edition. Shackleton (1874–1922) led the British Imperial Trans-Antarctic Expedition (1914–16), the aim of which was to cross Antarctica via the South Pole. His ship was trapped in the pack ice, and his party survived for five months on ice floes. This episode occurs as Shackleton and two of his crew, having rowed and sailed 800 miles in a whale boat, cross South Georgia Island on foot to find help.

feels "the dearth of human words, the roughness of mortal speech"[1] in trying to describe things intangible, but a record of our journeys would be incomplete without a reference to a subject very near to our hearts.

HERMANN HESSE

[The Downfall of Europe]†

It appears to me that what I call the Downfall of Europe is foretold and explained with extreme clearness in Dostoevsky's works and in the most concentrated form in "The Brothers Karamazoff."[1]

It seems to me that European and especially German youth are destined to find their greatest writer in Dostoevsky—not in Goethe, not even in Nietzsche.[2] In the most modern poetry, there is everywhere an approach to Dostoevsky, even though it is sometimes callow and imitative. The ideal of the Karamazoff, primeval, Asiatic and occult, is already beginning to consume the European soul. That is what I mean by the downfall of Europe. This downfall is a returning home to the mother, a turning back to Asia, to the source, to the "Faustischen Müttern"[3] and will necessarily lead, like every death on earth, to a new birth.

We contemporaries see a "downfall" in these events in the same way as the aged who, compelled to leave the home they love, mourn a loss to them irreparable while the young only think of the future, care only for what is new.

What is the Asiatic Ideal that I find in Dostoevsky, the effect of which will be, as I see it, to overwhelm Europe?

Briefly, it is the rejection of every strongly held Ethic and Moral in favor of a comprehensive LAISSEZ-FAIRE. This is the new and dangerous faith. . . .

*   *   *

And do these developments in the souls of imagined characters of fiction really signify the Downfall of Europe? Certainly. They signify it as surely as the mind's eye perceives life and eternity in the

---

1. From *Endymion* (1820), ll. 816–17, by John Keats.
† From *In Sight of Chaos*, tr. Stephen Hudson (Zurich: Verlag Seldwyla, 1923), pp. 13–14, 38–39, 44–46. Notes are by the editor of this Norton Critical Edition.
1. Novel (1880) by the Russian writer Fyodor Dostoevsky (1821–1881).
2. Johann Wolfgang von Goethe (1749–1832), German poet, playwright, novelist, etc. Friedrich Nietzsche (1844–1900), German philosopher and writer.
3. Faustian Mothers (German). A reference to an episode in *Faust* (Part II) by Goethe, in which Faust must enter the underground realm of the Mothers. They are associated by Hesse with a prehistoric, preconscious chaos.

grass-blade of spring and death and its inevitability in every falling leaf of autumn. It is possible the whole "Downfall of Europe" will play itself out "only" inwardly, "only" in the souls of a generation, "only" in changing the meaning of worn out symbols, in the disvaluation of spiritual values. Thus, the ancient world, that first brilliant coming of European culture, did not go down under Nero. Its destruction was not due to Spartacus nor to the Germanic tribes. But "only" to a thought out of Asia, that simple, subtle thought, that had been there very long but which took the form the teacher Christ gave to it.

*   *   *

I said Dostoevsky is not a poet, or he is a poet only in the secondary sense. I called him a prophet. It is difficult to say exactly what a prophet means. It seems to me something like this. A prophet is a sick man, like Dostoevsky, who was an epileptic. A prophet is the sort of sick man who has lost the sound sense of taking care of himself, the sense which is the saving of the efficient citizen. It would not do if there were many such, for the world would go to pieces. This sort of sick man, be he called Dostoevsky or Karamazoff, has that strange occult, godlike faculty, the possibility of which the Asiatic venerates in every maniac. He is a seer and an oracle. A people, a period, a country, a continent has fashioned out of its corpus an organ, a sensory instrument of infinite sensitiveness, a very rare and delicate organ. Other men, thanks to their happiness and health, can never be troubled with this endowment. This sensory instrument, this mantological[4] faculty is not crudely comprehensible like some sort of telepathy or magic, although the gift can also show itself in such confusing forms. Rather is it that the sick man of this sort interprets the movement of his own soul in terms of the universal and of mankind. Every man has visions, every man has fantasies, every man has dreams. And every vision, every dream, every idea and thought of a man on the road from the unconscious to the conscious, can have a thousand different meanings, of which every one can be right. But the appearances and visions of the seer and the prophet are not his own. The nightmare of visions which oppresses him does not warn him of a personal illness, of a personal death but of the illness, the death of that corpus whose sensory organ he is. This corpus can be a family, a clan, a people or it can be all mankind. In the soul of Dostoevsky a certain sickness and sensitiveness to suffering in the bosom of mankind which is otherwise called hysteria, found at once its means of expression and its barometer. Mankind is now on the point of realising this. Already half Europe,

---

4. Having to do with divination or the interpretation of signs.

at all events half Eastern Europe, is on the road to Chaos. In a state of drunken illusion she is reeling into the abyss and, as she reels, she sings a drunken hymn such as Dmitri Karamazoff sang. The insulted citizen laughs that song to scorn, the saint and seer hear it with tears.[5]

FROM BRIHADĀRANYAKA UPANISHAD[†]

The Three Great Disciplines

Prajāpati[1] had three kinds of offspring: gods, men, and demons (asuras). They lived with Prajāpati, practising the vows of brahmachārins.[2] After finishing their term, the gods said to him: "Please instruct us, Sir." To them, he uttered the syllable *da* [and asked]: "Have you understood?" They replied: "We have. You said to us, 'Control yourselves (dāmyata).'"[3] He said: "Yes, you have understood."

2

Then the men said to him: "Please instruct us, Sir." To them he uttered the same syllable *da* [and asked]: "Have you understood?" They replied: "We have. You said to us, 'Give (datta).'"[4] He said: "Yes, you have understood."

3

Then the demons said to him: "Please instruct us, Sir." To them he uttered the same syllable *da* [and asked]: "Have you understood?" They replied: "We have. You said to us: "Be compassionate (dayadhvam.)'"[5] He said: "Yes, you have understood."

---

5. The last three sentences of the passage are quoted in Eliot's note to ll. 366–76. Eliot was so impressed by this passage, which he had read while convalescing in Switzerland in 1921, that he wrote to Hesse, arranged to meet him in 1922, and commissioned his friend Sidney Schiff (who wrote under the name of Stephen Hudson) to translate the work into English.

† From *The Upanishads*, tr. Swami Nikhilananda, 4 vols. (New York: Harper and Brothers, 1949–59), pp. 321–22. Reprinted by permission of Ramakrishna-Vivekananda Center. Copyright © 1956. Notes are by the translator. The Upanishads are a series of commentaries on the Vedas, ancient Sanskrit texts recorded from the 15th to the 5th centuries BCE. The religion based on these ancient texts evolved into Hinduism, and the texts became the sacred literature of that religion.

1. The Creator God.

2. A celibate student who lives with his teacher and devotes himself to the practice of spiritual discipline.

3. The gods, in spite of possessing many virtues, are naturally unruly.

4. The Sanskrit word datta begins with the syllable da. Men are naturally avaricious; so they are asked to distribute their wealth to the best of their power.

5. Prajāpati asked the demons to show kindness to all; for the demons are naturally cruel and given to injuring others.

That very thing is repeated [even today] by the heavenly voice, in
the form of thunder, as "Da," "Da," "Da," which means: "Control
yourselves," "Give," and "Have compassion." Therefore one should
learn these three: self-control, giving, and mercy.[6]

FROM PERVIGILIUM VENERIS[†]

XXI

Now hoarse-mouthed swans crash trumpeting over the pools;
the maid of Tereus[1] makes descant under the poplar shade,
that you would think tunes of love issued trilling from her mouth,
and not a sister's complaint of a barbarous lord.

To-morrow shall be love for the loveless, and for the lover
to-morrow shall be love.

XXII

She sings, we are mute: when is my spring coming?
when shall I be as the swallow, that I may cease to be voiceless?
I have lost the Muse in silence, nor does Apollo regard me:
so Amyclae,[2] being mute, perished by silence.

---

6. Gods and demons ° ° ° may be found among men. Those human beings who are want-
   ing in self-control, but otherwise endowed with many good qualities, are the gods;
   those who are particularly greedy are men; while those who are cruel and given to
   injuring others are the demons. So the same species of human beings, according to
   their lack of self-control, charity, or mercy ° ° ° are distinguished as gods, men, and
   demons. Hence it is human beings who should be guided by the three instructions
   mentioned above; for Prajāpati intended his advice for them alone: men are observed to
   be unrestrained, greedy, and cruel. Though Prajāpati uttered the same syllable *da* in
   order to teach all his children, yet each one understood the instruction differently,
   according to his limitations.
† From *Catullus, Tibullus, and Pervigilium Veneris*, tr. F. W. Cornish, J. P. Postgate, and
   J. W. Mackail (Cambridge, MA: Harvard University Press, 1913), pp. 361–62. Notes
   are by the editor of this Norton Critical Edition. According to Mackail's introduction,
   the *Pervigilium Veneris* (which he translates as *The Eve of St. Venus*) is "the earliest
   known poem belonging in spirit to the Middle Ages." The date and authorship of the
   poem are unknown, and the text is traced back to the *Anthologia Latina*, a collection
   formed in the 4th century. Mackail regularizes the very disorderly remains of this
   ancient poem so that they form twenty-two stanzas with a regular refrain. Eliot was
   apparently attracted by the lament, attributed to Philomela, that ends the poem: "when
   shall I be as the swallow" ("*quando fiam uti chelidon*," l. 428).
1. I.e., Philomela. For the story of Tereus and Philomela, see pp. 87–91.
2. Most probably the Roman city of that name, proverbial for its silence. According to one
   story, a law passed there against the spread of false rumors prevented warnings of a
   real attack from reaching the authorities.

To-morrow shall be love for the loveless, and for the lover
to-morrow shall be love.

THOMAS KYD

From The Spanish Tragedie†

BALTHAZAR   It pleased you   60
  At the entertainment of the ambassador,
  To grace the King so much as with a show;
  Now, were your study so well furnishèd
  As, for the passing of the first night's sport,
  To entertain my father with the like,   65
  Or any such-like pleasing motion,
  Assure yourself it would content them well.
HIERONIMO
  Is this all?
BALTHAZAR Ay, this is all.
HIERONIMO
  Why then I'll fit you, say no more.
  When I was young, I gave my mind   70
  And plied myself to fruitless poetry:
  Which, though it profit the professor naught,
  Yet is it passing pleasing to the world.
LORENZO
  And how for that?
HIERONIMO   Marry, my good lord, thus—
  And yet methinks you are too quick with us—   75
  When in Toledo there I studièd,
  It was my chance to write a tragedy—
  See here, my lords—   *He shows them a book.*
  Which long forgot, I found this other day.
  Now, would your lordships favor me so much   80

---

† From *The Spanish Tragedy: A Norton Critical Edition*, ed. Michael Neill (New York:
  Norton, 2014), pp. 95–97, 99–100. Copyright © 2014 by W. W. Norton & Company,
  Inc. Used by permission of W. W. Norton & Company, Inc. The notes, by Michael
  Neill, are identified by line numbers in the original.
62. **grace:** give pleasure to (*OED v.* 6).
63. **furnishèd:** stocked.
66. **motion:** Usually a puppet show; perhaps as an alternative to the regular forms of the-
  atrical performance denoted by "show" (line 62) or perhaps (as most editors suggest)
  meant to refer generally to any form of entertainment—though *OED* offers no exam-
  ples of such a usage.
69. **I'll fit you:** (1) I'll provide what you need; (2) I'll punish you as you deserve * * *.
72. **professor:** exponent, practitioner.
75. **too quick:** "too pressing; perhaps with a pun on *quick* meaning alive" * * *.

As but to grace me with your acting it—
I mean each one of you to play a part—
Assure you it will prove most passing strange
And wondrous plausible to that assembly.

BALTHAZAR
What, would you have us play a tragedy?   85

HIERONIMO
Why, Nero thought it no disparagement,
And kings and emperors have ta'en delight
To make experience of their wits in plays?

LORENZO
Nay, be not angry, good Hieronimo,
The prince but asked a question.   90

BALTHAZAR
In faith, Hieronimo, and you be in earnest,
I'll make one.

LORENZO   And I another.

HIERONIMO
Now, my good lord, could you entreat
Your sister Bel-Imperia to make one?
For what's a play without a woman in it?   95

BEL-IMPERIA
Little entreaty shall serve me, Hieronimo,
For I must needs be employed in your play.

HIERONIMO
Why, this is well; I tell you, lordings,
It was determined to have been acted
By gentlemen and scholars too,   100
Such as could tell what to speak.

BALTHAZAR
And now it shall be played by princes and courtiers—
Such as can tell how to speak

❊ ❊ ❊

83. **strange:** wonderful, astonishing, unexpected (with an ironic double entendre).
84. **plausible:** deserving of applause; pleasing, agreeable (*OED* n. 1–2).
85. **us:** the next speech suggests that Balthazar uses a haughty royal plural here.
86–88. **Nero . . . plays:** The emperor Nero was known to have been a passionate amateur actor; Hieronimo may also have covertly in mind the occasional Roman practice of killing condemned criminals in the course of a theatrical performance.
86. **disparagement:** dishonor, loss of dignity.
91. **and:** if.
92. **make one:** be one (of the cast).
95. **For . . . it:** An ironic metatheatrical joke: in English theaters all women's parts were played by boys.
97. **employed:** stress on the first syllable.
99. **determined:** intended.
101–103. **what to speak . . . how to speak:** the distinction is a social one, between "gentlemen and scholars," educated men concerned with content, and denizens of the court, whose primary concern is with formal elegance.

HIERONIMO
* * *

There's one thing more that rests for us to do.

BALTHAZAR

What's that, Hieronimo? Forget not anything.

HIERONIMO

Each one of us must act his part   170
In unknown languages,
That it may breed the more variety—
As you, my lord, in Latin, I in Greek,
You in Italian; and, for because I know
That Bel-Imperia hath practised the French,   175
In courtly French shall all her phrases be.

BEL-IMPERIA

You mean to try my cunning, then, Hieronimo?

BALTHAZAR

But this will be a mere confusion,
And hardly shall we all be understood.

HIERONIMO

It must be so, for the conclusion   180
Shall prove the invention and all was good;
And I myself in an oration—
And with a strange and wondrous show besides,
That I will have there behind a curtain—
Assure yourself shall make the matter known;   185
And all shall be concluded in one scene,
For there's no pleasure ta'en in tediousness.

BALTHAZAB

How like you this?

LORENZO   Why thus my lord
We must resolve to soothe his humors up.

BALTHAZAR

On then, Hieronimo! Farewell till soon.   190

170–71. act . . . languages: Scholars are divided as to whether Kyd intended this instruc-
  tion to be carried out in actual performance * * *.
177. cunning: (1) learning; (2) skill in deceiving, craft (*OED* n. l; 5b).
178–79. But . . . understood: cf. God's words in Genesis 11.7 (Geneva version) "Come on,
  let vs goe downe, and there confound their language, that euery one perceiue not
  anothers speache." (*Marginal gloss*: "By this great plague of the confusion of tongues,
  appeareth Gods horrible judgement against mans pride and vaine glorie.")
181. invention: (1) devising or treatment of a subject; (2) device, contrivance, scheme
  (*OED* n. 3b; 6).
185. matter: * * * Playing on the sense "material cause" (*OED* n. 15); i.e., the murdered
  boy of Horatio.
189. soothe . . . up: humor him.

Composition and Publication of *The Waste Land*

LYNDALL GORDON

[The Composition of *The Waste Land*]†

It is not easy to follow the sequence of *The Waste Land*'s composition during 1921, but some facts are clear. After resolving to write the poem at the end of 1919 Eliot did nothing about it during 1920. That year he busied himself with a volume of criticism, *The Sacred Wood*. The reviews were disappointing and he went about looking pale and ill. Then, in the autumn of 1920, Vivienne's[1] father became dangerously ill and she and Eliot sat up night after night nursing him. The anxiety was too much for Vivienne, who broke down. Though in March and April 1921 she was in bed and complaining of pain that made her scream continuously for several days, Eliot began to see there would be no end to domestic crises, and that he must keep a part of his mind intact if he wished to get on with his long-delayed poem.

There were two periods of composition in 1921. New evidence reveals activity at the beginning of the year, for in an unpublished letter of 6 February, Wyndham Lewis reports to Mrs Schiff[2] that Eliot, whom he had seen at a production of *Volpone,* 'seems to be engaged in some obscure & intricate task of late'. Lewis must have pressed him further, for the very next day Lewis writes again to tell Schiff that Eliot had shown him 'a new long poem (in 4 parts) which I think will be not only very good, but a new departure for him'. Between then and May, there are repeated indications that Eliot was pulling it together: in April he was revising, and hoped to have it in

---

† From *The Imperfect Life of T. S. Eliot* (London: Virago, 2012), pp. 164–70, 177–83. Copyright © 1998 by Lyndall Gordon. Used by permission of W. W. Norton & Company, Inc. Unless otherwise indicated, notes are by the author. Some of the author's notes have been omitted.
1. Vivien Haigh-Wood (1888–1947), Eliot's first wife [*Editor*].
2. Violet Schiff (1876–1962), a friend of the Eliots. Wyndam Lewis (1887–1957), English artist and author, publisher of the avant-garde magazine *Blast*, which contained some of Eliot's early poetry [*Editor*].

a final form by June. May, while Vivienne was away at the seaside, was an opportunity to get more on paper.

It is not possible to know for sure what he had in hand at this point, but it was not the poem as we know it. He continued to envisage a poem in four parts, and it is likely that, by now, he had written the first version of parts I and II, drawing heavily on scenes from his own life. These he rehearsed years later when he drove about London with Mary Trevelyan.[3] He told her that in 1921 he went to dine in Hampstead or Primrose Hill with a woman he had met at the poetry circle of the Lyceum Club, who had showed him her tarot pack, the only time he had seen one. Eliot transformed this into the fortune-teller who introduces the characters of *The Waste Land* through her tarot cards. In 1942, as Eliot and Mary Trevelyan passed the dingy flats of Crawford Mansions on the border of Paddington, he said: 'We lived there—I was very unhappy. There was a pub—I used to watch people coming out at Closing Time. That's the origin of "HURRY UP PLEASE IT'S TIME".' In Trafalgar Square, he said, pointing: 'It was from there that Vivienne threw her nightdress out of the window into the street in the middle of the night.' Her power to shame his sense of propriety was transformed into the frenzied wife in part II who threatens, 'I shall rush out as I am, and walk the street / With my hair down, so.' Vivienne remarked at the time of publication that *The Waste Land* became 'a part of me (or I of it)'.

The second period of composition came in the autumn, from October to December, a more concentrated stretch of writing. For, finally, Eliot himself broke down, and during his recuperation at Margate and Lausanne at the end of 1921 he had, at last, the continuous time he needed to complete his poem.

The event that immediately preceded his breakdown was a long-awaited visit from his mother, accompanied by his sister Marian and brother Henry. He had not seen his mother for six years. He feared that Charlotte, now seventy-seven, would be old and weak, but when they arrived he was taken aback by his mother's formidable energy. Most of the strain was keeping marital problems under wraps and Vivienne at a distance in the country. When she did appear she strove to preserve the even manners an Eliot would take for granted, but Charlotte could tell that her son was afraid of his wife, and at the very last moment Vivienne exploded. She wrote regretfully, and rather touchingly, to Henry Eliot:

3. English musician (1897–1983), choir leader, and founder/head of organizations representing overseas students in the U.K. She was a close friend of Eliot from 1938 to 1957 [Editor].

Wigmore Street
Tuesday 23 [August 1921]

Dear Henry,

. . . Now I want you to tell me something truly. You are not to lie. Did your mother and sister show, think, say or intimate that I behaved like 'no lady', and just like a wild animal when [we] saw you off? I was perfectly stunned on that occasion. I had no idea what I was doing. I have been more or less stunned for many months now and when I come to, I suppose it seems dreadful, to an American. I have worried all the time since. Tom said it was perfectly allright, etc, but I am sure he has lived here so long he hardly realises how *very* much less English people mind showing their emotions than Americans—or perhaps he does realise it so perfectly. But I was extremely anxious to show no emotion before your family at any time, and then I ended in a fit!

I found the emotionless condition a great strain, all the time. I used to think I should burst out and scream and dance. That's why I used to think you were so terribly failing me. But I won't talk about that now, except to ask you if ever two people made *such* a fearful mess of their obvious possibilities. I don't understand, and I never shall . . . Both flats are equally unbearable to us [they had moved to Lucy Thayer's flat, so as to leave Clarence Gate Gardens to their visitors], so we stay here morosely . . .

Good-bye Henry. And *be personal*, you must be personal, or else it's no good. Nothing's any good.

Vivien

Henry took a cool view. 'I have a feeling that subconsciously (or unconsciously) she likes the role of invalid,' he remarked to his mother, 'and that, liking it as she does to be petted, "made a fuss over", condoled and consoled, she . . . encourages her breakdowns, instead of throwing them off by a sort of nervous resistance. It is hard to tell how much is physical and how much mental and controllable by will power; but I think that if she had more of "the Will to Be Well" she would have less suffering . . . She needs something to take her mind off herself; something to absorb her entire attention.'

After his mother left, Eliot collapsed. 'I really feel very shaky', he wrote to Aldington,[4] 'and seem to have gone down rapidly since my family left.' He felt as though he might lose self-control, but it was 'impossible to describe these feelings even if one wants to'. When overstrained, he said, he used to suffer from a vague but acute sense of horror and apprehension. Clarence Gate Gardens without his

4. Richard Aldington (1892–1962), English writer and editor.

family seemed no home, and his brother's departure seemed 'as unreal as death'. Vivienne's lamentations over missing his mother seemed to vie with his own. In late September he went to see a nerve specialist. Though it was Vivienne who proposed the specialist, she was taken aback by the serious view he took of Eliot's case. '. . . Look at *my* position,' she urged Scofield Thayer.[5] 'I have not nearly finished my own nervous breakdown yet.'

When Henry Eliot heard of his brother's condition, he was inclined to blame Vivienne. He put it to their mother: 'I am afraid he finds it impossible to do creative work (other than critical) at home. Vivien demands a good deal of attention, and I imagine is easily offended if she does not get it well buttered with graciousness and sympathy.'

Henry took the view that his brother suffered also from his disguise. 'The strain of going out among people who after all are foreigners to him, and, I believe, always must be to an American—even Henry James never became a complete Englishman—has, I think, been pretty heavy. I remember a year or more ago, in a letter to me, he spoke of always having to be . . . alert to the importance of appearances, always wearing a mask among people. To me he seemed like a man playing a part.'

On 12 October, Eliot was given three months' sick-leave from the bank. It now became clear to him that he was suffering neither from 'nerves' or insanity, but from 'psychological troubles' which, he complained, English doctors at that time simply did not acknowledge. He decided to seek help abroad, and the biologist Julian Huxley and Ottoline Morrell[6] recommended Dr Vittoz in Lausanne. Both had been his patients. Roger Vittoz was an austere Catholic, to some a living saint, who trained his patients in meditation, similar to yoga and Buddhism. His book, *Treatment of Neurasthenia by Means of Brain Control* (1913), appeared in English in 1921. He did not advocate lengthy psychoanalysis, rather mastery, through reason and will, of what he termed *clichés*, the painful thoughts in which a diseased mind had become imprisoned. The method was not to suppress memories and desires, but through a return to moral equilibrium, to free a patient of his pain.

In the meantime, on 22 October, Eliot moved to the Albemarle Hotel, Cliftonville, Margate. Vivienne bought him a mandolin and accompanied him, at his request; after two weeks, she left him to follow the rest-cure his doctor prescribed. He was to be alone, and in the open air, and not think of the future. It is likely that it was

---

5. American art collector (1889–1982), poet, and editor, most notably of *The Dial* when it published *The Waste Land*. It was through Thayer, an old schoolmate of his, that Eliot met Vivien [*Editor*].

6. Huxley (1887–1975) was a frequent visitor, along with Eliot, at Garsington Manor, the home of the literary hostess Ottoline Morrell (1873–1938) [*Editor*].

during the last of his three weeks there, after Vivienne left, that he did 'a rough draft of part of part III',[7] calling it 'The Fire Sermon'. 'I do not know whether it will do, & must wait for Vivien's opinion as to whether it is printable,' he informed Schiff. 'I have done this while sitting in a shelter on the front—as I am out all day except when taking rest.'

Eliot attached his hotel bill to the manuscript: the work he did at Margate cost him about £16 in all. The first week he indulged himself in the 'white room' and took all his meals. The next two weeks were spent rather more frugally in a modest room *en pension*. Vivienne, reporting to Russell,[8] said that he seemed to like Margate. He was in a precarious state, but the purposeful letters he wrote at this time suggest that he was convalescing rather than declining. Pound,[9] briefly in England in early October, found him enlivened by the prospect of leisure. There was evidently no discussion of Eliot's poem, and I doubt that Eliot showed it to him before he went to Margate.

During the final stages of *The Waste Land*'s composition Eliot put himself under Pound's direction. On 18 November, on his way to Switzerland, Eliot passed through Paris and left his wife with the Pounds, who were then living there. It seems likely that Eliot now showed Pound what he had done in Margate. Pound called Eliot's Swiss draft 'the 19 page version', which implies that he had previously seen another. He marked certain sheets on two occasions: once in pencil, probably on 18 November; once in ink, on Eliot's return from Lausanne early in January.[1] Pound undoubtedly improved particular passages: his excisions of another anti-Semitic portrait of Bleistein and a misogynist portrait of a woman writer called Fresca curbed Eliot's excessive animus, and his feel for the right word improved odd lines throughout. Pound was proud of his hand in *The Waste Land* and wrote:

> *If you must needs enquire*
> *Know diligent Reader*
> *That on each Occasion*
> *Ezra performed the caesarian Operation.*

* * *

7. The reference to 'part III' confirms the supposition that parts I and II were already by then in existence.
8. The English philosopher Bertrand Russell (1872–1970), Eliot's one-time teacher and adviser, had an ongoing affair with Vivien at this time [*Editor*].
9. See above, p. 43 [*Editor*].
1. 'Exequy' and 'The Fire Sermon' are typed with Eliot's brother's typewriter on yellowish sheets with a 'Verona' watermark. The carbon of 'The Fire Sermon', with Pound's marginalia in pencil, was clearly shown first. Eliot then revised the top copy in accordance with Pound's suggestions before submitting it for further consideration on his return from Lausanne.

'Death by Water', part IV, which Eliot completed at Lausanne, was initially a narrative of a fishing expedition from Cape Ann to the Grand Banks, off Nova Scotia.[2] In the London of 'The Fire Sermon' someone fishes futilely in the polluted canal; here, in the North Atlantic, the New England fishermen lead purposeful, honest lives, far from the contamination of cities. They are constantly in danger of death off some remote shore, but to Eliot this is preferable to death-in-life, like Gerontion's, in a soiled corner of familiar trade-routes.[3]

The transition from the London of 'The Fire Sermon' to the New England of 'Death by Water' revives an ancestral sense of release from the sinfulness of the Old World. Eliot's North Atlantic is unexplored territory, a testing-ground. He thinks of the New Englander as pure will confronting the sea, 'something inhuman, clean and dignified'. As the vessel flies north, far off course, the voyage turns into an allegorical dream. As the stars become invisible, the voyager sees three crosses and, in front of them, three women with foaming hair, singing a siren's song. Prufrock longed for mermaids to sing to him; Londoners were charmed by the Thames daughters' 'la la' to their senses; but the voyager rejects women. For him, their song blends with the 'illimitable scream' of the whole natural world. At the height of the storm, it occurs to him that the shrill world with its provocative women is simply an illusion:

> . . . while I was
> Frightened beyond fear, horrified past horror, calm
> (Nothing was real) for, I thought, now when
> I like, I can wake up and end the dream.[4]

No sooner does he reject this world as a dream than he knocks up against it. Literally, the vessel drives against an iceberg. One moment he looks into infinity, a meeting of sea and sky; the next, a long white line breaks into it like 'a wall, a barrier'. The drowning at the end of 'Death by Water' is not seen to be a disaster but a stage of purification and metamorphosis.

*   *   *

2. ***Eliot did his handwritten drafts at Lausanne on quadruled paper. These were 'What the Thunder Said', fair copies of 'Death by Water' and 'Dirge', and a rough draft of 'Venus Anadyomene' (which was soon discarded along with the Fresca episode for which it was designed). Eliot used the same black ink for the two fair copies.
3. See above, p. 25 [*Editor*].
4. Excised lines in *The Waste Land: A Facsimile and Transcript of the Original Drafts including the Annotations of Ezra Pound*, ed. Valerie Eliot (New York: Harcourt Brace Jovanovich, 1974), p. 59 [*Editor*].

At the same time as Eliot made his fair copy of the New England voyage, he found the pilgrim's journey of 1914[5] reviving in his imagination—the sunbaked road winding among the mountains, the bells and chanting voices, the reversed point of view of the saint. Eliot said that part V was the only part of *The Waste Land* 'that justifies the whole at all'. Here, in 'What the Thunder Said', the heroes of the spirit in the earliest manuscript fragments are depersonalised. In place of a man with extraordinary powers there is now a 'form' and, in a later revision, merely a bat. And instead of a voice saying plainly 'I am the Resurrection', the thunder now rumbles obscure Sanskrit words.

In the sanatorium in Lausanne, Dr Vittoz saw Eliot for half-an-hour each day when he would place his hand on a patient's forehead to determine the agitation of what he believed were physical brain waves. The cure was to concentrate on a simple word with a view to 'calm' and 'control'. Vittoz abjured learned words in favour of 'quelques paroles, nette et lumineuses',[6] which he hoped would heal by their clarity—for Vittoz, simplicity was based on religious belief. The final part of *The Waste Land*, written at one sitting at the Hotel Ste Luce, carries out this meditative exercise, choosing to focus on 'water' to the point when agitation is dissolved in 'calm', 'beating obedient / To controlling hands'.

* * *

Eliot wrote this 'in a trance', and explained his extraordinary facility in terms of the 'illness' from which he was, at this time, recuperating. 'It is a commonplace that some forms of illness are extremely favourable, not only to religious illumination, but to artistic and literary composition. A piece of writing mediated without progress for months or years, may suddenly take shape and word, and in this state long passages may be produced which require little or no touch.'[7]

The thunder prompts the speaker to put a psychological waste behind him. He might shore up his 'ruin' through attention to instructive moments in others' lives: Arnaut Daniel suffering for lust in the flames of purgatory, and Nerval's disinherited prince who experienced hell and returned to life, and conceived his *mélancolie* to be the sign of a saint. A vengeful rage could drive one into madness—that possibility remains. An alternative is a prayer for

5. Reference to three visionary poems composed in 1914 but not finished or published. One of these includes a sequence based on Jesus's proclamation "I am the resurrection and the life" (John 11:25) [*Editor*].
6. A few words, clean and bright (French) [*Editor*].
7. T.S. Eliot, "The *Pensées* of Pascal," in *Essays Ancient and Modern*, 142 [*Editor*].

mental peace: 'Shantih'. Eliot again uses Sanskrit to convey an untranslatable truth 'which passeth understanding'.[8]

On 2 January 1922, Eliot stopped again in Paris and stayed about two weeks en route for home. At this late stage, Pound's emphatic criticisms cut the poem by half (in Lausanne, Eliot spoke of 800–1,000 lines, double its final length).

Pound thought badly of the narrative in 'Death by Water'. He drew a thick line through the focal 'London' fragment of 'The Fire Sermon' and cancelled the churches, St Mary Woolnoth and Michael Paternoster. What excited Pound was not private hallucinations and spiritual hopes but helpless submission ('deploring action') to the stings of fortune, to London's odour of putrefaction and dull routines. He congratulated Eliot on the outline he had found for their 'deformative secretions'.

*   *   *

On 20 January 1922, when Eliot offered *The Waste Land* to his friend Scofield Thayer, editor of the New York *Dial*, he said it had been three times through the sieve by Pound and himself and should soon be in its final form. Eliot probably left the manuscript, or part of it, in Paris so that Pound might consider it a third time. With the last sieving of the manuscript Eliot cut the whole of the fisherman's voyage in response to Pound's numerous cancellations on the typescript copy, though doubts lingered as to the effect of this on the poem as a whole. This was a sustained counter to urban stagnation, but Pound was hostile to narrative, and had his way. He thought Conrad was not 'weighty enough', and Eliot dropped the telling epigraph.[9] But the main force of Pound's attack in his late-January letters was directed against the three closing lyrics of the Lausanne draft: 'Song', 'Dirge', and 'Exequy'. On 24 January Pound advised Eliot repeatedly 'to abolish 'em altogether'. Eliot replied that he accepted criticism 'so far as understood'. They were not impressive pieces, aesthetically, but essential facets of Eliot's emotional ensemble. What Pound called 'superfluities' were cut.

8. Eliot's original note to the line, 'The Peace which passeth understanding', attempts to translate 'Shantih'. Cleo McNelly Kearns, in *T. S Eliot and Indic Tradition*, 228–9, explains 'the full context of *shantih* in Hindu tradition, where it is . . . simultaneously a mantra, a closing prayer for many ritual occasions, and one of the most prestigious terms in the Sanskrit language for the goal of meditative truth'.
9. Before setting on the current epigraph, Eliot had considered using "The horror! The horror!" from Joseph Conrad's novella *Heart of Darkness* (1899) [*Editor*].

LAWRENCE RAINEY

[Publishing *The Waste Land*]†

A core of basic facts about the publication of *The Waste Land* has long been known. In October 1922 it was simultaneously published in two journals: the *Criterion* in England, on 16 October, and the *Dial* in the United States, around 20 October (though in the November issue). In December it appeared a third time, now an independent book that for the first time included line numbers and Eliot's explanatory notes, published by the American firm of Boni and Liveright.[1] Ten months later, in September 1923, it appeared a fourth time, once more as an independent book that included Eliot's explanatory notes, now published by the Hogarth Press, a British firm run by Leonard and Virginia Woolf. Together these constituted an event that has acquired almost mythical status, a legend that recounts the story of modernism's troubled or difficult emergence, its initial repudiation by a purblind critical establishment and a benighted public, and its slow but irreversible triumph. "Eliot," writes one critic when surveying the transition *From Modern to Contemporary American Poetry, 1945–1965*, "had been reviled in the twenties as a drunken Bolshevik," but by 1945 he "had ascended . . . to the status of a kind of grandfatherly literary institution." True, the author concedes, it might be difficult to pinpoint the author of that epithet "drunken Bolshevik"; but "even if the story is

---

† From *Revisiting* The Waste Land (New Haven, CT: Yale University Press, 2005), pp. 72–86. Reprinted by permission of Yale University Press. Unless otherwise indicated, notes are the author's. Some of the author's notes have been omitted.

1. For the English publication, see T. S. Eliot to Henry Ware Eliot, 11 October 1922: "The Criterion is due to appear next Monday [16 October]," in [*Letters of T.S. Eliot*, ed. Valerie Eliot (New York: Harcourt Brace Jovanovich, 1988), hereafter *LOTSE*, 580]. See also Eliot to Richard Cobden-Sanderson, 16 October 1922, in *LOTSE*, 582. The exact date of the American publication in the *Dial* is less clear. "We are to publish the text of the poem, without the notes, in the November Dial, which will be published about October 20th" (carbon copy of Gilbert Seldes to Horace Liveright, 7 September 1922, Yale, Beinecke Library, *Dial* Papers, box 41, folder 1153; hereafter *Dial* Papers). With a delay of perhaps one or two days, the *Dial* apparently met its schedule: * * *. More mystery surrounds the exact date of the Liveright release. In a letter to Seldes of 12 September, Liveright confirmed that his firm was "not to publish The Waste Land prior to its appearance in The Dial," and speculated, "I don't think that we'll publish it before January" (*Dial* Papers, ms. 34, box 41, folder 1153). * * * Apparently Liveright hastened to release it on 15 December in order to capitalize on the publicity generated by the announcement of the Dial Award in its December issue (presumably released around 20 November). For the date, see Donald Gallup, *T. S. Eliot: A Bibliography*, rev. ed. (New York: Harcourt, 1969), A6, 29–32. For an earlier study on *The Waste Land*'s publication, see Daniel Woodward, "Notes on the Publishing History and Text of The Waste Land," *Papers of the Bibliographical Society of America* 58 (1964): 252–269.

apocryphal, it accurately evokes the public reception of 'The Waste Land.'"[2] But does it?

To reexamine that complex event, we might begin by exploring not where the poem was ultimately published but where it was *not* published—in the witty and sophisticated pages of *Vanity Fair*, or in the intransigent leaves of that avant-garde journal the *Little Review*. For both were considered as potential publishers at various points in 1922 as negotiations for the poem followed their unpredictable course. And together these possibilities, with the stories that lie behind them, set out a spectrum of modernist publishing practices— the halting steps that modernism took as it groped its way through the darkened corridors of its own production.

One might begin by examining an unnoticed occasion in early August 1922, when John Peale Bishop visited the Paris studio of Ezra Pound. Two weeks earlier Bishop had resigned his post as managing editor of *Vanity Fair*, and ostensibly he was traveling on an extended honeymoon after his recent marriage. Unofficially, however, Bishop had come to visit the savage god of modern experimentalism—and to talk business.[3] The topic was the publication of *The Waste Land*, a work that Bishop had never read but whose vicissitudes he had been following for five months. In early March, while still in New York and laboring for *Vanity Fair*, he had received an essay from Aldous Huxley[4] that reported the poem's composition and announced—mistakenly, it turned out—its imminent publication in the *Dial*. An astute and conscientious editor, Bishop had phoned to confirm the report with his colleague and counterpart at the *Dial*, Gilbert Seldes. Seldes was puzzled, having heard nothing about the poem; on 6 March he cabled *Dial* co-owner and chief editor Scofield Thayer, who was then residing in Vienna: CABLE WHETHER ELIOT POETRY COMING SELDES. Three days later

---

2. James E. B. Breslin, *From Modern to Contemporary: American Poetry, 1945–1965* (Chicago: University of Chicago Press, 1984), 11 and 11 n. 53. Breslin cannot assign the epithet "drunken Bolshevik" to a source because it has none. The ultimate source of the phrase is a book review by Arthur Waugh (1866–1943), father of the two novelists Alec and Evelyn. [See p. 175—*Editor*.] * * * Ezra Pound, in an angry defense of Eliot's work, seized upon the phrase "drunken slave," transformed it ever so slightly into "drunken helot," and charged Waugh with applying it to Eliot. From there, in the lore of the young, it went on to become "drunken Bolshevik" and lodged itself in the memory of Stephen Spender, and from Spender it was taken up by Breslin and turned into a comment representing public opinion of the 1920s, or even a judgment on *The Waste Land*. For the review by Waugh and the counterblast by Pound, see *T. S. Eliot: The Critical Heritage*, ed. Michael Grant (London: Routledge, 1942), 67–73. For Spender's contribution, see his essay "The New Orthodoxies," in Robert Richman, ed., *The Arts at Mid-Century* (New York: Horizon, 1954), 11, which in turn is the source that is cited by Breslin.
3. On Bishop see Elizabeth Carroll Spindler, *John Peale Bishop* (Morgantown: West Virginia University Library, 1980), chapters 5–7. It should be noted that Spindler often errs on points of detail, especially in transcribing letters. * * *
4. See above, p. 81 [*Editor*].

Thayer replied in French: ELIOT REFUSA THAYER. Seldes immediately contacted Bishop and urged him to alter Huxley's article to indicate that the poem's appearance in the *Dial* was, as Seldes expressed it, "problematical but probable."[5] More important, Bishop had now glimpsed the growing rift between Eliot and the *Dial*.

By late April 1922, in fact, relations between Eliot and Thayer had completely broken down, and in the wake of their collapse Pound had begun to intervene actively in the search for a publisher. On 6 May 1922 he wrote to Jeanne Foster, who was the beloved companion of the New York lawyer and cultural patron John Quinn, but also an occasional contributor to *Vanity Fair* and a friend of Bishop's.[6] Pound was soliciting an offer of publication for the poem in the bluntest possible terms: "What wd. Vanity Fair pay Eliot for 'Waste Land.' Cd. yr. friend there [Bishop] get in touch with T. S. E., address 12 Wigmore St., London W.1." By August, when he visited Pound, Bishop was clearly apprised of the situation—indeed, was responding to a suggestion advanced by Pound himself. The two met on 3 August, and two days later Bishop reported their conversation to Edmund Wilson, his closest friend and his successor as managing editor at *Vanity Fair*:

> Pound I met the other afternoon. I found him extended on a bright green couch, swathed in a hieratic bathrobe made of a maiden aunt's shit-brown blanket. His head is quite fine, but his voice is offensively soft, almost effeminate and [illegible word], and his body is rather disagreeably soft. However, he was quite gracious, and the twinkle of his eyes whenever he makes a point is worth something. He held forth for two hours on the intellectual moribundity of England—the old stuff. Here's the thing however—Eliot is starting a quarterly review: he is to run 'Waste Land,' the new series of lyrics in the first number: he and Thayer have split and the *Dial* will not publish it. Perhaps you might want to arrange for the American publication. Pound says they are as fine as anything written in English since 1900. I'm lunching with EP tomorrow [6 August] and will report further.

Whether Bishop wrote again to Wilson as he promised is unknown. On 7 August he left for Vienna, and by the time his letter could have reached Wilson in New York (around 16 August) and Wilson could have replied, his proposal had already been overtaken by events

5. Gilbert Seldes to Scofield Thayer, cable of 6 March 1922 ([Yale, Beinecke Library,] *Dial* Papers, box 40, folder 1138); Thayer to Seldes, cable of 9 March 1922; Seldes to Thayer, letter of 11 March 1922 (both in the *Dial* Papers, box 40, folder 1139). [Thayer's cable indicates that Eliot has refused to submit his poem—*Editor*.]
6. Ezra Pound to Jeanne Foster, 6 May 1922 (Harvard University, Houghton Library, bMS Am 1635). * * *

previously set in motion.[7] Yet the seriousness with which it was advanced by both Bishop and Pound should indicate that *Vanity Fair* was considered a serious contender to publish the poem. How serious, indeed, we shall see later.

Bishop's meeting in August also indicates the centrality of Pound's role in prompting and facilitating this abortive plan, recapitulating a story that grows increasingly familiar: Pound was the cultural impresario who, precisely by virtue of this role, occupied a critical position at the heart of modernism. It is this position, in fact, that informs the rhetoric in which he articulated his advocacy of *The Waste Land*'s publication: "Pound says they are as fine as anything written in English since 1900," wrote Bishop, evidently quoting him verbatim. A month earlier Pound had written to Felix Schelling, his former professor at the University of Pennsylvania: "Eliot's *Waste Land* is I think the justification of the 'movement,' of our modern experiment, since 1900."[8] Bishop had clearly been subjected to a variant of that argument: the poem was important precisely for its representative quality, and to publish it did not require that one appreciate its aesthetic qualities or sympathize with its contents—however one defined those terms—but that one be eager to stake out a position as the spokesperson for a field of cultural production, the voice of an array of institutions ("the justification of the 'movement,' of our modern experiment, since 1900"). How much this animated Bishop's interest in the poem is underscored by a curious anomaly in the nature of his enthusiasm, for Bishop was praising a poem that he had yet to read—indeed, whose exact title was still a bit obscure to him ("'Waste Land,' the new series of lyrics").[9]

Bishop's imperfect knowledge was not unique. Indeed, insofar as he knew the title of the poem at all, he knew more than Horace Liveright had known when he first advanced his own offer of publication for the poem on 3 January 1922—the date being notable because it was before the poem had been completed, before it had even acquired its present title. Liveright's interest, like Bishop's, was the consequence not of an aesthetic encounter with a work he had read

7. John Peale Bishop to Edmund Wilson, 5 August 1922 (Yale, Beinecke Library, Edmund Wilson Papers, Series 2). * * *
8. Pound to Felix Schelling, 8–9 July 1922, in Ezra Pound, *Selected Letters, 1907–1941,* ed. D. D. Paige (New York: New Directions, 1971), 180.
9. It should be stressed that Pound did not at this time have a copy of the manuscript and so could not lend it to Bishop. One week before their meeting, on 27 July, Pound had written to Eliot requesting a copy of the manuscript precisely because he had none available to show James Sibley Watson, Jr., who was then visiting Pound and wished to read it. This can be inferred from Eliot's reply of 18 July, when he stated that he had only one copy to hand but would make another and send it as soon as he could (see *LOTSE,* 552). Equally important, the typescript did not arrive until 14 August, or seven days after Bishop's departure, as reported by Watson to Thayer when he sent it on to him in Vienna (James Sibley Watson to Thayer, 16 August 1922, *Dial* Papers, box 44, folder 1260).

and admired but of an eagerness to buy a product that promised to meet a series of minimum conditions. Yet what were these conditions?

Like Bishop's, Liveright's access to Eliot's poem had been mediated by Pound. It was he who assumed the function of stage director cuing the characters in their parts: the reserved and diffident poet played by T. S. Eliot, the brash young publisher acted by Horace Liveright. Eliot had arrived in Paris on 2 January 1922 and was to stay for two weeks, until 16 January. He had come from Lausanne, bearing the disorderly sheaf of manuscripts that he and Pound began to edit and revise, producing a quasi-final version of *The Waste Land*.[1] His arrival coincided with the visit of Liveright, the partner who was guiding editorial policy at Boni and Liveright. Liveright was touring Europe to acquire new works of literature, and his visit to Pound was designed to set their relations on firmer ground. In 1919 he had published Pound's *Instigations*; in 1920 he had undertaken *Poems, 1918–1921*, a volume released only three weeks before his arrival in Paris; and in the summer of 1921 he had paid Pound for a translation of Remy de Gourmont's *Physique de l'amour*, an engagement that had rescued Pound from dire financial straits. Now Liveright hoped to establish more stable relations; he trusted Pound's capacity to recognize new talent, saw him as a valuable link to other authors whose work interested him, and even entertained the idea that Pound's work might prove commercially viable at some point in the future.[2] In turn, Pound thought that he might make Liveright into the principal publisher of modernism and hoped to secure a long-term agreement guaranteeing financial security and time for work.

Poet and publisher courted one another actively. During the six days of Liveright's stay in Paris (30 December 1921–4 January 1922),

---

1. The dates of Eliot's arrival and departure are inferred from Vivien Eliot to Mary Hutchinson, 12 January 1922, in *LOTSE*, 501. She reports that "Tom has been here ten days," implying that he arrived on 2 January; and she states that "he will be back [in London] on Monday," 17 January 1922, suggesting that he would leave the day before, or 16 January. The new dates also make clear that all of Pound's editorial interventions occurred between 2 and 16 January 1922. Further, as scholars have previously suspected, these consisted principally of two editorial sessions. This hypothesis is confirmed by Eliot's letter of 20 January 1922 to Scofield Thayer, in which he reports that his poem "will have been three times through the sieve by Pound as well as myself" (*LOTSE*, 503). In other words, in addition to the two times that Pound had already gone over the poem while the two men were in Paris, Eliot was planning to send it to him for yet a third time. Eliot probably sent the poem to Pound on 19 or 20 January, at roughly the same time he was writing to Thayer, and in response Pound wrote his letter dated "24 Saturnus," or 24 January 1922 (mistakenly assigned to 24 December 1921 by Valerie Eliot, and printed in *LOTSE*, 497–498).

2. On *Instigations*, see Gallup, *Eliot*, A18. For Liveright's acceptance of *Poems, 1918–1921*, see Liveright to Pound, 13 September 1920, Indiana University, Lilly Library, Pound Mss. II, Liveright. For his helpful role in Pound's personal finances in 1921, see Lawrence Rainey, *Ezra Pound and the Monument of Culture* (Chicago: University of Chicago Press, 1991), 48.

they saw each other daily.[3] Pound treated Liveright to visits with
Paul Morand and Constantin Brancusi,[4] and the young publisher
left "a good impression" on Pound, who felt that he was "going toward
the light[,] not from it." He was "much more of a man than publish-
ers usually are," and indeed "perhaps the only man in the business."[5]
He was "a pearl among publishers."[6] The pearly and masculine pub-
lisher had arrived at an opportune moment. Joyce was seeking an
American publisher for *Ulysses,* and Eliot would need a publisher
for his unfinished poem. On 3 January 1922, Liveright had an
extraordinary dinner with Joyce, Eliot, and Pound to discuss a
milestone publishing program. The encounter was productive. With
Joyce he agreed to publish *Ulysses* and to give $1,000 against royal-
ties. To Pound he offered a contract guaranteeing $500 annually for
two years in addition to translator's fees for any work from French
agreed upon by both parties. To Eliot he offered $150 advance
against 15 percent royalties and promised publication in the fall list.
Liveright was nervous only about length; in a brief note dated 11
January, a week before Eliot had even left Paris, he worried that the
poem might not be long enough. "I'm disappointed that Eliot's mate-
rial is as short. Can't he add anything?" he pleaded with Pound.[7]

   Pound, it is clear, was eager to gather under one roof the princi-
pal authors and works of modernism, including Yeats, whom he
encouraged to abandon a long-standing contract with Macmillan in
favor of Liveright.[8] At stake in these efforts was an attempt to pre-
sent modernist writings as the articulation of an idiom, a serviceable
language that was shared (and in this sense collective in character),

3. Copy of Liveright to John Quinn, 24 March 1922, Indiana University, Lilly Library,
   Pound Mss. I, Quinn: "I am attaching to this letter a card which James Joyce gave me
   in Paris one evening when I had dinner with him. . . . Ezra Pound and T. S. Eliot had
   dinner with us that night and as I am publishing Ezra Pound, and I'm about to publish
   Eliot, providing that Knopf has no legal claim on his next book, I think Joyce belongs
   in the Boni and Liveright fold."
4. Morand (1888–1976), French author; Brancusi (1876–1957), Romanian sculptor
   [*Editor*].
5. Pound to Jeanne Foster, 5 April 1992[, Harvard University, Houghton Library, bMS
   Am 1635].
6. Pound to Quinn, 20 June 1920, New York Public Library, Quinn Papers, box 34, folder
   4.
7. Liveright to Pound, 11 January 1922, Yale, Beinecke Library, Bird Papers, folder 23;
   hereafter Bird Papers. It is Liveright's concern with the length of the poem that
   explains Eliot's repeated proposals designed to make the book longer by adding as pref-
   atory material to *The Waste Land:* (1) three minor pieces, a suggestion that Pound
   rejected on 24 January, (2) a reprint of "Gerontion," an idea advanced to Pound in a
   letter circa 26 January (assigned to "24? January" by Valerie Eliot), and (3) one or two
   poems by Pound, also advanced in the same letter of circa 26 January to Pound. * * *
8. See Liveright to Pound, 12 October 1922, [Yale, Beinecke Library,] Bird Papers, folder
   23: "It doesn't seem that we've found the right thing yet, does it? . . . And if Yeats insists
   on sticking to Macmillan, and I firmly believe that Yeats has more to do with it than
   Watt [his agent] because I did have a long talk with Watt and he seemed inclined to let
   me have a look-in,—well, all the worse for Yeats." [William Butler Yeats (1863–1939),
   Irish poet and dramatist—*Editor*.]

yet also amenable to a high degree of individuation: the voice of a "'movement,' of our modern experiment since 1900." In short, his activity was characterized by programmatic ambitions and a coherent sense of their interaction with market conditions.

The same traits surface in his dealings with Scofield Thayer, the editor of the *Dial* who was eventually to purchase *The Waste Land*. Pound lobbied forcefully for the poem's publication from the outset, invoking a rhetoric by now familiar. On 18 February 1922, when Thayer and Eliot were still at a preliminary stage of discussion, Pound wrote to Thayer: "Eliot's poem is very important, almost enough to make everyone else shut up shop." When Thayer replied (5 March) that he could not comment on the poem's merits, since Eliot had not yet sent him the text, Pound persisted: "His poem is as good in its way as Ulysses in its way, and there is so DAMN little genius, so DAMN little work that one can take hold of and say, 'This at any rate stands, makes a definite part of literature.'" *The Waste Land* was represented as a verse equivalent of *Ulysses,* a work that epitomized not just the experiences of an individual, whether author or protagonist, but the modernist claim to a preeminent position in the institution of "literature," an ambiguous entity that was both distinct and yet inseparable from the commercial production of reading matter. Its merits resided not just in a specific set of words or text but in its capacity to articulate this collective aspiration of a small but influential group.

Pound's letter of 9–10 March also outlined practical suggestions that would prove pivotal both for *The Waste Land* and for subsequent literature: "I wish to Christ he had had the December award," he hinted, referring to the influential prize which the *Dial* had recently founded, the annual Dial Award. But other solutions were also available. Eliot might be granted "a professorship," as Robert Frost[9] had recently been. Or he might be given a job on the *Century* or the *Atlantic,* since "he is not an alarming revolutionary, and he don't, as I at moments, get mistaken for a labour-leader or bolshy bombthrower."[1] Yet it was his suggestion of "the December award," the Dial Award for services in the cause of letters, that would ultimately bear fruit both for Eliot and for modernism.

Pound's suggestions were advanced just when communications between Eliot and Thayer were breaking down. On 8 March, Eliot had telegraphed Thayer that he could not accept less than £50 ($250). Unfortunately, the message was distorted in transmission,

9. American poet (1874–1963), who taught English at Amherst College 1917–20 and later.
1. Pound to Thayer, 18 February 1922, *Dial* Papers, box 38, folder 1070; Thayer to Pound, 5 March 1922, and Pound to Thayer, 9–10 March 1922, *Dial* Papers, box 38, folder 1071.

and Thayer had received a shocking request for an unprecedented sum: "cannot accept under !8!56 pounds = eliot + [sic]." In reply, on 12 March, Thayer reiterated his offer of $150 for the poem, a figure that was advanced without sight of the manuscript and was 25 percent higher than the $110 to $120 he normally would have paid.[2] * * * Not unreasonably, Thayer also asked to receive a copy of the manuscript. In addition, he pointed out the staggering deficits the *Dial* was incurring and argued that it could not alter its policy of "pay[ing] all contributors famous and unknown at the same rates." In reply Eliot was curt and frankly insulting, and he proceeded to withdraw the poem entirely:

> Please excuse my not replying sooner to your letter, except by my wire; but I have had a good deal of trouble over letting my flat furnished and moving here, where I shall be till the 20th June. In addition, there have been engrossing personal affairs, and I have been prevented from dealing with any correspondence.
>
> I also took some days to think about your offer, during which time I happened to hear on good authority that you paid £.100 to George Moore[3] for a short story, and I must confess that this influenced me in declining $150 [£30] for a poem which has taken me a year to write and which is my biggest work. To have it published in a journal was not in any case the way I should choose for bringing it out; and certainly if I am to be offered only 30 to 35 pounds for such a publication it is out of the question.
>
> I have written to Ezra Pound to explain my reasons for refusing to dispose of the poem to the Dial at that price and he concurs with me. . . .
>
> You have asked me several times to give you the right of first refusal of any new work of mine, and I gave you the first refusal of this poem.

When Thayer received Eliot's letter, he wrote in pencil on the margin, opposite Eliot's charge about George Moore: "novellette length / serially." At the bottom of the letter he also noted: "Seen Moore work[,] exception for him[;] and because review had offended[,] Moore had already sacrificed several hundred dollars." True, the *Dial* had paid Moore a higher than usual fee, but in part this was

2. Thayer's marginalia on Eliot's letter of 20 January 1922 (*Dial* Papers, box 31, folder 810) record his diligent calculations of the poem's price at normal rates: if typeset at thirty-five lines per page, the poem would come to slightly less than twelve pages, yielding a price of $120; if typeset at forty lines per page, it would come to eleven and a quarter pages, yielding a price slightly more than $110. Summarizing his results, Thayer firmly concludes: "12 pp. $120." His offer of $150, then, was already 25 percent higher than normal rates.
3. Irish poet, novelist, and critic (1852–1933) [*Editor*].

because of the work's length, in part because the *Dial* had been remiss in fulfilling earlier obligations to Moore ("had offended"), thereby forcing him to sacrifice "several hundred dollars," for which the larger payment had been a form of compensation. But more important was Thayer's remark opposite Eliot's last sentence withdrawing the offer to publish. Thayer vented his tart indignation: "Not submitted."[4]

Eliot's allegations about Moore appeared to invoke a principle of equal pay for all contributors. In fact, it was precisely the opposite principle that interested him, as he had explained a few days earlier to Pound: "I think these people should learn to recognize Merit instead of Senility, and I think it is an outrage that we should be paid less merely because Thayer thinks we will take less and be thankful for it, and I thought that somebody ought to take steps to point this out."[5] At first sight Eliot's argument may strike us as sympathetic, if only because it seems so familiar. But the issues were rather more complicated: in an important sense the question of aesthetic value is inseparable from commercial success in a market economy, a difficulty that beset every argument for the intrinsic merit of literary modernism. By 1922 literary modernism desperately required a financial-critical success that would seem comparable to the stunning achievement of modernist painting; yet every step in this direction was hampered by market constraints less amenable to the kinds of pressure from elite patronage and investment that had secured the fortunes of Cubism and modern painting. The legal definition of intellectual property—which continued to belong to the author after its purchase by the consumer, in contrast to a painting or a statue, which became the property of the purchaser—posed a series of intractable dilemmas. Patronage could nurture literary modernism only to the threshold of its confrontation with a wider public; beyond that point, however, only commercial success could ratify its viability as a significant idiom. That was the question that permeated discussion about publication of *The Waste Land*: assuming that the poem epitomized the investment of twenty years in the creation of a collective idiom—"our modern experiment, since 1900"—the protagonists were obliged to find a return on their investment in modernity.

Thayer was shocked and insulted by Eliot's letter of 16 March and refused to engage in further communications with him. Instead he turned to Pound, who was more vulnerable to the threat of losing his job with the *Dial* and might be reproached for having encouraged Eliot's intransigence. On 10 April, Thayer demanded that he

4. Eliot to Thayer, 16 March 1922, *Dial* Papers, box 31, folder 810.
5. Eliot to Pound, 12 March 1922, *LOTSE*, 507.

explain himself: "Perhaps you will be able to enlighten me as to why you concur with Eliot in his refusal to let The Dial have his poem."[6] In reply Pound rehearsed the same charge (which Eliot had communicated to him), that George Moore was "getting special rates from *The Dial* (also Sherwood Anderson[7])," and he concluded: "That being the case I can hardly reprove Eliot—if you have put the thing on a commercial basis, for holding out for as high a price as he can get. [Added in autograph in margin:] (i.e. if The Dial is a business house, it gets business treatment. If The Dial is a patron of literature T. contends it should not pay extra rates for 'mere senility,' all of which is extreme theory-ism, perhaps, on his part.)" But in passing, Pound added another point. While he could hardly attest to the veracity of Eliot's or Thayer's claims, in general he preferred that the poem be published in the *Dial:* "I shd. perhaps prefer one good review to several less good ones. I have, as I think you know, always wanted to see a concentration of the authors I believe in, in one review. The Dial perhaps looks better to me than it does to Eliot. (Life in general does.)"[8] As always, Pound displayed a keen understanding of the nexus between cultural ambitions and their institutional actualization. Implicit in his remarks to Thayer was his view that literary modernism could best present itself as a shared language through a centralization suggesting the coherence of its ambitions— the same project that animated his endeavor to unite the works of Joyce, Eliot, Yeats, and himself under the umbrella of a single publisher. Such a project would facilitate the perception of modernism as an idiom both collective and capable of individuation: an identifiable, distinctive, and serviceable language. Yet with equal acuteness Pound also articulated a central dilemma that characterized the *Dial* and the role it might play in any such project. Was the *Dial* a form of patronage, or was it a commercial venture? Unlike traditional journals that were the organs of publishing houses, the *Dial* could shun the diversity and heterogeneity that increasingly typified a literary journal, presenting itself as a patron of letters that was benign and "disinterested." Its owners, Scofield Thayer and James Sibley Watson, Jr., however, were also active purchasers of modern painting and sculpture, and in this sense were investors in

6. Thayer visited Pound for the first time on 12 July 1921. Pound's initial contract to serve as writer and talent scout for the *Dial* had expired twelve days earlier, and Thayer had advised him that it would not be renewed. When the two met for a second time on 13 July, however, the contract was renewed, though only in part: Pound would continue to write for the *Dial* but not serve as talent scout, and he would receive roughly half his former salary. These meetings were only part of a series that continued throughout the month: 12 July, 13 July, circa 20 July, 26 July, and 28 July. For the meetings, see Pound to Dorothy Shakespear Pound, 12 July, 14 July, 21 July, 26 July, 30 July 1921, Indiana University, Lilly Library, Pound Mss. III, 1921.
7. American novelist and short-story writer (1876–1941) [*Editor*].
8. Pound to Thayer, 23 April 1922, *Dial* Papers, box 38, folder 1072.

a market commodity whose value was rapidly rising, in part through the efforts of the publicity apparatus that they themselves owned and controlled. Literary modernism, by analogy, was now courting the risk of becoming "smart art," an investment that would pay and pay big if successful in an expanding market. But pay whom?

The contradictions were irreconcilable. Driven by conflicting imperatives, the participants muddled through the summer of 1922. On 30 April, Thayer summarized the state of his relations with Eliot: "We now correspond only through Pound with whom my relations are also strained, but who seems to desire to keep his job." Pound himself was more cavalier. On 6 May, while traveling through Italy, he paused to send Thayer a postcard: "My present impression of the case is 'Oh you two Bostonians.'"[9] The surface gaiety, however, was a pose. The same day he also posted his letter to Jeanne Foster, inquiring about the price that *Vanity Fair* might be willing to pay for *The Waste Land.*

Discussions remained stalled throughout the rest of May and June as the participants reconsidered their strategies. On 2 June, Pound and Eliot met in Verona, a meeting recorded a few weeks later by Pound in a series of drafts and draft fragments suggesting the substance of their conversations. One of these (later incorporated into *The Cantos*[1]) makes clear that they considered the editorial program of Eliot's new review (still un-titled, but soon to be named the *Criterion*) a topic that probably led to another: where to publish *The Waste Land.*[2] From the outset of his undertaking the *Criterion,* Eliot had entertained the idea that it might collaborate with American reviews in simultaneous publication; his first letter announcing the new journal to Pound, written on 12 March, had proposed exactly this: "I also see no reason why some things should not appear in this and in the Little Review concurrently."[3] The timing of this suggestion should be noted: it was four days after Eliot had sent his provocative telegram to Thayer and four days before he withdrew his offer of publication to the *Dial.* It was a curious proposal: Eliot had not published in the *Little Review* since 1918 and had never evinced particular interest in its fortunes. Yet if Eliot was already assuming that *The Waste Land* would be published by his own journal in England, then his 12 March reference to the *Little Review*— addressed to Pound, a force behind its current editorial activity—was probably an effort to suggest a replacement for the *Dial.* The same

9. Pound to Thayer, 6 May 1922, *Dial* Papers, box 38, folder 1073.
1. Pound's epic poem, published in separate "Cantos" between 1917 and 1969 [*Editor*].
2. The visit is mentioned in Eliot to Sydney Schiff, attributed to "early June 1922" by Valerie Eliot in *LOTSE*, 528: "I also went to Verona and saw Pound." * * *
3. Eliot to Pound, 12 March 1922, *LOTSE*, 508. Eliot mentions the *Little Review* only twice in his correspondence for 1922, both times in letters to Pound. Clearly he considered the journal to be largely Pound's.

idea, we may suppose, arose in their discussions at Verona. And quite
naturally so, since the editors of the *Little Review* were now in Paris
and often in touch with Pound, who had recently assembled a spe-
cial Brancusi issue for them. Like *Vanity Fair,* the *Little Review* was
also a possible candidate for what had now become a project of
simultaneous publication.

In the wake of the Verona meeting, the decisive episodes in the
story unfolded quickly. Pound returned to Paris on 2 July 1922 and
two weeks later received a personal visit from James Sibley Wat-
son, Jr., the co-owner and co-editor of the *Dial* and the partner of
Thayer. Two days later Pound reported the meeting to his wife, Dor-
othy, who was away in London: "Usual flood [of people visiting]:
Lunch with Watson of Dial, on Wed. [19 July], amiable . . . wants
T's poem for Dial, etc." The report leaves no doubt about the pur-
pose of Watson's visit: he had come to purchase *The Waste Land.*[4]
Presumably he was treated to a variant of Pound's argument that
the poem was "as good in its way as Ulysses in its way"—resonant,
even haunting terms to Watson now that he was in Paris. For when
Watson had gone to Sylvia Beach's bookstore to pick up his own copy
of *Ulysses* (number 33, at 350 francs), he had learned that the last of
the 150-franc copies had already soared in value to 500 francs. Wat-
son and Thayer, after all, had ordered nine copies of the first edi-
tion for themselves, the *Dial,* and various staff members (Thayer had
purchased copy number 73). And Thayer understood the kind of
publicity such a work could generate: he had been called as a wit-
ness at the *Little Review* trial[5] and seen at first hand its sensational
newspaper coverage. Influenced by these events and the assumption
that the poem vindicated the project of modern experimentalism,
Watson was seized with anxiety that the *Dial* would suffer an igno-
minious defeat in its effort to position itself as *the* representative of
advanced cultural life. What if the poem were published in the *Little
Review* or even *Vanity Fair?* The day after his meeting with Pound,
Watson flew to Berlin and met with Thayer.[6]

The chief subject of discussion in Berlin was *The Waste Land*
and the *Dial*'s prospects for publishing it. Increasingly fearful and
excited, the two editors reached an unprecedented decision: they
would offer Eliot the second annual Dial Award with its $2,000 prize
as payment for the poem, in confidence, while officially they would

---

4. Pound to Dorothy Shakespear Pound, 21 July 1922, Indiana University, Lilly Library,
   Pound Mss. III, 1922.
5. Trial of 1921 in which the American literary magazine, which had been publishing
   chapters of *Ulysses,* was prosecuted for obscenity [*Editor*].
6. Thayer to Seldes, 20 July 1922, *Dial* Papers, box 40, folder 1148. Thayer reports that
   Watson "is present as I dictate," leaving no doubt that Watson departed within hours of
   his meeting with Pound on 19 July (date of meeting from Pound to Dorothy Shake-
   spear Pound, 21 July 1922).

pay only the $150 that had been their original offer.[7] Literary history records few spectacles so curious or so bizarre as this: two editors of a major review offering a figure nearly three times the national income per capita—in 2003 dollars, the payment would exceed $83,000—for a poem that neither of them had seen or read. What they had decided to purchase was less a specific poem, more a bid for a preeminent position in the field of cultural production. Moreover, their strategy for reaching that goal was exquisitely self-fulfilling: since news of the Dial Award would attract media attention, it would augment the sales of the work and further redound to the credit of the *Dial*.

Seven days after his encounter with Thayer, Watson returned to Paris and met with Pound a second time. Two accounts of the meeting survive, one by Pound addressed to Dorothy: "Watson in Thursday [27 July] with Cummings. . . . Wat. troubled at not having T. S.'s poem for Dial."[8] More revealing is Watson's account, addressed to Thayer:

> Pound has written a [autograph addition: *very*] veiled hint to Eliot. He took me to see Brancusi, who [illegible word] appears very anxious not to be reproduced anymore. I gather this is mostly a pose. Such chittering and apologizing and kowtowing as Pound indulged in I have never before seen. It was disgusting. I pointed out several things I thought you would like, but no, I must take what the master will give. "You win the victory," says Brancusi, as though I had been beseeching him for a week. A dam' Pyrrhic victory, by me! . . . He will, of course, be furious if we don't take any; and Pound will say that we have destroyed his only remaining Parisian friendship. I hope you will write Brancusi rather than have me go to see him again; if I go, I shan't take Pound, that's sure. . . . Pound looks pretty unhealthy. He handed me two lemons which he recommends very highly and which I send to you on the [canceled: hope] chance you may like one of them.[9]

Pound's letter to Eliot, which has not survived, was written immediately after Watson's visit on 27 July. And though his "hint" had been "*very* veiled" when issued from Paris, a certain rending evidently took place as it crossed the channel. Eliot understood fully the implications of his request for a typescript: "I will let you have

7. Thayer to Eliot, 5 October 1922, *Dial* Papers, box 31, folder 810: "I have been very glad to learn from New York that the suggestion I made to Mr. Watson while he was with me in Berlin last July has borne fruit and that we are despite your asperity to have the pleasure of recognizing publicly your contribution to contemporary letters."
8. Pound to Dorothy Shakespear Pound, 29 July 1922, Indiana University, Lilly Library, Pound Mss. III, 1922.
9. Watson to Thayer, 29 July 1922, *Dial* Papers, box 44, folder 1260.

a copy of the Waste Land for confidential use as soon as I can make one. . . . I infer from your remarks that Watson is at present in Paris. I have no objection to either his or Thayer's seeing the manuscript."[1] Evidently it took Eliot some two weeks to arrange (or type himself) a copy of the typescript, and it was not until 12 or 13 August that he sent it to Watson in Paris. When it arrived, Watson hastily read it and reported the news to Thayer in Vienna:

> In response to Pound's letter Eliot has assumed a more concil- iatory attitude and has sent on a copy of Wasteland for our perusal. I am forwarding it to you. . . . Anyway I wrote him more plainly about the prize and await his answer. I found the poem disappointing on first reading but after a third shot I think it up to his usual—all the styles are there, somewhat toned down in language [autograph addition: *adjectives*!] and theatricalized in sentiment—at least I thought.[2]

Here again, one is struck by the discrepancy between Watson's initial assessment of the poem and views of it enshrined in later criticism. "On first reading" Watson found the poem "disappointing," and after perusing it three times he considered it merely "up to [Eliot's] usual." In some respects, his letter implies, it was perhaps below his usual: the diction seemed flat ("somewhat toned down"), while the tone was overdone ("theatricalized"). Yet all this makes only more remarkable Watson's decision to advance a publication proposal that entailed an unprecedented scale of payment, which he pre- sented to Eliot in a letter of 13 or 14 August.

Eliot responded on 15 August: "Subject to Mr. Liveright's consent, I would let the *Dial* publish the poem for $150, not before Novem- ber 1st. In this event I would forego the $150 advance from Mr. Live- right, and he would delay publication as a book until the new year. Possibly he would be glad to do this, on the possibility of the book's getting the prize, which might increase the sales."[3] His proposal reached Watson late in the afternoon of 16 August. The next day, however, he was seized with panic at the audacity of his proposal and sent a telegram reporting that he could not make up his mind. On 19 August, Watson reported both events to Thayer:

> Got a letter from Eliot [received 16 August] regretting his haste in thinking we were trying to rob him, and offering us the right of publishing his poem simultaneously in Dial with its pub. in the Criterion. I find from Pound that Bel Esprit hasn't enough yet for one year, that it goes to Eliot only when he leaves his

1. Eliot to Pound, 28 July 1922, *LOTSE*, 552.
2. Watson to Thayer, 16 August 1922, *Dial* Papers, box 44, folder 1260.
3. Eliot to Watson, 15 August 1922, *LOTSE*, 560.

bank and engages in writing exclusively. He gets only a nomi-
nal salary from Lady Rothermere. In other words I don't see why
we shouldn't be doing something moderately popular in giving
him the award. But the next day [17 August] I got a [canceled:
cable] telegram saying "don't act till you receive a second let-
ter." Haven't received it yet, though it may come on board tonight
when we touch at Plymouth. So the matter is still in the air.
Please don't do anything definitive without letting me know
first. I reach New York probably August 26, and there is also
the telegraphie sans fil.[4]

Pound, clearly, had informed him about the difficult state of Eliot's
personal finances. Watson, in turn, hoped these circumstances
might be exploited to the advantage of the *Dial*, that it might be
viewed as "doing something moderately popular in giving him the
award." Eliot's actual services to letters (the ostensible justification
for the award) and the merits of *The Waste Land* were issues that
never appeared in his discussion of the Dial Award. Instead, Wat-
son cheerily admitted his view that the proposal was a device
intended to garner goodwill for the *Dial,* a tactic in its struggle to
consolidate its position as the dominant journal of advanced
culture.

Meanwhile, on 21 August, Eliot sent his own letter to Quinn,
apprising him of the recent developments and leaving open the pos-
sibility for action: "A few days ago I had an attractive proposal from
Mr. Watson of the *Dial* who are very anxious to publish the poem. . . .
They suggested getting Liveright to say postpone the date of publi-
cation as a book, but I have written to them to say that it seemed to
me too late to be proper to make any change now and that I should
not care to trouble either Mr. Liveright or yourself with any ques-
tions of alterations in the contract."[5] Nine days later Eliot wrote to
Pound and reported his letters to Watson and Quinn:

I received a letter from your friend Watson most amiable in
tone. . . . offering $150 for the "Waste Land" (not "Waste Land,"
please, but "*The* Waste Land," and (in the strictest confidence)
the award for virtue also. Unfortunately, it seemed considerably
too late, as I had the preceding day [14 August] got contract,
signed by Liveright and Quinn, book to be out by Nov. 1st, etc.)
I can't bother Quinn any more about it, I don't see why Live-
right should find it to his advantage to postpone publication in
order to let the Dial kill the sale by printing it first, and there

4. Watson to Thayer, 19 August 1922, *Dial* Papers, box 44, folder 1260. [Wireless telegra-
phy (French); Bel Esprit was Pound's scheme to raise a pension for Eliot; Lady Rother-
mere was the patron of the *Criterion—Editor.*]
5. Eliot to Quinn, 21 August 1922, *LOTSE,* 564.

has been so much fluster and business about this contract that I don't want to start the whole thing up again, so I see nothing but to hope that the Dial will be more businesslike with other people. Watson's manner was charming, if Thayer had behaved in the same way the Dial might have published it long ago, instead of pretending that I had given him the lie as if he was *ehrenfähig*[6] anyhow. Anyway, it's my loss, I suppose; if Watson wants to try to fix it up with Liveright I suppose he can, that's his affair. I suppose the move was entirely due to your beneficent and pacific efforts, which are appreciated. Dam but why don't they give the prize to you? More presently.[7]

Notwithstanding the disingenuous demurral by Eliot, the issue was already all but settled. The suggestion he had advanced—that the *Dial* undertake to arrange terms with Liveright—was rapidly realized through the agency of Watson. On 29 August his ship arrived in New York; the next day he received Eliot's letter of 21 August broaching the new arrangement. He set to work immediately, as Gilbert Seldes duly reported to Thayer: "Watson has just come back and the Eliot affair is taking up much of our time."[8] A week later he and Seldes met with Liveright in the New York office of the lawyer John Quinn, and there the deal was concluded. Liveright required that the *Dial* purchase 350 copies of the volume at standard discounts, assuring himself an advance sale and adding $315 to the *Dial*'s costs for procuring the poem. But the *Dial* had achieved its victory, and the outcome would be a remarkable success.

Liveright reported on these later events in a letter to Pound written on 5 February 1923, eleven weeks after the poem's publication in the *Dial*, seven weeks after his own release of the book-cum-notes: "God bless you and Cantos IX to XII. If we can get as much publicity from them as The Waste Land has received, you will be a millionaire. The Waste Land has sold 1000 copies to date and who knows, it may go up to 2000 or 3000 copies. Just think, Eliot may make almost $500 on the book rights of this poem. And Gene Stratton Porter makes $40,000.00 to $60,000 a year out of her books. Well, it's all in a life time, so who cares."[9]

Liveright's estimate of the poem's sales was too low, according to his biographer, for in fact "more than 5,000 copies were . . . sold."[1] More important, though, was the tenor of his comments, insofar as

6. Honorable (German) [*Editor*].
7. Eliot to Pound, 30 August 1922, *LOTSE*, 567.
8. Eliot to Watson, 21 August 1922, *LOTSE*, 564–565; Seldes to Thayer, 31 August 1922, *Dial* Papers, box 40, folder 1151.
9. Liveright to Pound, 5 February 1922, Indiana University, Lilly Library, Pound Mss. I, Liveright.
1. Tom Dardis, *Firebrand: The Life of Horace Liveright* (New York: Random House, 1995), 97.

it tended to echo Watson's rationale in urging Thayer to take on the poem: the argument that the *Dial* would "be doing something moderately popular in giving him the award." Liveright's stress on how much publicity the award-and-publication package received is telling. For by now it should be clear that the publication of *The Waste Land* marked the crucial moment in the transition of modernism from a minority culture to one supported by an important institutional and financial apparatus.

Eliot on *The Waste Land*

[The Disillusionment of a Generation]†

I dislike the word "generation", which has been a talisman for the last ten years; when I wrote a poem called *The Waste Land* some of the more approving critics said that I had expressed the 'disillusionment of a generation',[1] which is nonsense. I may have expressed for them their own illusion of being disillusioned, but that did not form part of my intention.

[A Piece of Rhythmical Grumbling]‡

'Various critics have done me the honour to interpret the poem in terms of criticism of the contemporary world, have considered it, indeed, as an important bit of social criticism. To me it was only the relief of a personal and wholly insignificant grouse against life; it is just a piece of rhythmical grumbling.'—*Quoted by the late Professor Theodore Spencer during a lecture at Harvard University, and recorded by the late Henry Ware Eliot, Jr., the poet's brother.*

† From *Thoughts after Lambeth* (London: Faber, 1931), p. 10. Reprinted by permission of Faber and Faber Ltd.
1. A reference to the following footnote in I. A. Richards's *Science and Poetry* (New York: Norton, 1926): "He seems to me by this poem to have performed two considerable services for this generation. He has given a perfect emotive description of a state of mind which is probably inevitable for a while to all meditative people. Secondly, by effecting a complete severance between his poetry and *all* beliefs, and this without any weakening of the poetry, he has realised what might otherwise have remained largely a speculative possibility, and has shown the way to the only solution of these difficulties" (p. 76). Richards repeats the same argument in slightly different words at the end of "The Poetry of T. S. Eliot." See p. 218.
‡ From *"The Waste Land": A Facsimile and Transcript of the Original Drafts Including the Annotations of Ezra Pound,* ed. Valerie Eliot (New York: Harcourt Brace Jovanovich, 1971), p. 1, epigraph. Reprinted by permission of Faber and Faber Ltd.

[On the *Waste Land* Notes][†]

Here I must admit that I am, on one conspicuous occasion, not guiltless of having led critics into temptation. The notes to *The Waste Land*! I had at first intended only to put down all the references for my quotations, with a view to spiking the guns of critics of my earlier poems who had accused me of plagiarism. Then, when it came to print *The Waste Land* as a little book—for the poem on its first appearance in *The Dial* and in *The Criterion* had no notes whatever—it was discovered that the poem was inconveniently short, so I set to work to expand the notes, in order to provide a few more pages of printed matter, with the result that they became the remarkable exposition of bogus scholarship that is still on view to-day. I have sometimes thought of getting rid of these notes; but now they can never be unstuck. They have had almost greater popularity than the poem itself—anyone who bought my book of poems, and found that the notes to *The Waste Land* were not in it, would demand his money back. But I don't think that these notes did any harm to other poets: certainly I cannot think of any good contemporary poet who has abused this same practice. (As for Miss Marianne Moore, *her* notes to poems are always pertinent, curious, conclusive, delightful and give no encouragement whatever to the researcher of origins.) No, it is not because of my bad example to other poets that I am penitent; it is because my notes stimulated the wrong kind of interest among the seekers of sources. It was just, no doubt, that I should pay my tribute to the work of Miss Jessie Weston; but I regret having sent so many enquirers off on a wild goose chase after Tarot cards and the Holy Grail.

[Allusions to Dante][‡]

Certainly I have borrowed lines from [Dante], in the attempt to reproduce, or rather to arouse in the reader's mind the memory, of some Dantesque scene, and thus establish a relationship between the medieval inferno and modern life. Readers of my *Waste Land* will perhaps remember that the vision of my city clerks trooping over London Bridge from the railway station to their offices

---

† From "The Frontiers of Criticism," in *On Poetry and Poets* (London: Faber, 1957), pp. 109–10. Reprinted by permission of Faber and Faber Ltd.
‡ From "What Dante Means to Me," in *To Criticize the Critic* (New York: Farrar, Straus, & Giroux, 1965), p. 128. Copyright © 1965 by T. S. Eliot. Copyright renewed 1993 by Valerie Eliot. Reprinted by permission of Farrar, Straus and Giroux. All Rights Reserved.

evoked the reflection "I had not thought death had undone so many": and that in another place I deliberately modified a line of Dante by altering it—"sighs, short and infrequent, were exhaled." And I gave the references in my notes, in order to make the reader who recognized the allusion, know that I meant him to recognize it, and know that he would have missed the point if he did not recognize it.

Reflections on *Vers Libre*†

*Ceux qui possedent leur vers libre y tiennent: on n'abandonne que
le vers libre.*—DUHAMEL ET VILDRAC.[1]

A lady, renowned in her small circle for the accuracy of her stop-
press information of literature, complains to me of a growing poco-
curantism.[2] "Since the Russians came in I can read nothing else. I
have finished Dostoevski, and I do not know what to do." I suggested
that the great Russian was an admirer of Dickens, and that she also
might find that author readable. "But Dickens is a sentimentalist;
Dostoevski is a realist." I reflected on the amours of Sonia and Rash-
kolnikov, but forbore to press the point, and I proposed *It Is Never
Too Late To Mend.*[3] "But one cannot read the Victorians at all!"
While I was extracting the virtues of the proposition that Dostoevski
is a Christian, while Charles Reade is merely pious, she added that
she could no longer read any verse but *vers libre.*

It is assumed that *vers libre* exists. It is assumed that *vers libre* is
a school; that it consists of certain theories; that its group or groups
of theorists will either revolutionise or demoralise poetry if their
attack upon the iambic pentameter meets with any success. *Vers libre*
does not exist, and it is time that this preposterous fiction followed
the *élan vital*[4] and the eighty thousand Russians into oblivion.

When a theory of art passes it is usually found that a groat's worth
of art has been bought with a million of advertisement. The theory
which sold the wares may be quite false, or it may be confused and
incapable of elucidation, or it may never have existed. A mythical
revolution will have taken place and produced a few works of art

† From *The New Statesman* (March 3, 1917): 518–19. Notes are by the editor of this
   Norton Critical Edition.
1. From *Notes on Poetic Technique* (1910) by Georges Duhamel and Charles Vildrac.
2. Indifference, nonchalance.
3. An 1856 novel by Charles Reade (1814–1884). Sonia and Raskolnikov are characters in
   Dostoevsky's novel *Crime and Punishment* (1867).
4. Life force (French). The notion, popularized by Henri Bergson (1859–1914) in *Creative
   Evolution* (1910), that some principle common to all living things accounts for their
   evolutionary development. Once quite taken with Bergson's ideas, Eliot is now
   skeptical.

which perhaps would be even better if still less of the revolutionary theories clung to them. In modern society such revolutions are almost inevitable. An artist happens upon a method, perhaps quite unreflectingly, which is new in the sense that it is essentially different from that of the second-rate people about him, and different in everything but essentials from that of any of his great predecessors. The novelty meets with neglect; neglect provokes attack; and attack demands a theory. In an ideal state of society one might imagine the good New growing naturally out of the good Old, without the need for polemic and theory; this would be a society with a living tradition. In a sluggish society, as actual societies are, tradition is ever lapsing into superstition, and the violent stimulus of novelty is required. This is bad for the artist and his school, who may become circumscribed by their theory and narrowed by their polemic; but the artist can always console himself for his errors in his old age by considering that if he had not fought nothing would have been accomplished.

Vers libre has not even the excuse of a polemic; it is a battle-cry of freedom, and there is no freedom in art. And as the so-called *vers libre* which is good is anything but "free," it can better be defended under some other label. Particular types of *vers libre* may be supported on the choice of content, or on the method of handling the content. I am aware that many writers of *vers libre* have introduced such innovations, and that the novelty of their choice and manipulation of material is confused—if not in their own minds, in the minds of many of their readers—with the novelty of the form. But I am not here concerned with imagism,[5] which is a theory about the use of material; I am only concerned with the theory of the verse-form in which imagism is cast. If *vers libre* is a genuine verse-form it will have a positive definition. And I can define it only in negatives: (1) absence of pattern, (2) absence of rhyme, (3) absence of metre.

The third of these qualities is easily disposed of. What sort of a line that would be which would not scan at all I cannot say. Even in the popular American magazines, whose verse columns are now largely given over to *vers libre*, the lines are usually explicable in terms of prosody. Any line can be divided into feet and accents. The simpler metres are a repetition of one combination, perhaps a long and a short, or a short and a long syllable, five times repeated. There is, however, no reason why, within the single line, there should be any repetition; why there should not be lines (as there are) divisible only into feet of different types. How can the grammatical exercise of scansion make a line of this sort more intelligible? Only by isolating elements which occur in other lines, and the sole purpose of

---

5. A movement in poetry publicized and to a great extent concocted by Ezra Pound, starting in 1913.

doing this is the production of a similar effect elsewhere. But repetition of effect is a question of pattern.

Scansion tells us very little. It is probable that there is not much to be gained by an elaborate system of prosody, by the erudite complexities of Swinburnian metre. With Swinburne,[6] once the trick is perceived and the scholarship appreciated, the effect is somewhat diminished. When the unexpectedness, due to the unfamiliarity of the metres to English ears, wears off and is understood, one ceases to look for what one does not find in Swinburne; the inexplicable line with the music which can never be recaptured in other words. Swinburne mastered his technique, which is a great deal, but he did not master it to the extent of being able to take liberties with it, which is everything. If anything promising for English poetry is hidden in the metres of Swinburne, it probably lies far beyond the point to which Swinburne has developed them. But the most interesting verse which has yet been written in our language has been done either by taking a very simple form, like the iambic pentameter, and constantly withdrawing from it, or taking no form at all, and constantly approximating to a very simple one. It is this contrast between fixity and flux, this unperceived evasion of monotony, which is the very life of verse.

I have in mind two passages of contemporary verse which would be called *vers libre*. Both of them I quote because of their beauty:

> Once, in finesse of fiddles found I ecstasy,
> In the flash of gold heels on the hard pavement.
> Now see I
> That warmth's the very stuff of poesy.
> Oh, God, make small
> The old star-eaten blanket of the sky,
> That I may fold it round me and in comfort lie.[7]

This is a complete poem. The other is part of a much longer poem.

> There shut up in his castle, Tairiran's,
> She who had nor ears nor tongue save in her hands,
> Gone—ah, gone—untouched, unreachable!
> She who could never live save through one person,
> She who could never speak save to one person,
> And all the rest of her a shifting change,
> A broken bundle of mirrors . . .[8]

6. Algernon Charles Swinburne (1837–1909). English poet, considered by later generations as overly devoted to purely musical effects.
7. "The Embankment," by the English poet T. E. Hulme (1883–1917); originally titled "The fantasia of a fallen gentleman on a cold, bitter night."
8. From Ezra Pound's "Near Perigord" (1915).

It is obvious that the charm of these lines could not be, without the constant suggestion and the skilful evasion of iambic pentameter.

At the beginning of the seventeenth century, and especially in the verse of John Webster,[9] who was in some ways a more cunning technician than Shakespeare, one finds the same constant evasion and recognition of regularity. Webster is much freer than Shakespeare, and that his fault is not negligence is evidenced by the fact that it is often at moments of the highest intensity that his verse acquires this freedom. That there is also carelessness I do not deny, but the irregularity of carelessness can be at once detected from the irregularity of deliberation. (In the White Devil Brachiano dying, and Cornelia mad, deliberately rupture the bonds of pentameter.)

> I recover, like a spent taper, for a flash,
> And instantly go out.

> Cover her face; mine eyes dazzle; she died young.

> You have cause to love me, I did enter you in my heart
> Before you would vouchsafe to call for the keys.

> This is a vain poetry: but I pray you tell me
> If there were proposed me, wisdom, riches, and beauty,
> In three several young men, which should I choose?

These are not lines of carelessness. The irregularity is further enhanced by the use of short lines and the breaking up of lines in dialogue, which alters the quantities. And there are many lines in the drama of this time which are spoilt by regular accentuation.

> I loved this woman in spite of my heart. (*The Changeling.*)
> I would have these herbs grow up in his grave. (*The White Devil.*)
> Whether the spirit of greatness or of woman. . . . (*The Duchess of Malfi.*)

The general charge of decadence cannot be preferred. Tourneur and Shirley, who I think will be conceded to have touched nearly the bottom of the decline of tragedy, are much more regular than Webster or Middleton.[1] Tourneur will polish off a fair line of iambics even at the cost of amputating a preposition from its substantive,

---

9. English dramatist (ca. 1580–ca. 1632), author of *The White Devil* and *The Duchess of Malfi*, the grim tragedy of which had a particular fascination for Eliot.
1. The English dramatists Cyril Tourneur (d. 1626), James Shirley (1596–1666), and Thomas Middleton (1580–1627) worked in the same tragic vein as Webster. Middleton cowrote *The Changeling.*

and in the *Atheist's Tragedy* he has a final "of" in two lines out of five together.

We may therefore formulate as follows: the ghost of some simple metre should lurk behind the arras in even the "freest" verse; to advance menacingly as we doze, and withdraw as we rouse. Or, freedom is only truly freedom when it appears against the background of an artificial limitation.

Not to have perceived the simple truth that *some* artificial limitation is necessary except in moments of the first intensity is, I believe, a capital error of even so distinguished a talent as that of Mr. E. L. Masters.[2] The *Spoon River Anthology* is not material of the first intensity; it is reflective, not immediate; its author is a moralist, rather than an observer. His material is so near to the material of Crabbe[3] that one wonders why he should have used a different form. Crabbe is, on the whole, the more intense of the two; he is keen, direct, and unsparing. His material is prosaic, not in the sense that it would have been better done in prose, but in the sense of requiring a simple and rather rigid verse-form, and this Crabbe has given it. Mr. Masters requires a more rigid verse-form than either of the two contemporary poets quoted above, and his epitaphs suffer from the lack of it.

So much for metre. There is no escape from metre; there is only mastery. But while there obviously is escape from rhyme, the *vers librists* are by no means the first out of the cave.

> The boughs of the trees
> Are twisted
> By many bafflings;
> Twisted are
> The small-leafed boughs.
> But the shadow of them
> Is not the shadow of the mast head
> Nor of the torn sails.[4]
>
> .   .   .
>
> When the white dawn first
> Through the rough fir-planks
> Of my hut, by the chestnuts,
> Up at the valley-head,
> Came breaking, Goddess,

2. American poet (1868–1950). His most famous work, *Spoon River Anthology*, a collection of short free verse poems, appeared in 1915.
3. George Crabbe (1754–1832), English poet who specialized in realistic depictions of working-class subjects.
4. From "Hermes of the Ways," by the American poet H.D. (Hilda Doolittle, 1886–1961).

> I sprang up, I threw round me
> My dappled fawn-skin. . . .[5]

Except for the more human touch in the second of these extracts a hasty observer would hardly realise that the first is by a contemporary, and the second by Matthew Arnold.

I do not minimise the services of modern poets in exploiting the possibilities of rhymeless verse. They prove the strength of a Movement, the utility of a Theory. What neither Blake nor Arnold could do alone is being done in our time. "Blank verse" is the only accepted rhymeless verse in English—the inevitable iambic pentameter. The English ear is (or was) more sensitive to the music of the verse and less dependent upon the recurrence of identical sounds in this metre than in any other. There is no campaign against rhyme. But it is possible that excessive devotion to rhyme has thickened the modern ear. The rejection of rhyme is not a leap at facility; on the contrary, it imposes a much severer strain upon the language. When the comforting echo of rhyme is removed, success or failure in the choice of words, in the sentence structure, in the order, is at once more apparent. Rhyme removed, the poet is at once held up to the standards of prose. Rhyme removed, much ethereal music leaps up from the word, music which has hitherto chirped unnoticed in the expanse of prose. And rhyme forbidden, many Shagpats were unwigged.[6]

And this liberation from rhyme might be as well a liberation *of* rhyme. Freed from its exacting task of supporting lame verse, it could be applied with greater effect where it is most needed. There are often passages in an unrhymed poem where rhyme is wanted for some special effect, for a sudden tightening-up, for a cumulative insistence, or for an abrupt change of mood. But formal rhymed verse will certainly not lose its place. We only need the coming of a Satirist—no man of genius is rarer—to prove that the heroic couplet has lost none of its edge since Dryden and Pope laid it down. As for the sonnet I am not so sure. But the decay of intricate formal patterns has nothing to do with the advent of *vers libre*. It had set in long before. Only in a closely-knit and homogeneous society, where many men are at work on the same problems, such a society as those which produced the Greek chorus, the Elizabethan lyric, and the Troubadour canzone, will the development of such forms ever be carried to perfection. And as for *vers libre*, we conclude that it is not defined by absence of pattern or absence of rhyme, for other verse is without these; that it is not defined by non-existence of metre, since even the *worst* verse can be scanned; and we conclude

---

5. From "Empedocles on Etna," by the English poet Matthew Arnold (1822–1888).
6. A reference to *The Shaving of Shagpat*, an 1856 fantasy novel by George Meredith (1828–1909). The title character is a tyrant whose power derives from his magical hair.

that the division between Conservative Verse and *Vers Libre* does not exist, for there is only good verse, bad verse, and chaos.

From Reflections on Contemporary Poetry[†]

It is not true that the development of a writer is a function of his development as a man, but it is possible to say that there is a close analogy between the sort of experience which develops a man and the sort of experience which develops a writer. Experience in living may leave the literary embryo still dormant, and the progress of literary development may to a considerable extent take place in a soul left immature in living. But similar types of experience form the nourishment of both. There is a kind of stimulus for a writer which is more important than the stimulus of admiring another writer. Admiration leads most often to imitation; we can seldom remain long unconscious of our imitating another, and the awareness of our debt naturally leads us to hatred of the object imitated. If we stand toward a writer in this other relation of which I speak we do not imitate him, and though we are quite as likely to be accused of it, we are quite unperturbed by the charge. This relation is a feeling of profound kinship, or rather of a peculiar personal intimacy, with another, probably a dead author. It may overcome us suddenly, on first or after long acquaintance; it is certainly a crisis; and when a young writer is seized with his first passion of this sort he may be changed, metamorphosed almost, within a few weeks even, from a bundle of second-hand sentiments into a person. The imperative intimacy arouses for the first time a real, an unshakeable confidence. That you possess this secret knowledge, this intimacy, with the dead man, that after few or many years or centuries you should have appeared, with this indubitable claim to distinction; who can penetrate at once the thick and dusty circumlocutions about his reputation, can call yourself alone his friend: it is something more than *encouragement* to you. It is a cause of development, like personal relations in life. Like personal intimacies in life, it may and probably will pass, but it will be ineffaceable.

The usefulness of such a passion is various. For one thing it secures us against forced admiration, from attending to writers simply because they are great. We are never at ease with people who, to us, are merely great. We are not ourselves great enough for that: probably not one man in each generation is great enough to be intimate with Shakespeare. Admiration for the great is only a sort of

† From *The Egoist* (July 1919): 39–40. Notes are by the editor of this Norton Critical Edition.

discipline to keep us in order, a necessary snobbism to make us mind our places. We may not be great lovers; but if we had a genuine affair with a real poet of any degree we have acquired a monitor to avert us when we are not in love. Indirectly, there are other acquisitions; our friendship gives us an introduction to the society in which our friend moved; we learn its origins and its endings; we are broadened. We do not imitate, we are charged; and our work is the work of the changed man; we have not borrowed, we have been quickened, and we become bearers of a tradition.

I feel that the traces of this sort of experience are conspicuously lacking from contemporary poetry, and that contemporary poetry is deficient in tradition. We can raise no objection to "experiments" if the experimenters are qualified; but we can object that almost none of the experimenters hold fast to anything permanent under the varied phenomena of experiment. Shakespeare was one of the slowest, if one of the most persistent, of experimenters; even Rimbaud[1] shows process. And one never has the tremendous satisfaction of meeting a writer who is more original, more independent, than he himself knows. No dead voices speak through the living voice; no reincarnation, no re-creation. Not even the *saturation* which sometimes combusts spontaneously into originality.

> fly where men feel
> The cunning axletree: and those that suffer
> Beneath the chariot of the snowy Bear[2]

is beautiful; and the beauty only appears more substantial if we conjecture that Chapman may have absorbed the recurring phrase of Seneca in

> signum celsi glaciale poli
> septem stellis Arcados ursae
> lucem verso termone vocat. . . . .
>   sub cardine
> glacialis ursae . . .[3]

a union, at a point at least, of the Tudor and the Greek through the Senecan phrase.

---

1. Arthur Rimbaud (1854–1891), French poet.
2. George Chapman, *Bussy D'Ambois* (1607) 5.4. Eliot alludes to the same passage in "Gerontion" (see above, p. 25).
3. "The icy constellation of the lofty pole / The bear of Arcados with seven stars / Turns on its axle and calls down the light . . . under the turning point of the icy bear" (Latin). Seneca (4 BCE–65 CE), *Hercules Furens*, lines 129–36. "Termone" should be "temone."

From Tradition and the Individual Talent[†]

I

In English writing we seldom speak of tradition, though we occasionally apply its name in deploring its absence. We cannot refer to "the tradition" or to "a tradition"; at most, we employ the adjective in saying that the poetry of So-and-so is "traditional" or even "too traditional." Seldom, perhaps, does the word appear except in a phrase of censure. If otherwise, it is vaguely approbative, with the implication, as to the work approved, of some pleasing archæological reconstruction. You can hardly make the word agreeable to English ears without this comfortable reference to the reassuring science of archæology.

Certainly the word is not likely to appear in our appreciations of living or dead writers. Every nation, every race, has not only its own creative, but its own critical turn of mind; and is even more oblivious of the shortcomings and limitations of its critical habits than of those of its creative genius. We know, or think we know, from the enormous mass of critical writing that has appeared in the French language the critical method or habit of the French; we only conclude (we are such unconscious people) that the French are "more critical" than we, and sometimes even plume ourselves a little with the fact, as if the French were less spontaneous. Perhaps they are; but we might remind ourselves that criticism is as inevitable as breathing, and that we should be none the worse for articulating what passes in our minds when we read a book and feel an emotion about it, for criticizing our own minds in their work of criticism. One of the facts that might come to light in this process is our tendency to insist, when we praise a poet, upon those aspects of his work in which he least resembles anyone else. In these aspects or parts of his work we pretend to find what is individual, what is the peculiar essence of the man. We dwell with satisfaction upon the poet's difference from his predecessors, especially his immediate predecessors; we endeavour to find something that can be isolated in order to be enjoyed. Whereas if we approach a poet without his prejudice we shall often find that not only the best, but the most individual parts of his work may be those in which the dead poets, his ancestors, assert their immortality most vigorously. And I do not mean the impressionable period of adolescence, but the period of full maturity.

[†] From *The Sacred Wood* (London: Methuen, 1920), pp. 42–53. Notes are by the editor of this Norton Critical Edition.

Yet if the only form of tradition, of handing down, consisted in following the ways of the immediate generation before us in a blind or timid adherence to its successes, "tradition" should positively be discouraged. We have seen many such simple currents soon lost in the sand; and novelty is better than repetition. Tradition is a matter of much wider significance. It cannot be inherited, and if you want it you must obtain it by great labour. It involves, in the first place, the historical sense, which we may call nearly indispensable to anyone who would continue to be a poet beyond his twenty-fifth year; and the historical sense involves a perception, not only of the pastness of the past, but of its presence; the historical sense compels a man to write not merely with his own generation in his bones, but with a feeling that the whole of the literature of Europe from Homer and within it the whole of the literature of his own country has a simultaneous existence and composes a simultaneous order. This historical sense, which is a sense of the timeless as well as of the temporal and of the timeless and of the temporal together, is what makes a writer traditional. And it is at the same time what makes a writer most acutely conscious of his place in time, of his contemporaneity.

No poet, no artist of any art, has his complete meaning alone. His significance, his appreciation is the appreciation of his relation to the dead poets and artists. You cannot value him alone; you must set him, for contrast and comparison, among the dead. I mean this as a principle of æsthetic, not merely historical, criticism. The necessity that he shall conform, that he shall cohere, is not one-sided; what happens when a new work of art is created is something that happens simultaneously to all the works of art which preceded it. The existing monuments form an ideal order among themselves, which is modified by the introduction of the new (the really new) work of art among them. The existing order is complete before the new work arrives; for order to persist after the supervention of novelty, the *whole* existing order must be, if ever so slightly, altered; and so the relations, proportions, values of each work of art toward the whole are readjusted; and this is conformity between the old and the new. Whoever has approved this idea of order, of the form of European, of English literature, will not find it preposterous that the past should be altered by the present as much as the present is directed by the past. And the poet who is aware of this will be aware of great difficulties and responsibilities.

In a peculiar sense he will be aware also that he must inevitably be judged by the standards of the past. I say judged, not amputated, by them; not judged to be as good as, or worse or better than, the dead; and certainly not judged by the canons of dead critics. It is a judgment, a comparison, in which two things are measured by each other. To conform merely would be for the new work not really to conform at all; it would not be new, and would therefore not be a work of art. And we do not quite say that the new is more valuable because it fits in; but its fitting in is a test of its value—a test, it is true, which can only be slowly and cautiously applied, for we are none of us infallible judges of conformity. We say: it appears to conform, and is perhaps individual, or it appears individual, and may conform; but we are hardly likely to find that it is one and not the other.

To proceed to a more intelligible exposition of the relation of the poet to the past: he can neither take the past as a lump, an indiscriminate bolus, nor can he form himself wholly on one or two private admirations, nor can he form himself wholly upon one preferred period. The first course is inadmissible, the second is an important experience of youth, and the third is a pleasant and highly desirable supplement. The poet must be very conscious of the main current, which does not at all flow invariably through the most distinguished reputations. He must be quite aware of the obvious fact that art never improves, but that the material of art is never quite the same. He must be aware that the mind of Europe—the mind of his own country—a mind which he learns in time to be much more important than his own private mind—is a mind which changes, and that this change is a development which abandons nothing *en route*, which does not superannuate either Shakespeare, or Homer, or the rock drawing of the Magdalenian draughtsmen.[1] That this development, refinement perhaps, complication certainly, is not, from the point of view of the artist, any improvement. Perhaps not even an improvement from the point of view of the psychologist or not to the extent which we imagine; perhaps only in the end based upon a complication in economics and machinery. But the difference between the present and the past is that the conscious present is an awareness of the past in a way and to an extent which the past's awareness of itself cannot show.

Some one said: "The dead writers are remote from us because we *know* so much more than they did." Precisely, and they are that which we know.

I am alive to a usual objection to what is clearly part of my programme for the *métier* of poetry. The objection is that the doctrine requires a ridiculous amount of erudition (pedantry), a claim which can be rejected by appeal to the lives of poets in any pantheon. It will even be affirmed that much learning deadens or perverts poetic sensibility. While, however, we persist in believing that a poet ought

---

1. Anonymous artists responsible for the cave paintings at Altamira, Spain, and La Madeleine, France.

to know as much as will not encroach upon his necessary receptivity and necessary laziness, it is not desirable to confine knowledge to whatever can be put into a useful shape for examinations, drawing-rooms, or the still more pretentious modes of publicity. Some can absorb knowledge, the more tardy must sweat for it. Shakespeare acquired more essential history from Plutarch[2] than most men could from the whole British Museum. What is to be insisted upon is that the poet must develop or procure the consciousness of the past and that he should continue to develop this consciousness throughout his career.

What happens is a continual surrender of himself as he is at the moment to something which is more valuable. The progress of an artist is a continual self-sacrifice, a continual extinction of personality.

There remains to define this process of depersonalization and its relation to the sense of tradition. It is in this depersonalization that art may be said to approach the condition of science. I shall, therefore, invite you to consider, as a suggestive analogy, the action which takes place when a bit of finely filiated platinum is introduced into a chamber containing oxygen and sulphur dioxide.

II

Honest criticism and sensitive appreciation is directed not upon the poet but upon the poetry. If we attend to the confused cries of the newspaper critics and the susurrus of popular repetition that follows, we shall hear the names of poets in great numbers; if we seek not Blue-book knowledge but the enjoyment of poetry, and ask for a poem, we shall seldom find it. In the last article I tried to point out the importance of the relation of the poem to other poems by other authors, and suggested the conception of poetry as a living whole of all the poetry that has ever been written. The other aspect of this Impersonal theory of poetry is the relation of the poem to its author. And I hinted, by an analogy, that the mind of the mature poet differs from that of the immature one not precisely in any valuation of "personality," not being necessarily more interesting, or having "more to say," but rather by being a more finely perfected medium in which special, or very varied, feelings are at liberty to enter into new combinations.

The analogy was that of the catalyst. When the two gases previously mentioned are mixed in the presence of a filament of platinum, they form sulphurous acid. This combination takes place only if the platinum is present; nevertheless the newly formed acid

2. Greek biographer and historian (1st century CE), whose most famous work, the *Lives*, provided biographical information for a number of Shakespeare's history plays.

contains no trace of platinum, and the platinum itself is apparently unaffected; has remained inert, neutral, and unchanged. The mind of the poet is the shred of platinum. It may partly or exclusively operate upon the experience of the man himself; but, the more perfect the artist, the more completely separate in him will be the man who suffers and the mind which creates; the more perfectly will the mind digest and transmute the passions which are its material.

The experience, you will notice, the elements which enter the presence of the transforming catalyst, are of two kinds: emotions and feelings. The effect of a work of art upon the person who enjoys it is an experience different in kind from any experience not of art. It may be formed out of one emotion, or may be a combination of several; and various feelings, inhering for the writer in particular words or phrases or images, may be added to compose the final result. Or great poetry may be made without the direct use of any emotion whatever: composed out of feelings solely. * * * The poet's mind is in fact a receptacle for seizing and storing up numberless feelings, phrases, images, which remain there until all the particles which can unite to form a new compound are present together.

If you compare several representative passages of the greatest poetry you see how great is the variety of types of combination, and also how completely any semi-ethical criterion of "sublimity" misses the mark. For it is not the "greatness," the intensity, of the emotions, the components, but the intensity of the artistic process, the pressure, so to speak, under which the fusion takes place, that counts. The episode of Paolo and Francesca[3] employs a definite emotion, but the intensity of the poetry is something quite different from whatever intensity in the supposed experience it may give the impression of. It is no more intense, furthermore, than Canto XXVI, the voyage of Ulysses, which has not the direct dependence upon an emotion. Great variety is possible in the process of transmution of emotion: the murder of Agamemnon,[4] or the agony of Othello, gives an artistic effect apparently closer to a possible original than the scenes from Dante. In the *Agamemnon*, the artistic emotion approximates to the emotion of an actual spectator; in *Othello* to the emotion of the protagonist himself. But the difference between art and the event is always absolute; the combination which is the murder of Agamemnon is probably as complex as that which is the voyage of Ulysses. In either case there has been a fusion of elements. The ode of Keats contains a number of feelings

3. Paolo Malaesta and his sister-in-law Francesca da Rimini, illicit lovers whom Dante meets in Canto 5 of the *Inferno*. Line 404 of *The Waste Land* bears a trace of their story. In Canto 26, Dante meets Ulysses (mentioned in the next sentence).
4. By his wife, Clytemnestra, on his return from the Trojan War. Eliot loaned his copy of Aeschylus's *Agamemnon* to Ezra Pound while they were editing *The Waste Land*.

which have nothing particular to do with the nightingale, but which the nightingale, partly, perhaps, because of its attractive name, and partly because of its reputation, served to bring together.

The point of view which I am struggling to attack is perhaps related to the metaphysical theory of the substantial unity of the soul: for my meaning is, that the poet has, not a "personality" to express, but a particular medium, which is only a medium and not a personality, in which impressions and experiences combine in peculiar and unexpected ways. Impressions and experiences which are important for the man may take no place in the poetry, and those which become important in the poetry may play quite a negligible part in the man, the personality.

I will quote a passage which is unfamiliar enough to be regarded with fresh attention in the light—or darkness—of these observations:

> And now methinks I could e'en chide myself
> For doating on her beauty, though her death
> Shall be revenged after no common action.
> Does the silkworm expend her yellow labours
> For thee? For thee does she undo herself?
> Are lordships sold to maintain ladyships
> For the poor benefit of a bewildering minute?
> Why does yon fellow falsify highways,
> And put his life between the judge's lips,
> To refine such a thing—keeps horse and men
> To beat their valours for her? . . .[5]

In this passage (as is evident if it is taken in its context) there is a combination of positive and negative emotions: an intensely strong attraction toward beauty and an equally intense fascination by the ugliness which is contrasted with it and which destroys it. This balance of contrasted emotion is in the dramatic situation to which the speech is pertinent, but that situation alone is inadequate to it. This is, so to speak, the structural emotion, provided by the drama. But the whole effect, the dominant tone, is due to the fact that a number of floating feelings, having an affinity to this emotion by no means superficially evident, have combined with it to give us a new art emotion.

It is not in his personal emotions, the emotions provoked by particular events in his life, that the poet is in any way remarkable or interesting. His particular emotions may be simple, or crude, or flat. The emotion in his poetry will be a very complex thing, but not with the complexity of the emotions of people who have very complex or unusual emotions in life. One error, in fact, of eccentricity in poetry

5. From *The Revenger's Tragedy* (1607), by Thomas Middleton (1580–1627).

is to seek for new human emotions to express: and in this search for novelty in the wrong place it discovers the perverse. The business of the poet is not to find new emotions, but to use the ordinary ones and, in working them up into poetry, to express feelings which are not in actual emotions at all. And emotions which he has never experienced will serve his turn as well as those familiar to him. Consequently, we must believe that "emotion recollected in tranquillity"[6] is an inexact formula. For it is neither emotion, nor recollection, nor, without distortion of meaning, tranquillity. It is a concentration, and a new thing resulting from the concentration, of a very great number of experiences which to the practical and active person would not seem to be experiences at all; it is a concentration which does not happen consciously or of deliberation. These experiences are not "recollected," and they finally unite in an atmosphere which is "tranquil" only in that it is a passive attending upon the event. Of course this is not quite the whole story. There is a great deal, in the writing of poetry, which must be conscious and deliberate. In fact, the bad poet is usually unconscious where he ought to be conscious, and conscious where he ought to be unconscious. Both errors tend to make him "personal." Poetry is not a turning loose of emotion, but an escape from emotion; it is not the expression of personality, but an escape from personality. But, of course, only those who have personality and emotions know what it means to want to escape from these things.

III

ὁ δὲ νοῦς ἴσως θειότερόν τι καὶ ἀπαθές ἐστιῦ[7]

This essay proposes to halt at the frontier of metaphysics or mysticism, and confine itself to such practical conclusions as can be applied by the responsible person interested in poetry. To divert interest from the poet to the poetry is a laudable aim: for it would conduce to a juster estimation of actual poetry, good and bad. There are many people who appreciate the expression of sincere emotion in verse, and there is a smaller number of people who can appreciate technical excellence. But very few know when there is expression of *significant* emotion, emotion which has its life in the poem and not in the history of the poet. The emotion of art is impersonal. And the poet cannot reach this impersonality without surrendering himself wholly to the work to be done. And he is not likely to know what is to be done unless he lives in what is not merely the present,

---

6. From the preface to *Lyrical Ballads* (1800), by William Wordsworth (1770–1850).
7. The mind is doubtless more divine and less subject to passion (Greek). From Aristotle's *De Anima* ("On the Soul") 1.4.

but the present moment of the past, unless he is conscious, not of
what is dead, but of what is already living.

Hamlet and His Problems[†]

Few critics have even admitted that *Hamlet* the play is the primary
problem, and Hamlet the character only secondary. And Hamlet the
character has had an especial temptation for that most dangerous
type of critic: the critic with a mind which is naturally of the cre-
ative order, but which through some weakness in creative power
exercises itself in criticism instead. These minds often find in
Hamlet a vicarious existence for their own artistic realization.
Such a mind had Goethe, who made of Hamlet a Werther; and such
had Coleridge, who made of Hamlet a Coleridge; and probably nei-
ther of these men in writing about Hamlet remembered that his first
business was to study a work of art.[1] The kind of criticism that
Goethe and Coleridge produced, in writing of Hamlet, is the
most misleading kind possible. For they both possessed unques-
tionable critical insight, and both make their critical aberrations
the more plausible by the substitution—of their own Hamlet
for Shakespeare's—which their creative gift effects. We should
be thankful that Walter Pater did not fix his attention on this
play.

Two recent writers, Mr. J. M. Robertson and Professor Stoll of the
University of Minnesota, have issued small books which can be
praised for moving in the other direction. Mr. Stoll performs a ser-
vice in recalling to our attention the labours of the critics of the sev-
enteenth and eighteenth centuries,[2] observing that

> they knew less about psychology than more recent Hamlet crit-
> ics, but they were nearer in spirit to Shakespeare's art; and as
> they insisted on the importance of the effect of the whole rather
> than on the importance of the leading character, they were
> nearer, in their old-fashioned way, to the secret of dramatic art
> in general.

Qua work of art, the work of art cannot be interpreted; there is
nothing to interpret; we can only criticize it according to standards,
in comparison to other works of art; and for "interpretation" the

---

[†] From *The Sacred Wood* (London: Methuen, 1920), pp. 87–94. Unless otherwise indi-
cated, notes are by the editor of this Norton Critical Edition.
1. These interpretations of *Hamlet* are to be found in *Wilhelm Meister's Apprenticeship*
(1795), by Johann Wolfgang von Goethe (1799–1832), and "Lecture on Hamlet" (1811),
by Samuel Taylor Coleridge (1772–1834).
2. I have never, by the way, seen a cogent refutation of Thomas Rymer's objections to
Othello [*Author*].

chief task is the presentation of relevant historical facts which the reader is not assumed to know. Mr. Robertson points out, very pertinently, how critics have failed in their "interpretation" of *Hamlet* by ignoring what ought to be very obvious: that *Hamlet* is a stratification, that it represents the efforts of a series of men, each making what he could out of the work of his predecessors. The *Hamlet* of Shakespeare will appear to us very differently if, instead of treating the whole action of the play as due to Shakespeare's design, we perceive his *Hamlet* to be superposed upon much cruder material which persists even in the final form.

We know that there was an older play by Thomas Kyd, that extraordinary dramatic (if not poetic) genius who was in all probability the author of two plays so dissimilar as the *Spanish Tragedy*[3] and *Arden of Feversham*; and what this play was like we can guess from three clues: from the *Spanish Tragedy* itself, from the tale of Belleforest upon which Kyd's *Hamlet* must have been based, and from a version acted in Germany in Shakespeare's lifetime which bears strong evidence of having been adapted from the earlier, not from the later, play. From these three sources it is clear that in the earlier play the motive was a revenge-motive simply; that the action or delay is caused, as in the *Spanish Tragedy*, solely by the difficulty of assassinating a monarch surrounded by guards; and that the "madness" of Hamlet was feigned in order to escape suspicion, and successfully. In the final play of Shakespeare, on the other hand, there is a motive which is more important than that of revenge, and which explicitly "blunts" the latter; the delay in revenge is unexplained on grounds of necessity or expediency; and the effect of the "madness" is not to lull but to arouse the king's suspicion. The alteration is not complete enough, however, to be convincing. Furthermore, there are verbal parallels so close to the *Spanish Tragedy* as to leave no doubt that in places Shakespeare was merely *revising* the text of Kyd. And finally there are unexplained scenes—the Polonius-Laertes and the Polonius-Reynaldo scenes—for which there is little excuse; these scenes are not in the verse style of Kyd, and not beyond doubt in the style of Shakespeare. These Mr. Robertson believes to be scenes in the original play of Kyd reworked by a third hand, perhaps Chapman,[4] before Shakespeare touched the play. And he concludes, with very strong show of reason, that the original play of Kyd was, like certain other revenge plays, in two parts of five acts each. The upshot of Mr. Robertson's examination is, we believe, irrefragable: that Shakespeare's *Hamlet*, so far as it is Shakespeare's, is a play dealing with the effect of a mother's guilt upon her son, and

3. See above, p. 106.
4. George Chapman (1559?–1634).

that Shakespeare was unable to impose this motive successfully upon the "intractable" material of the old play.

Of the intractability there can be no doubt. So far from being Shakespeare's masterpiece, the play is most certainly an artistic failure. In several ways the play is puzzling, and disquieting as is none of the others. Of all the plays it is the longest and is possibly the one on which Shakespeare spent most pains; and yet he has left in it superfluous and inconsistent scenes which even hasty revision should have noticed. The versification is variable. Lines like

> Look, the morn, in russet mantle clad,
> Walks o'er the dew of yon high eastern hill,

are of the Shakespeare of *Romeo and Juliet*. The lines in Act v. sc. ii.,

> Sir, in my heart there was a kind of fighting
> That would not let me sleep . . .
> Up from my cabin,
> My sea-gown scarf'd about me, in the dark
> Grop'd I to find out them: had my desire;
> Finger'd their packet;

are of his quite mature. Both workmanship and thought are in an unstable condition. We are surely justified in attributing the play, with that other profoundly interesting play of "intractable" material and astonishing versification, *Measure for Measure*, to a period of crisis, after which follow the tragic successes which culminate in *Coriolanus*. *Coriolanus* may be not as "interesting" as *Hamlet*, but it is, with *Antony and Cleopatra*, Shakespeare's most assured artistic success. And probably more people have thought *Hamlet* a work of art because they found it interesting, than have found it interesting because it is a work of art. It is the "Mona Lisa" of literature.

The grounds of *Hamlet's* failure are not immediately obvious. Mr. Robertson is undoubtedly correct in concluding that the essential emotion of the play is the feeling of a son towards a guilty mother:

> [Hamlet's] tone is that of one who has suffered tortures on the score of his mother's degradation. . . . The guilt of a mother is an almost intolerable motive for drama, but it had to be maintained and emphasized to supply a psychological solution, or rather a hint of one.

This, however, is by no means the whole story. It is not merely the "guilt of a mother" that cannot be handled as Shakespeare handled the suspicion of Othello, the infatuation of Antony, or the pride of Coriolanus. The subject might conceivably have expanded into a tragedy like these, intelligible, self-complete, in the sunlight. *Hamlet*, like the sonnets, is full of some stuff that the writer could not drag to light, contemplate, or manipulate into art. And when we search for this feeling, we find it, as in the sonnets, very difficult to localize. You cannot point to it in the speeches; indeed, if you examine the two famous soliloquies you see the versification of Shakespeare, but a content which might be claimed by another, perhaps by the author[5] of the *Revenge of Bussy d'Ambois*, Act v. sc. i. We find Shakespeare's *Hamlet* not in the action, not in any quotations that we might select, so much as in an unmistakable tone which is unmistakably not in the earlier play.

The only way of expressing emotion in the form of art is by finding an "objective correlative"; in other words, a set of objects, a situation, a chain of events which shall be the formula of that *particular* emotion; such that when the external facts, which must terminate in sensory experience, are given, the emotion is immediately evoked. If you examine any of Shakespeare's more successful tragedies, you will find this exact equivalence; you will find that the state of mind of Lady Macbeth walking in her sleep has been communicated to you by a skilful accumulation of imagined sensory impressions; the words of Macbeth on hearing of his wife's death strike us as if, given the sequence of events, these words were automatically released by the last event in the series. The artistic "inevitability" lies in this complete adequacy of the external to the emotion; and this is precisely what is deficient in *Hamlet*. Hamlet (the man) is dominated by an emotion which is inexpressible, because it is in *excess* of the facts as they appear. And the supposed identity of Hamlet with his author is genuine to this point: that Hamlet's bafflement at the absence of objective equivalent to his feelings is a prolongation of the bafflement of his creator in the face of his artistic problem. Hamlet is up against the difficulty that his disgust is occasioned by his mother, but that his mother is not an adequate equivalent for it; his disgust envelops and exceeds her. It is thus a feeling which he cannot understand; he cannot objectify it, and it therefore remains to poison life and obstruct action. None of the possible actions can satisfy it; and nothing that Shakespeare can do with the plot can express Hamlet for him. And it must be noticed that the very nature of the *données* of the problem precludes objective equivalence. To have heightened the criminality of Gertrude would have been to provide the formula for a totally different emotion in Hamlet; it is just *because* her character is so negative and insignificant that she arouses in Hamlet the feeling which she is incapable of representing.

The "madness" of Hamlet lay to Shakespeare's hand; in the earlier play a simple ruse, and to the end, we may presume, understood as

---

5. I.e., Chapman.

a ruse by the audience. For Shakespeare it is less than madness and more than feigned. The levity of Hamlet, his repetition of phrase, his puns, are not part of a deliberate plan of dissimulation, but a form of emotional relief. In the character Hamlet it is the buffoonery of an emotion which can find no outlet in action; in the dramatist it is the buffoonery of an emotion which he cannot express in art. The intense feeling, ecstatic or terrible, without an object or exceeding its object, is something which every person of sensibility has known; it is doubtless a study to pathologists. It often occurs in adolescence: the ordinary person puts these feelings to sleep, or trims down his feeling to fit the business world; the artist keeps it alive by his ability to intensify the world to his emotions. The Hamlet of Laforgue[6] is an adolescent; the Hamlet of Shakespeare is not, he has not that explanation and excuse. We must simply admit that here Shakespeare tackled a problem which proved too much for him. Why he attempted it at all is an insoluble puzzle; under compulsion of what experience he attempted to express the inexpressibly horrible, we cannot ever know. We need a great many facts in his biography; and we should like to know whether, and when, and after or at the same time as what personal experience, he read Montaigne, II. xii., *Apologie de Raimond Sebond*.[7] We should have, finally, to know something which is by hypothesis unknowable, for we assume it to be an experience which, in the manner indicated, exceeded the facts. We should have to understand things which Shakespeare did not understand himself.

From The Metaphysical Poets[†]

Not only is it extremely difficult to define metaphysical poetry, but difficult to decide what poets practise it and in which of their verses. * * * It is difficult to find any precise use of metaphor, simile, or other conceit, which is common to all the poets and at the same time important enough as an element of style to isolate these poets as a group. Donne, and often Cowley,[1] employ a device which is sometimes considered characteristically "metaphysical"; the elaboration (contrasted with the condensation) of a figure of

---

6. Jules Laforgue (1860–1887), French symbolist poet, "to whom," Eliot says in "To Criticize the Critics" (1965), "I owe more than to any one poet in any language." One of Laforgue's *Moral Tales*, a set of experimental prose works, is entitled "Hamlet, or the Consequences of Filial Piety."

7. Michel de Montaigne (1533–1592), a Frenchman whose *Essais* established the essay as a literary form, wrote the *Apology for Raymond Sebond* (1580) as an oblique defense of his own skepticism.

† From *Times Literary Supplement* (October 20, 1921): 699–70. Notes are by the editor of this Norton Critical Edition.

1. John Donne (1572–1631) and Abraham Cowley (1618–1667), English poets.

speech to the furthest stage to which ingenuity can carry it. Thus Cowley develops the commonplace comparison of the world to a chess-board through long stanzas ("To Destiny"), and Donne, with more grace, in "A Valediction,"[2] the comparison of two lovers to a pair of compasses. But elsewhere we find, instead of the mere explication of the content of a comparison, a development by rapid association of thought which requires considerable agility on the part of the reader.

> On a round ball
> A workeman that hath copies by, can lay
> An Europe, Afrique, and an Asia,
> And quickly make that, which was nothing, *All*,
>> So doth each teare,
>> Which thee doth weare,
> A globe, yea world by that impression grow,
> Till thy tears mixt with mine doe overflow
> This world, by waters sent from thee, my heaven dissolved so.

Here we find at least two connexions which are not implicit in the first figure, but are forced upon it by the poet: from the geographer's globe to the tear, and the tear to the deluge. On the other hand, some of Donne's most successful and characteristic effects are secured by brief words and sudden contrasts—

> A bracelet of bright hair about the bone,[3]

where the most powerful effect is produced by the sudden contrast of associations of "bright hair" and of "bone". This telescoping of images and multiplied associations is characteristic of the phrase of some of the dramatists of the period which Donne knew: not to mention Shakespeare, it is frequent in Middleton, Webster, and Tourneur,[4] and is one of the sources of the vitality of their language.

Johnson, who employed the term "metaphysical poets," apparently having Donne, Cleveland, and Cowley chiefly in mind, remarks of them that "the most heterogeneous ideas are yoked by violence together."[5] The force of this impeachment lies in the failure of the conjunction, the fact that often the ideas are yoked but not united;

2. "A Valediction: Forbidding Mourning." The lines quoted below are from Donne's "A Valediction: Of Weeping."
3. From "The Relic."
4. Middleton and Webster are alluded to in *The Waste Land* and are identified in the notes to the poem. Cyril Tourneur (1575–1626) was an Irish dramatist known as a practitioner of revenge tragedy.
5. From Samuel Johnson's life of Cowley (one of his famous *Lives of the English Poets* [1779–81]), which influentially voices the neoclassical disapproval of the wit of the metaphysicals. John Cleveland (1613–1658) has always been considered the most extreme of the metaphysical poets.

and if we are to judge of styles of poetry by their abuse, enough examples may be found in Cleveland to justify Johnson's condemnation. But a degree of heterogeneity of material compelled into unity by the operation of the poet's mind is omnipresent in poetry. We need not select for illustration such a line as—

> Notre ame est un trois-mats cherchant son Icarie;[6]

we may find it in some of the best lines of Johnson himself ("The Vanity of Human Wishes"):—

> His fate was destined to a barren strand,
> A petty fortress, and a dubious hand;
> He left a name at which the world grew pale,
> To point a moral, or adorn a tale.

where the effect is due to a contrast of ideas, different in degree but the same in principle, as that which Johnson mildly reprehended.

Again, we may justly take these quatrains from Lord Herbert's Ode,[7] stanzas which would, we think, be immediately pronounced to be of the metaphysical school:—

> So when from hence we shall be gone,
> And be no more, nor you, nor I,
> As one another's mystery,
> Each shall be both, yet both but one.
>
> This said, in her up-lifted face,
> Her eyes, which did that beauty crown,
> Were like two starrs, that having faln down,
> Look up again to find their place:
>
> While such a moveless silent peace
> Did seize on their becalmed sense,
> One would have thought some influence
> Their ravished spirits did possess.

There is nothing in these lines (with the possible exception of the stars, a simile not at once grasped, but lovely and justified) which fits Johnson's general observations on the metaphysical poets in his essay on Cowley. A good deal resides in the richness of association which is at the same time borrowed from and given to the word "becalmed";

---

6. Our soul is a three-master seeking her Icarie (French); from the French poet Charles Baudelaire's "Le Voyage," the final poem in *Les Fleurs du Mal* (2nd ed., 1861). Icarie is an imaginary utopia, the subject of Étienne Cabet's *Voyage en Icarie* (1840) and inspiration for an experimental community established by Cabet in Illinois in 1849.
7. "Ode upon a Question Moved, Whether Love Should Continue Forever?" by Lord Herbert of Cherbury (1583–1648).

but the meaning is clear, the language simple and elegant. It is to be observed that the language of these poets is as a rule simple and pure; in the verse of George Herbert this simplicity is carried as far as it can go—a simplicity emulated without success by numerous modern poets. The *structure* of the sentences, on the other hand, is sometimes far from simple, but this is not a vice; it is a fidelity to thought and feeling. The effect, at its best, is far less artificial than that of an ode by Gray. And as this fidelity induces variety of thought and feeling, so it induces variety of music. We doubt whether, in the eighteenth century, could be found two poems in nominally the same metre, so dissimilar as Marvell's "Coy Mistress" and Crashaw's "Saint Teresa";[8] the one producing an effect of great speed by the use of short syllables, and the other an ecclesiastical solemnity by the use of long ones:—

> Love thou art absolute sole lord
> Of life and death.

If so shrewd and sensitive (though so limited) a critic as Johnson failed to define metaphysical poetry by its faults, it is worth while to inquire whether we may not have more success by adopting the opposite method: by assuming that the poets of the seventeenth century (up to the Revolution)[9] were the direct and normal development of the precedent age; and, without prejudicing their case by the adjective "metaphysical", consider whether their virtue was not something permanently valuable, which subsequently disappeared, but ought not to have disappeared. Johnson has hit, perhaps by accident, on one of their peculiarities, when he observed that "their attempts were always analytic"; he would not agree that, after the dissociation, they put the material together again in a new unity.

It is certain that the dramatic verse of the later Elizabethan and early Jacobean poets expresses a degree of development of sensibility which is not found in any of the prose, good as it often is. If we except Marlowe, a man of prodigious intelligence, these dramatists were directly or indirectly (it is at least a tenable theory) affected by Montaigne.[1] Even if we except also Jonson and Chapman, these two were notably erudite, and were notably men who incorporated their erudition into their sensibility: their mode of feeling was directly and freshly altered by their reading and thought. In Chapman especially there is a direct sensuous apprehension of thought,

---

8. Richard Crashaw (1613–1649), poet and convert to Catholicism, modeled his work on the devotional writings of St. Teresa of Avila.
9. England's Glorious Revolution of 1688, in which William of Orange was invited by Protestant forces to invade England and replace James II.
1. See above, p. 158, note 7.

or a re-creation of thought into feeling, which is exactly what we find in Donne:—

> in this one thing, all the discipline
> Of manners and of manhood is contained;
> A man to join himself with th' Universe
> In his main sway, and make in all things fit
> One with that All, and go on, round as it;
> Not plucking from the whole his wretched part,
> And into straits, or into nought revert,
> Wishing the complete Universe might be
> Subject to such a rag of it as he;
> But to consider great Necessity.[2]

We compare this with some modern passage:—

> No, when the fight begins within himself,
> A man's worth something. God stoops o'er his head,
> Satan looks up between his feet—both tug—
> He's left, himself, i' the middle; the soul wakes
> And grows. Prolong that battle through his life![3]

It is perhaps somewhat less fair, though very tempting (as both poets are concerned with the perpetuation of love by offspring), to compare with the stanzas already quoted from Lord Herbert's Ode the following from Tennyson:—

> One walked between his wife and child,
> With measured footfall firm and mild,
> And now and then he gravely smiled.
>   The prudent partner of his blood
>   Leaned on him, faithful, gentle, good,
>   Wearing the rose of womanhood.
> And in their double love secure,
> The little maiden walked demure,
> Pacing with downward eyelids pure.
>   These three made unity so sweet,
>   My frozen heart began to beat,
>   Remembering its ancient heat.[4]

The difference is not a simple difference of degree between poets. It is something which had happened to the mind of England between

2. From *The Revenge of Bussy d'Ambois* (1610–11), by the English dramatist and poet George Chapman (1559?–1634).
3. From "Bishop Blougram's Apology" (1855), by the English poet Robert Browning (1812–1889).
4. From "The Two Voices," begun by Alfred, Lord Tennyson (1809–1892) in 1833 somewhat in anticipation of *In Memoriam*.

the time of Donne or Lord Herbert of Cherbury and the time of Tennyson and Browning; it is the difference between the intellectual poet and the reflective poet. Tennyson and Browning are poets, and they think; but they do not feel their thought as immediately as the odour of a rose. A thought to Donne was an experience; it modified his sensibility. When a poet's mind is perfectly equipped for its work, it is constantly amalgamating disparate experience; the ordinary man's experience is chaotic, irregular, fragmentary. The latter falls in love, or reads Spinoza, and these two experiences have nothing to do with each other, or with the noise of the typewriter or the smell of cooking; in the mind of the poet these experiences are always forming new wholes.

We may express the difference by the following theory:—The poets of the seventeenth century, the successors of the dramatists of the sixteenth, possessed a mechanism of sensibility which could devour any kind of experience. They are simple, artificial, difficult, or fantastic, as their predecessors were; no less or more than Dante, Guido Cavalcanti, Guinicelli, or Cino.[5] In the seventeenth century a dissociation of sensibility set in, from which we have never recovered; and this dissociation, as is natural, was due to the influence of the two most powerful poets of the century, Milton and Dryden. Each of these men performed certain poetic functions so magnificently well that the magnitude of the effect concealed the absence of others. The language went on and in some respects improved; the best verse of Collins, Gray, Johnson, and even Goldsmith[6] satisfies some of our fastidious demands better than that of Donne or Marvell or King. But while the language became more refined, the feeling became more crude. The feeling, the sensibility, expressed in the "Country Churchyard" (to say nothing of Tennyson and Browning) is cruder than that in the "Coy Mistress."

The second effect of the influence of Milton and Dryden followed from the first, and was therefore slow in manifestation. The sentimental age began early in the eighteenth century, and continued. The poets revolted against the ratiocinative, the descriptive; they thought and felt by fits, unbalanced; they reflected. In one or two passages of Shelley's "Triumph of Life," in the second "Hyperion,"[7]

---

5. Italian poets of the 13th century. The four had been credited by Ezra Pound (in *The Spirit of Romance* [1910]) with reviving in their *canzoni*, or love songs, the pure poetic beauty of the medieval troubadours.
6. Poets associated with the neoclassical reaction against the excesses of metaphysical poetry. Thomas Gray is best known for his "Elegy Written in a Country Churchyard" (1750), disparaged by Eliot below. Oliver Goldsmith, interestingly, provides as many lines for *The Waste Land* as Marvell.
7. English poet Percy Shelley (1792–1822) left *The Triumph of Life* unfinished at his death. Keats (1795–1821) abandoned *Hyperion* in 1819.

there are traces of a struggle toward unification of sensibility. But Keats and Shelley died, and Tennyson and Browning ruminated.

After this brief exposition of a theory—too brief, perhaps, to carry conviction—we may ask, what would have been the fate of the "metaphysical" had the current of poetry descended in a direct line from them, as it descended in a direct line to them? They would not, certainly, be classified as metaphysical. The possible interests of a poet are unlimited; the more intelligent he is the better; the more intelligent he is the more likely that he will have interests: our only condition is that he turn them into poetry, and not merely meditate on them poetically. A philosophical theory which has entered into poetry is established, for its truth or falsity in one sense ceases to matter, and its truth in another sense is proved. The poets in question have, like other poets, various faults. But they were, at best, engaged in the task of trying to find the verbal equivalent for states of mind and feeling. And this means both that they are more mature, and that they wear better, than later poets of certainly not less literary ability.

It is not a permanent necessity that poets should be interested in philosophy, or in any other subject. We can only say that it appears likely that poets in our civilization, as it exists at present, must be *difficult*. Our civilization comprehends great variety and complexity, and this variety and complexity, playing upon a refined sensibility, must produce various and complex results. The poet must become more and more comprehensive, more allusive, more indirect, in order to force, to dislocate if necessary, language into his meaning. (A brilliant and extreme statement of this view, with which it is not requisite to associate oneself, is that of M. Jean Epstein, "La Poesie d'aujourd'hui.")[8] Hence we get something which looks very much like the conceit—we get, in fact, a method curiously similar to that of the "metaphysical poets," similar also in its use of obscure words and of simple phrasing.

*   *   *

It is interesting to speculate whether it is not a misfortune that two of the greatest masters of diction in our language, Milton and Dryden, triumph with a dazzling disregard of the soul. If we continued to produce Miltons and Drydens it might not so much matter, but as things are it is a pity that English poetry has remained so incomplete. Those who object to the "artificiality" of Milton or Dryden sometimes tell us to "look into our hearts and write." But that is not looking deep enough; Racine or Donne looked into a good

---

8. "Poetry of Today" (French), published by filmmaker and critic Jean Epstein (1899–1953) as a letter to Blaise Cendrars (1887–1961) in Paris in 1921.

deal more than the heart. One must look into the cerebral cortex, the nervous system, and the digestive tracts.

May we not conclude, then, that Donne, Crashaw, Vaughan, Herbert and Lord Herbert, Marvell, King, Cowley at his best, are in the direct current of English poetry, and that their faults should be reprimanded by this standard rather than coddled by antiquarian affection? They have been enough praised in terms which are implicit limitations because they are "metaphysical" or "witty," "quaint" or "obscure," though at their best they have not these attributes more than other serious poets. On the other hand we must not reject the criticism of Johnson (a dangerous person to disagree with) without having mastered it, without having assimilated the Johnsonian canons of taste. In reading the celebrated passage in his essay on Cowley we must remember that by wit he clearly means something more serious than we usually mean to-day; in his criticism of their versification we must remember in what a narrow discipline he was trained, but also how well trained; we must remember that Johnson tortures chiefly the chief offenders, Cowley and Cleveland. It would be a fruitful work, and one requiring a substantial book, to break up the classification of Johnson (for there has been none since) and exhibit these poets in all their difference of kind and of degree, from the massive music of Donne to the faint, pleasing tinkle of Aurelian Townshend—whose "Dialogue between a Pilgrim and Time" is one of the few regrettable omissions from this excellent anthology.[9]

Ulysses, Order, and Myth[†]

Ulysses. By James Joyce. 8vo. 752 pages. Shakespeare and Company, Paris. Limited edition.

Mr Joyce's book has been out long enough for no more general expression of praise, or expostulation with its detractors, to be necessary; and it has not been out long enough for any attempt at a complete measurement of its place and significance to be possible. All that one can usefully do at this time, and it is a great deal to do, for such a book, is to elucidate any aspect of the book—and the number of aspects is indefinite—which has not yet been fixed. I hold this book to be the most important expression which the present age has

9. This essay was originally a review of *Metaphysical Lyrics and Poems of the Seventeenth Century: Donne to Butler,* an anthology edited by Herbert J. C. Grierson, which included two other poems by Aurelian Townshend (ca. 1583–ca. 1649), a little-known follower of Donne whose few works survived only in manuscript collections.

† From *The Dial* (November 1923): 480–83. Unless otherwise indicated, notes are by the editor of this Norton Critical Edition.

found; it is a book to which we are all indebted, and from which none of us can escape. These are postulates for anything that I have to say about it, and I have no wish to waste the reader's time by elaborating my eulogies; it has given me all the surprise, delight, and terror that I can require, and I will leave it at that.

Amongst all the criticisms I have seen of the book, I have seen nothing—unless we except, in its way, M Valery Larbaud's[1] valuable paper which is rather an Introduction than a criticism—which seemed to me to appreciate the significance of the method employed—the parallel to the Odyssey, and the use of appropriate styles and symbols to each division. Yet one might expect this to be the first peculiarity to attract attention; but it has been treated as an amusing dodge, or scaffolding erected by the author for the purpose of disposing his realistic tale, of no interest in the completed structure. The criticism which Mr Aldington directed upon Ulysses several years ago seems to me to fail by this oversight—but, as Mr Aldington wrote before the complete work had appeared, fails more honourably than the attempts of those who had the whole book before them. Mr Aldington treated Mr Joyce as a prophet of chaos; and wailed at the flood of Dadaism which his prescient eye saw bursting forth at the tap of the magician's rod. Of course, the influence which Mr Joyce's book may have is from my point of view an irrelevance. A very great book may have a very bad influence indeed; and a mediocre book may be in the event most salutary. The next generation is responsible for its own soul; a man of genius is responsible to his peers, not to a studio-full of uneducated and undisciplined coxcombs. Still, Mr Aldington's pathetic solicitude for the half-witted seems to me to carry certain implications about the nature of the book itself to which I cannot assent; and this is the important issue. He finds the book, if I understand him, to be an invitation to chaos, and an expression of feelings which are perverse, partial, and a distortion of reality. But unless I quote Mr Aldington's words I am likely to falsify. "I say, moreover," he says,[2] "that when Mr Joyce, with his marvellous gifts, uses them to disgust us with mankind, he is doing something which is false and a libel on humanity." It is somewhat similar to the opinion of the urbane Thackeray upon Swift. "As for the moral, I think it horrible, shameful, unmanly, blasphemous: and giant and great as this Dean is, I say we should hoot him."[3] (This, of the conclusion of the Voyage to the Houyhnhnms—which

---

1. French novelist (1881–1957), whose early lecture on *Ulysses* helped build an audience for the book. It was published in *Nouvelle Revue Française* in 1921 and then in Eliot's journal, *The Criterion*.
2. English Review, April 1921 [*Author*].
3. William Makepeace Thackeray (1811–1863), "The English Humorists of the Eighteenth Century," originally delivered as a lecture in 1851.

seems to me one of the greatest triumphs that the human soul has ever achieved.—It is true that Thackeray later pays Swift one of the finest tributes that a man has ever given or received: "So great a man he seems to me that thinking of him is like thinking of an empire falling." And Mr Aldington, in his time, is almost equally generous.)

Whether it is possible to libel humanity (in distinction to libel in the usual sense, which is libelling an individual or a group in contrast with the rest of humanity) is a question for philosophical societies to discuss; but of course if Ulysses were a "libel" it would simply be a forged document, a powerless fraud, which would never have extracted from Mr Aldington a moment's attention. I do not wish to linger over this point: the interesting question is that begged by Mr Aldington when he refers to Mr Joyce's "great *undisciplined* talent."

I think that Mr Aldington and I are more or less agreed as to what we want in principle, and agreed to call it classicism. It is because of this agreement that I have chosen Mr Aldington to attack on the present issue. We are agreed as to what we want, but not as to how to get it, or as to what contemporary writing exhibits a tendency in that direction. We agree, I hope, that "classicism" is not an alternative to "romanticism," as of political parties, Conservative and Liberal, Republican and Democrat, on a "turn-the-rascals-out" platform. It is a goal toward which all good literature strives, so far as it is good, according to the possibilities of its place and time. One can be "classical," in a sense, by turning away from nine-tenths of the material which lies at hand, and selecting only mummified stuff from a museum—like some contemporary writers, about whom one could say some nasty things in this connexion, if it were worth while (Mr Aldington is not one of them). Or one can be classical in tendency by doing the best one can with the material at hand. The confusion springs from the fact that the term is applied to literature and to the whole complex of interests and modes of behaviour and society of which literature is a part; and it has not the same bearing in both applications. It is much easier to be a classicist in literary criticism than in creative art—because in criticism you are responsible only for what you want, and in creation you are responsible for what you can do with material which you must simply accept. And in this material I include the emotions and feelings of the writer himself, which, for that writer, are simply material which he must accept—not virtues to be enlarged or vices to be diminished. The question, then, about Mr Joyce, is: how much living material does he deal with, and how does he deal with it: deal with, not as a legislator or exhorter, but as an artist?

It is here that Mr Joyce's parallel use of the Odyssey has a great importance. It has the importance of a scientific discovery. No one else has built a novel upon such a foundation before: it has never before been necessary. I am not begging the question in calling Ulysses a "novel"; and if you call it an epic it will not matter. If it is not a novel, that is simply because the novel is a form which will no longer serve; it is because the novel, instead of being a form, was simply the expression of an age which had not sufficiently lost all form to feel the need of something stricter. Mr Joyce has written one novel—the Portrait; Mr Wyndham Lewis[4] has written one novel—Tarr. I do not suppose that either of them will ever write another "novel." The novel ended with Flaubert and with James. It is, I think, because Mr Joyce and Mr Lewis, being "in advance" of their time, felt a conscious or probably unconscious dissatisfaction with the form, that their novels are more formless than those of a dozen clever writers who are unaware of its obsolescence.

In using the myth, in manipulating a continuous parallel between contemporaneity and antiquity, Mr Joyce is pursuing a method which others must pursue after him. They will not be imitators, any more than the scientist who uses the discoveries of an Einstein in pursuing his own, independent, further investigations. It is simply a way of controlling, of ordering, of giving a shape and a significance to the immense panorama of futility and anarchy which is contemporary history. It is a method already adumbrated by Mr Yeats, and of the need for which I believe Mr Yeats to have been the first contemporary to be conscious. It is a method for which the horoscope is auspicious. Psychology (such as it is, and whether our reaction to it be comic or serious), ethnology, and The Golden Bough[5] have concurred to make possible what was impossible even a few years ago. Instead of narrative method, we may now use the mythical method. It is, I seriously believe, a step toward making the modern world possible for art, toward that order and form which Mr Aldington so earnestly desires. And only those who have won their own discipline in secret and without aid, in a world which offers very little assistance to that end, can be of any use in furthering this advance.

The True Church and the Nineteen Churches[†]

While the poetry lovers have been subscribing to purchase for the nation the Keats house in Hampstead as a museum, the Church of England has apparently persisted in its design to sell for demolition

---

4. English writer, painter, and critic (1882–1957). *Tarr* was first published in 1918.
5. Major work by Sir James George Frazer (1854–1941), which Eliot credited with significant influence on *The Waste Land*. For selections, see above, pp. 69–75.
† From "London Letter," *The Dial* 70 (June 1921): 690–91. Notes are by the editor of this Norton Critical Edition.

nineteen religious edifices in the City of London.[1] Probably few American visitors, and certainly few natives, ever inspect these disconsolate fanes; but they give to the business quarter of London a beauty which its hideous banks and commercial houses have not quite defaced. Some are by Christopher Wren[2] himself, others by his school; the least precious redeems some vulgar street, like the plain little church of All Hallows at the end of London Wall. Some, like St Michael Paternoster Royal, are of great beauty. As the prosperity of London has increased, the City Churches have fallen into desuetude; for their destruction the lack of congregation is the ecclesiastical excuse, and the need of money the ecclesiastical reason. The fact that the erection of these churches was apparently paid for out of a public coal tax and their decoration probably by the parishioners, does not seem to invalidate the right of the True Church to bring them to the ground. To one who, like the present writer, passes his days in this City of London (*quand'io sentii chiavar l'uscio di sotto*)[3] the loss of these towers, to meet the eye down a grimy lane, and of these empty naves, to receive the solitary visitor at noon from the dust and tumult of Lombard Street, will be irreparable and unforgotten. A small pamphlet issued for the London County Council (Proposed Demolition of Nineteen City Churches: P. S. King & Son, Ltd., 2–4 Gt. Smith Street, Westminster, S.W.1, 3s.6d. net) should be enough to persuade of what I have said.

[*The Rite of Spring* and *The Golden Bough*][†]

Looking back upon the past season in London—for no new season has yet begun—it remains certain that Strawinsky[1] was our two months' lion. He has been the greatest success since Picasso. In London all the stars obey their seasons, though these seasons no more conform to the almanac than those which concern the weather. A mysterious law of appearance and disappearance governs everybody—or at least everybody who is wise enough to obey it. * * * Why this should have happened this year rather than last year, perhaps

---

1. See both Eliot's note and the editorial note to *The Waste Land*, l. 264.
2. English architect and scientist (1632–1723). Probably the most widely known of all English architects, he designed St. Paul's Cathedral and fifty-two other London churches, which were rebuilt after the Great Fire of 1666.
3. When I heard them nailing up the door (Italian). A reference to Canto 33 of Dante's *Inferno*, in which Count Ugolino is imprisoned in a tower for treason. See Eliot's note to l. 411 of *The Waste Land*, in which he quotes the same passage.
† From "London Letter," *The Dial* 71 (October 1921): 452–53. Notes are by the editor of this Norton Critical Edition.
1. Igor Stravinsky (1882–1971), Russian composer, whose ballet *Le Sacre du Printemps* (French for *The Rite of Spring*) premiered in Paris in 1913. Eliot uses the transliteration of his name common at the time.

rather than next year, I for one cannot tell. Even very insignificant people feel the occult influence; one knows, oneself, that there are times when it is desirable to be seen and times when it is felicitous to vanish.

But Strawinsky, Lucifer of the season, brightest in the firmament[2] took the call many times, small and correctly neat in pince-nez. His advent was well prepared by Mr Eugene Goossens[3]—also rather conspicuous this year—who conducted two Sacre du Printemps concerts, and other Strawinsky concerts were given before his arrival. The music was certainly too new and strange to please very many people; it is true that on the first night it was received with wild applause, and it is to be regretted that only three performances were given. If the ballet was not perfect, the fault does not lie either in the music, or in the choreography—which was admirable, or in the dancing—where Madame Sokolova[4] distinguished herself. To me the music seemed very remarkable—but at all events struck me as possessing a quality of modernity which I missed from the ballet which accompanied it. The effect was like Ulysses with illustrations by the best contemporary illustrator.

Strawinsky, that is to say, had done his job in the music. But music that is to be taken like operatic music, music accompanying and explained by an action, must have a drama which has been put through the same process of development as the music itself. The spirit of the music was modern, and the spirit of the ballet was primitive ceremony. The Vegetation Rite upon which the ballet is founded remained, in spite of the music, a pageant of primitive culture. It was interesting to any one who had read The Golden Bough and similar works, but hardly more than interesting. In art there should be interpenetration and metamorphosis. Even The Golden Bough can be read in two ways: as a collection of entertaining myths, or as a revelation of that vanished mind of which our mind is a continuation. In everything in the Sacre du Printemps, except in the music, one missed the sense of the present. Whether Strawinsky's music be permanent or ephemeral I do not know; but it did seem to transform the rhythm of the steppes into the scream of the motor horn, the rattle of machinery, the grind of wheels, the beating of iron and steel, the roar of the underground railway, and the other barbaric cries of modern life; and to transform these despairing noises into music.

---

2. Lucifer, literally "lightbearer" (Latin), is traditionally the name given to Satan before his fall from heaven. In classical times, and in Isaiah 14:12, he is associated with the morning star, Venus.
3. English conductor and composer (1893–1962).
4. Lydia Sokolova (1896–1974), English ballerina, born Hilda Munnings.

CRITICISM

Reviews and First Reactions

ARTHUR WAUGH

From The New Poetry[†]

Cleverness is, indeed, the pitfall of the New Poetry.[1] There is no question about the ingenuity with which its varying moods are exploited, its elaborate symbolism evolved, and its sudden, disconcerting effects exploded upon the imagination. Swift, brilliant images break into the field of vision, scatter like rockets, and leave a trail of flying fire behind. But the general impression is momentary; there are moods and emotions, but no steady current of ideas behind them. Further, in their determination to surprise and even to puzzle at all costs, these young poets are continually forgetting that the first essence of poetry is beauty; and that, however much you may have observed the world around you, it is impossible to translate your observation into poetry, without the intervention of the spirit of beauty, controlling the vision, and reanimating the idea.

The temptations of cleverness may be insistent, but its risks are equally great: how great indeed will, perhaps, be best indicated by the example of the 'Catholic Anthology,' which apparently represents the very newest of all the new poetic movements of the day. This strange little volume bears upon its cover a geometrical device, suggesting that the material within holds the same relation to the art of poetry as the work of the Cubist school holds to the art of painting and design.[2] The product of the volume is mainly American in origin, only one or two of the contributors being of indisputably English birth. But it appears here under the auspices of a house associated with some of the best poetry of the younger generation, and

† From *Quarterly Review* (October 1916): 384–86. Notes are by the editor of this Norton Critical Edition.
1. Waugh's essay is a review of two volumes of *Georgian Poetry* (1912, 1915) and *The Catholic Anthology* (1915), a collection edited by Ezra Pound that included "The Love Song of J. Alfred Prufrock" and four other poems by Eliot.
2. The cover design, of simple black and white parallelograms, was by Dorothy Shakespear, Pound's wife.

is prefaced by a short lyric by Mr W. B. Yeats,[3] in which that honoured representative of a very different school of inspiration makes bitter fun of scholars and critics, who

> 'Edit and annotate the lines
> That young men, tossing on their beds,
> Rhymed out in love's despair
> To flatter beauty's ignorant ear.'

The reader will not have penetrated far beyond this warning notice before he finds himself in the very stronghold of literary rebellion, if not of anarchy. Mr Orrick Johns may be allowed to speak for his colleagues, as well as for himself:

> 'This is the song of youth,
> This is the cause of myself;
> I knew my father well and he was a fool,
> Therefore will I have my own foot in the path before
>   I take a step;
> I will go only into new lands,
> And I will walk on no plank-walks.
> The horses of my family are wind-broken,
> And the dogs are old,
> And the guns rust;
> I will make me a new bow from an ash-tree,
> And cut up the homestead into arrows.'

And Mr Ezra Pound takes up the parable in turn, in the same wooden prose, cut into battens:

> 'Come, my songs, let us express our baser passions.
> Let us express our envy for the man with a steady job and
>   no worry about the future.
> You are very idle, my songs,
> I fear you will come to a bad end.
> You stand about the streets. You loiter at the corners and
>   bus-stops,
> You do next to nothing at all.
> You do not even express our inner nobility,
> You will come to a very bad end.
> And I? I have gone half cracked.'

It is not for his audience to contradict the poet, who for once may be allowed to pronounce his own literary epitaph. But this, it is to

---

3. Irish poet (1865–1939). The quotation is from "The Scholars." The following quotations are from "Song of Youth," by the American poet Orrick Johns (1887–1946), and "Further Instructions," by Ezra Pound.

be noted, is the 'poetry' that was to say nothing that might not be said 'actually in life—under emotion,'[4] the sort of emotion that settles down into the banality of a premature decrepitude:

'I grow old. . . . I grow old . . .
I shall wear the bottoms of my trousers rolled.
Shall I part my hair behind? Do I dare to eat a peach?
I shall wear white flannel trousers, and walk upon the beach.
I have heard the mermaids singing, each to each.
I do not think that they will sing to me.'[5]

Here, surely, is the reduction to absurdity of that school of literary license which, beginning with the declaration

'I knew my father well and he was a fool,'

naturally proceeds to the convenient assumption that everything which seemed wise and true to the father must inevitably be false and foolish to the son. Yet if the fruits of emancipation are to be recognised in the unmetrical, incoherent banalities of these literary 'Cubists,' the state of Poetry is indeed threatened with anarchy which will end in something worse even than 'red ruin and the breaking up of laws.'[6] From such a catastrophe the humour, commonsense, and artistic judgment of the best of the new 'Georgians' will assuredly save their generation; nevertheless, a hint of warning may not be altogether out of place. It was a classic custom in the family hall, when the feast was at its height, to display a drunken slave among the sons of the household, to the end that they, being ashamed at the ignominious folly of his gesticulations, might determine never to be tempted into such a pitiable condition themselves.[7] The custom had its advantages; for the wisdom of the younger generation was found to be fostered more surely by a single example than by a world of homily and precept.

---

4. Paraphrasing Pound's introduction to *The Poems of Lionel Johnson* (1915).
5. See above, p. 8.
6. From *Idylls of the King* (1859–85), by Alfred, Lord Tennyson (1809–1892).
7. According to the 1st–2nd-century Greek philosopher and historian Plutarch's *Life of Lycurgus*, one of many humiliations visited on slaves in Sparta.

EZRA POUND

[Review of *Prufrock and Other Observations*]†

I should like the reader to note how complete is Mr. Eliot's depiction of our contemporary condition. He has not confined himself to genre nor to society portraiture. His

> lonely men in shirt-sleeves leaning out of windows [p. 7]

are as real as his ladies who

> come and go
> Talking of Michelangelo. [p. 6]

His "one night cheap hotels" are as much "there" as are his

> four wax candles in the darkened room,
> Four rings of light upon the ceiling overhead,
> An atmosphere of Juliet's tomb. [p. 9]

And, above all, there is no rhetoric, although there is Elizabethan reading in the background. Were I a French critic, skilled in their elaborate art of writing books about books, I should probably go to some length discussing Mr. Eliot's two sorts of metaphor: his wholly unrealizable, always apt, half ironic suggestion, and his precise realizable picture. It would be possible to point out his method of conveying a whole situation and half a character by three words of a quoted phrase; his constant aliveness, his mingling of very subtle observation with the unexpectedness of a backhanded cliché. It is, however, extremely dangerous to point out such devices. The method is Mr. Eliot's own, but as soon as one has reduced even a fragment of it to formula, someone else, not Mr. Eliot, someone else wholly lacking in his aptitudes, will at once try to make poetry by mimicking his external procedure. And this indefinite "someone" will, needless to say, make a botch of it.

For what the statement is worth, Mr. Eliot's work interests me more than that of any other poet now writing in English. The most interesting poems in Victorian English are Browning's *Men and Women*,[1] or, if that statement is too absolute, let me contend that the form of these poems is the most vital form of that period of English, and that the poems written in that form are the least like each other in content. Antiquity gave us Ovid's *Heroides* and Theocritus'

---

† From *Poetry* 10 (August 1917): 265–71. Notes are by the editor of this Norton Critical Edition. Bracketed page numbers refer to this volume.
1. Dramatic monologues published by Robert Browning (1812–1889) in 1855.

woman using magic.[2] The form of Browning's *Men and Women* is more alive than the epistolary form of the *Heroides*. Browning included a certain amount of ratiocination and of purely intellectual comment, and in just that proportion he lost intensity. Since Browning there have been very few good poems of this sort. Mr. Eliot has made two notable additions to the list. And he has placed his people in contemporary settings, which is much more difficult than to render them with mediaeval romantic trappings. If it is permitted to make comparison with a different art, let me say that he has used contemporary detail very much as Velasquez used contemporary detail in *Las Meninas*;[3] the cold gray-green tones of the Spanish painter have, it seems to me, an emotional value not unlike the emotional value of Mr. Eliot's rhythms, and of his vocabulary.

James Joyce has written the best novel of my decade, and perhaps the best criticism of it has come from a Belgian who said, "All this is as true of my country as of Ireland". Eliot has a like ubiquity of application. Art does not avoid universals, it strikes at them all the harder in that it strikes through particulars. Eliot's work rests apart from that of the many new writers who have used the present freedoms to no advantage, who have gained no new precisions of language, and no variety in their cadence. His men in shirt-sleeves, and his society ladies, are not a local manifestation; they are the stuff of our modern world, .and true of more countries than one. I would praise the work for its fine tone, its humanity, and its realism; for all good art is realism of one sort or another.

It is complained that Eliot is lacking in emotion. *La Figlia che Piange* [p. 24] is sufficient confutation to that rubbish.

⁂   ⁂   ⁂

[T]he supreme test of a book is that we should feel some unusual intelligence working behind the words. By this test various other new books, that I have, or might have, beside me, go to pieces. The barrels of sham poetry that every decade and school and fashion produce, go to pieces. It is sometimes extremely difficult to find any other particular reason for their being so unsatisfactory. I have expressly written here not "intellect" but "intelligence." There is no intelligence without emotion. The emotion may be anterior or concurrent. There may be emotion without much intelligence, but that does not concern us.

2. The *Heroides* are epistolary poems in which the Latin poet Ovid (43 BCE–17/18 CE) takes on various female voices. Similarly, the Second Idyll of Theocritus (Greek, ca. 300 BCE–ca. 260 BCE) is written in the voice of a woman using magic to regain the lover who has abandoned her.
3. A 1656 painting depicting the Infanta Margaret Theresa and her ladies-in-waiting (*las meninas*).

Versification:

A conviction as to the rightness or wrongness of *vers libre* is no guarantee of a poet. I doubt if there is much use trying to classify the various kinds of *vers libre*, but there is an anarchy which may be vastly overdone; and there is a monotony of bad usage as tiresome as any typical eighteenth or nineteenth century flatness.

In a recent article Mr. Eliot contended, or seemed to contend, that good *vers libre* was little more than a skilful evasion of the better known English metres.[4] His article was defective in that he omitted all consideration of metres depending on quantity, alliteration, etc.; in fact he wrote as if metres were measured by accent. This may have been tactful on his part, it may have brought his article nearer to the comprehension of his readers (that is, those of the *New Statesman*, in which the article appeared, people who are chiefly concerned with sociology of the "button" and "unit" variety). But he came nearer the fact when he wrote elsewhere: "No *vers* is *libre* for the man who wants to do a good job."

Alexandrine and other grammarians[5] have made cubbyholes of various groupings of syllables; they have put names upon them, and have given various labels to "metres" consisting of combinations of these different groups. Thus it would be hard to escape contact with some group or other; only an encyclopedist could ever be half sure he had done so. The known categories would allow a fair liberty to the most conscientious traditionalist. The most fanatical vers-librist will escape them with difficulty. However, I do not think there is any crying need for verse with absolutely no rhythmical basis.

On the other hand, I do not believe that Chopin wrote to a metronome. There is undoubtedly a sense of music that takes count of the "shape" of the rhythm in a melody rather than of bar divisions, which came rather late in the history of written music and were certainly not the first or most important thing that musicians tried to record. The creation of such shapes is part of thematic invention. Some musicians have the faculty of invention, rhythmic, melodic. Likewise some poets.

Treatises full of musical notes and of long and short marks have never been convincingly useful. Find a man with thematic invention and all he can say is that he gets what the Celts call a "chune" in his head, and that the words "go into it," or when they don't "go into it" they "stick out and worry him."

You can not force a person to play a musical masterpiece correctly, even by having the notes correctly printed on the paper before him;

4. A reference to "Reflections on *Vers Libre*," published in the *New Statesman* in 1917. See above, pp. 139–45.
5. Textual scholars associated with the great library at Alexandria in the 2nd–3rd centuries BCE.

neither can you force a person to feel the movement of poetry, be the metre "regular" or "irregular." I have heard Mr. Yeats trying to read Burns, struggling in vain to fit the *Birks o' Aberfeldy* and *Bonnie Alexander* into the mournful keen of the *Wind among the Reeds*.[6] Even in regular metres there are incompatible systems of music.

I have heard the best orchestral conductor in England read poems in free verse, poems in which the rhythm was so faint as to be almost imperceptible. He read them with the author's cadence, with flawless correctness. A distinguished statesman read from the same book, with the intonations of a legal document, paying no attention to the movement inherent in the words before him. I have heard a celebrated Dante scholar and mediaeval enthusiast read the sonnets of the *Vita Nuova*[7] as if they were not only prose, but the ignominious prose of a man devoid of emotions: an utter castration.

The leader of orchestra said to me, "There is more for a musician in a few lines with something rough or uneven, such as Byron's

> There be none of Beauty's daughters
> With a magic like thee;

than in whole pages of regular poetry."[8]

Unless a man can put some thematic invention into *vers libre*, he would perhaps do well to stick to "regular" metres, which have certain chances of being musical from their form, and certain other chances of being musical through his failure in fitting the form. In *vers libre* his sole musical chance lies in invention.

Mr. Eliot is one of the very few who have brought in a personal rhythm, an identifiable quality of sound as well as of style. And at any rate, his book is the best thing in poetry since . . . (for the sake of peace I will leave that date to the imagination). I have read most of the poems many times; I last read the whole book at breakfast time and from flimsy and grimy proof-sheets: I believe these are "test conditions." Confound it, the fellow can write—we may as well sit up and take notice.

6. An Irish poet (W. B. Yeats [1865–1939]) attempting to scan the works of a Scottish poet (Robert Burns [1759–1796]).
7. A poetic sequence, published by Dante Alighieri in 1294, in which the poems are interspersed with prose commentary.
8. In Lord Byron's 16-line poem, first published in 1816, the alternate lines are in a very free iambic trimeter.

MAY SINCLAIR

Prufrock and Other Observations: A Criticism[†]

So far I have seen two and only two reviews of Mr. Eliot's poems: one by Ezra Pound in *The Egoist*, one by an anonymous writer in *The New Statesman*.[1] I learn from Mr. Pound's review that there is a third, by Mr. Arthur Waugh, in the *Quarterly*.

To Mr. Ezra Pound Mr. Eliot is a poet with genius as incontestable as the genius of Browning. To the anonymous one he is an insignificant phenomenon that may be appropriately disposed of among the "Shorter Notices." To Mr. Waugh, quoted by Mr. Pound, he is a "drunken Helot."[2] I do not know what Mr. Pound would say to the anonymous one, but I can imagine. Anyhow, to him the *Quarterly* reviewer is "the silly old Waugh." And that is enough for Mr. Pound.

It ought to be enough for me. Of course I know that genius does inevitably provoke these outbursts of silliness. I know that Mr. Waugh is simply keeping up the good old manly traditions of the *Quarterly*, "so savage and tartarly," with its war-cry: "'Ere's a stranger, let's 'eave 'arf a brick at 'im!" And though the behaviour of *The New Statesman* puzzles me, since it has an editor who sometimes knows better, and really ought to have known better this time, still *The New Statesman* also can plead precedent. But when Mr. Waugh calls Mr. Eliot "a drunken Helot," it is clear that he thinks he is on the track of a tendency and is making a public example of Mr. Eliot. And when the anonymous one with every appearance of deliberation picks out his "*Boston Evening Transcript*," the one insignificant, the one neglible and trivial thing in a very serious volume, and assures us that it represents Mr. Eliot at his finest and his best, it is equally clear that we have to do with something more than mere journalistic misadventure. And I think it is something more than Mr. Eliot's genius that has terrified *The Quarterly* into exposing him in the full glare of publicity and *The New Statesman* into shoving him and his masterpieces away out of the public sight.

For "The Love-Song of J. Alfred Prufrock", and the "Portrait of a Lady" are masterpieces in the same sense and in the same degree

---

† From *The Little Review* 4 (December 1917): 8–14. Notes are by the editor of this Norton Critical Edition.

1. This short notice, published in the *New Statesman* on August 18, 1917, maintains that Eliot's work is "unrecognizable as poetry."
2. Pound's rejoinder to Arthur Waugh, published in *The Egoist* in June 1917, uses the phrase "drunken Helot," which did not actually appear in Waugh's comparison of Eliot to a drunken Spartan slave (see above, p. 175).

as Browning's "Romances" and "Men and Women";[3] the "Preludes" and "Rhapsody on a Windy Morning" are masterpieces in a profounder sense and a greater degree than Henley's "London Voluntaries";[4] "La Figlia Che Piange" is a masterpiece in its own sense and in its own degree. It is a unique masterpiece.

But Mr. Eliot is dangerous. Mr. Eliot is associated with an unpopular movement and with unpopular people. His "Preludes" and his "Rhapsody" appeared in *Blast*.[5] They stood out from the experimental violences of *Blast* with an air of tranquil and triumphant achievement; but, no matter; it was in *Blast* that they appeared. That circumstance alone was disturbing to the comfortable respectability of Mr. Waugh and *The New Statesman*.

And apart from this purely extraneous happening, Mr. Eliot's genius is in itself disturbing. It is elusive; it is difficult; it demands a distinct effort of attention. Comfortable and respectable people could see, in the first moment after dinner, what Mr. Henley and Mr. Robert Louis Stevenson and Mr. Rudyard Kipling[6] would be at; for the genius of these three travelled, comfortably and fairly respectably, along the great high roads. They could even, with a little boosting, follow Francis Thompson's[7] flight in mid-air, partly because it was signalled to them by the sound and shining of his wings, partly because Thompson had hitched himself securely to some well-known starry team. He was in the poetic tradition all right. People knew where they were with him, just as they know now where they are with Mr. Davies[8] and his fields and flowers and birds.

But Mr. Eliot is not in any tradition at all; not even in Browning's and Henley's tradition. His resemblances to Browning and Henley are superficial. His difference is twofold; a difference of method and technique; a difference of sight and aim. He does not see anything between him and reality, and he makes straight for the reality he sees; he cuts all his corners and his curves; and this directness of method is startling and upsetting to comfortable, respectable people accustomed to going superfluously in and out of corners and carefully round curves. Unless you are prepared to follow with the same nimbleness and straightness you will never arrive with Mr. Eliot at

3. Like Pound (see above, p. 176), Sinclair compares Eliot's poems to Robert Browning's dramatic monologues, which he referred to as dramatic lyrics or dramatic romances.
4. William Ernest Henley (1849–1903) was a well-known poet, critic, and editor at the time, highly regarded for his poems in a realist mode. His "London Voluntaries" (1893) is a free-verse sequence modeled on the improvised organ music performed before and after a church service.
5. The avant-garde journal edited by Ezra Pound and Wyndham Lewis, in two issues (1914–15).
6. Stevenson (1850–1894), Scottish novelist and travel writer; Kipling (1865–1936), English poet and novelist.
7. English poet (1859–1907), known for visionary, religious poems such as *The Hound of Heaven* (1893).
8. W. H. Davies (1871–1940), well-known nature poet.

his meaning. Therefore the only comfortable thing is to sit down and pretend, either that Mr. Eliot is a "Helot" too drunk to have any meaning, or that his "Boston Evening Transcript" which you do understand is greater than his "Love Song of Prufrock" which you do not understand. In both instances you have successfully obscured the issue.

Again, the comfortable and respectable mind loves conventional beauty, and some of the realities that Mr. Eliot sees are not beautiful. He insists on your seeing very vividly, as he sees them, the streets of his "Preludes" and "Rhapsody." He insists on your smelling them.

> "Regard that woman
> Who hesitates towards you in the light of the door
> Which opens on her like a grin.
> You see the border of her dress
> Is torn and stained with sand,
> And you see the corner of her eye
> Twists like a crooked pin.
>
> Remark the cat which flattens itself in the gutter,
> Slips out its tongue
> And devours a morsel of rancid butter."

He is

> "aware of the damp souls of housemaids
> Sprouting despondently at area gates."

And these things are ugly. The comfortable mind turns away from them in disgust. It identifies Mr. Eliot with a modern tendency; it labels him securely "Stark Realist", so that lovers of "true poetry" may beware.

It is nothing to the comfortable mind that Mr. Eliot is

> ". . . moved by fancies that are curled
> Around these images, and cling:
> The notion of some infinitely gentle
> Infinitely suffering thing."

It is nothing to it that the emotion he disengages from his ugliest image is unbearably poignant. His poignancy is as unpleasant as his ugliness, disturbing to comfort.

We are to observe that Mr. Eliot's "Observations" are ugly and unpleasant and obscure.

Now there is no earthly reason why Mr. Eliot should not be ugly and unpleasant if he pleases, no reason why he should not do in words what Hogarth did in painting, provided he does it well enough. Only, the comfortable mind that prefers So and So and So and So

to Mr. Eliot ought to prefer Hogarth's "Paul Before Felix" to his
"Harlot's Progress".[9] Obscurity, if he were really obscure, would be
another matter. But there was a time when the transparent Tenny-
son was judged obscure; when people wondered what under heaven
the young man was after; they couldn't tell for the life of them
whether it was his "dreary gleams" or his "curlews" that were fly-
ing over Locksley Hall! Obscurity may come from defective syn-
tax, from a bad style, from confusion of ideas, from involved thinking,
from irrelevant association, from sheer piling on of ornament.
Mr. Eliot is not obscure in any of these senses.

There is also an obscurity of remote or unusual objects, or of
familiar objects moving very rapidly. And Mr. Eliot's trick of cutting
his corners and his curves makes him seem obscure where he is clear
as daylight. His thoughts move very rapidly and by astounding cuts.
They move not by logical stages and majestic roundings of the full
literary curve, but as live thoughts move in live brains. Thus "La
Figlia Che Piange:"

> "Stand on the highest pavement of the stair—
> Lean on a garden urn—
> Weave, weave the sunlight in your hair—
> Clasp your flowers to you with a pained surprise,
> Fling them to the ground and turn
> With a fugitive resentment in your eyes:
> But weave, weave the sunlight in your hair.
>
> So I would have had him leave,
> So would have had her stand and grieve,
> So he would have left
> As the soul leaves the body torn and bruised,
> As the mind deserts the body it has used.
> I should find
> Some way incomparably light and deft.
> Some way we both should understand,
> Simple and faithless as a smile or a shake of the hand.
>
> She turned away, but with the autumn weather
> Compelled my imagination many days,
> Many days and many hours,
> Her hair over her arms and her arms full of flowers.

9. *Paul Before Felix* (1748) is an oil painting on a religious theme, whereas *A Harlot's Pro-
   gress* (1731) is a series of paintings, distributed as engravings, on the theme announced
   in its title.
1. "'T is the place, and all around it, as of old, the curlews call, / Dreary gleams about the
   moorland flying over Locksley Hall": lines 3–4 of Tennyson's poem, first published in
   1842.

> And I wonder how they should have been together!
> I should have lost a gesture and a pose.
> Sometimes these cogitations still amaze
> The troubled midnight and the moon's repose."

I suppose there are minds so comfortable that they would rather not be disturbed by new beauty and by new magic like this. I do not know how much Mr. Eliot's beauty and magic is due to sheer imagination, how much to dexterity of technique, how much to stern and sacred attention to reality; but I do know that without such technique and such attention the finest imagination is futile, and that if Mr. Eliot had written nothing but that one poem he would rank as a poet by right of its perfection.

But Mr. Eliot is not a poet of one poem; and if there is anything more astounding and more assured than his performance it is his promise. He knows what he is after. Reality, stripped naked of all rhetoric, of all ornament, of all confusing and obscuring association, is what he is after. His reality may be a modern street or a modern drawing-room; it may be an ordinary human mind suddenly and fatally aware of what is happening to it; Mr. Eliot is careful to present his street and his drawing-room as they are, and Prufrock's thoughts as they are: live thoughts, kicking, running about and jumping, nervily, in a live brain.

Prufrock, stung by a longing for reality, escapes from respectability into the street and the October fog.

> "The yellow fog that rubs its back upon the window-panes,
> The yellow smoke that rubs its muzzle on the window panes,
> Licked its tongue into the corners of the evening,
> Lingered upon the pools that stand in drains,
> Let fall upon its back the soot that falls from chimneys,
> Slipped by the terrace, made a sudden leap,
> And seeing that it was a soft October night,
> Curled once about the house and fell asleep."

Prufrock has conceived the desperate idea of disturbing the universe. He wonders

> "Do I dare
> Disturb the universe?
> In a minute there is time
> For decisions and revisions which a minute will reverse.
>
> For I have known them all already, known them all:
> Have known the evenings, mornings, afternoons;
> I have measured out my life with coffee spoons;
> I know the voices dying with a dying fall

> Beneath the music from a farther room.
> So how should I presume?"

Prufrock realises that it is too late. He is middle-aged. The horrible drawing-room life he has entered has got him.

> "And the afternoon, the evening, sleeps so peacefully!
> Smoothed by long fingers,
> Asleep . . . tired . . . or it malingers,
> Stretched on the floor, here between you and me.
> Should I, after tea and cakes and ices,
> Have the strength to force the moment to its crisis?
> But though I have wept and fasted, wept and prayed.
> Though I have seen my head (grown slightly bald) brought
>   in upon a platter,
> I am no prophet—and here's no great matter;
> I have seen the moment of my greatness flicker,
> And I have seen the eternal Footman hold my coat and
>   snicker,
> And, in short, I was afraid."

His soul can only assert itself in protests and memories. He would have had more chance in the primeval slime.

> "I should have been a pair of ragged claws
> Scuttling across the floors of silent seas."

As he goes downstairs he is aware of his futility, aware that the noticeable thing about him is the "bald spot in the middle of my hair". He has an idea; an idea that he can put into action:—

> "I shall wear the bottoms of my trousers rolled."

He is incapable, he knows that he is incapable of any action more momentous, more disturbing.
And yet—and yet—

> "I have heard the mermaids singing, each to each.
>
> I have seen them riding seaward on the waves
> Combing the white hair of the waves blown back
> When the wind blows the water white and black.
> We have lingered in the chambers of the sea,
> By sea-girls wreathed with seaweed red and brown
> Till human voices wake us and we drown."

Observe the method. Instead of writing round and round about Prufrock, explaining that his tragedy is the tragedy of submerged passion, Mr. Eliot simply removes the covering from Prufrock's mind: Prufrock's mind, jumping quickly from actuality to memory and back again, like an animal, hunted, tormented, terribly and poignantly alive. The Love-Song of Prufrock is a song that Balzac might have sung if he had been as great a poet as he was a novelist.

It is nothing to the *Quarterly* and to the *New Statesman* that Mr. Eliot should have done this thing. But it is a great deal to the few people who care for poetry and insist that it should concern itself with reality. With ideas, if you like, but ideas that are realities and not abstractions.

VIRGINIA WOOLF

Is This Poetry?[†]

There are people who write what they wish to write, though it misses by a thousand words or exceeds by five hundred and fifty the accustomed measure. And, when they write, they have for audience in their mind's eye—five people, three, nobody at all perhaps. But the invisible audience is the most exacting. The little books issued by the Hogarth Press are, to judge by the present examples, of this uncompromising nature, designed to please no one in particular, addressed to no public save that which has in it the ghosts of Plato and Sir Thomas Browne, and one or two living writers who are certainly unaware of their distinction.[1] Thus it comes about that Mr. Murry and Mr. Eliot, who have nothing in common save the sincerity of their passion, are issued by the same press and fall to be reviewed on the same day. "Reviewed" is written, but it is scarcely felt. Whether or not it is to be charged to the writer's merit, the reviewer of these two books must feel himself decidedly more fallible than usual. Perhaps all writing with an honest intention behind it is thus teasing and destructive. Perhaps poetry pays less surface deference to rules than prose.

At any rate, to deal with Mr. Murry first, we have to recognize in our own mind as little serenity and certainty as is compatible with what we have done our best to make a thorough understanding of his work. As a first step towards understanding, rub out as many years as divide you from the youth which, stark, stiff, severe, terribly sanguine, has not yet been absorbed into the main activities of

† From *The Athenaeum* (June 20, 1919): 491. Notes are by the editor of this Norton Critical Edition.
1. In 1919, Hogarth Press was a small operation owned and run by Woolf and her husband, Leonard. In this article, Woolf is reviewing books she had just published: *The Critic in Judgment* by John Middleton Murry (1889–1957) and *Poems* by Eliot. Sir Thomas Browne (1605–1682) wrote complex and deeply learned books, including *Religio Medici* (1643) and *Pseudodoxia Epidemica* (1646).

the world. Never again is one so serious, so uncompromising and so clear-sighted. That is Mr. Murry's position. He stands upright, surveys the prospect, in which as yet he plays no part, and asks himself, What is the aim of life? What can one believe? * * *

* * * But does Mr. Murry make the journey worth while? Is he, that is to say, what, for convenience sake, we call a poet? Does he give us what after all matters so much more than the end of any journey or the truth of any argument? This, indeed, is what we find it difficult to decide. * * * In part, of course, the subtle English logic carries us along. Beyond that, however, there are passages and phrases where the glow and heat that we require appear, giving us, not the easy beauty that we are used to call inspiration, but a more difficult variety born of friction which, from the effort that it exacts, makes us ask in the midst of our exaltation, "Is this poetry?"

The "ordinary man," the ghostly master or terror of most writers, would certainly ask the same question about Mr. Eliot, and answer it with a decided negative.

> Polyphiloprogenitive
> The sapient sutlers of the Lord
> Drift across the window-panes.
> In the beginning was the Word.

Thus begins one of Mr. Eliot's poems, provocative of the question and of the jeering laugh which is the easy reaction to anything strange, whether it be a "damned foreigner" or a Post-Impressionist picture. Mr. Eliot is certainly damned by his newness and strangeness; but those two qualities, which in most art are completely unimportant, because ephemeral, in him claim the attention of even the serious critic. For they are part of the fabric of his poetry. Mr. Eliot is always quite consciously "trying for" something, and something which has grown out of and developed beyond all the poems of all the dead poets. Poetry to him seems to be not so much an art as a science, a vast and noble and amusing body of communal feeling upon which the contemporary poet must take a firm stand and then launch himself into the unknown in search of new discoveries. That is the attitude not of the conventional poet, but of the scientist who with the help of working hypotheses hopes to add something, a theory perhaps or a new microbe, to the corpus of human knowledge. If we accept, provisionally, Mr. Eliot's attitude, we must admit that he comes well equipped to his task. The poetry of the dead is in his bones and at the tips of his fingers: he has the rare gift of being able to weave, delicately and delightfully, an echo or even a line of the past into the pattern of his own poem. And at the same time he is always trying for something new, something which has evolved—one drops instinctively into the scientific terminology—out of the echo or the line, out of the last poem of the last dead poet, something subtly intellectual and spiritual, produced by the careful juxtaposition of words and the even more careful juxtaposition of ideas. The cautious critic, warned by the lamentable record of his tribe, might avoid answering the question: "And is this poetry?" by asking to see a little more of Mr. Eliot than is shown in these seven short poems and even "Prufrock." But, to tell the truth, seven poems reveal a great deal of any poet. There is poetry in Mr. Eliot, as, for instance, in the stanzas:

> The host with someone indistinct
> Converses at the door apart,
> The nightingales are singing near
> The Convent of the Sacred Heart,
>
> And sang within the bloody wood
> When Agamemnon cried aloud,
> And let their liquid siftings fall
> To stain the stiff dishonoured shroud.

Yet the poetry often seems to come in precisely at the moment when the scientist and the science, the method and the newness, go out. A poem like "The Hippopotamus," for all its charm and cleverness and artistry, is perilously near the pit of the jeu d'esprit. And so scientific and scholarly a writer as Mr. Eliot might with advantage consider whether his method was not the method of that "terrible warning," P. Papinius Statius.[2] We hope that Mr. Eliot will quickly give us more and remove our melancholy suspicion that he is the product of a Silver Age.

[Eliot Chants *The Waste Land*][†]

Eliot dined last Sunday & read his poem. He sang it & chanted it rhythmed it. It has great beauty & force of phrase: symmetry; & tensity. What connects it together, I'm not so sure. But he read till he had to rush—letters to write about the London Magazine—& discussion thus was curtailed. One was left, however, with some strong

2. Publius Papinius Statius (ca. 45 CE–ca. 96 CE), Roman poet known for learned, allusive poetry. A Silver Age follows a Golden one and is less spontaneous and natural and therefore less illustrious. Traditionally, the Silver Age of Latin poetry was supposed to have extended from the death of Emperor Augustus (14 CE) to that of Trajan (117 CE) or perhaps Marcus Aurelius (180 CE).

† From *The Diary of Virginia Woolf* (New York: Harcourt Brace, 1978), 2:178. Copyright © 1978 by Quentin Bell and Angelica Garnett. Reprinted by permission of Houghton Mifflin Harcourt Publishing Company and The Society of Authors as the Literary Representative the Estate of Virginia Woolf. All rights reserved.

emotion. The Waste Land, it is called; & Mary Hutch,[1] who has heard it more quietly, interprets it to be Tom's autobiography—a melancholy one.

TIMES LITERARY SUPPLEMENT

[Mr. Eliot's Poem][†]

Mr. Eliot's poem is also a collection of flashes, but there is no effect of heterogeneity, since all these flashes are relevant to the same thing and together give what seems to be a complete expression of this poet's vision of modern life. We have here range, depth, and beautiful expression. What more is necessary to a great poem? This vision is singularly complex and in all its labyrinths utterly sincere. It is the mystery of life that it shows two faces, and we know of no other modern poet who can more adequately and movingly reveal to us the inextricable tangle of the sordid and the beautiful that make up life. Life is neither hellish nor heavenly; it has a purgatorial quality. And since it is purgatory, deliverance is possible. Students of Mr. Eliot's work will find a new note, and a profoundly interesting one, in the latter part of this poem.

EDMUND WILSON

The Poetry of Drouth[‡]

Mr T. S. Eliot's first meagre volume of twenty-four poems was dropped into the waters of contemporary verse without stirring more than a few ripples. But when two or three years had passed, it was found to stain the whole sea. Or, to change the metaphor a little, it became evident that Mr Eliot had fished a murex[1] up. His productions, which had originally been received as a sort of glorified *vers de société*, turned out to be unforgettable poems, which everyone was trying to rewrite. There might not be very much of him, but what there was had come somehow to seem precious and now the publication of his long poem, The Waste Land, confirms the opinion

1. Mary Hutchinson (1889–1977), short-story writer and a close friend of the Eliots in the early years of their marriage [*Editor*].
† From an anonymous review of *The Criterion* (October 26, 1922): 690.
‡ From *The Dial* 73 (December 1922): 611–16. Notes are by the editor of this Norton Critical Edition. Bracketed page numbers refer to this volume.
1. A sea snail (*Murex brandaris*) sought after in ancient times as the source of Tyrian purple dye.

which we had begun gradually to cherish, that Mr Eliot, with all his
limitations, is one of our only authentic poets. For this new poem—
which presents itself as so far his most considerable claim to
eminence—not only recapitulates all his earlier and already famil-
iar motifs, but it sounds for the first time in all their intensity, untem-
pered by irony or disguise, the hunger for beauty and the anguish at
living which lie at the bottom of all his work.

Perhaps the best point of departure for a discussion of The Waste
Land is an explanation of its title. Mr Eliot asserts that he derived
this title, as well as the plan of the poem "and much of the inciden-
tal symbolism," from a book by Miss Jessie L. Weston called From
Ritual to Romance. The Waste Land, it appears, is one of the many
mysterious elements which have made of the Holy Grail legend a
perennial puzzle of folk-lore; it is a desolate and sterile country, ruled
over by an impotent king, in which not only have the crops ceased
to grow and the animals to reproduce their kind, but the very human
inhabitants have become unable to bear children. The renewal of
the Waste Land and the healing of the "Fisher King's" wound depend
somehow upon the success of the Knight who has come to find the
Holy Grail.

Miss Weston, who has spent her whole life in the study of the
Arthurian legends, has at last propounded a new solution for
the problems presented by this strange tale. Stimulated by Frazer's
Golden Bough—of which this extraordinarily interesting book is a
sort of offshoot—she has attempted to explain the Fisher King as
a primitive vegetable god—one of those creatures who, like Attis
and Adonis, is identified with Nature herself and in the temporary
loss of whose virility the drouth or inclemency of the season is sym-
bolized; and whose mock burial is a sort of earnest of his coming to
life again. Such a cult, Miss Weston contends, became attached to
the popular Persian religion of Mithraism and was brought north
to Gaul and Britain by the Roman legionaries. When Christianity
finally prevailed, Attis was driven underground and survived only
as a secret cult, like the Venus of the Venusberg.[2] The Grail legend,
according to Miss Weston, had its origin in such a cult; the Lance
and Grail are the sexual symbols appropriate to a fertility rite and
the eerie adventure of the Chapel Perilous is the description of an
initiation.

Now Mr Eliot uses the Waste Land as the concrete image of a
spiritual drouth. His poem takes place half in the real world—the
world of contemporary London, and half in a haunted wilderness—
the Waste Land of the mediaeval legend; but the Waste Land is only

2. The secret mountain cavern sacred to Venus, discovered in Richard Wagner's opera
   Tannhäuser (1845).

the hero's arid soul and the intolerable world about him. The water which he longs for in the twilit desert is to quench the thirst which torments him in the London dusk.—And he exists not only upon these two planes, but as if throughout the whole of human history. Miss Weston's interpretation of the Grail legend lent itself with peculiar aptness to Mr Eliot's extraordinarily complex mind (which always finds itself looking out upon the present with the prouder eyes of the past and which loves to make its oracles as deep as the experience of the race itself by piling up stratum upon stratum of reference, as the Italian painters used to paint over one another); because she took pains to trace the Buried God not only to Attis and Adonis, but further back to the recently revealed Tammuz of the Sumerian-Babylonian civilization and to the god invited to loosen the waters in the abysmally ancient Vedic Hymns.[3] So Mr Eliot hears in his own parched cry the voices of all the thirsty men of the past—of the author of Ecclesiastes in majestic bitterness at life's futility, of the Children of Israel weeping for Zion by the unrefreshing rivers of Babylon, of the disciples after the Crucifixion meeting the phantom of Christ on their journey; of Buddha's renunciation of life and Dante's astonishment at the weary hordes of Hell, and of the sinister dirge with which Webster blessed the "friendless bodies of unburied men." In the centre of his poem he places the weary figure of the blind immortal prophet Tiresias, who, having been woman as well as man, has exhausted all human experience and, having "sat by Thebes below the wall and walked among the lowest of the dead," knows exactly what will happen in the London flat between the typist and the house-agent's clerk; and at its beginning the almost identical figure of the Cumaean Sibyl mentioned in Petronius, who—gifted also with extreme longevity and preserved as a sort of living mummy—when asked by little boys what she wanted, replied only "I want to die." Not only is life sterile and futile, but men have tasted its sterility and futility a thousand times before. T. S. Eliot, walking the desert of London, feels profoundly that the desert has always been there. Like Tiresias, he has sat below the wall of Thebes; like Buddha, he has seen the world as an arid conflagration; like the Sibyl, he has known everything and known everything vain.

Yet something else, too, reaches him from the past: as he wanders among the vulgarities which surround him, his soul is haunted by heroic strains of an unfading music. Sometimes it turns suddenly and shockingly into the jazz of the music-halls, sometimes it breaks in the middle of a bar and leaves its hearer with dry ears again, but

3. Ancient Sanskrit poems, on which the Upanishads (including the *Brihadāranyaka Upanishad* from which Eliot quotes in "What the Thunder Said") are elaborations and commentaries.

still it sounds like the divine rumour of some high destiny from which he has fallen, like indestructible pride in the citizenship of some world which he never can reach. In a London boudoir, where the air is stifling with a dust of futility, he hears, as he approaches his hostess, an echo of Anthony and Cleopatra and of Aeneas coming to the house of Dido—and a painted panel above the mantel gives his mind a moment's swift release by reminding him of Milton's Paradise and of the nightingale that sang there.—Yet though it is most often things from books which refresh him, he has also a slight spring of memory. He remembers someone who came to him with wet hair and with hyacinths in her arms, and before her he was stricken senseless and dumb—"looking into the heart of light, the silence." There were rain and flowers growing then. Nothing ever grows during the action of the poem and no rain ever falls. The thunder of the final vision is "dry sterile thunder without rain." But as Gerontion in his dry rented house thinks wistfully of the young men who fought in the rain [p. 25], as Prufrock longs to ride green waves and linger in the chambers of the sea [p. 5], as Mr Apollinax is imagined drawing strength from the deep sea-caves of coral islands [p. 21], so in this new poem Mr Eliot identifies water with all freedom and illumination of the soul. He drinks the rain that once fell on his youth as—to use an analogy in Mr Eliot's own manner— Dante drank at the river of Eunoë that the old joys he had known might be remembered. But—to note also the tragic discrepancy, as Mr Eliot always does—the draught, so far from renewing his soul and leaving him pure to rise to the stars, is only a drop absorbed in the desert; to think of it is to register its death. The memory is the dead god whom—as Hyacinth—he buries at the beginning of the poem and which—unlike his ancient prototype—is never to come to life again. Hereafter, fertility will fail; we shall see women deliberately making themselves sterile; we shall find that love has lost its life-giving power and can bring nothing but an asceticism of disgust. He is travelling in a country cracked by drouth in which he can only dream feverishly of drowning or of hearing the song of the hermit-thrush which has at least the music of water. The only reappearance of the god is as a phantom which walks beside him, the delirious hallucination of a man who is dying of thirst. In the end the dry-rotted world is crumbling about him—his own soul is falling apart. There is nothing left to prop it up but some dry stoic Sanskrit maxims and the broken sighs from the past, of singers exiled or oppressed. Like de Nerval, he is disinherited; like the poet of the Pervigilium Veneris, he is dumb; like Arnaut Daniel in Purgatory, he begs the world to raise a prayer for his torment, as he disappears in the fire.

It will be seen from this brief description that the poem is complicated; and it is actually even more complicated than I have made it appear. It is sure to be objected that Mr Eliot has written a puzzle rather than a poem and that his work can possess no higher interest than a full-rigged ship built in a bottle. It will be said that he depends too much upon books and borrows too much from other men and that there can be no room for original quality in a poem of little more than four hundred lines which contains allusions to, parodies of, or quotations from, the Vedic Hymns, Buddha, the Psalms, Ezekiel, Ecclesiastes, Luke, Sappho, Virgil, Ovid, Petronius, the Pervigilium Veneris, St Augustine, Dante, the Grail Legends, early English poetry, Kyd, Spenser, Shakespeare, John Day, Webster, Middleton, Milton, Goldsmith, Gérard de Nerval, Froude, Baudelaire, Verlaine, Swinburne, Wagner, The Golden Bough, Miss Weston's book, various popular ballads, and the author's own earlier poems. It has already been charged against Mr Eliot that he does not feel enough to be a poet and that the emotions of longing and disgust which he does have belong essentially to a delayed adolescence. It has already been suggested that his distate for the celebrated Sweeney [pp. 30, 40] shows a superficial mind and that if he only looked more closely into poor Sweeney he would find Eugene O'Neill's Hairy Ape; and I suppose it will be felt in connexion with this new poem that if his vulgar London girls had only been studied by Sherwood Anderson they would have presented a very different appearance.[4] At bottom, it is sure to be said, Mr Eliot is timid and prosaic like Mr Prufrock; he has no capacity for life, and nothing which happens to Mr Prufrock can be important.

Well: all these objections are founded on realities, but they are outweighed by one major fact—the fact that Mr Eliot is a poet. It is true his poems seem the products of a constricted emotional experience and that he appears to have drawn rather heavily on books for the heat he could not derive from life. There is a certain grudging margin, to be sure, about all that Mr Eliot writes—as if he were compensating himself for his limitations by a peevish assumption of superiority. But it is the very acuteness of his suffering from this starvation which gives such poignancy to his art. And, as I say, Mr Eliot is a poet—that is, he feels intensely and with distinction and speaks naturally in beautiful verse—so that, no matter within what walls he lives, he belongs to the divine company. His verse is sometimes much too scrappy—he does not dwell long enough upon one idea to give it its proportionate value before passing on to the next— but these drops, though they be wrung from flint, are none the less authentic crystals. They are broken and sometimes infinitely tiny,

---

4. The American fiction writer Sherwood Anderson (1876–1941) was thought at this time to be rather daring, especially on sexual themes. *The Hairy Ape* (1922), by the American playwright Eugene O'Neill (1888–1953), is about a coal stoker on a steamship.

but they are worth all the rhinestones on the market. I doubt whether there is a single other poem of equal length by a contemporary American which displays so high and so varied a mastery of English verse. The poem is—in spite of its lack of structural unity—simply one triumph after another—from the white April light of the opening and the sweet wistfulness of the nightingale passage—one of the only successful pieces of contemporary blank verse—to the shabby sadness of the Thames Maidens, the cruel irony of Tiresias' vision, and the dry grim stony style of the descriptions of the Waste Land itself.

That is why Mr Eliot's trivialities are more valuable than other people's epics—why Mr Eliot's detestation of Sweeney is more precious than Mr Sandburg's[5] sympathy for him, and Mr Prufrock's tea-table tragedy more important than all the passions of the New Adam[6]—sincere and carefully expressed as these latter emotions indubitably are. That is also why, for all its complicated correspondences and its recondite references and quotations, The Waste Land is intelligible at first reading. It is not necessary to know anything about the Grail Legend or any but the most obvious of Mr Eliot's allusions to feel the force of the intense emotion which the poem is intended to convey—as one cannot do, for example, with the extremely ill-focussed Eight Cantos of his imitator Mr Ezra Pound, who presents only a bewildering mosaic with no central emotion to provide a key. In Eliot the very images and the sound of the words— even when we do not know precisely why he has chosen them—are charged with a strange poignancy which seems to bring us into the heart of the singer. And sometimes we feel that he is speaking not only for a personal distress, but for the starvation of a whole civilization—for people grinding at barren office-routine in the cells of gigantic cities, drying up their souls in eternal toil whose products never bring them profit, where their pleasures are so vulgar and so feeble that they are almost sadder than their pains. It is our whole world of strained nerves and shattered institutions, in which "some infinitely gentle, infinitely suffering thing" is somehow being done to death—in which the maiden Philomel "by the barbarous king so rudely forced" can no longer even fill the desert "with inviolable voice." It is the world in which the pursuit of grace and beauty is something which is felt to be obsolete—the reflections which reach us from the past cannot illumine so dingy a scene; that heroic prelude has ironic echoes among the streets and the drawing-rooms where we live. Yet the race of the poets—though grown rarer—is

5. Reference to the democratic principles of the American poet Carl Sandburg (1878–1967).
6. Reference to *The New Adam* (1920), by the American poet Louis Untermeyer (1885–1977).

not yet quite dead: there is at least one who, as Mr Pound says, has brought a new personal rhythm into the language and who has lent even to the words of his great predecessors a new music and a new meaning.

ELINOR WYLIE

Mr. Eliot's Slug-Horn[†]

The reviewer who must essay, within the limits of a few hundred temperate and well-chosen words, to lead even a willing reader into the ensorcelled[1] mazes of Mr. T. S. Eliot's 'Waste Land' perceives, as the public prints have it, no easy task before him. He will appear to the mental traveller as dubious a guide as Childe Roland's hoary cripple with malicious eye;[2] he lies in every word, unless by some stroke of luck, some lightning flash of revelation, he succeeds in showing forth the tragic sincerity and true power of that mysterious and moving spectacle, 'The Waste Land,' the mind of Mr. Eliot, the reflected and refracted mind of a good—or rather a bad—quarter of the present generation.

Amazing comparisons have been drawn between Mr. Eliot and certain celebrated poets; his admirers do not couple him with Pound nor his detractors with Dante, and both are justified in any annoyance which they may feel when others do so. His detractors say that he is obscure; his friends reply that he is no more cryptic than Donne and Yeats; his detractors shift their ground and point out with perfect truth that he has not the one's incomparable wit nor the other's incomparable magic; his friends, if they are wise, acquiesce. It is stated that he is not so universal a genius as Joyce; the proposition appears self-evident to any one who believes with the present reviewer, that Joyce is the sea from whose profundity Eliot has fished up that very Tyrian murex with which Mr. Wilson rightly credits him.[3] Some comparisons, indeed, suggest the lunatic asylums where gentlemen imagine themselves to be the authors of Caesar's Commentaries and the Code Napoléon.

But when we begin to inquire what Mr. Eliot is, instead of what he is not—then if we fail to respond to his accusing cry of '*Mon*

[†] From *New York Evening Post Literary Review* (January 20, 1923): 396. Notes are by the editor of this Norton Critical Edition.

1. Bewitched.

2. From Robert Browning's poem "Childe Roland to the Dark Tower Came" (1855), in which the protagonist confronts such a cripple at the beginning of his quest.

3. See Wilson's essay "The Poetry of Drouth," p. 189 above.

semblable—mon frère!'[4] I am inclined to think that we are really
either hypocrite readers or stubborn ones closing deliberate eyes
against beauty and passion still pitifully alive in the midst of horror.
I confess that once upon a time I believed Mr. Eliot to be a brutal
person: this was when I first read the 'Portrait of a Lady.' I now
recognize my error, but my sense of the hopeless sadness and
humiliation of the poor lady was perfectly sound. I felt that
Mr. Eliot had torn the shrinking creature's clothes from her back
and pulled the drawing-room curtains aside with a click to admit a
flood of shameful sunlight, and I hated him for his cruelty. Only now
that I know he is Tiresias have I lost my desire to strike him blind as
Peeping Tom.

   This power of suggesting intolerable tragedy at the heart of the
trivial or the sordid is used with a skill little less than miraculous in
'The Waste Land,' and the power is the more moving because of the
attendant conviction, that this terrible resembling contrast between
nobility and baseness is an agony in the mind of Mr. Eliot of which
only a portion is transferred to that of the reader. He is a cadaver,
dissecting himself in our sight; he is the god Atthis who was buried
in Stetson's garden[5] and who now arises to give us the benefit of an
anatomy lesson. Of course it hurts him more than it does us, and
yet it hurts some of us a great deal at that. If this is a trick, it is an
inspired one. I do not believe that it is a trick; I think that Mr. Eliot
conceived 'The Waste Land' out of an extremity of tragic emotion
and expressed it in his own voice and in the voices of other unhappy
men not carefully and elaborately trained in close harmony, but com-
ing as a confused and frightening and beautiful murmur out of the
bowels of the earth. 'I did not know death had undone so many.' If
it were merely a piece of virtuosity it would remain astonishing; it
would be a work of art like a fine choir of various singers or a rose
window executed in bright fragments of glass. But it is far more than
this; it is infused with spirit and passion and despair, and it shoots
up into stars of brilliance or flows down dying falls of music which
nothing can obscure or silence. These things, rather than other
men's outcries, are shored against any ruin which may overtake
Mr. Eliot at the hands of Fate or the critics. As for the frequently
reiterated statement that Mr. Eliot is a dry intellectual, without
depth or sincerity of feeling, it is difficult for me to refute an idea
which I am totally at a loss to understand; to me he seems almost
inexcusably sensitive and sympathetic and quite inexcusably poi-
gnant, since he forces me to employ this horrid word to describe
certain qualities which perhaps deserve a nobler tag in mingling pity

4. See above, p. 47.
5. See above, p. 47.

with terror. That he expresses the emotion of an intellectual is perfectly true, but of the intensity of that emotion there is, to my mind, no question, nor do I recognize any reason for such a question. A very simple mind expresses emotion by action: a kiss or a murder will not make a song until they have passed through the mind of a poet, and a subtle mind may make a simple song about a murder because the murder was a simple one. But the simplicity of the song will be most apparent to the subtlest minds; it will be like a queer masquerading as a dairy maid. But as for Mr. Eliot, he has discarded all disguises; nothing could be more personal and direct than his method of presenting his weariness and despair by means of a stream of memories and images the like of which, a little dulled and narrowed, runs through the brain of any educated and imaginative man whose thoughts are sharpened by suffering. I should perhaps have doubted the suitability of such a stream as material for poetry, just as I do now very much doubt the suitability of Sanskrit amens and abracadabras, but these dubieties are matters of personal taste and comparatively unimportant beside the fact that, though Mr. Eliot may speak with the seven tongues of men and of angels, he has not become as sounding brass and tinkling cymbal. His gifts, whatever they are, profit him much; his charity, like Tiresias, has suffered and foresuffered all. If he is intellectually arrogant and detached—and I cannot for the life of me believe that he is—he is not spiritually either the one or the other; I could sooner accuse him of being sentimental. Indeed, in his tortured pity for ugly and ignoble things he sometimes comes near to losing his hardness of outline along with his hardness of heart; his is not a kindly tolerance for weakness and misery, but an obsessed and agonized sense of kinship with it which occasionally leads him into excesses of speech, ejaculations whose flippancy is the expression of profound despair.

Were I unable to feel this passion shaking the dry bones of 'The Waste Land' like a great wind I would not give a penny for all the thoughts and riddles of the poem; the fact that Mr. Eliot has failed to convince many readers that he has a soul must be laid as a black mark against him. Either you see him as a parlor prestidigitator, a character in which I am personally unable to visualize him, or else you see him as a disenchanted wizard, a disinherited prince. When he says *Shantih* three times as he emerges from 'The Waste Land' you may not think he means it: my own impulse to write *Amen* at the end of a poem has been too often and too hardly curbed to leave any doubt in my mind as to Mr. Eliot's absorbed seriousness; he is fanatically in earnest. His 'Waste Land' is Childe Roland's evil ground, the names of all the lost adventurers his peers toll in his mind increasing like a bell. He has set the slug-horn to his lips and

blown it once and twice: the squat, round tower, blind as the fool's
heart, is watching him, but he will blow the horn again.[6]

CONRAD AIKEN

An Anatomy of Melancholy[†]

Mr. T. S. Eliot is one of the most individual of contemporary poets,
and at the same time, anomalously, one of the most 'traditional.' By
individual I mean that he can be, and often is (distressingly, to some)
aware in his own way; as when he observes of a woman (in 'Rhap-
sody on a Windy Night') that the door 'opens on her like a grin' and
that the corner of her eye 'Twists like a crooked pin.' Everywhere, in
the very small body of his work, is similar evidence of a delicate sen-
sibility, somewhat shrinking, somewhat injured, and always sharply
itself. But also, with this capacity or necessity for being aware in his
own way, Mr. Eliot has a haunting, a tyrannous awareness that there
have been many other awarenesses before; and that the extent of his
own awareness, and perhaps even the nature of it, is a consequence
of these. He is, more than most poets, conscious of his roots. If this
consciousness had not become acute in 'Prufrock' or the 'Portrait
of a Lady,' it was nevertheless probably there: and the roots were
quite conspicuously French, and dated, say, 1870–1900. A little later,
as if his sense of the past had become more pressing, it seemed that
he was positively redirecting his roots—urging them to draw a mor-
bid dramatic sharpness from Webster and Donne, a faded dry gilt
of cynicism and formality from the Restoration. This search of the
tomb produced "Sweeney' and 'Whispers of Immortality.' And finally,
in 'The Waste Land,' Mr. Eliot's sense of the literary past has become
so overmastering as almost to constitute the motive of the work. It
is as if, in conjunction with the Mr. Pound of the 'Cantos,'[1] he
wanted to make a 'literature of literature'—a poetry not more actu-
ated by life itself than by poetry; as if he had concluded that the
characteristic awareness of a poet of the 20th century must inevita-
bly, or ideally, be a very complex and very literary awareness able to
speak only, or best, in terms of the literary past, the terms which
had moulded its tongue. This involves a kind of idolatry of

---

6. At the end of Browning's poem, Roland blows his "slug-horn." The word is in fact an
   early form of the word "slogan," but Browning uses it as if it means trumpet. In any
   case, the blowing of it is supposed to be a doomed, romantic gesture.
† From *The New Republic* (February 7, 1923): 294–95. Notes are by the editor of this
   Norton Critical Edition.
1. Ezra Pound published his modernist literary epic in separate "Cantos" between 1917
   and 1969.

literature with which it is a little difficult to sympathize. In posit-
ing, as it seems to, that there is nothing left for literature to do but
become a kind of parasitic growth on literature, a sort of mistletoe, it
involves, I think, a definite astigmatism—a distortion. But the the-
ory is interesting if only because it has colored an important and
brilliant piece of work.

'The Waste Land' is unquestionably important, unquestionably
brilliant. It is important partly because its 433 lines summarize
Mr. Eliot, for the moment, and demonstrate that he is an even bet-
ter poet than most had thought; and partly because it embodies the
theory just touched upon, the theory of the 'allusive' method in
poetry. 'The Waste Land' is, indeed, a poem of allusion all compact.
It purports to be symbolical; most of its symbols are drawn from liter-
ature or legend; and Mr. Eliot has thought it necessary to supply, in
notes, a list of the many quotations, references, and translations
with which it bristles. He observes candidly that the poem presents
'difficulties,' and requires 'elucidation.' This serves to raise at once,
the question whether these difficulties, in which perhaps Mr. Eliot
takes a little pride, are so much the result of complexity, a fine elab-
orateness, as of confusion. The poem has been compared, by one
reviewer, to a 'full-rigged ship built in a bottle,' the suggestion being
that it is a perfect piece of construction. But *is* it a perfect piece of
construction? Is the complex material mastered, and made coher-
ent? Or, if the poem is not successful in that way, in what way *is* it
successful? Has it the formal and intellectual complex unity of a
microscopic 'Divine Comedy'; or is its unity—supposing it to have
one—of another sort?

If we leave aside for the moment all other considerations, and read
the poem solely with the intention of understanding, with the aid of
the notes, the symbolism, of making out what it is that is symbol-
ized, and how these symbolized feelings are brought into relation
with each other and with the other matters in the poem; I think we
must, with reservations, and with no invidiousness, conclude that
the poem is not, in any formal sense, coherent. We cannot feel
that all the symbolisms belong quite inevitably where they have been
put; that the order of the parts is an inevitable order; that there is any-
thing more than a rudimentary progress from one theme to another;
nor that the relation between the more symbolic parts and the less
is always as definite as it should be. What we feel is that Mr. Eliot
has not wholly annealed the allusive matter, has left it unabsorbed,
lodged in gleaming fragments amid material alien to it. Again, there
is a distinct weakness consequent on the use of allusions which may
have both intellectual and emotional value for Mr. Eliot, but (even
with the notes) none for us. The 'Waste Land,' of the Grail Legend,
might be a good symbol, if it were something with which we were

sufficiently familiar. But it can never, even when explained, be a
good symbol, simply because it has no immediate associations for
us. It might, of course, be a good *theme*. In that case it would be
given us. But Mr. Eliot uses it for purposes of overtone; he refers to
it; and as overtone it quite clearly fails. He gives us, superbly, a waste
land—not *the* Waste Land. Why, then, refer to the latter at all—if
he is not, in the poem, really going to use it? Hyacinth fails in the
same way. So does the Fisher King. So does the Hanged Man, which
Mr. Eliot tells us he associates with Frazer's Hanged God—we take
his word for it. But if the precise association is worth anything, it is
worth *putting into the poem*; otherwise there can be no purpose in
mentioning it. Why, again, Datta, Dayadhvam, Damyata? Or Shan-
tih. Do they not say a good deal less for us than 'Give: sympathize:
control' or 'Peace'? Of course; but Mr. Eliot replies that he wants
them not merely to mean those particular things, but also to mean
them in a particular way—that is, to be remembered in connection
with a Upanishad. Unfortunately, we have none of us this memory,
nor can he give it to us; and in the upshot he gives us only a series
of agreeable sounds which might as well have been nonsense. What
we get at, and I think it is important, is that in none of these partic-
ular cases does the reference, the allusion, justify itself intrinsically,
make itself felt. When we are aware of these references at all (some-
times they are unidentifiable) we are aware of them simply as some-
thing unintelligible but suggestive. When they have been explained,
we are aware of the material referred to, the fact, (for instance, a
vegetation ceremony,) as something useless for our enjoyment or
understanding of the poem, something distinctly 'dragged in,' and
only, perhaps, of interest as having suggested a pleasantly ambigu-
ous line. For unless an allusion is made to live identifiably, to flower,
where transplanted, it is otiose. We admit the beauty of the impli-
cational or allusive method; but the key to an implication should be
in the implication itself, not outside of it. We admit the value of eso-
teric pattern: but the pattern should itself disclose its secret, should
not be dependent on a cypher. Mr. Eliot assumes for his allusions,
and for the fact that they actually allude to something, an impor-
tance which the allusions themselves do not, as expressed, aestheti-
cally command, nor, as explained, logically command; which is
pretentious. He is a little pretentious, too, in his 'plan,'—'qui
pourtant n'existe pas.'[2] If it is a plan, then its principle is oddly akin
to planlessness. Here and there, in the wilderness, a broken finger-
post.

I enumerate these objections not, I must emphasize, in deroga-
tion of the poem, but to dispel, if possible, an illusion as to its nature.

---

2. Which, nonetheless, does not exist (French).

It is perhaps important to note that Mr. Eliot, with his comment on the 'plan,' and several critics, with their admiration of the poem's woven complexity, minister to the idea that 'The Waste Land' is, precisely, a kind of epic in a walnut shell: elaborate, ordered, unfolded with a logic at every joint discernible; but it is also important to note that this idea is false. With or without the notes the poem belongs rather to that symbolical order in which one may justly say that the 'meaning' is not explicitly, or exactly, worked out. Mr. Eliot's net is wide, its meshes are small; and he catches a good deal more—thank heaven—than he pretends to. If space permitted one could pick out many lines and passages and parodies and quotations which do not demonstrably, in any 'logical' sense, carry forward the theme, passages which unjustifiably, but happily, 'expand' beyond its purpose. Thus the poem has an emotional value far clearer and richer than its arbitrary and rather unworkable logical value. One might assume that it originally consisted of a number of separate poems which have been telescoped—given a kind of forced unity. The Waste Land conception offered itself as a generous net which would, if not unify, at any rate contain these varied elements. We are aware of a superficial 'binding'—we observe the anticipation and repetition of themes, motifs; 'Fear death by water' anticipates the episode of Phlebas, the cry of the nightingale is repeated, but these are pretty flimsy links, and do not genuinely bind because they do not reappear naturally, but arbitrarily. This suggests, indeed, that Mr. Eliot is perhaps attempting a kind of program music in words, endeavoring to rule out 'emotional accidents' by supplying his readers, in notes, with only those associations which are correct. He himself hints at the musical analogy when he observes that 'In the first part of Part V three themes are employed.'

I think, therefore, that the poem must be taken,—most invitingly offers itself,—as a brilliant and kaleidoscopic confusion; as a series of sharp, discrete, slightly related perceptions and feelings, dramatically and lyrically presented, and violently juxtaposed, (for effect of dissonance) so as to give us an impression of an intensely modern, intensely literary consciousness which perceives itself to be not a unit but a chance correlation or conglomerate of mutually discolorative fragments. We are invited into a mind, a world, which is a 'broken bundle of mirrors'; a 'heap of broken images,' Isn't it that Mr. Eliot, finding it 'impossible to say just what he means,'[3]—to recapitulate, to enumerate all the events and discoveries and memories that make a consciousness,—has emulated the 'magic lantern' that throws 'the nerves in patterns on a screen'? If we perceive the poem in this light, as a series of brilliant, brief, unrelated or dimly

3. A reference to l. 104 of "The Love Song of J. Alfred Prufrock" (see above, p. 8).

related pictures by which a consciousness empties itself of its characteristic contents, then we also perceive that, anomalously, though the dropping out of any one picture would not in the least affect the logic or 'meaning' of the whole, it would seriously detract from the value of the portrait. The 'plan' of the poem would not greatly suffer, one makes bold to assert, by the elimination of 'April is the cruellest month,' or Phlebas, or the Thames daughters, or Sosostris or 'You gave me hyacinths' or 'A woman drew her long black hair out tight'; nor would it matter if it did. These things are not important parts of an important or careful intellectual pattern, but they are important parts of an important emotional ensemble. The relations between Tiresias (who is said to unify the poem, in a sense, as spectator) and the Waste Land, or Mr. Eugenides, or Hyacinth, or any other fragment, is a dim and tonal one, not exact. It will not bear analysis, it is not always operating, nor can one with assurance, at any given point, say how much it is operating. In this sense 'The Waste Land' is a series of separate poems or passages, not perhaps all written at one time or with one aim, to which a spurious but happy sequence has been given. This spurious sequence has a value—it creates the necessary superficial formal unity; but it need not be stressed, as the Notes stress it. Could one not wholly rely for one's unity,—as Mr. Eliot *has* largely relied—simply on the dim unity of 'personality' which would underlie the retailed contents of a single consciousness? Unless one is going to carry unification very far, weave and interweave very closely, it would perhaps be as well not to unify at all; to dispense, for example, with arbitrary repetitions.

We reach thus the conclusion that the poem succeeds—as it brilliantly does—by virtue of its incoherence, not of its plan; by virtue of its ambiguities, not of its explanations. Its incoherence is a virtue because its 'donnée' is incoherence. Its rich, vivid, crowded use of implication is a virtue, as implication is *always* a virtue;—it shimmers, it suggests, it gives the desired strangeness. But when, as often, Mr. Eliot uses an implication beautifully—conveys by means of a picture-symbol or action-symbol a feeling—we do not require to be told that he had in mind a passage in the Encyclopedia, or the color of his nursery wall; the information is disquieting, has a sour air of pedantry. We 'accept' the poem as we would accept a powerful, melancholy tone-poem. We do not want to be told what occurs; nor is it more than mildly amusing to know what passages are, in the Straussian manner, echoes or parodies. We cannot believe that every syllable has an algebraic inevitability, nor would we wish it so. We could dispense with the French, Italian, Latin and Hindu phrases—they are irritating. But when our reservations have all been made, we accept 'The Waste Land' as one of the most moving and original poems of our time. It captures us. And we sigh, with a dubious eye

on the 'notes' and 'plan,' our bewilderment that after so fine a per-
formance Mr. Eliot should have thought it an occasion for calling
'Tullia's ape a marmosyte.' Tullia's ape is good enough.[4]

MALCOLM COWLEY

[The Dilemma of *The Waste Land*]†

No other American poet had so many disciples as Eliot, in so many
stages of his career. Until 1925 his influence seemed omnipresent,
and it continued to be important in the years that followed. But in
1922, at the moment when he was least known to the general public
and most fervently worshiped by young poets, there was a sudden
crisis. More than half of his disciples began slowly to drop away.

When *The Waste Land* first appeared, we were confronted with a
dilemma. Here was a poem that agreed with all our recipes and pre-
scriptions of what a great modern poem should be. Its form was not
only perfect but was far richer musically and architecturally than
that of Eliot's earlier verse. Its diction was superb. It employed in a
magisterial fashion the technical discoveries made by the French
writers who followed Baudelaire.[1] Strangeness, abstractness, simpli-
fication, respect for literature as an art with traditions—it had all
the qualities demanded in our slogans. We were prepared fer-
vently to defend it against the attacks of the people who didn't
understand what Eliot was trying to do—but we made private res-
ervations. The poem had forced us into a false position, had brought
our consciously adopted principles into conflict with our instincts.
At heart—not intellectually, but in a purely emotional fashion—we
didn't like it. We didn't agree with what we regarded as the princi-
pal idea that the poem set forth.

The idea was a simple one. Beneath the rich symbolism of *The
Waste Land*, the wide learning expressed in seven languages,
the actions conducted on three planes, the musical episodes, the
geometrical structure—beneath and by means of all this, we felt
the poet was saying that the present is inferior to the past. The past
was dignified; the present is barren of emotion. The past was a land-
scape nourished by living fountains; now the fountains of spiritual

---

4. "He tickles this age that can / Call Tullia's ape a marmosite / And Leda's goose a swan"
(from an anonymous 17th-century song).
† From *Exile's Return: A Literary Odyssey of the 1920's* (New York: Viking, 1951), pp. 112–15.
Copyright © 1934, 1935, 1941, 1951, renewed © 1962, 1963, 1969, 1979 by Malcolm
Cowley. Used by permission of Viking Books, an imprint of Penguin Publishing Group,
a division of Penguin Random House LLC. All rights reserved. Unless otherwise indi-
cated, notes are by the editor of this Norton Critical Edition.
1. See above, p. 83.

grace are dry. . . . Often in his earlier poems Eliot had suggested this idea; he had used such symbols of dead glory as the Roman eagles and trumpets or the Lion of St. Mark's to emphasize the vulgarities of the present. In those early poems, however, the present was his real subject. Even though he seemed to abhor it, even though he thought "of all the hands that are raising dingy shades in a thousand furnished rooms"[2] and was continually "aware of the damp souls of housemaids sprouting despondently at area gates," still he was writing about the life that all of us knew—and more than that, he was endowing our daily life with distinction by means of the same distinguished metaphors in which he decried and belittled it. *The Waste Land* marked a real change. This time he not only expressed the idea with all his mature resources but carried it to a new extreme. He not only abused the present but robbed it of vitality. It was as if he were saying, this time, that our age was prematurely senile and could not even find words of its own in which to bewail its impotence; that it was forever condemned to borrow and patch together the songs of dead poets.

The seven-page appendix to *The Waste Land*, in which Eliot paraded his scholarship and explained the Elizabethan or Italian sources of what had seemed to be his most personal phrases, was a painful dose for us to swallow. But the truth was that the poet had not changed so much as his younger readers. We were becoming less preoccupied with technique and were looking for poems that portrayed our own picture of the world. As for the question proposed to us by Eliot, whether the values of past ages were superior or inferior to present values, we could bring no objective evidence to bear on it. Values are created by living men. If they believe—if their manner of life induces them to believe—that greatness died with Virgil or Dante or Napoleon, who can change their opinion or teach them new values? It happened that we were excited by the adventure of living in the present. The famous "postwar mood of aristocratic disillusionment" was a mood we had never really shared. It happened that Eliot's subjective truth was not our own.

I say "it happened" although, as a matter of fact, our beliefs grew out of the lives we had led. I say "we" although I can refer only to a majority, perhaps two-thirds, of those already influenced by Eliot's poems. When *The Waste Land* was published it revealed a social division among writers that was not a division between rich and poor or—in the Marxian terms that would later be popular—between

2. "Preludes." The next line quoted comes from "Morning at the Window." Both poems appeared originally in *Prufrock and Other Observations* (1917); see above, pp. 13 and 17.

capitalist and proletarian.[3] Not many of the younger writers belonged to either the top or the bottom layer of society. Some of them, it is true, were the children of factory workers or tenant farmers, but even those few had received the education of the middle class and had for the most part adopted its standards. The middle class had come to dominate the world of letters; the dominant educational background was that of the public high school and the big Midwestern university. And the writers of this class—roughly corresponding to Marx's petty bourgeoisie—were those who began to ask where Eliot was leading and whether they should follow.

But there were also many young writers who had been sent to good preparatory schools, usually Episcopalian, before they went on to Yale, Harvard, Princeton, Williams or Dartmouth. Whether rich or poor, they had received the training and acquired the standards of the small but powerful class in American society that might be described as the bourgeoisie proper. These, in general, were the "young poets old before their time" who not only admired *The Waste Land* but insisted on dwelling there in spirit; as Edmund Wilson said, they "took to inhabiting exclusively barren beaches, cactus-grown deserts and dusty attics overrun with rats."[4] Their special education, their social environment and also, I think, their feeling of mingled privilege and insecurity had prepared them to follow Eliot in his desert pilgrimage toward the shrines of tradition and authority.

There were exceptions in both groups, and Eliot continued to be recited and praised behind the dingy shades of a thousand furnished rooms, but most of the struggling middle-class writers were beginning to look for other patterns of literary conduct. We were new men, without inherited traditions, and we were entering a new world of art that did not impress us as being a spiritual desert. Although we did not see our own path, we instinctively rejected Eliot's. In the future we should still honor his poems and the clearness and integrity of his prose, but the Eliot picture had ceased to be our guide.

---

3. It seems to me now that the division was more a matter of temperament, and less a result of social background, than I believed in 1934. The division was real, however, and it reflected attitudes toward life in our own time. When *The Waste Land* appeared, complete with notes, E. E. Cummings asked me why Eliot couldn't write his own lines instead of borrowing from dead poets. In his remarks I sensed a feeling almost of betrayal. Hemingway said in the *Transatlantic Review*, "If I knew that by grinding Mr. Eliot into a fine dry powder and sprinkling that powder over Mr. Conrad's grave Mr. Conrad would shortly appear, looking very annoyed at the forced return, and commence writing, I would leave for London early tomorrow with a sausage grinder." On the other hand John Peale Bishop, of Princeton, who was also in Paris at the time, told me that he was studying Italian so that he could get the full force of the quotations from Dante identified in Eliot's notes [*Author*].

4. From Wilson's essay on Eliot in *Axel's Castle* (New York: Charles Scribner's Sons, 1931), p. 114.

RALPH ELLISON

[*The Waste Land* and Jazz][†]

Mrs. L. C. McFarland had taught us much of Negro history in grade school and from her I'd learned of the New Negro Movement of the twenties, of Langston Hughes, Countee Cullen, Claude McKay, James Weldon Johnson and the others.[1] They had inspired pride and had given me a closer identification with poetry * * * but with music so much on my mind it never occurred to me to try to imitate them. Still I read their work and was excited by the glamour of the Harlem which emerged from their poems and it was good to know that there were Negro writers.—Then came *The Waste Land*.

I was much more under the spell of literature than I realized at the time. *Wuthering Heights* had caused me an agony of unexpressible emotion and the same was true of *Jude the Obscure*, but *The Waste Land* seized my mind. I was intrigued by its power to move me while eluding my understanding. Somehow its rhythms were often closer to those of jazz than were those of the Negro poets, and even though I could not understand then, its range of allusion was as mixed and as varied as that of Louis Armstrong. Yet there were its discontinuities, its changes of pace and its hidden system of organization which escaped me.

There was nothing to do but look up the references in the footnotes to the poem, and thus began my conscious education in literature.

---

† From *Shadow and Act* (New York: Random House, 1964), pp. 159–60. Copyright © 1962 and renewed 1990 by Ralph Ellison. Used by permission of Vintage Books, an imprint of the Knopf Doubleday Publishing Group, a division of Penguin Random House LLC. All rights reserved. Note is by the editor of this Norton Critical Edition.
1. Hughes (1902–1967), Cullen (1903–1946), McKay (1889–1948), and Johnson (1871–1938) published writings in the celebrated anthology *The New Negro* (1925).

Twentieth-Century Criticism

LAURA RIDING AND ROBERT GRAVES

["Burbank with a Baedeker: Bleistein with a Cigar"]†

A poem by Mr. Eliot may be quoted in full as an example of how limited the humorous appeal of modernist verse may become. The extreme particularity of some of the references may be called the teasing element of modernist wit. Here is our poor understanding of the poem. We do not pretend to be wise to all the jokes in Mr. Eliot's poem; undoubtedly the pertinaceous and joke-shrewd reader will be able to carry the scent further; and of course Mr. Eliot himself could, if pressed, make everything clear:

BURBANK WITH A BAEDEKER:
BLEISTEIN WITH A CIGAR.

Tra-la-la-la-la-la-laire—nil nisi divinum stabile est; caetera fumus—the gondola stopped, the old palace was there, how charming its grey and pink—goats and monkeys with such hair too!—so the countess passed on until she came through the little park, where Niobe presented her with a casket, and so departed.

Burbank crossed a little bridge
    Descending at a small hotel;
Princess Volupine arrived,
    They were together, and he fell.

Defunctive music under sea
    Passed seaward with the passing bell
Slowly: the God Hercules
    Had left him, that had loved him well

† From *A Survey of Modern Poetry* (Garden City, NY: Doubleday, Doran, 1928), pp. 235–43. Notes are by the editor of this Norton Critical Edition.

The horses, under the axle-tree
  Beat up the dawn from Istria
With even feet. Her shuttered barge
  Burned on the water all the day.

This is evidently modern Venice visited by two tourists, one an American, who may or may not be called Burbank on account of Burbank the botanist, the other a caricature-Jew. The Latin quotation means: "Nothing is lasting unless it is divine: the rest is smoke." The rest of the introduction, with the exception of 'with such hair too' out of Browning, may be by Ruskin or by some obscure diarist or by Mr. Eliot himself: we cannot be bothered to discover whom.[1] The best that we can do for it is to apply it to the poem. The old palace is one of the many show-places on the Grand Canal: the one possibly where Lord Byron's intrigue with the Countess Guiccoli took place.[2] The goats and monkeys may be part of the zoo that Lord Byron kept there and later conveyed to Pisa; but also may symbolise lechery. Not only are monkeys permanent features, like gargoyles, of Venetian palaces; but monkeys play a symbolic part in the *Merchant of Venice*, and the *Merchant of Venice* is a suppressed *motif*, shaping the poem from behind the scenes, so to speak. Jessica, it will be remembered, turned her back on Jewry, took up with Christians and immediately bought a monkey.[3] The little parks are features of these Venetian palaces. Niobe is the Greek emblem of sorrow; her children were slain as a punishment for her pride in them. The casket is a memorial of Niobe's sympathy with Venice, whose pride has also been brought low. Princess Volupine evidently represents the degenerate aristocratic romanticism of Venice: she has an intrigue with Burbank who stands for the element of sentiment in modern civilization—a sort of symbolical 'decent chap'. 'Defunctive music' is from Shakespeare's *Phoenix and Turtle*. The last line of the first stanza, like the last two of the second and the first two of the third, is possibly also a quotation, but here again we leave pedigrees to more reference-proud critics than ourselves. Burbank's power leaves him. (The God Hercules is the Latin god of strength and also the guardian of money.) The third stanza marks an increase from the second in the mock-grandeur of the writing: at this point it seems to fall in love with itself and threatens to become serious. This in turn demands the sudden bathetic drop of the fourth

---

1. For other possibilities, see editorial notes to the poem, pp. 61–66 above.
2. Teresa, Countess Guiccioli (1800–1873), met the English poet Lord Byron (1788–1824) three days after marrying the Count, who was 50 years her elder.
3. In Shakespeare's *Merchant of Venice*, Jessica turns her back on her father, Shylock, and his faith because of her love for Lorenzo, a Christian. In Act 3, scene 1, she is described as having traded a precious ring belonging to Shylock for a monkey.

stanza. The manner of the third stanza accounts for the especial artificiality of the symbols used: their grandiosity and the obscurity of their source throw a cloud over their precise significance. The horses under the axle-tree may be the horses of the sun under the axle-tree of heaven; but they may also suggest the little heraldic horses fixed at the side of every Venetian gondola, which may be said to be under the axle-tree of the gondola, *i.e.* the oar. So this may be a conceit that amounts to calling the sun a sky-gondola rather than a chariot. Or it may not. Istria lies East from Venice on the road to Vienna. Princess Volupine's shuttered barge burns significantly on the water all day, a sign that she is now closeted with someone else. There is an echo here from *Antony and Cleopatra*:

> 'The barge she sat in, like a burnished throne,
>   Burned on the water . . . !'

At this point the other half of the cast enters the poem: Bleistein the Jew. Burbank walks through Venice with a Baedeker, that is, with a melancholy respect for the past. Bleistein, on the contrary, walks through Venice with a cigar, a symbol of vulgar and ignorant self-enjoyment. The name Bleistein itself is a caricature of the common Goldstein or 'Goldstone': it means 'Leadstone'.

> But this or such was Bleistein's way.
>   A saggy bending of the knees
> And elbows, with the palms turned out,
>   Chicago Semite Viennese.
>
> A lustreless protrusive eye
>   Stares from the protozoic slime
> At a perspective of Canaletto.
>   The smoky candle end of time
>
> Declines. On the Rialto once.
>   The rats are underneath the piles.
> The jew is underneath the lot.
>   Money in furs. The boatman smiles,

Burbank sees the strength and wealth of Venice departed, the remnants of her glory enjoyed by an upstart Chicago Jew who probably started life as a tailor's apprentice in Galicia (whose origin is Austria, whither Hercules first went from Venice in 1814). Canaletto was a painter of the eighteenth century whose aristocratic pictures of Venice are a long way from Bleistein's kind. The smoky candle end recalls the Latin motto: 'the rest is smoke'. Burbank pictures sorrowfully the Rialto of other days. The rats are underneath the piles now, and the Jew (the eternal Shylock) is the rat of rats. The jew (Jew is written with a small initial letter like rat)[4] is apparently a rat because he has made money and because for some reason Jewish wealth, as opposed to Gentile wealth, has a mystical connection with the decline of Venice. This may not be Burbank's private opinion or even Mr. Eliot's. It at any rate expresses for Mr. Burbank and Mr. Eliot the way Venice at present feels or should feel about the modern Jew strutting through its streets. 'Money in furs' refers not only to the fact that the fur trade is largely in Jewish hands and that this is how Bleistein probably made his money, but also to some proverbial witticism, perhaps, about the ability of a Jew to make money even out of rats' skins, out of the instruments of decay, that is. The smiling boatman, who has for centuries seen everything, stands as an ironic fate between Bleistein and Princess Volupine.

> Princess Volupine extends
> A meagre, blue-nailed, pthisic hand
> To climb the waterstair. Lights, lights,
> She entertains Sir Ferdinand

> Klein. Who clipped the lion's wings
> And flea'd his rump and pared his claws?
> Thought Burbank, meditating on
> Time's ruins, and the seven laws.

Venice in the person of Princess Volupine (is this another French comic-opera character; or a coined word compounded of the Latin for 'pleasure,' *Voluptas*, and the name of a play of Ben Jonson's *Volpone, the Fox*; or a character from one of the obscurer dramatists of the *Mermaid Series*?[5] We confess we do not care) has now descended so low that, no longer content with Byronic intrigues with civilization, she actually admits the Jew (in the person of Sir Ferdinand Klein, an English financier) to her embraces. Sir Ferdinand's name is an epitome of contempt and pathetic comedy: the Jew, having made money, has likewise conquered and corrupted English society; his noble Christian name is stolen from the very country which most persecuted him (now also in decay); his family name means 'little' and is, appropriately enough, from the German (there is no sentimental condolence with the Germans because, presumably, they do not suffer from this peculiarly Mediterranean type of decay). So, in the person of Sir Ferdinand Klein, Bleistein succeeds where

---

4. The lowercase *j* was used in all printings of this poem until 1963.
5. A well-known collection of reprints of Elizabethan, Jacobean, and Restoration plays, launched in 1887. The Jonson volume did include his play *Volpone*, first produced in 1605.

Burbank fails; the implication being that the Jew is not an individual but an eternal symbol, each Jew always being the entire race. "Lights, lights!" is a Shakespearianism further evoking the *Merchant of Venice* atmosphere. The lion is the winged lion of St. Mark, the patron saint of Venice; but also, in a secondary sense, the British lion, whose wings have been clipped by the Jew. What the seven laws are in the Venetian context will probably be found in Baedeker or the Classical Dictionary or the *Merchant of Venice* (where rats, the Rialto and pet monkeys also occur).

This is not, of course, popular writing. It is aristocratic writing, and its jokes are exclusive; but only exclusive if the reader has no capacity or interest for sharing in them: the Baedeker is common to all men, so are the Classical Dictionary and La Rousse. The jokes are against modern civilization, against money, against classicism, against romanticism, against Mr. Eliot himself as a tourist in Venice with a Baedeker. One of the privileges of the comedian is to have prejudices without being held morally accountable for them; and the modernist poet is inclined to take full advantage of this privilege, to have caprices without being obliged to render a dull, rationalistic account of them. The anti-Jewish prejudice, for instance, occurs frequently in modernist poetry, and the anti-American prejudice also. It is part of the comedy that a Jew or an American may equally have these prejudices.

Although written in a mood of intellectual severity, modernist poetry retains the clown's privilege of having irrational prejudices in favour of a few things as well as against a few things. It assumes, indeed, the humorous championship of things that the last centuries have either hated, neglected or mishandled. Toward poetical items that have been worn out by spiritual elevation, such as motherhood, childhood, nature, national pride, the soul, fame, freedom and perfection, it maintains a policy of disinterested neutrality; not because of a prejudice against motherhood, nature, etc., but because of a feeling that they have had their day and that it is now the turn of other things like obscenity, lodging-house life, pedantry, vulgarity, frivolousness, failure, drunkenness, and so on, to be put into the scales. This is out of a desire not for sensationalism but for emotional equilibrium. The generation to which the modernist poet belongs is, as we have said, an exceedingly common-sense, 'sensible' generation, to which most things are equally poetic because equally commonplace.

HUGH KENNER

Prufrock of St. Louis[†]

The name of Prufrock-Littau, furniture wholesalers, appeared in advertisements in St. Louis, Missouri, in the first decade of the present century; in 1911 a young Missourian's whimsical feline humor prefixed the name of Prufrock to what has become the best-known English poem since the *Rubaiyat*.[1] The savor of that act had faded from the memory of the sexagenarian London man of letters who wrote to a mid-century enquirer that his appropriation of the now-famous German surname must have been "quite unconscious." There would be no point in denying that it probably was; but the unconscious mind of T. S. Eliot once glimmered with a rich mischief which for many years has been much more cautiously disclosed than it was in 1911.

The query itself must have amused him, however; Mr. Eliot's dealings with people who wanted to know what he was concealing have for two decades afforded some of the richest comedy in the annals of literary anecdote. Letter after letter, visitor after visitor, he answers with unfailing plangent courtesy. After *The Confidential Clerk* was produced, a journalist, teased by implications he couldn't pin down, or perhaps simply assigned a turn of duty at poet-baiting, wanted to know what it meant. It means what it says, said Mr. Eliot patiently. No more? Certainly, no more. But supposing, the journalist pursued, supposing you had meant *something else,* would you not have put some other meaning more plainly? "No," Mr. Eliot replied, "I should have put it just as obscurely."

No other writer's verse has inspired so tenacious a conviction that it means more than it seems to. Certainly no other modern verses so invade the mind, attracting to themselves in the months following their ingestion reminiscence, desire, and speculation. Eliot deals in effects, not ideas; and the effects are in an odd way wholly verbal, seemingly endemic to the language, scrupulously concocted out of the expressive gestures of what a reader whose taste has been educated in the 19th-century classics takes poetry to be.

[†] From *Prairie Schooner* 31.1 (Spring 1957): 24–30. Reprinted by permission of the University of Nebraska Press. Copyright 1957 by the University of Nebraska Press. Notes are by the editor of this Norton Critical Edition.
[1] A St. Louis furniture store by the name of Prufrock-Litton (not -Littau) placed advertisements in the school newspaper of Smith Academy in 1899–1900, when Eliot was a student there. Though Eliot did tell numerous inquirers that he did not remember such a store, he also said in 1959 that he had seen their sign as a boy (*St. Louis Post-Dispatch,* November 29, 1959). The *Rubaiyat*, first published in 1859, is a set of translations from the Persian by Edward FitzGerald. It was wildly popular in the late 19th century.

That is why they will not leave the mind, which grows bored with ideas but will never leave off fondling phrases. How much of the grotesque melancholy of *Prufrock* radiates from the protagonist's name would be difficult to estimate. It was surgical economy that used the marvellous name once only, in the title, and compounded it with a fatuous "J. Alfred." It was a talent already (aetat. 23) finely schooled that with nice audacity weighed in a single phrase the implications of this name against those of "Love Song." It was genius that separated the speaker of the monologue from the writer of the poem by the solitary device of affixing an unforgettable title. Having done that, Eliot didn't need to keep fending off his protagonist with facile irony; the result was a poised intimacy which could draw on every emotion the young author knew without incurring the liabilities of "self-expression."

This complex deftness in the title of his first long poem epitomizes the nature of Eliot's best early verse. Every phrase seems composed as though the destiny of the author's soul depended on it, yet it is unprofitable not to consider the phrases as arrangements of words before considering them as anything else. Like the thousand little gestures that constitute good manners, their meaning is contained in themselves alone. Eliot is the most verbal of the eminent poets: more verbal than Swinburne.[2] If he has carried verbalism far beyond the mere extirpation of jarring consonants, it is because of his intimate understanding of what language can do: how its "tentacular roots," as he once said, reach "down to the deepest terrors and desires."[3] Only a poet who came after the nineteenth century and grew up in its shadow could have acquired this understanding. Eliot acquired it early, and was able to coerce a small masterpiece into existence at a time when, according to his later standards, he understood very little else.

"Prufrock" exploits the 19th century's specialized plangencies at every turn.

> I grow old . . . I grow old . . .
> I shall wear the bottoms of my trousers rolled.

Everyone remembers these lines. They manage to be ridiculous without being funny (the speaker is not making a joke) or cruel (a joke is not being made about the speaker). Their mechanism is allied to the mock-heroic but it doesn't burlesque anything. Like a side-show

---

2. Charles Algernon Swinburne (1837–1909), English poet, generally deprecated by the poets of Eliot's generation as a purveyor of empty verbal and musical effects.
3. In his essay "Ben Jonson" (1919), Eliot compares Jonson unfavorably to Shakespeare and other Elizabethan and Jacobean dramatists who have "a depth, a third dimension, . . . a network of tentacular roots reaching down to the deepest terrors and desires."

mermaid, this non-sequitur of an aging Bostonian floats embalmed in dark sonorities whose cloudiness almost conceals the stitching between mammal and fish. We feel that the two halves won't con-join at the very instant of being persuaded they do. The vowels sound very fine, the syllables are impeccably cadenced; but vaguely within one's pleasure at Tennysonian excellence there struggles an intima-tion of the absurd, with no more chance of winging clear into view than a wasp in a jar of molasses.

The phenomenon of sound obscuring deficiencies of sense from writer and reader is often to be observed in English poetry; the Romantics may be said to have elevated it into a procédé.[4] Mr. Eliot's originality consisted in allowing the deficiency to be concealed only from the speaker. The writer is too cool not to have known what he was about, and as for the reader, his pleasure consists precisely in experiencing a disproportion difficult to isolate. The certainty that Prufrock himself understands it no better than we do checks any pursuit of "metaphysical" analogies between senility and trouser-bottoms; and as for Prufrock's mind, where the collocation is sup-posed to be taking place, its workings are nowhere very profoundly explored. His *sensibility* is plumbed to the uttermost, but that is not what is usually meant when a poet is praised for revealing a human soul. To say that Prufrock is contemplating a young blade's gesture, or alternatively an old castoff's, rolling up his trousers because he either hasn't learned to care for dignity or has out-grown its claims, is to substitute for the poetic effect a formula that fails to exhaust it because incapable of touching it. For the pur-poses of the effect, the pathos of the character of Prufrock is no more than a *donnée*.[5] And the effect is unique, and no reader has ever forgotten it.

"The Love Song of J. Alfred Prufrock" most clings to the memory whenever it exploits, as a foil to undistinguished middle age, the authorized sonorities of the best English verse, circa 1870:

> In the room the women come and go
> Talking of Michelangelo.

The closed and open o's, the assonances of room, women, and come, the pointed caesura before the polysyllabic burst of "Michelangelo" weave a context of grandeur within which our feeling about these trivial women determines itself. The heroic sound, and especially the carefully dramatized sound of the painter's name is what muf-fles these women. The lines scale down severely in French:

---

4. A method or technique (French).
5. Borrowed from the French to designate those aspects of a literary text too fundamental and necessary to be stated explicitly.

> Dans la pièce les femmes vont et viennent
> En parlant des maîtres de Sienne.[6]

That the translator has caught the sense and approximated the movement is an achievement strangely insufficient for lines whose poetic mechanism, one might have thought, depended on so simple a contrast of conceptions: talking women, and a heroic visionary. But Eliot's effects traffic only marginally with conceptions. Hence—again—the elusive disproportion from which his humor arises, a delicate vapor in whose aura the lights twinkle.

* * *

What was bequeathed to the young poets of 1910 by their predecessors in England was a world made out of words; much of Tennyson and most of Swinburne has no more bite on the realities outside the dictionary than have the verses of *Jabberwocky*.[7] It cohered by exploiting the sounds of the words and the implications concealed in their sounds; "A cry that shivered to the tingling stars"[8] would be a strikingly impoverished line if the English language could be suddenly purged of the words "twinkling" and "tinkling." T. S. Eliot from the first has leaned on words in that way; it was the *name* of Prufrock that attracted him; no information about the St. Louis bearers of that name can throw the smallest light on his poem. In the few juvenilia that have been preserved we find him manipulating sounds in Johnson's way—

> The Flowers I sent thee when the dew
>   Was trembling on the vine
> Were withered ere the wild bee flew
>   To pluck the eglantine. . . .   (1905)[9]

or Swinburne's—

> Their petals are fanged and red
> With hideous streak and stain. . . .   (1908)[1]

or Tennyson's—

> The moonflower opens to the moth,
> The mist crawls in from the sea;

---

6. From a 1917 translation by Pierre Leyris.
7. Nonsense poem, originally published in *Through the Looking-Glass* (1871), by Lewis Carroll (1832–1898).
8. From "The Passing of Arthur" in Tennyson's *Idylls of the King* (1869).
9. From "Song," published in *The Harvard Advocate* (June 3, 1907). The Johnson referred to is the English poet Lionel Johnson (1868–1902).
1. From "Circe's Palace," published in *The Harvard Advocate* (November 25, 1908).

> A great white bird, a snowy owl,
> Slips from the alder tree. . . .   (1909)[2]

Two years later he wrote "Prufrock." It was the Tennysonian medium that he learned to use; characteristically, he took what it seemed proper to take at the time, the manner of his immediate elders. He learned to use it; he never made the mistake of trying to think in it. Aware both of its limitations and of its extraordinary emotional inclusiveness, he contrives instead to give the impression that thought is going on alongside the poetic process, that sardonic eyes are being frequently bent on the pretensions toward which rhythmic speech incorrigibly reaches, and that whole areas of human life which the sentiments of romantic verbalism have appropriated are patently, to a rational vision, entoiled in richly muffled absurdity—

> They will say "But how his arms and legs are thin!"

Such is the situation that "Prufrock" dramatizes: a muffling of rational behavior by rhetoric. To the aggrandizement of that situation the poet brings every conceivable wile. The epigraph is a piece of calculated opportunism:

> *S'io credisse che ma risponse fosse. . . .*

> "If I thought that my response would be addressed to one
> who might go back alive, this flame would shake no more;
> but since no one ever goes back alive out of these deeps (if
> what I hear be true), without fear of infamy I answer you."

> *Senza tema d'infamia ti risponso.*

From these Italian words the English speech moves forward without a break—

> Let us go then, you and I. . . .

—effecting a liaison between this situation and Dante's which is all the smoother for the reflective, lingering rhythm of the opening phrase. For the next twenty lines Eliot brings all his melodic resources to the incantation of a quiet fin-de-siècle inferno, equipped with nightmare streets that "follow" and are ominously "half-deserted," and inimical clouds of yellow fog. It is a hell neither sustained by a theology nor graduated by degrees of crime; a genteel accumulation of stage effects, nothing quite in excess. It isn't a punishment so much as a state. Somewhere beyond or around it lies the

---

2. From "Song," published in *The Harvard Advocate* (January 26, 1909).

world where questions have answers, but the moment an "over-whelming question" is mentioned we are cautioned,

Oh, do not ask, "What is it?"

Above this monotonous emotional pedal-point runs a coruscating texture of effects. For twelve lines the word "time" reverberates, struck again and again, while (punctuated once by the startling precision of "To prepare a face to meet the faces that you meet") por-tentousness overlays mere sonority:

> And indeed there will be time
> For the yellow smoke that slides along the street
> Rubbing its back upon the window-panes;
> There will be time, there will be time
> To prepare a face to meet the faces that you meet;
> There will be time to murder and create
> And time for all the works and days of hands
> That lift and drop a question on your plate;
> Time for you and time for me,
> And time yet for a hundred indecisions
> And for a hundred visions and revisions,
> Before the taking of a toast and tea.

What "murder and create" may mean we cannot tell, though it is plain what the phrase can *do*; the words have lost their connection with the active world, lost in fact everything but their potential for neurasthenic shock. "Time for you and time for me" is as hypnotic and as meaningless as a phrase on the cellos. The yellow smoke rub-bing its back upon windowpanes is a half-realizable picture; the detail about the hands and the plate has the air of being a picture but in fact isn't, the thing that is dropped on the plate being "a ques-tion," and the hands—blurred by the phrase "works and days" which is a fusion of Hesiod[3] and Ecclesiastes (III, 1–8)—being not quite those of God and not quite those of a butler.

> And time for all the works and days of hands
> That lift and drop a question on your plate . . .

These gravely irrational words evoke a nervous system snubbed by the Absolute without committing themselves as to whether that Absolute is the moral rigor of an implacable Creator or the system-atized social discomfort of a Boston tea-party.

---

3. *Works and Days* is a didactic poem by the Greek poet Hesiod, who is thought to have lived sometime between 750 and 650 BCE.

The first half of "Prufrock," in fact, is devoted to a systematic con-
fusion of temporal and eternal disciplines; this man's doom is an
endless party-going—

> For I have known them all already, known them all—
> Have known the evenings, mornings, afternoons,

—which he is no more at liberty to modify than one of Dante's sub-
jects can desert his circle of Hell. As he moves wearily through the fog
toward yet another entrance-hall he can toy with images of rebellion

> And indeed there will be time
> To wonder "Do I dare?" and "Do I dare?"
> Time to turn back and descend the stair
> With a bald spot in the middle of my hair
> (They will say: "How his hair is growing thin!")

But one doesn't—the switch from social to cosmic is typical—
"disturb the universe." In Hell you do what you are doing.

I. A. RICHARDS

From The Poetry of T. S. Eliot[†]

Mr. Eliot's poetry has occasioned an unusual amount of irritated or
enthusiastic bewilderment. The bewilderment has several sources.
The most formidable is the unobtrusiveness, in some cases the
absence, of any coherent intellectual thread upon which the items
of the poem are strung. A reader of 'Gerontion,' of 'Preludes,' or of
'The Waste Land,' may, if he will, after repeated readings, introduce
such a thread. Another reader after much effort may fail to contrive
one. But in either case energy will have been misapplied. For the
items are united by the accord, contrast, and interaction of their
emotional effects, not by an intellectual scheme that analysis must
work out. The value lies in the unified response which this interac-
tion creates in the right reader. The only intellectual activity required
takes place in the realisation of the separate items. We can, of
course, make a 'rationalisation' of the whole experience, as we can
of any experience. If we do, we are adding something which does
not belong to the poem. Such a logical scheme is, at best, a scaf-
folding that vanishes when the poem is constructed. But we have so
built into our nervous systems a demand for intellectual coherence,
even in poetry, that we find a difficulty in doing without it.

[†] From *Principles of Literary Criticism* (1926; rpt. New York: Harcourt Brace, 1949),
pp. 289–95. The note is by the editor of this Norton Critical Edition.

This point may be misunderstood, for the charge most usually brought against Mr. Eliot's poetry is that it is overintellectualised. One reason for this is his use of allusion. A reader who in one short poem picks up allusions to *The Aspern Papers, Othello,* 'A Toccata of Galuppi's,' Marston, *The Phœnix and the Turtle, Antony and Cleopatra* (twice), 'The Extasie,' *Macbeth, The Merchant of Venice,* and Ruskin, feels that his wits are being unusually well exercised. He may easily leap to the conclusion that the basis of the poem is in wit also. But this would be a mistake. These things come in, not that the reader may be ingenious or admire the writer's erudition (this last accusation has tempted several critics to disgrace themselves), but for the sake of the emotional aura which they bring and the attitudes they incite. Allusion in Mr. Eliot's hands is a technical device for compression. 'The Waste Land' is the equivalent in content to an epic. Without this device twelve books would have been needed. But these allusions and the notes in which some of them are elucidated have made many a petulant reader turn down his thumb at once. Such a reader has not begun to understand what it is all about.

This objection is connected with another, that of obscurity. To quote a recent pronouncement upon 'The Waste Land' from Mr. Middleton Murry: 'The reader is compelled, in the mere effort to understand, to adopt an attitude of intellectual suspicion, which makes impossible the communication of feeling. The work offends against the most elementary canon of good writing: that the immediate effect should be unambiguous.'[1] Consider first this 'canon.' What would happen, if we pressed it, to Shakespeare's greatest sonnets or to *Hamlet?* The truth is that very much of the best poetry is necessarily ambiguous in its immediate effect. Even the most careful and responsive reader must reread and do hard work before the poem forms itself clearly and unambiguously in his mind. An original poem, as much as a new branch of mathematics, compels the mind which receives it to grow, and this takes time. Anyone who upon reflection asserts the contrary for his own case must be either a demigod or dishonest; probably Mr. Murry was in haste. His remarks show that he has failed in his attempt to read the poem, and they reveal, in part, the reason for his failure—namely, his own overintellectual approach. To read it successfully he would have to discontinue his present self-mystifications.

The critical question in all cases is whether the poem is worth the trouble it entails. For 'The Waste Land' this is considerable. There is Miss Weston's *From Ritual to Romance* to read, and its 'astral' trimmings to be discarded—they have nothing to do with Mr. Eliot's

---

1. J. Middleton Murry, "The 'Classical' Revival," *Adelphi* 3 (February 1926): 585–95; and (March 1926): 648–53.

poem. There is Canto xxvi of the *Purgatorio* to be studied—the rel-
evance of the close of that canto to the whole of Mr. Eliot's work
must be insisted upon. It illuminates his persistent concern with sex,
the problem of our generation, as religion was the problem of the
last. There is the central position of Tiresias in the poem to be puz-
zled out—the cryptic form of the note which Mr. Eliot writes on
this point is just a little tiresome. It is a way of underlining the fact
that the poem is concerned with many aspects of the one fact of sex,
a hint that is perhaps neither indispensable nor entirely successful.

When all this has been done by the reader, when the materials
with which the words are to clothe themselves have been collected,
the poem still remains to be read. And it is easy to fail in this under-
taking. An 'attitude of intellectual suspicion' must certainly be
abandoned. But this is not difficult to those who still know how to
give their feelings precedence to their thoughts, who can accept and
unify an experience without trying to catch it in an intellectual net
or to squeeze out a doctrine. One form of this attempt must be men-
tioned. Some, misled no doubt by its origin in a Mystery, have
endeavoured to give the poem a symbolical reading. But its symbols
are not mystical, but emotional. They stand, that is, not for ineffa-
ble objects, but for normal human experience. The poem, in fact, is
radically naturalistic; only its compression makes it appear other-
wise. And in this it probably comes nearer to the original Mystery
which it perpetuates than transcendentalism does.

If it were desired to label in three words the most characteristic
feature of Mr. Eliot's technique, this might be done by calling his
poetry a 'music of ideas.' The ideas are of all kinds, abstract and con-
crete, general and particular, and, like the musician's phrases, they
are arranged, not that they may tell us something, but that their
effects in us may combine into a coherent whole of feeling and atti-
tude and produce a peculiar liberation of the will. They are there to
be responded to, not to be pondered or worked out. * * *

How this technique lends itself to misunderstandings we have
seen. But many readers who have failed in the end to escape bewil-
derment have begun by finding on almost every line that Mr. Eliot
has written—if we except certain youthful poems on American
topics—that personal stamp which is the hardest thing for the crafts-
man to imitate and perhaps the most certain sign that the experi-
ence, good or bad, rendered in the poem is authentic. Only those
unfortunate persons who are incapable of reading poetry can resist
Mr. Eliot's rhythms. The poem as a whole may elude us while every
fragment, as a fragment, comes victoriously home. It is difficult to
believe that this is Mr. Eliot's fault rather than his reader's, because
a parallel case of a poet who so constantly achieves the hardest part
of his task and yet fails in the easier is not to be found. It is much

more likely that we have been trying to put the fragments together on a wrong principle.

Another doubt has been expressed. Mr. Eliot repeats himself in two ways. The nightingale, Cleopatra's barge, the rats, and the smoky candle-end, recur and recur. Is this a sign of a poverty of inspiration? A more plausible explanation is that this repetition is in part a consequence of the technique above described, and in part something which many writers who are not accused of poverty also show. Shelley, with his rivers, towers, and stars, Conrad, Hardy, Walt Whitman, and Dostoevski spring to mind. When a writer has found a theme or image which fixes a point of relative stability in the drift of experience, it is not to be expected that he will avoid it. Such themes are a means of orientation. And it is quite true that the central process in all Mr. Eliot's best poems is the same; the conjunction of feelings which, though superficially opposed,—as squalor, for example, is opposed to grandeur,—yet tend as they develop to change places and even to unite. If they do not develop far enough the intention of the poet is missed. Mr. Eliot is neither sighing after vanished glories nor holding contemporary experience up to scorn.

Both bitterness and desolation are superficial aspects of his poetry. There are those who think that he merely takes his readers into the Waste Land and leaves them there, that in his last poem he confesses his impotence to release the healing waters. The reply is that some readers find in his poetry not only a clearer, fuller realisation of their plight, the plight of a whole generation, than they find elsewhere, but also through the very energies set free in that realisation a return of the saving passion.

F. R. LEAVIS

[The Significance of the Modern Waste Land][†]

[*The Waste Land*] appeared first in the opening numbers of *The Criterion* (October 1922 and January 1923). The title, we know, comes from Miss J. L. Weston's book, *From Ritual to Romance,* the theme of which is anthropological: the Waste Land there has a significance in terms of Fertility Ritual. What is the significance of the modern Waste Land? The answer may be read in what appears as the rich disorganization of the poem. The seeming disjointedness is intimately related to the erudition that has annoyed so many

---

† From *New Bearings in English Poetry* (London: Chatto and Windus, 1932), pp. 90–113. Reprinted courtesy of the Leavis Literary Estate. Unless otherwise indicated, notes are the author's.

readers and to the wealth of literary borrowings and allusions. These characteristics reflect the present state of civilization. The traditions and cultures have mingled, and the historical imagination makes the past contemporary; no one tradition can digest so great a variety of materials, and the result is a breakdown of forms and the irrevocable loss of that sense of absoluteness which seems necessary to a robust culture. * * *

In considering our present plight we have also to take account of the incessant rapid change that characterizes the Machine Age. The result is breach of continuity and the uprooting of life. This last metaphor has a peculiar aptness, for what we are witnessing to-day is the final uprooting of the immemorial ways of life, of life rooted in the soil. * * *

The remoteness of the civilization celebrated in *The Waste Land* from the natural rhythms is brought out, in ironical contrast, by the anthropological theme. Vegetation cults, fertility ritual, with their sympathetic magic, represent a harmony of human culture with the natural environment, and express an extreme sense of the unity of life. In the modern Waste Land

> April is the cruellest month, breeding
> Lilacs out of the dead land,

but bringing no quickening to the human spirit. Sex here is sterile, breeding not life and fulfilment but disgust, accidia and unanswerable questions. It is not easy to-day to accept the perpetuation and multiplication of life as ultimate ends.

But the anthropological background has positive functions. It plays an obvious part in evoking that particular sense of the unity of life which is essential to the poem. It helps to establish the level of experience at which the poem works, the mode of consciousness to which it belongs. In *The Waste Land* the development of impersonality that *Gerontion* shows in comparison with *Prufrock* reaches an extreme limit: it would be difficult to imagine a completer transcendence of the individual self, a completer projection of awareness. We have, in the introductory chapter, considered the poet as being at the conscious point of his age.[1] There are ways in which it is possible to be too conscious; and to be so is, as a result of the breakup of forms and the loss of axioms noted above, one of the troubles of the present age (if the abstraction may be permitted, consciousness being in any case a minority affair). We recognize in modern literature the accompanying sense of futility.

---

1. "Poetry matters because of the kind of poet who is more alive than other people, more alive in his own age. He is, as it were, at the most conscious point of his race in his time" (Leavis, *New Bearings*, p. 13) [*Editor*].

The part that science in general has played in the process of dis-integration is matter of commonplace: anthropology is, in the present context, a peculiarly significant expression of the scientific spirit. To the anthropological eye beliefs, religions and moralities are human habits—in their odd variety too human. Where the anthropological outlook prevails, sanctions wither. In a contemporary consciousness there is inevitably a great deal of the anthropological, and the background of *The Waste Land* is thus seen to have a further significance.

To be, then, too much conscious and conscious of too much—that is the plight:

> After such knowledge, what forgiveness?

At this point Mr. Eliot's note on Tiresias deserves attention:

> Tiresias, although a mere spectator and not indeed a 'character,' is yet the most important personage in the poem, uniting all the rest. Just as the one-eyed merchant, seller of currants, melts into the Phoenician Sailor, and the latter is not wholly distinct from Ferdinand Prince of Naples, so all the women are one woman, and the two sexes meet in Tiresias. What Tiresias *sees*, in fact, is the substance of the poem.

If Mr Eliot's readers have a right to a grievance, it is that he has not given this note more salience; for it provides the clue to *The Waste Land*. It indicates plainly enough what the poem is: an effort to focus an inclusive human consciousness. The effort, in ways suggested above, is characteristic of the age; and in an age of psychoanalysis, an age that has produced the last section of *Ulysses*, Tiresias—'venus huic erat utraque nota'[2]—presents himself as the appropriate impersonation. A cultivated modern is (or feels himself to be) intimately aware of the experience of the opposite sex.

Such an undertaking offers a difficult problem of organization, a distinguishing character of the mode of consciousness that promotes it being a lack of organizing principle, the absence of any inherent direction. A poem that is to contain all myths cannot construct itself upon one. It is here that *From Ritual to Romance* comes in. It provides a background of reference that makes possible something in the nature of a musical[3] organization. Let us start by considering the use of the Tarot pack. Introduced in the first section, suggesting, as it does, destiny, chance and the eternal mysteries, it at once intimates the scope of the poem, the mode of its contemplation of

---

2. For he knew both sides of love (Latin). From the account of Tiresias in Ovid's *Metamorphoses*. For the context, see Sources, "[The Blinding of Tiresias]," p. 86 [*Editor*].

3. Mr I. A. Richards uses the analogy from music in some valuable notes on Mr Eliot that are printed in an appendix to the later editions of *The Principles of Literary Criticism*.

life. It informs us as to the nature of the characters: we know that they are such as could not have relations with one another in any narrative scheme, and could not be brought together on any stage, no matter what liberties were taken with the Unities. The immediate function of the passage introducing the pack, moreover, is to evoke, in contrast with what has preceded, cosmopolitan 'high life,' and the charlatanism that battens upon it:

> Madame Sosostris, famous clairvoyante,
> Had a bad cold, nevertheless
> Is known to be the wisest woman in Europe,
> With a wicked pack of cards.

Mr Eliot can achieve the banality appropriate here, and achieve at the same time, when he wants it, a deep undertone, a resonance, as it were, of fate:

> . . . and this card,
> Which is blank, is something he carries on his back,
> Which I am forbidden to see. I do not find
> The Hanged Man. Fear death by water.
> I see crowds of people, walking round in a ring.

The peculiar menacing undertone of this associates it with a passage in the fifth section:

> Who is the third who walks always beside you?
> When I count, there are only you and I together
> But when I look ahead up the white road
> There is always another one walking beside you
> Gliding wrapt in a brown mantle, hooded
> I do not know whether a man or a woman
> —But who is that on the other side of you?

The association establishes itself without any help from Mr Eliot's note; it is there in any case, as any fit reader of poetry can report; but the note helps us to recognize its significance:

> The Hanged Man, a member of the traditional pack, fits my purpose in two ways: because he is associated in my mind with the Hanged God of Frazer, and because I associate him with the hooded figure in the passage of the disciples to Emmaus in Part V.

The Tarot pack, Miss Weston has established, has affiliations with fertility ritual, and so lends itself peculiarly to Mr Eliot's purpose: the instance before us illustrates admirably how he has used its possibilities. The hooded figure in the passage just quoted is Jesus. Perhaps our being able to say so depends rather too much upon Mr

Eliot's note; but the effect of the passage does not depend so much upon the note as might appear. For Christ has figured already in the opening of the section (see *What the Thunder Said*):

> After the torchlight red on sweaty faces
> After the frosty silence in the gardens
> After the agony in stony places
> The shouting and the crying
> Prison and palace and reverberation
> Of thunder of spring over distant mountains
> He who was living is now dead
> We who were living are now dying
> With a little patience

The reference is unmistakable. Yet it is not only Christ; it is also the Hanged God and all the sacrificed gods: with the 'thunder of spring' 'Adonis, Attis, Osiris' and all the others of *The Golden Bough* come in. And the 'agony in stony places' is not merely the Agony in the Garden; it is also the agony of the Waste Land, introduced in the first section: (*The Burial of the Dead*, ll. 19 ff.).

> What are the roots that clutch, what branches grow
> Out of this stony rubbish? Son of man,
> You cannot say, or guess, for you know only
> A heap of broken images, where the sun beats,
> And the dead tree gives no shelter, the cricket no relief,
> And the dry stone no sound of water.

In *What the Thunder Said* the drouth becomes (among other things) a thirst for the waters of faith and healing, and the specifically religious enters into the orchestration of the poem. But the thunder is 'dry sterile thunder without rain'; there is no resurrection or renewal; and after the opening passage the verse loses all buoyancy, and takes on a dragging, persistent movement as of hopeless exhaustion—

> Here is no water but only rock
> Rock and no water and the sandy road
> The road winding above among the mountains
> Which are mountains of rock without water

—the imagined sound of water coming in as a torment. There is a suggestion of fever here, a sultry ominousness—

> There is not even solitude in the mountains

—and it is this which provides the transition to the passage about the hooded figure quoted above. The ominous tone of this last passage associates it, as we have seen, with the reference (ll. 55–56) to the Hanged Man in the Tarot passage of *The Burial of the Dead.* So Christ becomes the Hanged Man, the Vegetation God; and at the same time the journey through the Waste Land along 'the sandy road' becomes the Journey to Emmaus. Mr Eliot gives us a note on the 'third who walks always beside you':

> The following lines were stimulated by the account of one of the Antarctic expeditions (I forget which, but I think one of Shackleton's): it was related that the party of explorers, at the extremity of their strength, had the constant delusion that there was *one more member* than could actually be counted.

This might be taken to be, from our point of view, merely an interesting irrelevance, and it certainly is not necessary. But it nevertheless serves to intimate the degree of generality that Mr Eliot intends to accompany his concrete precision: he is both definite and vague at once. 'Just as the one-eyed merchant, seller of currants, melts into the Phoenician Sailor, and the latter is not wholly distinct from Ferdinand Prince of Naples'—so one experience is not wholly distinct from another experience of the same general order; and just as all experiences 'meet in Tiresias,' so a multitude of experiences meet in each passage of the poem. Thus the passage immediately in question has still further associations. That same hallucinatory quality which relates it to what goes before recalls also the neurasthenic episode (ll. 111 ff.) in *A Game of Chess* (the second section):

> 'What is that noise?'
>   The wind under the door.
> 'What is that noise now? . . .'

All this illustrates the method of the poem, and the concentration, the depth of orchestration that Mr Eliot achieves; the way in which the themes move in and out of one another and the predominance shifts from level to level. The transition from this passage is again by way of the general ominousness, which passes into hallucinated vision and then into nightmare:

> —But who is that on the other side of you?
>
> What is that sound high in the air
> Murmur of maternal lamentation
> Who are those hooded hordes swarming
> Over endless plains, stumbling in cracked earth
> Ringed by the flat horizon only
> What is the city over the mountains
> Cracks and reforms and bursts in the violet air
> Falling towers

> Jerusalem Athens Alexandria
> Vienna London
> Unreal.

The focus of attention shifts here to the outer disintegration in its large, obvious aspects, and the references to Russia and to post-war Europe in general are plain. The link between the hooded figure of the road to Emmaus and the 'hooded hordes swarming' is not much more than verbal (though appropriate to a fevered consciousness), but this phrase has an essential association with a line (56) in the passage that introduces the Tarot pack:

> I see crowds of people, walking round in a ring.

These 'hooded hordes,' 'ringed by the flat horizon only,' are not merely Russians, suggestively related to the barbarian invaders of civilization; they are also humanity walking endlessly round in a ring, a further illustration of the eternal futility. 'Unreal' picks up the 'Unreal city' of *The Burial of the Dead* (l. 60), where 'Saint Mary Woolnoth kept the hours,' and the unreality gets further development in the nightmare passage that follows:

> And upside down in air were towers
> Tolling reminiscent bells, that kept the hours
> And voices singing out of empty cisterns and exhausted wells.

Then, with a transitional reference (which will be commented on later) to the theme of the Chapel Perilous, the focus shifts inwards again. 'Datta,' 'dayadhvam,' and 'damyata,' the admonitions of the thunder, are explained in a note, and in this case, at any rate, the reliance upon the note justifies itself. We need only be told once that they mean 'give, sympathize, control,' and the context preserves the meaning. The Sanscrit lends an appropriate portentousness, intimating that this is the sum of wisdom according to a great tradition, and that what we have here is a radical scrutiny into the profit of life. The irony, too, is radical:

> *Datta*: what have we given?
> My friend, blood shaking my heart
> The awful daring of a moment's surrender
> Which an age of prudence can never retract
> By this, and this only, we have existed

—it is an equivocal comment. And for comment on 'sympathize' we have a reminder of the irremediable isolation of the individual. After all the agony of sympathetic transcendence, it is to the individual, the focus of consciousness, that we return:

> Shall I at least set my lands in order?

The answer comes in the bundle of fragments that ends the poem, and, in a sense, sums it up.

Not that the *poem* lacks organization and unity. The frequent judgments that it does betray a wrong approach. * * * The unity the poem aims at is that of an inclusive consciousness: the organization it achieves as a work of art is of the kind that has been illustrated, an organization that may, by analogy, be called musical. It exhibits no progression:

> I sat upon the shore
> Fishing, with the arid plain behind me

—the thunder brings no rain to revive the Waste Land, and the poem ends where it began.

At this point the criticism has to be met that, while all this may be so, the poem in any case exists, and can exist, only for an extremely limited public equipped with special knowledge. The criticism must be admitted. But that the public for it is limited is one of the symptoms of the state of culture that produced the poem. Works expressing the finest consciousness of the age in which the word 'high-brow' has become current are almost inevitably such as to appeal only to a tiny minority. It is still more serious that this minority should be more and more cut off from the world around it—should, indeed, be aware of a hostile and overwhelming environment. This amounts to an admission that there must be something limited about the kind of artistic achievement possible in our time: even Shakespeare in such conditions could hardly have been the 'universal' genius. And *The Waste Land*, clearly, is not of the order of *The Divine Comedy* or of *Lear*. The important admission, then, is not that *The Waste Land* can be appreciated only by a very small minority (how large in any age has the minority been that has really comprehended the masterpieces?), but that this limitation carries with it limitations in self-sufficiency.

These limitations, however, are easily overstressed. Most of the 'special knowledge,' dependence upon which is urged against *The Waste Land*, can fairly be held to be common to the public that would in any case read modern poetry. The poem does, indeed, to some extent lean frankly upon *From Ritual to Romance*. And sometimes it depends upon external support in ways that can hardly be justified. Let us take, for instance, the end of the third section, *The Fire Sermon:*

> la la

> To Carthage then I came

> Burning, burning, burning, burning

> O Lord Thou pluckest me out
> O Lord Thou pluckest

> burning

It is plain from Mr Eliot's note on this passage—'The collocation of these two representatives of eastern and western asceticism, as the culmination of this part of the poem, is not an accident'—that he intends St Augustine and the Buddha to be actively present here. But whereas one cursory reading of *From Ritual to Romance* does all (practically) that is assigned as function to that book, no amount of reading of the *Confessions* or *Buddhism in Translation* will give these few words power to evoke the kind of presence of 'eastern and western asceticism' that seems necessary to the poem: they remain, these words, mere pointers to something outside. We can only conclude that Mr Eliot here has not done as much as he supposes. And so with the passage (ll. 385 ff.) in *What the Thunder Said* bringing in the theme of the Chapel Perilous: it leaves too much to Miss Weston; repeated recourse to *From Ritual to Romance* will not invest it with the virtue it would assume. The irony, too, of the

> Shantih   shantih   shantih

that ends the poem is largely ineffective, for Mr Eliot's note that '"The Peace which passeth understanding" is a feeble translation of the content of this word' can impart to the word only a feeble ghost of that content for the Western reader.

Yet the weaknesses of this kind are not nearly as frequent or as damaging as critics of *The Waste Land* seem commonly to suppose. It is a self-subsistent poem, and should be obviously such. The allusions, references and quotations usually carry their own power with them as well as being justified in the appeal they make to special knowledge. 'Unreal City' (l. 60), to take an extreme instance from one end of the scale, owes nothing to Baudelaire (whatever Mr Eliot may have owed); the note is merely interesting—though, of course, it is probable that a reader unacquainted with Baudelaire will be otherwise unqualified. The reference to Dante that follows—

> A crowd flowed over London Bridge, so many,
> I had not thought death had undone so many

—has an independent force, but much is lost to the reader who does not catch the implied comparison between London and Dante's Hell. Yet the requisite knowledge of Dante is a fair demand. The knowledge of *Antony and Cleopatra* assumed in the opening of *A Game of Chess,* or of *The Tempest* in various places elsewhere, no one will boggle at. The main references in *The Waste Land* come within the classes represented by these to Dante and Shakespeare; while of the many others most of the essential carry enough of their power with them. By means of such references and quotations Mr Eliot attains a compression, otherwise unattainable, that is essential to his aim; a compression approaching simultaneity—the co-presence in the mind of a number of different orientations, fundamental attitudes, orders of experience.

This compression and the methods it entails do make the poem difficult reading at first, and a full response comes only with familiarity. Yet the complete rout so often reported, or inadvertently revealed * * * can be accounted for only by a wrong approach, an approach with inappropriate expectations. For the general nature and method of the poem should be obvious at first reading. Yet so commonly does the obvious seem to be missed that perhaps a little more elucidation (this time of the opening section) will not be found offensively superfluous. What follows is a brief analysis of *The Burial of the Dead*, the avowed intention being to point out the obvious themes and transitions: anything like a full analysis would occupy many times the space.

The first seven lines introduce the vegetation theme, associating it with the stirring of 'memory and desire.' The transition is simple: 'April,' 'spring,' 'winter,'—then

> Summer surprised us, coming over the Starnbergersee
> With a shower of rain . . .

We seem to be going straight forward, but (as the change of movement intimates) we have modulated into another plane. We are now given a particular 'memory,' and a representative one. It introduces the cosmopolitan note, a note of empty sophistication:

> In the mountains, there you feel free.
> I read, much of the night, and go south in the winter.
> [Cf. 'Winter kept us warm']

The next transition is a contrast and a comment, bringing this last passage into relation with the first. April may stir dull roots with spring rain, but

> What are the roots that clutch, what branches grow
> Out of this stony rubbish?

And there follows an evocation of the Waste Land, with references to *Ezekiel* and *Ecclesiastes*, confirming the tone that intimates that this is an agony of the soul ('Son of man' relates with the Hanged Man and the Hanged God: with him 'who was living' and 'is now dead' at the opening of *What the Thunder Said*). The 'fear'—

> I will show you fear in a handful of dust

—recurs, in different modes, in the neurasthenic passage (ll. 111 ff.) of *A Game of Chess,* and in the episode of the hooded figure in *What the Thunder Said.* The fear is partly the fear of death, but still more a nameless, ultimate fear, a horror of the completely negative.

Then comes the verse from *Tristan und Isolde,* offering a positive in contrast—the romantic absolute, love. The 'hyacinth girl,' we may say, represents 'memory and desire' (the hyacinth, directly evocative like the lilacs bred out of the Waste Land, was also one of the flowers associated with the slain vegetation god), and the 'nothing' of the Waste Land changes into the ecstasy of passion—a contrast, and something more:

> —Yet when we came back, late, from the Hyacinth garden,
> Your arms full, and your hair wet, I could not
> Speak, and my eyes failed, I was neither
> Living nor dead, and I knew nothing,
> Looking into the heart of light, the silence.

In the Waste Land one is neither living nor dead. Moreover, the neurasthenic passage referred to above recalls these lines unmistakably, giving them a sinister modulation:

> Speak to me. Why do you never speak. Speak.
> 'What are you thinking of? What thinking? What?
> 'I never know what you are thinking. Think.'
>
> .   .   .   .
>
>   'Do
> 'You know nothing? Do you see nothing? Do you remember
> 'Nothing?'

The further line from *Tristan und Isolde* ends the passage of romantic love with romantic desolation. Madame Sosostris, famous clairvoyante, follows; she brings in the demi-monde, so offering a further contrast—

> Here is Belladonna, the Lady of the Rocks,
> The lady of situations

—and introduces the Tarot pack. This passage has already received some comment, and it invites a great deal more. The 'lady of situations,' to make an obvious point, appears in the *Game of Chess.* The admonition, 'Fear death by water,' gets its response in the fourth section, *Death by Water:* death is inevitable, and the life-giving water thirsted for (and the water out of which all life comes) cannot save. But enough has been said to indicate the function of the Tarot pack, the way in which it serves in the organization of the poem.

With the 'Unreal City' the background of urban—of 'megalopolitan'—civilization becomes explicit. The allusion to Dante has already been remarked upon, and so has the way in which Saint Mary Woolnoth is echoed by the 'reminiscent bells' of *What the Thunder Said*. The portentousness of the 'dead sound on the final stroke of nine' serves as a transition, and the unreality of the City turns into the intense but meaningless horror, the absurd inconsequence, of a nightmare:

> There I saw one I knew, and stopped him, crying: 'Stetson!
> 'You who were with me in the ships at Mylae!
> 'That corpse you planted last year in your garden,
> 'Has it begun to sprout? Will it bloom this year? . . .'

These last two lines pick up again the opening theme. The corpse acquires a kind of nightmare association with the slain god of *The Golden Bough*, and is at the same time a buried memory. Then, after a reference to Webster (Webster's sepulchral horrors are robust), *The Burial of the Dead* ends with the line in which Baudelaire, having developed the themes of

> La sottise, l'erreur, le péché, la lésine[4]

and finally *L'Ennui*, suddenly turns upon the reader to remind him that he is something more.

The way in which *The Waste Land* is organized, then, should be obvious even without the aid of notes. And the poet's mastery should be as apparent in the organization as in the parts (where it has been freely acclaimed). The touch with which he manages his difficult transitions, his delicate collocations, is exquisitely sure. His tone, in all its subtle variations, exhibits a perfect control. If there is any instance where this last judgment must be qualified, it is perhaps here (from the first passage of *The Fire Sermon*):

> Sweet Thames, run softly till I end my song,
> Sweet Thames, run softly, for I speak not loud or long.
> But at my back in a cold blast I hear
> The rattle of the bones, and chuckle spread from ear to ear.

These last two lines seem to have too much of the caricature quality of *Prufrock* to be in keeping—for a certain keeping is necessary (and Mr Eliot commonly maintains it) even in contrasts. But even if the comment is just, the occasion for it is a very rare exception.

The Waste Land, then, whatever its difficulty, is, or should be, obviously a poem.[5] It is a self-subsistent poem. Indeed, though it would lose if the notes could be suppressed and forgotten, yet the

---

4. The first line of Baudelaire's "Au Lecteur." For an English translation of the whole poem, see "To the Reader," p. 83 [*Editor*].
5. 'It is a test (a positive test, I do not assert that it is always valid negatively), that genuine poetry can communicate before it is understood.'—T. S. Eliot, *Dante,* p. 16.

more important criticism might be said to be, not that it depends upon them too much, but rather that without them, and without the support of *From Ritual to Romance,* it would not lose more. It has, that is, certain limitations in any case; limitations inherent in the conditions that produced it. Comprehensiveness, in the very nature of the undertaking, must be in some sense at the cost of structure: absence of direction, of organizing principle, in life could hardly be made to subserve the highest kind of organization in art.

But when all qualifications have been urged, *The Waste Land* remains a great positive achievement, and one of the first importance for English poetry. In it a mind fully alive in the age compels a poetic triumph out of the peculiar difficulties facing a poet in the age. And in solving his own problem as a poet Mr Eliot did more than solve the problem for himself. Even if *The Waste Land* had been, as used to be said, a 'dead end' for him, it would still have been a new start for English poetry.

CLEANTH BROOKS, JR.

The Waste Land: An Analysis[†]

To venture to write anything further on *The Waste Land,* particularly after the work of F. R. Leavis and F. O. Matthiessen, may call for some explanation and even apology. I am obviously indebted to both critics. The justification for such a commentary as this must be made primarily in terms of a difference of intention. Leavis is interested predominantly in Eliot's method of organization. One or two passages in the poem are treated in detail and are highly valuable for a knowledge of the "meaning" of the poem, but the bulk of the poem does not receive this kind of examination. Moreover, I believe, Leavis makes some positive errors. Matthiessen examines more of the poem in detail, and, as far as it goes, his account is excellent. But the plan of his *Achievement of T. S. Eliot* does not allow for a consecutive examination either. He puts his finger on the basic theme, death-in-life, but I do not think that he has given it all the salience which it deserves.

I prefer not to raise here the question of how important it is for the reader of the poem to have an explicit intellectual account of the various symbols, and a logical account of their relationships. It may well be that such rationalization is no more than a scaffolding to be got out of the way before we contemplate the poem itself as a

† From *Southern Review* 3 (Summer 1937): 106–36. Reprinted by permission of the Estate of Cleanth Brooks. Notes are by the editor of this Norton Critical Edition.

poem. But many readers (including myself) find the erection of such a scaffolding valuable—if not absolutely necessary—and if some readers will be tempted to lay more stress on the scaffolding than they properly should, there are perhaps still more readers who will be prevented from getting at the poem at all without the help of such a scaffolding. Furthermore, an interest attaches to Mr. Eliot's own mental processes, and whereas Mr. Matthiessen has quite properly warned us that Eliot's poetry cannot be read as autobiography, many of the symbols and ideas which occur in *The Waste Land* are ideas which are definitely central to Eliot's general intellectual position.

The basic symbol used, that of the waste land, is taken, of course, from Miss Jessie Weston's *From Ritual to Romance*. In the legends which she treats there, the land has been blighted by a curse. The crops do not grow, and the animals cannot reproduce. The plight of the land is summed up by, and connected with, the plight of the lord of the land, the Fisher King, who has been rendered impotent by maiming or sickness. The curse can only be removed by the appearance of a knight who will ask the meanings of the various symbols which are displayed to him in the castle. The shift in meaning from physical to spiritual sterility is easily made, and was, as a matter of fact, made in certain of the legends. A knowledge of this symbolism is, as Eliot has already pointed out, essential for an understanding of the poem.

Of hardly less importance to the reader, however, is a knowledge of Eliot's basic method. *The Waste Land* is built on a major contrast—a device which is a favorite of Eliot's and to be found in many of his poems, particularly his later poems. The contrast is between two kinds of life and two kinds of death. Life devoid of meaning is death; sacrifice, even the sacrificial death, may be life-giving, an awaking to life. The poem occupies itself to a great extent with this paradox, and with a number of variations on it.

Eliot has stated the matter quite explicitly himself in one of his essays. In his "Baudelaire" he says: "One aphorism which has been especially noticed is the following: *la volupté unique et suprême de l'amour gît dans la certitude de faire le mal*.[1] This means, I think, that Baudelaire has perceived that what distinguishes the relations of man and woman from the copulation of beasts is the knowledge of Good and Evil (of *moral* Good and Evil which are not natural Good and Bad or puritan Right and Wrong). Having an imperfect, vague romantic conception of Good, he was at least able to understand that the sexual act as evil is more dignified, less boring, than

---

1. The most singular and the highest delight of love lies in the certainty of doing evil (French). A line from Baudelaire's *Intimate Journals*, quoted by Eliot in "Baudelaire" (1930).

as the natural, 'life-giving,' cheery automatism of the modern world . . . So far as we are human, what we do must be either evil or good; so far as we do evil or good, we are human; and it is better, in a paradoxical way, to do evil than to do nothing: at least, *we exist* [*italics mine*]." The last statement is highly important for an understanding of *The Waste Land*. The fact that men have lost the knowledge of good and evil, keeps them from being alive, and is the justification for viewing the modern waste land as a realm in which people do not even exist.

This theme is stated in the quotation which prefaces the poem. The Sybil says: "I wish to die." Her statement has several possible interpretations. For one thing, she is saying what the people who inhabit the waste land are saying. But she also may be saying what the speaker says in "The Journey of the Magi," . . . "this Birth was / Hard and bitter agony for us, like Death, our death / . . . I should be glad of another death."

I

The first section of "The Burial of the Dead" develops the theme of the attractiveness of death, or of the difficulty in rousing oneself from the death in life in which the people of the waste land live. Men are afraid to live in reality. April, the month of rebirth, is not the most joyful season but the cruelest. Winter at least kept us warm in forgetful snow. The idea is one which Eliot has stressed elsewhere. Earlier in "Gerontion" he had written

> In the juvescence of the year
> Came Christ the tiger
> . . . .
> The tiger springs in the new year. Us he devours.

More lately, in *Murder in the Cathedral,* he has the chorus say

> We do not wish anything to happen.
> Seven years we have lived quietly,
> Succeeded in avoiding notice,
> Living and partly living.

And in another passage: "Now I fear disturbance of the quiet seasons." Men dislike to be aroused from their death-in-life.

The first part of "The Burial of the Dead" introduces this theme through a sort of reverie on the part of the protagonist—a reverie in which speculation on life glides off into memory of an actual conversation in the Hofgarten and back into speculation again. The function of the conversation is to establish to some extent the class and character of the protagonist. The reverie is resumed with line 19.

> What are the roots that clutch, what branches grow
> Out of this stony rubbish?

The protagonist answers for himself:

> Son of man,
> You cannot say, or guess, for you know only
> A heap of broken images, where the sun beats,
> And the dead tree gives no shelter, the cricket no relief,
> And the dry stone no sound of water.

In this passage there are references to *Ezekiel* and to *Ecclesiastes,* and these references indicate what it is that men no longer know: the passage referred to in *Ezekiel,* II, pictures a world thoroughly secularized:

> 1. And he said unto me, Son of man, stand upon thy feet, and I will speak unto thee. 2. And the spirit entered into me when he spake unto me, and set me upon my feet, that I heard him that spake unto me. 3. And he said unto me, Son of man, I send thee to the children of Israel, to a rebellious nation that hath rebelled against me: they and their fathers have transgressed against me, even unto this very day.

The following passage from *Ecclesiastes,* XII, is not only referred to in this passage; a reference to it also is evidently made in the nightmare vision of Section V of the poem:

> 1. Remember now thy Creator in the days of thy youth, while the evil days come not, nor the years draw nigh, when thou shalt say, I have no pleasure in them; 2. While the sun, or the light, or the moon, or the stars, be not darkened, nor the clouds return after the rain: 3. In the day when the keepers of the house shall tremble, and the strong men shall bow themselves, and the grinders cease because they are few, and those that look out of the windows be darkened, 4. And the doors shall be shut in the streets, when the sound of the grinding is low, and he shall rise up at the voice of the bird, and all the daughters of music shall be brought low; 5. Also when they shall be afraid of that which is high, and fears shall be in the way, and the almond tree shall flourish, and the grasshopper shall be a burden, *and desire shall fail* [*italics mine*]: because man goeth to his long home, and the mourners go about the streets; 6. Or ever the silver cord be loosed, or the golden bowl be broken, or the pitcher be broken at the fountain, or the wheel broken at the cistern. 7. Then shall the dust return to the earth as it was: and the spirit shall return unto God who gave it. 8. Vanity of vanities, saith the preacher; all is vanity.

The next section which begins with the scrap of song quoted from Wagner (perhaps another item in the reverie of the protagonist), states the opposite half of the paradox which underlies the poem: namely, that life at its highest moments of meaning and intensity resembles death. The song from Act I of Wagner's *Tristan und Isolde,* "*Frisch weht der Wind,*" is sung in the opera by a young sailor aboard the ship which is bringing Isolde to Cornwall. The *"Irisch kind"* of the song does not properly apply to Isolde at all. The song is merely one of happy and naïve love. It brings to the mind of the protagonist an experience of love—the vision of the hyacinth girl as she came back from the hyacinth garden. The poet says

> . . . . my eyes failed, I was neither
> Living nor dead, and I knew nothing,
> Looking into the heart of light, the silence.

The line which immediately follows this passage, "*Oed' und leer das Meer,*" seems at first to be simply an extension of the last figure: that is, "Empty and wide the sea [of silence]." The line, however, as a matter of fact, makes an ironic contrast; for the line, as it occurs in Act III of the opera, is the reply of the watcher who reports to the wounded Tristan that Isolde's ship is nowhere in sight; the sea is empty. And, though the *"Irisch kind"* of the first quotation is not Isolde, the reader familiar with the opera will apply it to Isolde when he comes to the line "*Oed' und leer das Meer.*" For the question in the song is in essence Tristan's question in Act III: My Irish child, where dwellest thou? The two quotations from the opera which frame the ecstasy-of-love passage thus take on a new meaning in the altered context. In the first, love is happy; the boat rushes on with a fair wind behind it. In the second, love is absent; the sea is wide and empty. And the last quotation reminds us that even love cannot exist in the waste land.

The next passage, that in which Madame Sosostris figures, calls for further reference to Miss Weston's book. As Miss Weston has shown, the Tarot cards were originally used to determine the event of the highest importance to the people, the rising of the waters. Madame Sosostris has fallen a long way from the high function of her predecessors. She is engaged merely in vulgar fortune-telling—is merely one item in a generally vulgar civilization. But the symbols of the Tarot pack are still unchanged. The various characters are still inscribed on the cards, and she is reading in reality, though she does not know it, the fortune of the protagonist. She finds that his card is that of the drowned Phoenician Sailor, and so she warns him against death by water, not realizing any more than do the other inhabitants of the modern waste land that the way into life may be by death itself. The drowned Phoenician Sailor is a type of the fertility god whose image was thrown into the sea annually as a symbol of the death of summer. As for the other figures in the pack: Belladonna, the Lady of the Rocks, is woman in the waste land. The man with three staves, Eliot says he associates rather arbitrarily with the Fisher King. The term *arbitrarily* indicates that we are not to attempt to find a logical connection here. (It may be interesting to point out, however, that Eliot seems to have given in a later poem his reason for making the association. In "The Hollow Men" he writes, speaking as one of the Hollow Men:

> Let me also wear
> Such deliberate disguises
> Rat's coat, crowskin, crossed staves
> In a field
> Behaving as the wind behaves.

The figure is that of a scarecrow, fit symbol of the man who possesses no reality, and fit type of the Fisher King, the maimed, impotent king who ruled over the waste land of the legend. The man with three staves in the deck of cards may thus have appealed to the poet as an appropriate figure to which to assign the function of the Fisher King, although the process of identification was too difficult to expect the reader to follow and although knowledge of the process was not necessary to an understanding of the poem.)

The Hanged Man, who represents the hanged god of Frazer (including the Christ), Eliot states in a note, is associated with the hooded figure who appears in "What the Thunder Said." That he is hooded accounts for Madame Sosostris' inability to see him; or rather, here again the palaver of the modern fortune-teller is turned to new and important account by the poet's shifting the matter into a new and serious context. The Wheel and the one-eyed merchant will be discussed later.

After the Madame Sosostris passage, Eliot proceeds to complicate his symbols for the sterility and unreality of the modern waste land by associating it with Baudelaire's *"fourmillante cité"* and with Dante's Limbo. The passages already quoted from Eliot's essay on Baudelaire will indicate one of the reasons why Baudelaire's lines are evoked here. In Baudelaire's city, dream and reality seem to mix, and it is interesting that Eliot in "The Hollow Men" refers to this same realm of death-in-life as "death's dream kingdom" in contradistinction to "death's other kingdom."

The references to Dante are most important. The line, "I had not thought death had undone so many," is taken from the Third Canto of the *Inferno;* the line, "Sighs, short and infrequent, were exhaled," from the Fourth Canto. Mr. Matthiessen has already pointed out that the Third Canto deals with Dante's Limbo which is occupied by those who on earth had "lived without praise or blame." They share this abode with the angels, "Who were not rebels, nor were faithful to God, but were for themselves." They exemplify almost perfectly the secular attitude which dominates the modern world. Their grief, according to Dante, arises from the fact that they "have no hope of death; and their blind life is so debased, that they are envious of every other lot." But though they may not hope for death, Dante calls them "these wretches who never were alive." The people who are treated in the Fourth Canto are those who lived virtuously but who died before the proclamation of the Gospel—they are the unbaptized. This completes the categories of people who inhabit the modern waste land: those who are secularized and those who have no knowledge of the faith. Without a faith their life is in reality a death. To repeat the sentence from Eliot previously quoted: "So far as we do evil or good, we are human; and it is better, in a paradoxical way, to do evil than to do nothing: at least we exist."

The Dante and Baudelaire references, then, come to the same thing as the allusion to the waste land of the medieval legends; and these various allusions drawn from widely differing sources enrich the comment on the modern city so that it becomes "unreal" on a number of levels: as seen through "the brown fog of a winter dawn"; as the medieval waste land and Dante's Limbo and Baudelaire's Paris are unreal.

The reference to Stetson stresses again the connection between the modern London of the poem and Dante's hell. After the statement, "I could never have believed death had undone so many," follow the words "After I had distinguished some among them, I saw and knew the shade of him who made, through cowardice, the great refusal." The protagonist, like Dante, sees among the inhabitants of the contemporary waste land one whom he recognizes. (The name "Stetson" I take to have no ulterior significance. It is merely an ordinary name such as might be borne by the friend one might see in a crowd in a great city.) Mylae, as Mr. Matthiessen has pointed out to us, is the name of a battle between the Romans and the Carthaginians in the Punic War. The Punic War was a trade war—might be considered a rather close parallel to our late war. At any rate, it is plain that Eliot in having the protagonist address the friend in a London street as one who was with him in the Punic War rather than as one who was with him in the World War is making the point that all the wars are one war; all experience, one experience. As Eliot put the idea in *Murder in the Cathedral*:

> We do not know very much of the future
> Except that from generation to generation
> The same things happen again and again.

I am not sure that Leavis and Matthiessen are correct in inferring that the line, "That corpse you planted last year in your garden," refers to the attempt to bury a memory. But whether or not this is true, the line certainly refers also to the buried god of the old fertility rites. It also is to be linked with the earlier passage—"What are the roots that clutch, what branches grow," etc. This allusion to the buried god will account for the ironical, almost taunting tone of the passage. The burial of the dead is now a sterile planting—without hope. But the advice to "keep the Dog far hence," in spite of the tone, is, I believe, well taken and serious. The passage in Webster goes as follows

> O keep the wolf far hence, that's foe to men,
> Or with his nails he'll dig it up again.

Why does Eliot turn the wolf into a dog? And why does he reverse the point of importance from the animal's normal hostility to men to its friendliness? If, as some critics have suggested, he is merely interested in making a reference to Webster's darkest play, why alter the line? I am inclined to take the Dog (the capital letter is Eliot's) as Humanitarianism and the related philosophies which in their concern for man extirpate the supernatural—dig up the corpse of the buried god and thus prevent the rebirth of life. For the general idea, see Eliot's essay, "The Humanism of Irving Babbitt."[2]

The last line of "The Burial of the Dead"—"You! *hypocrite lecteur!—mon semblable,—mon frère!*"—the quotation from Baudelaire, completes the universalization of Stetson begun by the reference to Mylae. Stetson is every man including the reader and Mr. Eliot himself.

II

If "The Burial of the Dead" gives the general abstract statement of the situation, the second part of *The Waste Land,* "A Game of Chess," gives a more concrete illustration. The easiest contrast in this section—and one which may easily blind the casual reader to a continued emphasis on the contrast between the two kinds of life, or the two kinds of death, already commented on—is the contrast between life in a rich and magnificent setting, and life in the low and vulgar setting of a London pub. But both scenes, however antithetical they may appear superficially, are scenes taken from the contemporary waste land. In both of them life has lost its meaning.

I am particularly indebted to Mr. Allen Tate's brilliant comment on the first part of this section. To quote from him, "the woman . . .

2. First published in 1927.

is, I believe, the symbol of man at the present time. He is surrounded by the grandeurs of the past, but he does not participate in them; they don't sustain him." And to quote from another section of his commentary: "The rich experience of the great tradition depicted in the room receives a violent shock in contrast with a game that symbolizes the inhuman abstraction of the modern mind." Life has no meaning; history has no meaning; there is no answer to the question: "what shall we ever do?" The only thing that has meaning is the abstract game which they are to play, a game in which the meaning is assigned and arbitrary, meaning by convention only—in short, a game of chess.

This interpretation will account in part for the pointed reference to Cleopatra in the first lines of the section. But there is, I believe, a further reason for the poet's having compared the lady to Cleopatra. The queen in Shakespeare's drama—"Age cannot wither her, nor custom stale / Her infinite variety"—is perhaps the extreme exponent of love for love's sake—the feminine member of the pair of lovers who threw away an empire for love. But the infinite variety of the life of the woman in "A Game of Chess" *has* been staled. There is indeed no variety at all, and love simply does not exist. The function of the sudden change in the description of the carvings and paintings in the room from the heroic and magnificent to the characterization of the rest of them as "other withered stumps of time" is obvious. But the reference to Philomela is particularly important, for Philomela, it seems to me, is one of the major symbols of the poem.

Miss Weston points out (in *The Quest of the Holy Grail*) that a section of one of the Grail manuscripts, which is apparently intended as a gloss of the Grail story, tells how the court of the rich Fisher King was withdrawn from the knowledge of men when certain of the maidens who frequented the shrine were raped and had their golden cups taken from them. The curse on the land follows from this act. Miss Weston conjectures that this may be a statement, in the form of parable, of the violation of the older mysteries which were probably once celebrated openly, but were later forced underground into secrecy. Whether or not Mr. Eliot noticed this passage or intends a reference, the violation of a woman makes a very good symbol of the process of secularization. John Crowe Ransom makes the point very neatly for us in his *God Without Thunder*. Love is the aesthetic of sex; lust is the science. Love implies a deferring of the satisfaction of the desire; it implies even a certain asceticism and a ritual. Lust drives forward urgently and scientifically to the immediate extirpation of the desire. Our contemporary waste land is in a large part the result of our scientific attitude—of our complete secularization. Needless to say, lust defeats its own ends. The portrayal of "The change of Philomel, by the barbarous king" is a fitting commentary on the scene which it ornaments. The waste land of the legend came in this way—the modern waste land has come in this way.

That this view is not mere fine-spun ingenuity is borne out somewhat by the change of tense which Eliot employs here and which Mr. Edmund Wilson has commented upon: "And still she cried, and still the world pursues." Apparently the "world" partakes in the barbarous king's action, and still partakes in that action.

To "dirty ears" the nightingale's song is not that which filled all the desert with inviolable voice—it is "jug, jug." Edmund Wilson has pointed out that the rendition of the bird's song here represents not merely the Elizabethans' neutral notation of the bird's song, but carries associations of the ugly and coarse. The passage is one therefore of many instances of Eliot's device of using something which in one context is innocent but in another context becomes loaded with a special meaning.

The Philomela passage has another importance, however. If it is a commentary on how the waste land became waste, it also repeats the theme of the death which is the door to life—the theme of the dying god. The raped woman becomes transformed through suffering into the nightingale; through the violation comes the "inviolable voice." The thesis that suffering is action, and that out of suffering comes poetry is a favorite one of Eliot's. For example, "Shakespeare, too, was occupied with the struggle—which alone constitutes life for a poet—to transmute his personal and private agonies into something rich and strange, something universal and impersonal."[3] Consider also his statement with reference to Baudelaire: "Indeed, in his way of suffering is already a kind of presence of the supernatural and of the superhuman. He rejects always the purely natural and the purely human; in other words, he is neither 'naturalist' nor 'humanist.'" The theme of the life which is death is stated specifically in the conversation between the man and the woman. She asks the question "Are you alive, or not?" and this time we are sufficiently prepared by the Dante references in "The Burial of the Dead" for the statement here to bear a special meaning. (She also asks "Is there nothing in your head?" He is one of the Hollow Men—"headpiece stuffed with straw.") These people, as people in the waste land, know nothing, see nothing, do not even live.

But the protagonist, after this reflection that in the waste land of modern life even death is sterile—"I think we are in rats' alley / Where the dead men lost their bones"—remembers a death which

---

3. From "Shakespeare and the Stoicism of Seneca" (1927). The following quotation is from "Baudelaire."

was not sterile, remembers a death that was transformed into something rich and strange, the death described in the song from *The Tempest*—"Those are pearls that were his eyes."

The reference to this section of *The Tempest* is, like the Philomela reference, one of Eliot's major symbols. We are to meet it twice more, in later sections of the poem. Some more general comment on it is therefore appropriate here. The song, one remembers, was sung by Ariel in luring Ferdinand, Prince of Naples, on to meet Miranda, and thus to find love, and through this love, to effect the regeneration and deliverance of all the people on the island. Ferdinand says of the song:

> The ditty doth remember my drowned father.
> This is no mortal business, nor no sound
> That the earth owes . . .

The allusion is an extremely interesting example of the device of Eliot's already commented upon, that of taking an item from one context and shifting it into another in which it assumes a new and powerful meaning. This description of a death which is a portal into a realm of the rich and strange—a death which becomes a sort of birth—assumes in the mind of the protagonist an association with that of the drowned god whose effigy was thrown into the water as a symbol of the death of the fruitful powers of nature but which was taken out of the water as a symbol of the revivified god. (See *From Ritual to Romance*.) The passage therefore represents the perfect antithesis to the passage in "The Burial of the Dead": "That corpse you planted last year in your garden," etc. It also, as we have already pointed out, finds its antithesis in the sterile and unfruitful death "in rats' alley" just commented upon. (We shall find that this contrast between the death in rats' alley and the death in *The Tempest* is made again in "The Fire Sermon.")

We have yet to treat the relation of the title of the section, "A Game of Chess," to Middleton's play, *Women beware Women*, from which the game of chess is taken. In the play, the game is used as a device to keep the widow occupied while her daughter-in-law is being seduced. The seduction amounts almost to a rape, and in a *double entendre*, the rape is actually described in terms of the game. We have one more connection with the Philomela symbol therefore. The abstract game is being used in the contemporary waste land, as in the play, to cover up a rape and is a description of the rape itself.

In the second part of "A Game of Chess" we are given a picture of spiritual emptiness, but this time, at the other end of the social scale, as reflected in the talk between two cockney women in a London pub. The account here is straightforward enough and the only matter which calls for comment is the line spoken by Ophelia in *Hamlet* which ends the passage. Ophelia, too, was very much concerned about love, the theme of conversation of the two ladies. As a matter of fact, she was in very much the same position as that of the woman who has been the topic of conversation between the two good ladies we have just heard. She had remarked too once that

> Young men will do 't, if they come to 't;
> By cock, they are to blame.

And her poetry (including the line quoted from her here), like Philomela's, had come out of suffering. I think that we are probably to look for the relevance of the allusion to her in some such matter as this rather than in an easy satiric contrast between Elizabethan glories and modern sordidness. After all (in spite of the Marxists) Eliot's objection to the present world is not merely the sentimental one that this happens to be the twentieth century after Christ and not the seventeenth.

III

"The Fire Sermon" makes much use of several of the symbols already developed. The fire is the sterile burning of lust, and the section is a sermon, although a sermon by example only. This section of the poem also contains some of the most easily apprehended uses of literary allusion. The poem opens on a vision of the modern river. In Spenser's "Prothalamion" the scene described is also a river scene at London, and it is dominated by nymphs and their paramours, and the nymphs are preparing for a bridal. The contrast between Spenser's scene and its twentieth century equivalent is jarring. The paramours are now "the loitering heirs of city directors," and, as for the bridals of Spenser's Elizabethan maidens, in the stanzas which follow we learn a great deal about those. At the end of the section the speech of the third of the Thames-nymphs summarizes the whole matter for us.

The waters of the Thames are also associated with those of Leman—the poet in the contemporary waste land is in a sort of Babylonian Captivity.

The castle of the Fisher King was always located on the banks of a river or on the sea shore. The title "Fisher King," Miss Weston shows, originates from the use of the fish as a fertility or life symbol. This meaning, however, was often forgotten, and so the title in many of the later Grail romances is accounted for by describing the king as fishing. Eliot uses the reference to fishing for reverse effect. The reference to fishing is part of the realistic detail of the scene— "While I was fishing in the dull canal." But to the reader who knows the Weston references, the reference is to that of the Fisher King of the Grail legends. The protagonist is the maimed and impotent king of the legends.

Eliot proceeds now to tie the waste-land symbol to that of *The Tempest*, by quoting one of the lines spoken by Ferdinand, Prince of Naples, which occurs just before Ariel's song, "Full Fathom Five," is heard. But he alters *The Tempest* passage somewhat, writing not, "Weeping again the king my father's wreck," but

> Musing upon the king my brother's wreck
> And on the king my father's death before him.

It is possible that the alteration has been made to bring the account taken from *The Tempest* into accord with the situation in the Percival stories. In Wolfram von Eschenbach's *Parzival*, for instance, Trevrezent, the hermit, is the brother of the Fisher King, Anfortas. He tells Parzival, "His name all men know as Anfortas, and I weep for him evermore." Their father, Frimutel, is of course dead.

The protagonist in the poem, then, imagines himself not only in the situation of Ferdinand in *The Tempest* but also in that of one of the characters in the Grail legend; and the wreck, to be applied literally in the first instance, applies metaphorically in the second.

After the lines from *The Tempest*, appears again the image of a sterile death from which no life comes, the bones, "rattled by the rat's foot only, year to year." (The collocation of this figure with the vision of the death by water in Ariel's song has already been commented on. The lines quoted from *The Tempest* come just before the song.)

The allusion to Marvell's "To His Coy Mistress" is of course one of the easiest allusions in the poem. Instead of "Time's winged chariot" the poet hears "the sound of horns and motors" of contemporary London. But the passage has been further complicated. The reference has been combined with an allusion to Day's "Parliament of Bees." "Time's winged chariot" of Marvell has not only been changed to the modern automobile; Day's "sound of horns and hunting" has changed to the horns of the motors. And Actaeon will not be brought face to face with Diana, goddess of chastity; Sweeney, type of the vulgar bourgeois, is to be brought to Mrs. Porter, hardly a type of chastity. The reference in the ballad to the feet "washed in soda water" reminds the poet ironically of another sort of foot-washing, the sound of the children singing in the dome heard at the ceremony of the foot-washing which precedes the restoration of the wounded Anfortas (the Fisher King) by Parzival and the taking away of the curse from the waste land. The quotation thus completes the allusion to the Fisher King commenced in line 189—"While I was fishing in the dull canal."

The pure song of the children also reminds the poet of the song of the nightingale which we have heard in "The Game of Chess."

The recapitulation of symbols is continued with a repetition of "Unreal city" and with the reference to the one-eyed merchant.

Mr. Eugenides, the Smyrna merchant, is the one-eyed merchant mentioned by Madame Sosostris. The fact that the merchant is one-eyed apparently means in Madame Sosostris' speech no more than that the merchant's face on the card is shown in profile. But Eliot applies the term to Mr. Eugenides for a totally different effect. The defect corresponds somewhat to Madame Sosostris' bad cold. The Syrian merchants, we learn from Miss Weston's book, were, with slaves and soldiers, the principal carriers of the mysteries which lie at the core of the Grail legends. But in the modern world we find both the representatives of the Tarot divining and the mystery cults in decay. What he carries on his back and what the fortune-teller was forbidden to see is evidently the knowledge of the mysteries (although Mr. Eugenides himself is hardly likely to be more aware of it than Madame Sosostris is aware of the importance of her function). Mr. Eugenides, in terms of his former function ought to be inviting the protagonist to an initiation into the esoteric cult which holds the secret of life, but on the realistic surface of the poem, in his invitation to "a week end at the Metropole" he is really inviting him to a homosexual debauch. The homosexuality is "secret" and now a "cult" but a very different cult from that which Mr. Eugenides ought to represent. The end of the new cult is not life but, ironically, sterility.

In the modern waste land, however, even the relation between man and woman is also sterile. The incident between the typist and the carbuncular young man is a picture of "love" so exclusively and practically pursued that it is not love at all. The scene, as Allen Tate puts it, is one of our most terrible insights into Western civilization. The tragic chorus to the scene is Tiresias, into whom perhaps Mr. Eugenides may be said to modulate, Tiresias, the historical "expert" on the relation between the sexes.

The allusions to Sappho's lines and to Goldsmith's made in this passage need little comment. The hour of evening, which in Sappho's poem brings rest to all and brings the sailor home, brings the typist to her travesty of home—"On the divan . . . at night her bed"— and brings the carbuncular young man, the meeting with whom ends not in peace but in sterile burning.

The reminiscence of the lines from Goldsmith's song in the description of the young woman's actions after the departure of her lover gives concretely and ironically the utter break-down of traditional standards.

It is the music of her gramophone which the protagonist hears "creep by" him "on the waters." Far from the music which Ferdinand heard bringing him to Miranda and love, it is, one is tempted to think, the music of "O O O O that Shakespeherian Rag" of "A Game of Chess."

But the protagonist says that he can *sometimes* hear "The pleasant whining of a mandoline." Significantly enough, it is the music of the fishmen (the fish again as a life symbol) and it comes from beside a church (though—if this is not to rely too much on Eliot's note—the church has been marked for destruction). Life on Lower Thames Street, if not on the Strand, still has meaning as it cannot have meaning for either the typist or the rich woman of "A Game of Chess."

The song of the Thames-daughters brings us back to the opening section of "The Fire Sermon" again, and once more we have to do with the river and the river-nymphs. Indeed, the typist incident is framed by the two river-nymph scenes.

The connection of the river-nymphs with the Rhine-daughters of Wagner's *Götterdämerung* is easily made. In the passage in Wagner's opera to which Eliot refers in his note, the opening of Act III, the Rhine-daughters bewail the loss of the beauty of the Rhine occasioned by the theft of the gold and then beg Siegfried to give them back the Ring made from this gold, finally threatening him with death if he does not give it up. Like the Thames-daughters they too have been violated; and like the maidens mentioned in the Grail legend, the violation has brought a curse on gods and men. The first of the songs depicts the modern river, soiled with oil and tar. (Compare also with the description of the river in the first part of "The Fire Sermon.") The second song depicts the Elizabethan river, also evoked in the first part of "The Fire Sermon." (Leicester and Elizabeth ride upon it in a barge of state. Incidentally, Spenser's "Prothalamion" from which quotation is made in the first part of "The Fire Sermon" mentions Leicester as having formerly lived in the house which forms the setting of the poem.)

In this second song there is also a definite allusion to the passage in *Antony and Cleopatra* already referred to in the opening line of "A Game of Chess."

> Beating oars
> The stern was formed
> A gilded shell

And if we still have any doubt of the allusion, Eliot's note on the passage with its reference to the *barge* and *poop* should settle the matter. We have already commented on the earlier allusion to Cleopatra as the prime example of love for love's sake. The symbol bears something of the same meaning here, and the note which Eliot supplies does something to reinforce the "Cleopatra" aspect of Elizabeth. Elizabeth in the presence of the Spaniard De Quadra, though negotiations were going on for a Spanish marriage, "went so far that Lord Robert at last said, as I [De Quadra was a bishop] was on the spot there was no reason why they should not be married if the queen pleased." The passage has a sort of double function. It reinforces the general contrast between Elizabethan magnificence and modern sordidness: in the Elizabethan age love for love's sake has some meaning and therefore some magnificence. But the passage gives something of an opposed effect too: the same sterile love, emptiness of love, obtained in this period too: Elizabeth and the typist are alike as well as different. (One of the reasons for the frequent allusion to Elizabethan poetry in this and the preceding section of the poem may be the fact that with the English Renaissance the old set of supernatural sanctions had begun to break up. See Eliot's various essays on Shakespeare and the Elizabethan dramatists.)

The third Thames-daughter's song depicts another sordid "love" affair, and unites the themes of the first two songs. It begins "Trams and *dusty* trees." With it we are definitely in the waste land again. Pia, whose words she echoes in saying "Highbury bore me. Richmond and Kew / Undid me" was in Purgatory and had hope. The woman speaking here has no hope—she too is in the Inferno: "I can connect / Nothing with nothing." She has just completed, floating down the river in the canoe, what Eliot has described in *Murder in the Cathedral* as

> . . . the effortless journey, to the empty land
>
> .   .   .   .
>
> Where the soul is no longer deceived, for there are no
>   objects, no tones,
> Where those who were men can no longer turn the mind
> To distraction, delusion, escape into dream, pretence,
> No colours, no forms to distract, to divert the soul
> From seeing itself, foully united forever, nothing with
>   nothing,
> Not what we call death, but what beyond death is not
>   death . . .

Now, "on Margate sands," like the Hollow Men, she stands "on this beach of the tumid river."

The songs of the three Thames-daughters, as a matter of fact, epitomize this whole section of the poem. With reference to the quotations from St. Augustine and Buddha at the end of "The Fire Sermon" Eliot states that "The collocation of these two representatives of eastern and western asceticism, as the culmination of this part of the poem, is not an accident."

It is certainly not an accident. The moral of all the incidents which we have been witnessing is that there must be an asceticism—something to check the drive of desire. The wisdom of the East and the West comes to the same thing on this point. Moreover, the imagery which both St. Augustine and Buddha use for lust is fire. What we have witnessed in the various scenes of "The Fire Sermon" is the sterile burning of lust. Modern man, freed from all restraints, in his cultivation of experience for experience's sake burns, but not with a "hard and gemlike flame."[4] One ought not to pound the point home in this fashion, but to see that the imagery of this section of the poem furnishes illustrations leading up to the Fire Sermon is the necessary requirement for feeling the force of the brief allusions here at the end to Buddha and St. Augustine.

IV

Whatever the specific meaning of the symbols, the general function of the section, "Death by Water," is readily apparent. The section forms a contrast with "The Fire Sermon" which precedes it—a contrast between the symbolism of fire and that of water. Also readily apparent is its force as symbol of surrender and relief through surrender.

Some specific connections can be made, however. The drowned Phoenician Sailor recalls the drowned god of the fertility cults. Miss Weston tells that each year at Alexandria an effigy of the head of the god was thrown into the water as a symbol of the death of the powers of nature, and that this head was carried by the current to Byblos where it was taken out of the water and exhibited as a symbol of the reborn god.

Moreover, the Phoenician Sailor is a merchant—"Forgot . . . the profit and loss." The vision of the drowned sailor gives a statement of the message which the Syrian merchants originally brought to Britain and which the Smyrna merchant, unconsciously and by ironical negatives, has brought. One of Eliot's notes states that the "merchant . . . melts into the Phoenician Sailor, and the latter is not wholly distinct from Ferdinand Prince of Naples." The death by water would seem to be equated with the death described in Ariel's song in *The Tempest*. There is a definite difference in the tone of the description of this death—"A current under sea / Picked his bones in whispers," as compared with the "other" death—"bones cast in a little low dry garret / Rattled by the rat's foot only, year to year."

Farther than this it would not be safe to go, but one may point out that whirling (the whirlpool here, the Wheel of Madame

4. A reference to the Conclusion of Walter Pater's *The Renaissance* (1893), which rather scandalously recommended, "To burn always with this hard, gem-like flame, to maintain this ecstasy, is success in life."

Sosostris' palaver) is one of Eliot's symbols frequently used in other poems (*Ash Wednesday,* "Gerontion," *Murder in the Cathedral,* and "Burnt Norton") to denote the temporal world. And one may point out, supplying the italics oneself, the following passage from *Ash Wednesday:*

> Although I do not hope to *turn* again
> . . . .
> Wavering between the *profit and the loss*
> In this brief transit where the dreams cross
> The dream crossed twilight *between birth and dying.*

At least, with a kind of hindsight, one may suggest that "Section IV" gives an instance of the conquest of death and time, the "perpetual recurrence of determined seasons," the "world of spring and autumn, birth and dying" through death itself.

V

The reference to the "torchlight red on sweaty faces" and to the "frosty silence in the gardens" obviously associates, as we have already pointed out, Christ in Gethsemane with the other hanged gods. The god has now died, and in referring to this, the basic theme finds another strong restatement:

> He who was living is now dead
> We who were living are now dying
> With a little patience

The poet does not say "We who *are* living." It is "We who *were* living." It is the death-in-life of Dante's Limbo. Life in the full sense has been lost.

The passage on the sterility of the waste land and the lack of water which follows, provides for the introduction later of two highly important passages:

> There is not even silence in the mountains
> But dry sterile thunder without rain—

lines which look forward to the introduction later of "what the thunder said" when the thunder, no longer sterile, but bringing rain speaks.

The second of these passages is, "There is not even solitude in the mountains," which looks forward to the reference to the Journey to Emmaus theme a few lines later: "Who is the third who walks always beside you?" The god has returned, has risen, but the travelers cannot tell whether it is really he, or mere illusion induced by their delirium.

The parallelism between the "hooded figure" who "walks always beside you," and the "hooded hordes" is another instance of the sort of parallelism that is really a contrast, one of the type of which Eliot is fond. In the first case, the figure is indistinct because spiritual; in the second, the hooded hordes are indistinct because completely *unspiritual*—they are the people of the waste land—

> Shape without form, shade without colour,
> Paralysed force, gesture without motion—

to take two lines from "The Hollow Men," where the people of the waste land once more appear. Or to take another line from the same poem, perhaps their hoods are the "deliberate disguises" which the Hollow Men, the people of the waste land, wear.

Eliot, as his notes tell us, has particularly connected the description here with the "decay of eastern Europe." The hordes represent then the general waste land of the modern world with a special application to the breakup of Eastern Europe, the region with which the fertility cults were especially connected and in which today the traditional values are thoroughly discredited. The cities, Jerusalem, Athens, Alexandria, Vienna, like the London of the first section of the poem are "unreal," and for the same reason.

The passage which immediately follows develops the unreality into nightmare, but it is a nightmare vision which is not only an extension of the passage beginning, "What is the city over the mountains"—in it appear other figures from earlier in the poem: the lady of "A Game of Chess" who, surrounded by the glory of history and art sees no meaning in either and threatens to rush out into the street "With my hair down, so," has here let down her hair and fiddles "whisper music on those strings." One remembers in "A Game of Chess" that it was the woman's hair that spoke:

> . . . her hair
> Spread out in fiery points
> Glowed into words, then would be savagely still.

The hair has been immemorially a symbol of fertility, and Miss Weston and Frazer mention sacrifices of hair in order to aid the fertility god.

As we have pointed out earlier in dealing with "The Burial of the Dead," this whole passage is to be connected with the twelfth chapter of *Ecclesiastes*. The doors "of mudcracked houses," and the cisterns in this passage are to be found in *Ecclesiastes,* and the woman fiddling music from her hair is one of "the daughters of music" brought low. The towers and bells from the Elizabeth and Leicester passage of "The Fire Sermon" also appear here, but the towers are upside down, and the bells, far from pealing for an actual occasion or ringing the hours, are "reminiscent." The civilization is breaking up.

The "violet light" also deserves comment. In "The Fire Sermon" it is twice mentioned as the "violet hour," and there it has little more than a physical meaning. It is a description of the hour of twilight. Here it indicates the twilight of the civilization, but it is perhaps something more. Violet is one of the liturgical colors of the Church. It symbolizes repentance and it is the color of baptism. The visit to the Perilous Chapel, according to Miss Weston, was an initiation—that is, a baptism. In the nightmare vision, the bats wear baby faces.

The horror built up in this passage is a proper preparation for the passage on the Perilous Chapel which follows it. The journey has not been merely an agonized walk in the desert, though it is that, or merely the journey after the god has died and hope has been lost; it is also the journey to the Perilous Chapel of the Grail story. In Miss Weston's account, the Chapel was part of the ritual, and was filled with horrors to test the candidate's courage. In some stories the perilous cemetery is also mentioned. Eliot has used both: "Over the tumbled graves, about the chapel." In many of the Grail stories the Chapel was haunted by demons.

The cock in the folk-lore of many peoples is regarded as the bird whose voice chases away the powers of evil. It is significant that it is after his crow that the flash of lightning comes and the "damp gust / Bringing rain." It is just possible that the cock has a connection also with *The Tempest* symbols. The first song which Ariel sings to Ferdinand as he sits "Weeping again the king my father's wreck" ends

> The strain of strutting chanticleer,
> Cry, cock-a-doodle-doo.

The next stanza is the "Full Fathom Five" song which Eliot has used as a vision of life gained through death. If this relation holds, here we have an extreme instance of an allusion, in itself innocent, forced into serious meaning through transference to a new context.

As Miss Weston has shown, the fertility cults go back to a very early period and are recorded in Sanscrit legends. Eliot has been continually in the poem linking up the Christian doctrine with the beliefs of as many peoples as he can. Here he goes back to the very beginnings of Aryan culture, and tells the rest of the story of the rain's coming, not in terms of the setting already developed but in its earliest form. The passage is thus a perfect parallel in method to the passage in "The Burial of the Dead":

> You who were with me in the ships *at Mylae!*
> That corpse you planted *last year* in your garden . . .

The use of Sanscrit in what the thunder says is thus accounted for. In addition, there is of course a more obvious reason for casting what the thunder said into Sanscrit here: onomatopoeia.

The comments on the three statements of the thunder imply an acceptance of them. The protagonist answers the first question, "what have we given?" with the statement:

> The awful daring of a moment's surrender
> Which an age of prudence can never retract
> By this, and this only, we have existed.

Here the larger meaning is stated in terms which imply the sexual meaning. Man cannot be absolutely self-regarding. Even the propagation of the race—even mere "existence"—calls for such a surrender. Living calls for—see the passage already quoted from Eliot's essay on Baudelaire—belief in something more than "life."

The comment on *dayadhvam* (sympathize) is obviously connected with the foregoing passage. The surrender to something outside the self is an attempt (whether on the sexual level or some other) to transcend one's essential isolation. The passage gathers up the symbols previously developed in the poem just as the foregoing passage reflects, though with a different implication, the numerous references to sex made earlier in the poem. For example, the woman in the first part of "A Game of Chess" has also heard the key turn in the door, and confirms her prison by thinking of the key:

> Speak to me. Why do you never speak. Speak.
> What are you thinking of? What thinking? What?
> I never know what you are thinking. Think.

The third statement made by the thunder, *damyata* (control) follows the logical condition for control, sympathy. The figure of the boat catches up the figure of control already given in "Death by Water"—"O you who turn the wheel and look to windward"—and from "The Burial of the Dead" the figure of happy love in which the ship rushes on with a fair wind behind it: *"Frisch weht der wind . . ."*

I cannot accept Mr. Leavis' interpretation of the passage, "I sat upon the shore / Fishing, with the arid plain behind me," as meaning that the poem "exhibits no progression." The comment upon what the thunder says would indicate, if other passages did not, that the poem does "not end where it began." It is true that the protagonist does not witness a revival of the waste land; but there are two important relationships involved in his case: a personal one as well as a general one. If secularization has destroyed, or is likely to destroy, modern civilization, the protagonist still has a private obligation to fulfill. Even if the civilization is breaking up—"London Bridge is falling down falling down falling down"—there remains the personal obligation: "Shall I at least set my lands in order?" Consider in this connection the last sentences of Eliot's "Thoughts After Lambeth": "The World is trying the experiment of attempting to form a non-Christian mentality. The experiment will fail; but we must be very patient awaiting its collapse; meanwhile redeeming the time: so that the Faith may be preserved alive through the dark ages before us; to renew and rebuild civilization, and save the World from suicide."[5]

The bundle of quotations with which the poem ends has a very definite relation to the general theme of the poem and to several of the major symbols used in the poem. Before Arnaut leaps back into the refining fire of Purgatory with joy he says: "I am Arnaut who weep and go singing; contrite I see my past folly, and joyful I see before me the day I hope for. Now I pray you by that virtue which guides you to the summit of the stair, at times be mindful of my pain." This note is carried forward by the quotation from *Pervigilium Veneris*: "When shall I be like the swallow." The allusion also connects with the Philomela symbol. (Eliot's note on the passage indicates this clearly.) The sister of Philomela was changed into a swallow as Philomela was changed into a nightingale. The protagonist is asking therefore when shall the spring, the time of love return, but also when will he be reborn out of his sufferings, and—with the special meaning which the symbol takes on from the preceding Dante quotation and from the earlier contexts already discussed—he is asking what is asked at the end of one of the minor poems: "When will Time flow away."

The quotation from "El Desdichado," as Edmund Wilson has pointed out, indicates that the protagonist of the poem has been disinherited, robbed of his tradition. The ruined tower is perhaps also the Perilous Chapel, "only the wind's home," and it is also the whole tradition in decay. The protagonist resolves to claim his tradition and rehabilitate it.

The quotation from *The Spanish Tragedy*—"Why then Ile fit you. Hieronymo's mad againe"—is perhaps the most puzzling of all these quotations. It means, I believe, this: the protagonist's acceptance of what is in reality the deepest truth will seem to the present world mere madness. ("And still she cried, and still the world pursues / 'Jug Jug' to dirty ears.") Hieronymo in the play, like Hamlet, was "mad" for a purpose. The protagonist is conscious of the interpretation which will be placed on the words which follow—words which will seem to many apparently meaningless babble, but which contain the oldest and most permanent truth of the race:

5. An essay published in 1931 after one of the Lambeth Conferences of the Church of England.

Datta.   Dayadhvam.   Damyata.

After this statement comes the benediction:

Shantih   Shantih   Shantih

The foregoing account of *The Waste Land* is, of course, not to be substituted for the poem itself. Moreover, it certainly is not to be considered as representing *the method by which the poem was composed*. Much which the prose expositor must represent as though it had been consciously contrived obviously was arrived at unconsciously and concretely.

The account given above is a statement merely of the "prose meaning," and bears the same relation to the poem as does the "prose meaning" of any other poem. But one need not perhaps apologize for setting forth such a statement explicitly, for *The Waste Land* has been almost consistently misinterpreted since its first publication. Even a critic so acute as Edmund Wilson has seen the poem as essentially a statement of despair and disillusionment, and this account sums up the stock interpretation of the poem. Indeed, the phrase, "the poetry of drouth," has become a *cliché* of left-wing criticism. It is such a misrepresentation of *The Waste Land* as this which allows Eda Lou Walton to entitle an essay on contemporary poetry, "Death in the Desert"; or which causes Waldo Frank to misconceive of Eliot's whole position and personality.[6] But more than the meaning of one poem is at stake. If *The Waste Land* is not a world-weary cry of despair or a sighing after the vanished glories of the past, then not only the popular interpretation of the poem will have to be altered but also the general interpretations of post-War poetry which begin with such a misinterpretation as a premise.

Such misinterpretations involve also misconceptions of Eliot's technique. Eliot's basic method may be said to have passed relatively unnoticed. The popular view of the method used in *The Waste Land* may be described as follows: Eliot makes use of ironic contrasts between the glorious past and the sordid present—the crashing irony of

> But at my back from time to time I hear
> The sound of horns and motors, which shall bring
> Sweeney to Mrs. Porter in the spring.

But this is to take the irony of the poem at the most superficial level, and to neglect the other dimensions in which it operates. And it is to neglect what are essentially more important aspects of his method.

6. Eda Lou Walton's "Death in the Desert" first appeared in *Saturday Review* (August 26, 1933), pp. 61–63. The offending Waldo Frank essay is perhaps "The 'Universe' of T. S. Eliot," *New Republic* (October 26, 1932), pp. 294–95.

Moreover, it is to overemphasize the difference between the method employed by Eliot in this poem and that employed by him in later poems.

The basic method used in *The Waste Land* may be described as the application of the principle of complexity. The poet works in terms of surface parallelisms which in reality make ironical contrasts, and in terms of surface contrasts which in reality constitute parallelisms. (The second group set up effects which may be described as the obverse of irony.) The two aspects taken together give the effect of chaotic experience ordered into a new whole though the realistic surface of experience is faithfully retained. The complexity of the experience is not violated by the apparent forcing upon it of a predetermined scheme.

The fortune-telling of "The Burial of the Dead" will illustrate the general method very satisfactorily. On the surface of the poem the poet reproduces the patter of the charlatan, Madame Sosostris, and there is the surface irony: the contrast between the original use of the Tarot cards and the use made here. But each of the details (justified realistically in the palaver of the fortune-teller) assumes a new meaning in the general context of the poem. There is then in addition to the surface irony something of a Sophoclean irony too, and the "fortune-telling" which is taken ironically by a twentieth-century audience becomes *true* as the poem develops—true in a sense in which Madame Sosostris herself does not think it true. The surface irony is thus reversed and becomes an irony on a deeper level. The items of her speech have only one reference in terms of the context of her speech: the "man with three staves," the "one-eyed merchant," the "crowds of people, walking round in a ring," etc. But transferred to other contexts they become loaded with special meanings. To sum up, all the central symbols of the poem head up here, but here, in the only section in which they are explicitly bound together, the binding is slight and accidental. The deeper lines of association only emerge in terms of the total context as the poem develops—and this is, of course, exactly the effect which the poet intends.

This transference of items from an "innocent" context into a context in which they become charged and transformed in meaning will account for many of the literary allusions in the poem. For example, the "change of Philomel" is merely one of the items in the decorative detail in the room in the opening of "A Game of Chess." But the violent change of tense—"And still she cried, and still the world pursues"—makes it a comment upon, and a symbol of, the modern world. And further allusions to it through the course of the poem gradually equate it with the general theme of the poem. The allusions to *The Tempest* display the same method. The parallelism between Dante's Hell and the waste land of the

Grail legends is fairly close; even the equation of Baudelaire's Paris to the waste land is fairly obvious. But the parallelism between the death by drowning in *The Tempest* and the death of the fertility god is, on the surface, merely accidental, and the first allusion to Ariel's song is merely an irrelevant and random association of the stream-of-consciousness:

> Is your card, the drowned Phoenician Sailor,
> (Those are pearls that were his eyes. Look!)

And on its second appearance in "A Game of Chess" it is still only an item in the protagonist's abstracted reverie. Even the association of *The Tempest* symbol with the Grail legends in the lines

> While I was fishing in the dull canal
>   . . . . .
> Musing upon the king my brother's wreck

and in the passage which follows, is ironical merely. But the associations have been established, even though they may seem to be made in ironic mockery, and when we come to the passage, "Death by Water," with its change of tone, they assert themselves positively. We have a sense of revelation out of material apparently accidentally thrown together. I have called the effect the obverse of irony, for the method, like that of irony, is indirect, though the effect is positive rather than negative.

The "melting" of the characters into each other is, of course, an aspect of this general process. Elizabeth and the girl born at Highbury both ride on the Thames, one in the barge of state, the other supine in a narrow canoe, and they are both Thames-nymphs, who are violated and thus are like the Rhine-nymphs who have also been violated, etc. With the characters as with the other symbols, the surface relationships may be accidental and apparently trivial and they may be made either ironically or through random association or in hallucination, but in the total context of the poem the deeper relationships are revealed. The effect is a sense of the oneness of experience, and of the unity of all periods, and with this, a sense that the general theme of the poem is true. But the theme has not been imposed—it has been revealed.

This complication of parallelisms and contrasts makes, of course, for ambiguity, but the ambiguity, in part, resides in the poet's fidelity to the complexity of experience. The symbols resist complete equation with a simple meaning. To take an example, "rock" throughout the poem seems to be one of the "desert" symbols. For example, the "dry stone" gives "no sound of water"; woman in the waste land is "the Lady of the Rocks," and most pointed of all, there is the long delirium passage in "What the Thunder Said": "Here is no water but

only rock," etc. So much for its general meaning, but in "The Burial
of the Dead" occur the lines

> Only
> There is shadow under this red rock,
> (Come in under the shadow of this red rock).

Rock here is a place of refuge. (Moreover, there may also be a refer-
ence to the Grail symbolism. In *Parzival,* the Grail is a stone: "And
this stone all men call the grail. . . . As children the Grail doth call
them, 'neath its shadow they wax and grow.") The paradox, life
through death, penetrates the symbol itself.

To take an even clearer case of this paradoxical use of symbols,
consider the lines which occur in the hyacinth girl passage. The
vision gives obviously a sense of the richness and beauty of life. It is
a moment of ecstasy (the basic imagery is obviously sexual); but the
moment in its intensity is like death. The protagonist looks in that
moment into the "heart of light, the silence," and so looks into—not
richness—but blankness: he is neither "living nor dead." The sym-
bol of life stands also for a kind of death. This duality of function
may, of course, extend to a whole passage. For example, consider:

> Where fishmen lounge at noon: where the walls
> Of Magnus Martyr hold
> Inexplicable splendour of Ionian white and gold.

The function of the passage is to indicate the poverty into which
religion has fallen: the splendid church now surrounded by the
poorer districts. But the passage has an opposed effect also: the fish-
men in the "public bar in Lower Thames Street" next to the church
have a meaningful life which has been largely lost to the secular-
ized upper and middle classes.

The poem would undoubtedly be "clearer" if every symbol had
one, unequivocal meaning; but the poem would be thinner, and less
honest. For the poet has not been content to develop a didactic alle-
gory in which the symbols are two-dimensional items adding up
directly to the sum of the general scheme. They represent drama-
tized instances of the theme, embodying in their own nature the fun-
damental paradox of the theme.

We shall better understand why the form of the poem is right and
inevitable if we compare Eliot's theme to Dante's and to Spenser's.
Eliot's theme is not the statement of a faith held and agreed upon
(Dante's *Divine Comedy*) nor is it the projection of a "new" system
of beliefs (Spenser's *Faerie Queene*). Eliot's theme is the rehabilita-
tion of a system of beliefs, known but now discredited. Dante did
not have to "prove" his statement; he could assume it and move
within it about a poet's business. Eliot does not care, like Spenser,

to force the didacticism. He prefers to stick to the poet's business. But, unlike Dante, he can not assume acceptance of the statement. A direct approach is calculated to elicit powerful "stock responses" which will prevent the poem's being *read* at all. Consequently, the only method is to work by indirection. The "Christian" material is at the center, but the poet never deals with it directly. The theme of resurrection is made on the surface in terms of the fertility rites; the words which the thunder speaks are Sanscrit words.

We have been speaking as if the poet were a strategist trying to win acceptance from a hostile audience. But of course this is true only in a sense. The poet himself is audience as well as speaker; we state the problem more exactly if we state it in terms of the poet's integrity rather than in terms of his strategy. He is so much a man of his own age that he can indicate his attitude toward the Christian tradition without falsity only in terms of the difficulties of a rehabilitation; and he is so much a poet and so little a propagandist that he can be sincere only as he presents his theme concretely and dramatically.

To put the matter in still other terms: the Christian terminology is for the poet here a mass of *clichés*. However "true" he may feel the terms to be, he is still sensitive to the fact that they operate superficially as *clichés,* and his method of necessity must be a process of bringing them to life again. The method adopted in *The Waste Land* is thus violent and radical, but thoroughly necessary. For the renewing and vitalizing of symbols which have been crusted over with a distorting familiarity demands the type of organization which we have already commented on in discussing particular passages: the statement of surface similarities which are ironically revealed to be dissimilarities, and the association of apparently obvious dissimilarities which culminates in a later realization that the dissimilarities are only superficial—that the chains of likeness are in reality fundamental. In this way the statement of beliefs emerges *through* confusion and cynicism—not in spite of them.

DELMORE SCHWARTZ

T. S. Eliot as the International Hero[†]

A culture hero is one who brings new arts and skills to mankind. Prometheus was a culture hero and the inventors of the radio may also be said to be culture heroes, although this is hardly to be confounded with the culture made available by the radio.

† From *Partisan Review* 12 (Spring 1945): 199–206. Reprinted by permission of Robert Phillips, Executor for the Literary Estate of Delmore Schwartz. Notes are by the editor of this Norton Critical Edition.

The inventors of the radio made possible a new range of experience. This is true of certain authors; for example, it is true of Wordsworth in regard to nature, and Proust in regard to time. It is not true of Shakespeare, but by contrast it is true of Surrey and the early Elizabethan playwrights who invented blank verse. Thus the most important authors are not always culture heroes, and thus no rank, stature, or scope is of necessity implicit in speaking of the author as a culture hero.

When we speak of nature and of a new range of experience, we may think of a mountain range: some may make the vehicles by means of which a mountain is climbed, some may climb the mountain, and some may apprehend the new view of the surrounding countryside which becomes possible from the heights of the mountain. T. S. Eliot is a culture hero in each of these three ways. This becomes clear when we study the relationship of his work to the possible experiences of modern life. The term, possible, should be kept in mind, for many human beings obviously disregard and turn their backs upon much of modern life, although modern life does not in the least cease to circumscribe and penetrate their existence.

The reader of T. S. Eliot by turning the dials of his radio can hear the capitals of the world, London, Vienna, Athens, Alexandria, Jerusalem. What he hears will be news of the agony of war. Both the agony and the width of this experience are vivid examples of how the poetry of T. S. Eliot has a direct relationship to modern life. The width and the height and the depth of modern life are exhibited in his poetry; the agony and the horror of modern life are represented as inevitable to any human being who does not wish to deceive himself with systematic lies. Thus it is truly significant that E. M. Forster, in writing of Eliot, should recall August 1914 and the beginning of the First World War; it is just as significant that he should speak of first reading Eliot's poems in Alexandria, Egypt, during that war, and that he should conclude by saying that Eliot was one who had looked into the abyss and refused hence forward to deny or forget the fact.[1]

We are given an early view of the international hero in the quasi-autobiographical poem which Eliot entitles: "Mélange Adultère Du Tout."[2] The title, borrowed from a poem by Corbière, is ironic, but the adulterous mixture of practically everything, every time and every place, is not ironic in the least: a teacher in America, the poem goes, a journalist in England, a lecturer in Yorkshire, a literary

1. See Forster's essay "T. S. Eliot," originally published in 1928 and later included in *Abinger Harvest* (New York: Harcourt, Brace, 1936).
2. A poem originally written in French after the example of Tristan Corbière (1845–1875), French symbolist poet. The description that follows is essentially a prose translation of the poem.

nihilist in Paris, overexcited by philosophy in Germany, a wanderer from Omaha to Damascus, he has celebrated, he says, his birthday at an African oasis, dressed in a giraffe's skin. Let us place next to this array another list of names and events as heterogeneous as a circus or America itself: St. Louis, New England, Boston, Harvard, England, Paris, the First World War, Oxford, London, the Russian Revolution, the Church of England, the post-war period, the world crisis and depression, the Munich Pact, and the Second World War. If this list seems far-fetched or forced, if it seems that such a list might be made for any author, the answer is that these names and events are *presences* in Eliot's work in a way which is not true of many authors, good and bad, who have lived through the same years.

Philip Rahv has shown how the heroine of Henry James is best understood as the heiress of all the ages. So, in a further sense, the true protagonist of Eliot's poems is the heir of all the ages. He is the descendant of the essential characters of James in that he is the American who visits Europe with a Baedeker[3] in his hand, just like Isabel Archer. But the further sense in which he is the heir of all the ages is illustrated when Eliot describes the seduction of a typist in a London flat from the point of view of Tiresias, a character in a play by Sophocles. To suppose that this is the mere exhibition of learning or reading is a banal misunderstanding. The important point is that the presence of Tiresias illuminates the seduction of the typist just as much as a description of her room. Hence Eliot writes in his notes to *The Waste Land* that "what Tiresias *sees* is the substance of the poem." The illumination of the ages is available at any moment, and when the typist's indifference and boredom in the act of love must be represented, it is possible for Eliot to invoke and paraphrase a lyric from a play by Oliver Goldsmith. Literary allusion has become not merely a Miltonic reference to Greek gods and Old Testament geography, not merely the citation of parallels, but a powerful and inevitable habit of mind, a habit which issues in judgment and the representation of different levels of experience, past and present.

James supposed that his theme was the international theme: would it not be more precise to speak of it as the transatlantic theme? This effort at a greater exactness defines what is involved in Eliot's work. Henry James was concerned with the American in Europe. Eliot cannot help but be concerned with the whole world and all history. Tiresias sees the nature of love in all times and all places and when Sweeney outwits a scheming whore, the fate of Agamemnon

3. See above, p. 28, note 1. Isabel Archer is the main character in *The Portrait of a Lady* (1881).

becomes relevant. So too, in the same way exactly, Eliot must recognize and use a correspondence between St. Augustine and Buddha in speaking of sensuality. And thus, as he writes again in his notes to *The Waste Land*, "The collocation of these two representatives of eastern and western asceticism as the culmination of this part of the poem is not an accident." And it is not an accident that the international hero should have come from St. Louis, Missouri, or at any rate from America. Only an American with a mind and sensibility which is cosmopolitan and expatriated could have seen Europe as it is seen in *The Waste Land*.

A literary work may be important in many ways, but surely one of the ways in which it is important is in its relationship to some important human interest or need, or in its relationship to some new aspect of human existence. Eliot's work is important in relationship to the fact that experience has become international. We have become an international people, and hence an international hero is possible. Just as the war is international, so the true causes of many of the things in our lives are world-wide, and we are able to understand the character of our lives only when we are aware of all history, of the philosophy of history, of primitive peoples and the Russian Revolution, of ancient Egypt and the unconscious mind. Thus again it is no accident that in *The Waste Land* use is made of *The Golden Bough,* and a book on the quest of the Grail; and the way in which images and associations appear in the poem illustrates a new view of consciousness, the depths of consciousness and the unconscious mind.

The protagonist of *The Waste Land* stands on the banks of the Thames and quotes the Upanishads, and this very quotation, the command to "give, sympathize, and control," makes possible a comprehensive insight into the difficulty of his life in the present. But this emphasis upon one poem of Eliot's may be misleading. What is true of much of his poetry is also true of his criticism. When the critic writes of tradition and the individual talent, when he declares the necessity for the author of a consciousness of the past as far back as Homer, when he brings the reader back to Dante, the Elizabethans and Andrew Marvell, he is also speaking as the heir of all the ages.

The emphasis on a consciousness of literature may also be misleading, for nowhere better than in Eliot can we see the difference between being merely literary and making the knowledge of literature an element in vision, that is to say, an essential part of the process of seeing anything and everything. Thus, to cite the advent of Tiresias again, the literary character of his appearance is matched by the unliterary actuality by means of which he refers to himself as being "like a taxi throbbing waiting." In one way, the subject of

The Waste Land is the sensibility of the protagonist, a sensibility which is literary, philosophical, cosmopolitan and expatriated. But this sensibility is concerned not with itself as such, but with the common things of modern life, with two such important aspects of existence as religious belief and making love. To summon to mind such profound witnesses as Freud and D. H. Lawrence is to remember how often, in modern life, love has been the worst sickness of human beings.

The extent to which Eliot's poetry is directly concerned with love is matched only by the extent to which it is concerned with religious belief and the crisis of moral values. J. Alfred Prufrock is unable to make love to women of his own class and kind because of shyness, self-consciousness, and fear of rejection. The protagonists of other poems in Eliot's first book are men or women laughed at or rejected in love, and a girl deserted by her lover seems like a body deserted by the soul.

In Eliot's second volume of poems, an old man's despair issues in part from his inability to make love,[4] while Sweeney, an antithetical character, is able to make love, but is unable to satisfy the woman with whom he copulates. In *The Waste Land,* the theme of love as a failure is again uppermost. Two lovers return from a garden after a moment of love, and the woman is overcome by despair or pathological despondency. A lady, perhaps the same woman who has returned from the garden in despair, becomes hysterical in her boudoir because her lover or her husband has nothing to say to her and cannot give her life any meaning or interest: "What shall I do now?" she says, "what shall I ever do?" The neurasthenic lady is succeeded in the poem by cockney women who gossip about another cockney woman who has been made ill by contraceptive pills taken to avoid the consequences of love; which is to say that the sickness of love has struck down every class in society: "What you get married for, if you don't want children?" And then we witness the seduction of the typist; and then other aspects of the sickness of love appear when, on the Thames bank, three girls ruined by love rehearse the sins of the young men with whom they have been having affairs. In the last part of the poem, the impossibility of love, the gulf between one human being and another, is the answer to the command to give, that is to say, to give oneself or surrender oneself to another human being in the act of making love.

*   *   *

4. A reference to "Gerontion."

* * * But we ought to remember that the difficulty of making love, that is to say, of entering into the most intimate of relationships, is not the beginning but the consequence of the whole character of modern life. That is why the apparatus of reference which the poet brings to bear upon failure in love involves all history ("And I Tiresias have foresuffered all") and is international. So too the old man who is the protagonist of "Gerontion" must refer to human beings of many nationalities, to Mr. Silvero at Limoges, Hakagawa, Madame de Tornquist, Fräulein von Kulp and Christ [the tiger] and he finds it necessary to speak of all history as well as his failure in love. History is made to illuminate love and love is made to illuminate history. In modern life, human beings are whirled beyond the circuit of the constellations: their intimate plight is seen in connection or relation with the anguish of the Apostles after Calvary, the murder of Agamemnon, the insanity of Ophelia and children who chant that London bridge is falling down. In the same way, the plight of Prufrock is illuminated by means of a rich, passing reference to Michelangelo, the sculptor of the strong and heroic man. Only when the poet is the heir of all the ages can he make significant use of so many different and distant kinds of experience. But conversely, only when experience becomes international, only when many different and distant kinds of experience are encountered by the poet, does he find it necessary to become the heir of all the ages.

Difficulty in love is inseparable from the deracination and the alienation from which the international man suffers. When the traditional beliefs, sanctions and bonds of the community and of the family decay or disappear in the distance like a receding harbor, then love ceases to be an act which is in relation to the life of the community, and in immediate relation to the family and other human beings. Love becomes purely personal. It is isolated from the past and the future, and since it is isolated from all other relationships, since it is no longer celebrated, evaluated and given a status by the community, love does become merely copulation. The protagonist of "Gerontion" uses one of the most significant phrases in Eliot's work when he speaks of himself as living in a *rented* house; which is to say, not in the house where his forbears lived. He lives in a rented house, he is unable to make love, and he knows that history has many cunning, deceptive, and empty corridors. The nature of the house, of love and of history are interdependent aspects of modern life.

* * *

To be international is to be a citizen of the world and thus a citizen of no particular city. The world as such is not a community and it has no constitution or government: it is the turning world in which the human being, surrounded by the consequences of all times and all places, must live his life as a human being and not as the citizen of any nation. Hence, to be the heir of all the ages is to inherit nothing but a consciousness of how all heirlooms are rooted in the past. Dominated by the historical consciousness, the international hero finds that all beliefs affect the holding of any belief (he cannot think of Christianity without remembering Adonis); he finds that many languages affect each use of speech (*The Waste Land* concludes with a passage in four languages).

*　*　*

Modern life may be compared to a foreign country in which a foreign language is spoken. Eliot is the international hero because he has made the journey to the foreign country and described the nature of the new life in the foreign country. Since the future is bound to be international, if it is anything at all, we are all the bankrupt heirs of the ages, and the moments of the crisis expressed in Eliot's work are a prophecy of the crises of our own future in regard to love, religious belief, good and evil, the good life and the nature of the just society. *The Waste Land* will soon be as good as new.

MAUD ELLMANN

A Sphinx without a Secret[†]

In a fable of Oscar Wilde's, Gerald, the narrator, finds his old companion Lord Murchison so puzzled and anxious that he urges him to unburden his mind. Murchison confides that he fell in love some time ago with the mysterious Lady Alroy, whose life was so entrenched in secrecy that every move she made was surreptitious, every word she spoke conspiratorial. Fascinated, he resolved to marry her. But on the day he planned for his proposal, he caught sight of her on the street, "deeply veiled", and walking swiftly towards a lodging house, where she let herself in with her own key. Suspecting a secret lover, he abandoned her in rage and stormed off to the Continent to forget her. Soon afterwards, however, he learnt that she was dead, having caught pneumonia in the theatre. Still tormented by her mystery, he returned to London to continue his investigations.

† From *The Poetics of Impersonality: T. S. Eliot and Ezra Pound* (Cambridge, MA: Harvard University Press, 1987), pp. 91–109. Copyright © 1987 by Maud Ellmann. Reprinted by permission of the licensor, Edinburgh University Press, through PLSclear. The author's notes have been edited.

He cross-examined the landlady of the lodging house, but she insisted that Lady Alroy always visited her rooms alone, took tea, and left as blamelessly as she had come. "'Now, what do you think it all meant?'" Murchison demands. For Gerald, the answer is quite simple: the lady was "'a sphinx without a secret.'"[1]

Now, *The Waste Land* is a sphinx without a secret, too, and to force it to confession may also be a way of killing it. This poem, which has been so thoroughly *explained*, is rarely *read* at all, and one can scarcely see the "waste" beneath the redevelopments. Most commentators have been so busy tracking its allusions down and patching up its tattered memories that they have overlooked its broken images in search of the totality it might have been. Whether they envisage the poem as a pilgrimage, a quest for the Holy Grail, an elegy to Europe or to Jean Verdenal, these readings treat the text as if it were a photographic negative, tracing the shadows of a lost or forbidden body.[2]

This is how Freud first undertook interpretation, too, but his patients forced him to revise his method, and his experience may shed a different kind of light upon *The Waste Land*. In *Studies on Hysteria,* Freud and Breuer argue that "hysterics suffer mainly from reminiscences" (and by this definition, *The Waste Land* is the most hysterical of texts).[3] Since the hysteric somatises her desire, enciphering her memories upon her flesh, Freud imagined that he could alleviate her suffering by salvaging the painful recollections. However, these archaeologies would leave her cold. For this reason, he shifted his attention from the past to the present, from reminiscence to resistance, from the secrets to the silences themselves.

Now, *The Waste Land,* like any good sphinx, lures the reader into hermeneutics, too: but there is no secret underneath its

---

1. Oscar Wilde, "A Sphinx without a Secret," *Complete Writings,* 10 vols. (New York: Nottingham Society, 1905–1909), Vol. 8, pp. 121–132.
2. In fact the criticism reads more like a quest for the Holy Grail than the poem does. For the Holy Grail interpretation, see Grover Smith, *T. S. Eliot's Poetry and Plays: A Study in Sources and Meaning* (Chicago: University of Chicago Press, 1956), pp. 69–70, 74–7; and Edmund Wilson, *Axel's Castle: A Study in the Imaginative Literature of 1870–1930* (New York and London: Scribner's, 1931), pp. 104–5. Helen Gardner subscribes to this position with some qualifications in *The Art of T. S. Eliot* (London: Cresset Press, 1949), p. 87. George Williamson reconstructs *The Waste Land* ingeniously in *A Reader's Guide to T. S. Eliot* (New York: H. Woolf, 1953), esp. pp. 129–130. For Jean Verdenal see John Peter, "A New Interpretation of *The Waste Land,*" in *Essays in Criticism,* 2 (1952), esp. p. 245; and James E. Miller, *T. S. Eliot's Personal Waste Land: Exorcism of the Demons* (University Park, Pennsylvania: Pennsylvania State University Press, 1977), *passim.*
3. Freud revises this formula, however, in *The Interpretation of Dreams,* where he states that "Hysterical symptoms are not attached to actual memories, but to phantasies erected on the basis of memories." *Complete Psychological Works of Sigmund Freud,* tr. James Strachey (London: Hogarth, 1953–1974), Vol. 5, p. 491.

hugger-muggery. Indeed, Hegel saw the Sphinx as the symbol of the symbolic itself, because it did not know the answer to its own question: and *The Waste Land*, too, is a riddle to *itself*.[4] Here it is more instructive to be scrupulously superficial than to dig beneath the surface for the poem's buried skeletons or sources. For it is in the silences *between* the words that meaning flickers, local, evanescent—in the very "wastes" that stretch across the page. These silences curtail the powers of the author, for they invite the *hypocrite lecteur* to reconstruct their broken sense. Moreover, the speaker cannot be identified with his creator, not because he has a *different* personality, like Prufrock, but because he has no stable identity at all. The disembodied "I" glides in and out of stolen texts, as if the speaking subject were merely the quotation of its antecedents. Indeed, this subject is the victim of a general collapse of boundaries. This chapter examines *The Waste Land* in the light of Freud—and ultimately in the darkness of *Beyond the Pleasure Principle*—to trace the poem's suicidal logic.

Throbbing between Two Lives

Let us assume, first of all, that *The Waste Land* is about what it declares—waste. A ceremonial purgation, it inventories all the "stony rubbish" that it strives to exorcise (20).[5] The "waste *land*" could be seen as the thunderous desert where the hooded hordes are swarming towards apocalypse. But it also means "waste ground", bomb sites or vacant lots, like those in "Rhapsody on a Windy Night", where ancient women gather the wreckage of Europe.[6] It means Jerusalem or Alexandria or London—any ravaged centre of a dying world—and it foreshadows the dilapidation of centricity itself. The poem teems with urban waste, butt-ends of the city's days and ways: "empty bottles, sandwich papers, / Silk handkerchiefs, cardboard boxes, cigarette ends" (177–8). However, it is difficult to draw taxonomies of waste, because the text conflates the city with the body and, by analogy, the social with the personal. Abortions, broken fingernails, carious teeth, and "female smells" signify the culture's decadence, as well as bodily decrepitude. The self is implicated in

---

4. See *Hegel's Aesthetics: Lectures on Fine Art*, trans. T. M. Knox (Oxford: Clarendon, 1975), pp. 360–1.
5. Just as "Ash-Wednesday" strives to be a prayer, *The Waste Land* aspires to the condition of ritual. This fascination with cathartic rites drew Eliot towards the theatre in his later work, but his poems also crave performance, incantation. [The numbers given in parentheses in the text are line numbers to *The Waste Land*—Editor.]
6. Suggested by Peter Middleton, "The Academic Development of *The Waste Land*," in *Demarcating the Disciplines: Philosophy, Literature, Art*, ed. Samuel Weber (Minneapolis: University of Minnesota Press, 1986), pp. 153–80.

the degradation of the race, because the filth without insinuates defilement within.[7]

It is waste *paper*, however, which appals and fascinates the poem, the written detritus which drifts into the text as randomly as picnics sink into the Thames (177–8). Many modernist writers comb the past in order to recycle its remains, and Joyce is the master of the scavengers: "Nothing but old fags and cabbage-stumps of quotations", in D. H. Lawrence's words.[8] Joyce treats the rubbish heap of literature as a fund of creativity ("The letter! The litter!"), disseminating writings as Eliot strews bones.[9] A funeral rather than a wake, *The Waste Land* is a lugubrious version of Joyce's jubilant "recirculation" of the past, in which all waste becomes unbiodegradable: "Men and bits of paper, whirled by the cold wind . . ."[1] Indeed, *The Waste Land* is one of the most abject texts in English literature, in every sense: for abjection, according to Bataille, "is merely the inability to assume with sufficient strength the imperative act of excluding abject things", an act that "establishes the foundations of collective existence."[2] Waste is what a culture casts away in order to determine what is not itself, and thus to establish its own limits. In the same way, the subject defines the limits of his body through the violent expulsion of its own excess: and ironically, this catharsis *institutes* the excremental. Similarly, Paul Ricoeur has pointed out that social rituals of "burning, removing, chasing, throwing, spitting out, covering up, burying" continuously *reinvent* the waste they exorcise.[3]

The word "abject" literally means "cast out", though commonly it means downcast in spirits: but "abjection" may refer to the waste itself, together with the violence of casting it abroad. It is the ambiguity of the "abject" that distinguishes it from the "object", which the subject rigorously jettisons (ob-jects). According to Julia Kristeva, the abject emerges when exclusions fail, in the sickening collapse of limits. Rather than disease or filth or putrefaction, the abject is that which "disturbs identity, system, order": it is the "inbetween, the ambiguous, the composite."[4] In the "brown fog" of *The Waste Land*, for example, or the yellow fog of "Prufrock", the in-between grows

7. Paul Ricoeur has pointed out that "impurity was never literally filthiness" and "defilement was never literally a stain", for the notion of impurity is "primordially symbolic". See Ricoeur, *The Symbolism of Evil*, trans. Emerson Buchanan (Boston: Beacon Press, 1967), pp. 35, 39.
8. Quoted by Jennifer Schiffer Levine in "Originality and Repetition in *Finnegans Wake* and *Ulysses*", PMLA, 94 (1979), 108.
9. James Joyce, *Finnegans Wake* (New York: Viking, 1967), p. 93, line 24.
1. The quotation is from Eliot's poem "Burnt Norton," section 3, line 15. The term "recirculation" is taken from *Finnegans Wake*, p. 3 [*Editor*].
2. Quoted in Julia Kristeva, *Powers of Horror: An Essay on Abjection*, trans. Leon S. Roudiez (New York: Columbia University Press, 1982), p. 56.
3. Ricoeur, *Symbolism of Evil*, p. 35.
4. Kristeva, *Powers of Horror*, p. 4; see also p. 9.

animate: and Madame Sosostris warns us to fear death by water, for sinking banks betoken glutinous distinctions. In fact, the "horror" of *The Waste Land* lurks in the osmoses, exhalations and porosities, in the dread of *epidemic* rather than the filth itself, for it is this miasma that bespeaks dissolving limits.[5] The corpses signify the "utmost of abjection", in Kristeva's phrase, because they represent "a border that has encroached upon everything": an outside that irrupts into the inside, and erodes the parameters of life.[6] It is impossible to keep them underground: Stetson's garden is an ossuary, and the dull canals, the garrets, and the alleys are littered with unburied bones. "Tumbled graves" (387) have overrun the city, for the living have changed places with the dead: "A crowd flowed over London Bridge, so many, / I had not thought death had undone so many" (62–3). *The Waste Land* does not fear the dead themselves so much as their invasion of the living; for it is the collapse of boundaries that centrally disturbs the text, be they sexual, national, linguistic, or authorial.

Kristeva derives her notion of abjection from Freud's *Totem and Taboo*, which was written ten years before the publication of *The Waste Land* and anticipates its itch for anthropology.[7] Like Eliot, Freud draws analogies between the psychic and the cultural, linking "civilised" obsessionality to "savage" rites. In both cases the ritual "is ostensibly a protection against the prohibited act; but *actually . . .* a repetition of it."[8] *The Waste Land* resembles this obsessive rite, because it surreptitiously repeats the horror that it tries to expiate. In particular, it desecrates tradition. The poem may be seen as an extended "blasphemy", in Eliot's conception of the term, an affirmation masked as a denial. For the text dismantles Western culture as if destruction were the final mode of veneration. As Terry Eagleton argues:

> behind the back of this ruptured, radically decentred poem runs an alternative text which is nothing less than the closed, coherent, authoritative discourse of the mythologies which frame it. The phenomenal text, to use one of Eliot's own metaphors, is merely the meat with which the burglar distracts the guard-dog while he proceeds with his stealthy business.[9]

5. Eliot originally quoted Kurtz's last words "The horror! the horror!" from Conrad's *Heart of Darkness* as the epigraph to *The Waste Land*: see *The Waste Land: A Facsimile and Transcript of the Original Drafts Including the Annotations of Ezra Pound*, ed. Valerie Eliot (London: Faber, 1971), p. 3.
6. Kristeva, *Powers of Horror*, pp. 4, 3.
7. For contemporary interest in anthropology, see Stephen Kern, *The Culture of Time and Space* (Cambridge: Harvard University Press, 1983), pp. 19–20, 32, 34.
8. Freud, *Complete Works*, Vol. 12, p. 50.
9. Terry Eagleton, *Criticism and Ideology: A Study in Marxist Literary Theory* (London: Verso, 1978), pp. 149–150.

However, Eagleton omits a further ruse: for the poem uses its nostalgia to conceal its vandalism, its pastiche of the tradition that it mourns. Indeed, a double consciousness pervades the text, as if it had been written by a vicar and an infidel. The speaker is divided from himself, unable to resist the imp within who cynically subverts his pieties. Thus, Cleopatra's burnished throne becomes a dressing table, time's winged chariot a grinning skull (77, 186): but there are many subtler deformations.

Take, for instance, the opening words. The line "April is the cruellest month" blasphemes (in Eliot's sense) against the first lines of *The Canterbury Tales,* which presented April's showers as so sweet. At once a nod to origins and a flagrant declaration of beginninglessness, this allusion grafts the poem to another text, vaunting its parasitic inbetweenness. Only the misquotation marks the change of ownership, but the author's personality dissolves in the citational abyss. This is why Conrad Aiken once complained that Eliot had created "'a literature of literature' . . . a kind of parasitic growth on literature, a sort of mistletoe . . ."[1] As blasphemy, *The Waste Land* is obliged to poach upon the past, caught in a perpetual allusion to the texts that it denies.[2] For it is only by corrupting Chaucer's language that Eliot can grieve the passing of his world:

> April is the cruellest month, breeding
> Lilacs out of the dead land, mixing
> Memory and desire, stirring
> Dull roots with spring rain.
> Winter kept us warm, covering
> Earth in forgetful snow, feeding
> A little life with dried tubers.
>
> (1–7)

Because these lines allude to Chaucer, they invoke the origin of the tradition as well as the juvescence of the year.[3] But words like "stirring", "mixing", and "feeding" profane beginnings, be they literary or organic, provoking us to ask what "cruelty" has exchanged them for uniting, engendering, or nourishing. Thus the passage whispers of the words *its* words deny, and sorrows for the things it cannot say. Most of the lines stretch beyond the comma where the cadence falls, as if the words themselves had overflown their bounds, straining towards a future state of being like the dull roots that they describe. They typify the way *The Waste Land* differs from itself, forever

---

1. See Conrad Aiken, "An Anatomy of Melancholy," p. 198 above [*Editor*].
2. Thus it could be said that writing *engenders* blasphemy, just as law is the prerequisite to crime.
3. See Chaucer, General Prologue to *The Canterbury Tales,* lines 1–4.

trembling towards another poem which has already been written, or else has yet to be composed.

This betweenness also overtakes the speaking subject, for the first-person pronoun roams from voice to voice.[4] The "us" in "Winter kept us warm" glides into the "us" of "Summer surprised us," without alerting "us", the readers, of any change of name or locus. At last, the "us" contracts into the couple in the Hofgarten, after having spoken for the human, animal and vegetable worlds. What begins as an editorial "we" becomes the mark of a migration, which restlessly displaces voice and origin. Throughout the poem, the "I" slips from persona to persona, weaves in and out of quoted speech, and creeps like a contagion through the *Prothalamion* or Pope or the debased grammar of a London pub, sweeping history into a heap of broken images.

However, Eliot insisted in the Notes to *The Waste Land* that Tiresias should stabilise this drifting subject, and rally the nomadic voices of the text:[5]

> 218. Tiresias, although a mere spectator and not indeed a "character", is yet the most important personage in the poem, uniting all the rest. Just as the one-eyed merchant, seller of currants, *melts into* the Phoenician Sailor, and the latter is *not wholly distinct* from Ferdinand Prince of Naples, so all the women are one woman, and the *two sexes meet* in Tiresias. What Tiresias *sees*, in fact, is the substance of the poem.[6]

But what *does* Tiresias see? Blind as he is, the prophet has a single walk-on part, when he spies on the typist and her lover indulging in carbuncular caresses.[7] In this Note, moreover, Eliot emphasises the *osmosis* of identities more than their reunion in a central consciousness. For Tiresias's role within the poem is to "melt" distinctions and confuse personae:

> I Tiresias, though blind, throbbing between two lives,
> Old man with wrinkled female breasts, can see
> At the violet hour, the evening hour that strives

---

4. Alick West pointed this out long ago: see *Crisis and Criticism* (London: Lawrence and Wishart, 1937), pp. 5–6, 28.

5. For critics who see Tiresias as an omniscient narrator, see *inter alia* Grover Smith, *Eliot's Poetry and Plays*, pp. 72–6; F. O. Matthiessen, *The Achievement of T. S. Eliot* (Boston: Houghton-Mifflin, 1935), p. 60. For critics more sceptical of Tiresias's role, see Graham Hough, *Image and Experience: Studies in a Literary Revolution* (London: Duckworth, 1960), p. 25; Juliet McLaughlin, "Allusion in *The Waste Land*", *Essays in Criticism*, 19 (1969), 456; Paul LaChance, "The Function of Voice in *The Waste Land*", *Style*, 5, no. 2 (1971), 107ff.

6. Emphasis added, except for "sees."

7. Genevieve W. Forster takes the extraordinary view that the scene with the typist is therefore the "substance of the poem": in "The Archetypal Imagery of T. S. Eliot", *PMLA*, 60 (1945), 573.

Homeward, and brings the sailor home from sea,
The typist home at teatime, clears her breakfast, lights
Her stove, and lays out food in tins.
Out of the window perilously spread
Her drying combinations touched by the sun's last rays,
On the divan are piled (at night her bed)
Stockings, slippers, camisoles, and stays.
I Tiresias, old man with wrinkled dugs
Perceived the scene, and foretold the rest—
I too awaited the expected guest.
He, the young man carbuncular, arrives. . . .

                                                    (218–31)

Here the seer turns into a peeping Tom, the most ambiguous of spectators. "Throbbing between two lives", Tiresias could be seen as the very prophet of abjection, personifying all the poem's porous membranes. A revisionary, he foresees what he has already foresuffered, mixing memory and desire, self and other, man and woman, pollution and catharsis. The Notes which exalt him are "abject" themselves, for they represent a kind of supplement or discharge of the text that Eliot could never get "unstuck", though he later wished the poem might stand alone.[8] Now that the manuscript has been released (1971), the poem throbs between two authors and three texts—the Notes, the published poem, and the drafts that Pound pruned so cunningly. The text's integrity dissolves under the invasion of its own disjecta. Just as its quotations confuse the past and present, parasite and poet, the poem leaks in supplements and prolegomena.

The typist symptomises this betweenness, too. Her profession parodies the poet's, demoted as he is to the typist or amanuensis of the dead. Too untidy to acknowledge boundaries, she strews her bed with stockings, slippers, camisoles, and stays, and even the bed is a divan by day, in a petit bourgeois disrespect for definition. She resembles the neurotic woman in "A Game of Chess", who cannot decide to go out or to stay in, as if she were at enmity with their distinction. Eliot himself declares that all the women in *The Waste Land* are one woman, and this is because they represent the very principle of unguency. "Pneumatic bliss" entails emulsive demarcations.[9] Yet the misogyny is so ferocious, particularly in the manuscript, that it begins to turn into a blasphemy against itself. For the poem is enthralled by the femininity that it reviles, bewitched by this odorous and shoreless flesh. In fact, woman is the spirit of its own

8. See Eliot's comments on the notes, p. 136. See also p. 61, n. 1 [*Editor*].
9. A quotation from Eliot's "Whispers of Immortality," originally published in *Poems* (1920). See p. 36 [*Editor*].

construction, the phantom of its own betweennesses. In "The Fire Sermon", Eliot personifies his broken images in a woman's bruised, defiled flesh; and it is as if the damsel Donne once greeted as his new found land had reverted to the old world and an urban wilderness:

> "Trams and dusty trees.
> Highbury bore me. Richmond and Kew
> Undid me. By Richmond I raised my knees
> Supine on the floor of a narrow canoe."
>
> "My feet are at Moorgate, and my heart
> Under my feet. After the event
> He wept. He promised 'a new start'.
> I made no comment. What should I resent?"
>
> "On Margate Sands.
> I can connect
> Nothing with nothing.
> The broken fingernails of dirty hands.
> My people humble people who expect
> Nothing."
>   la la
>
> To Carthage then I came
>
> Burning burning burning burning
> O Lord Thou pluckest me out
> O Lord Thou pluckest
>
> burning

                                   (292–311)

The body and the city melt together, no longer themselves but not yet other. It is as if the metaphor were stuck between the tenor and the vehicle, transfixed in an eternal hesitation. Both the woman and the city have been raped, but the "he" seems passive in his violence, weeping at his own barbarity. The victim, too, consents to degradation as if it were foredoomed: "I raised my knees / Supine. . . . What should I resent?" (As Ian Hamilton observes, "no one in *The Waste Land* raises her knees in any other spirit than that of dumb complaisance.")[1] "Undone", the woman's body crumbles in a synecdochic heap of knees, heart, feet, weirdly disorganised: "My feet are at Moorgate, and my heart / Under my feet." But the city which undid her decomposes, too, in a random concatenation

---

1. Ian Hamilton, "The Waste Land", in *Eliot in Perspective: A Symposium,* ed. Graham Martin (London: Macmillan, 1960), p. 109.

of its parts—Highbury, Richmond, Kew, Moorgate—and ends in broken fingernails on Margate Sands.

Itinerant and indeterminate, the "I" slips from the woman to the city, and then assumes the voice of Conrad's Harlequin in *Heart of Darkness*, who apologises for a humble and exploited race. At last it merges with the "I" who came to Carthage in St Augustine's *Confessions*. As the last faltering words suggest, it is impossible to "pluck" the speaking subject out of the conflagration of the poem's idioms. The I cannot preserve its own identity intact against the shrieking voices which assail it, "Scolding, mocking, or merely chattering" according to their whim.[2] In *The Waste Land*, the only voice which *is* "inviolable" is the voice that does not speak, but only sings that phatic, faint "la la."

These notes allude to the warblings of the nightingale, who fills the desert "with inviolable voice" (101). In Ovid, however, the nightingale was born in violation. Tereus, "the barbarous king" (99) raped his wife's sister Philomela, and cut out her tongue so that she could not even name her own defiler ("Tereu . . ." [206]). But Philomela weaves a picture of his crime into her loom so that her sister, Procne, can decode her wrongs.[3] In this way, her web becomes a kind of writing, a dossier to defend her speechless flesh. After reading it, Procne avenges Philomela by feeding Tereus the flesh of his own son. In *The Waste Land*, Eliot omits the web, and he ignores this violent retaliation, too. He alludes only to the ending of the myth, when the gods give both the sisters wings to flee from Tereus's wrath. They change Philomela into a nightingale to compensate her loss of speech with wordless song.[4] By invoking this story, Eliot suggests that woman is excluded from language through the sexual violence of a man. As Peter Middleton has pointed out, she is awarded for her pains with a pure art which is powerless and desolate—"la, la."

In *The Waste Land* as in Ovid, writing provides the only refuge from aphasia, but it is a weapon that turns against its own possessor. Rather than the record of the victim's wrongs, writing has become the very instrument of violation: and it invades the male narrator's speech as irresistably as the "female stench" with which it comes to be associated.[5] Although Eliot quotes Bradley to the effect that "my experience falls within my own circle, a circle closed on the outside",

---

2. Quoted from Eliot's "Burnt Norton," section 5, line 18 [*Editor*].
3. While Freud once said that weaving was woman's only contribution to civilisation, and that it originates in the "concealment of genital deficiency" (*Complete Works*, Vol. 22, p. 132), Ovid makes women's weaving into the invention of the *text*.
4. Ovid juxtaposes her story to Arachne's, another weaving tattle-tale, who fraught her web with "heavenly crimes", depicting Zeus in all the shapes he took to ravish nymphs and mortal women: *Metamorphoses*, VI, 103–33. [For the story of Philomela, see the selection from Ovid's *Metamorphoses*, pp. 86–91—*Editor*.]
5. *Facsimile*, p. 39.

this circle has been broken in *The Waste Land* (411n.). Here no experience is proper or exclusive to the subject. Moreover, the speaker is possessed by the writings of the dead, and seized in a cacophony beyond control.

Prince of Morticians

Curious, is it not, that Mr. Eliot
Has not given more time to Mr. Beddoes
(T. L.) prince of morticians
Pound, Canto LXXX

In "Tradition and the Individual Talent" Eliot celebrates the voices of the dead, but he comes to dread their verbal ambush in *The Waste Land*.[6] In the essay, he claimed that "not only the best, but the most individual poetry" is that which is most haunted by its own precursors. Only thieves can truly be original. For any new creation gains its meaning in relation to the poems of the past, and writing is a voyage to the underworld, to commune with the phantasmal voices of the dead. Eliot published this essay immediately after World War I, in 1919, the same year that Freud was writing *Beyond the Pleasure Principle*. As Middleton has pointed out, they both confront the same material: the unprecedented death toll of the First World War. Like Freud's theory of repetition, Eliot's account of influence attempts to salvage something of a past that had never been so ruthlessly annihilated—however fearsome its reanimation from the grave. Whereas Freud discovers the death drive in the compulsion to repeat, *The Waste Land* stages it in the compulsion to citation.

In 1919 Freud also wrote his famous essay on the "uncanny", which he defines as "whatever reminds us of this inner compulsion to repeat."[7] *The Waste Land* is uncanny in a double sense, for it is haunted by the repetition of the dead—in the form of mimicry, quotation and pastiche—but also by a kind of Hammer horror: bats with baby faces, whisper music, violet light, hooded hordes, witches, death's heads, bones, and zombies (378–81). According to Freud, "heimlich" literally means "homely" or familiar, but it develops in the direction of ambivalence until it converges with its opposite, *unheimlich* or uncanny. Thus the very word has grown unhomely and improper to itself. The passage Eliot misquotes from *The White Devil* provides a good example of the double meaning of uncanniness:

---

6. Helen Gardner argues that *The Waste Land* is an "exercise in ventriloquism", but she makes the dead the dummies, Eliot the ventriloquist. I suggest that the poem works the other way around. [For "Tradition," see above, p. 147—*Editor*.]
7. "The Uncanny," in *Complete Works*, Vol. 17, p. 238. The reference below to the *unheimlich* is from the same essay, pp. 222–6.

O keep the Dog far hence, that's friend to men,
Or with his nails he'll dig it up again!

(74–5)

Since the passage is purloined from Webster, the very words are
ghostly revenants, returning as extravagant and erring spirits. This
kind of verbal kleptomania subverts the myth that literary texts are
private property, or that the author can enjoy the sole possession of
his words. But Eliot writes Dog where Webster wrote Wolf, and
friend where Webster wrote foe. Thus he tames the hellhound in
the same misprision that domesticates the discourse of the past.
Friendly pet and wild beast, the Dog becomes the emblem of the
poem's literary necrophilia, and the familiar strangeness of the past
that Eliot himself has disinterred.

Quotation means that words cannot be anchored to their authors,
and the fortune-tellers in the text personify this loss of origin. For
prophecy means that we hear about a thing before it happens. The
report precedes the event. The bell echoes before it rings. Tiresias,
for instance, has not only foreseen but actually "foresuffered all",
as if he were a living misquotation. A fake herself, Madame Sosos-
tris lives in fear of imitators ("Tell her I bring the horoscope myself"),
nervous that her words may go astray ("One must be so careful these
days"). This anxiety about originality and theft resurges in the form
of Mr Eugenides. A Turkish merchant in London, he also speaks
demotic French: and the word "demotic", Greek in etymology,
alludes to Egyptian hieroglyphics. Being a merchant, he is not only
the product but the sinister conductor of miscegenation, intermin-
gling verbal, sexual and monetary currencies. Even his pocketful of
currants could be heard as "currents", which dissolve identities and
definitions, like the "current under sea" that picks the bones of Phle-
bas, his Phoenician alter ego.[8] His reappearances suggest that rep-
etition has become a virus, unwholesome as the personages who
recur. Indeed, the poem hints that literature is nothing but a plague
of echoes: that writing necessarily deserts its author, spreading like
an epidemic into other texts. Any set of written signs can fall into
bad company, into contexts which pervert their meaning and their
genealogy.

The worst company in *The Waste Land*, both socially and rhetori-
cally, is the London pub where Lil is tortured by her crony for her
bad teeth and her abortion. Here, the publican's cry, "HURRY UP
PLEASE ITS TIME", becomes as vagrant as a written sign, orphaned
from its author. Any British drinker knows its origin, of course, so

8. I owe this pun and some of the preceding formulations to my student John Reid at
Amherst College, 1986.

Eliot does not identify the speaker, but sets the phrase adrift on a semantic odyssey. When it interrupts the dialogue, the two discursive sites contaminate each other.

> You ought to be ashamed, I said, to look so antique.
> (And her only thirty-one.)
> I can't help it, she said, pulling a long face,
> It's them pills I took, to bring it off, she said.
> (She's had five already, and nearly died of young George.)
> The chemist said it would be all right, but I've never
>   been the same.
> You *are* a proper fool, I said.
> Well, if Albert won't leave you alone, there it is, I said,
> What you get married for if you don't want children?
> HURRY UP PLEASE ITS TIME
> Well, that Sunday Albert was home, they had a hot
>   gammon,
> And they asked me in to dinner, to get the beauty of
>   it hot—
> HURRY UP PLEASE ITS TIME
> HURRY UP PLEASE ITS TIME
> Goonight Bill. Goonight Lou. Goonight May. Goonight.
> Ta ta. Goonight. Goonight.
> Good night, ladies, good night, sweet ladies, good night,
>   good night.
>
> (156–72)

This is the same technique that Flaubert uses in the fair in *Madame Bovary*, where Emma and Rodolph wallow in romance, while the voice of the Minister of Agriculture splices their sentiment with swine. In *The Waste Land*, the more the publican repeats his cry, the more its meaning strays from his intentions. Instead of closing time, it now connotes perfunctory and brutal sexuality: it means that time is catching up with Lil, in the form of dentures and decay, and rushing her culture to apocalypse. There is no omniscient speaker here to monitor these meanings, no "pill" to control their pullulation. It is as if the words themselves had been demobbed and grown adulterous. When Ophelia's good-byes creep in, just as the dialogue is closing, the allusion dignifies Lil's slower suicide: "Good night, ladies, good night, sweet ladies, good night, good night." Yet at the same time, the text degrades Ophelia by suturing her words to Lil's, reducing Shakespeare to graffiti.[9]

---

9. Andrew Parker pointed out to me in conversation that "degradation" in the poem always occurs through the association with the lower classes.

In general, the poem's attitude towards Shakespeare and the canon resembles taboos against the dead, with their mixture of veneration and horror. As Freud says, "they are expressions of mourning; but on the other hand they clearly betray—what they seek to conceal—hostility against the dead . . .".[1] But he stresses that it is not the dead themselves so much as their "infection" which is feared, for they are charged with a kind of "electricity." The taboo arises to defend the living subject from their sly invasions. But strangely enough, the taboo eventually becomes prohibited itself, as if the ban were as infectious as the horrors it forbids. Prohibition spreads like a disease, tainting everything that touches it, "till at last the whole world lies under an embargo." A similar reversal takes place in *The Waste Land* where the rituals of purity are perverted into *ersatz* desecrations of themselves. When Mrs. Porter and her daughter wash their feet in soda water, the ceremony of innocence is drowned, and the baptismal rite becomes its own defilement.

According to Freud, there are two ways in which taboo can spread, through contact and through mimesis. To touch a sacred object is to fall under its interdict. But the offender must also be tabooed because of "the risk of imitation", for others may follow his example.[2] These two forms of "transference" work like tropes, since the first, like metonymy, depends on contiguity, the second on similitude like metaphor. Freud adds that taboo usages resemble obsessional symptoms in that "the prohibitions lack any assignable motive", and they are "easily displaceable". It is as if the spread of the taboo depended on the power of rhetorical displacement: and underneath the fear of the contagion is the fear of tropes, the death-dealing power of figuration.

Displacement is indeed the malady the poem strives to cure, but its own figures are the source of the disorder. Though Eliot condemns Milton for dividing sound from sense, it is precisely this dissociation which produces the semantic epidemic of *The Waste Land*. It is the rats, appropriately, who carry the infection. They make their first appearance in "rats' alley"; but here a note refers us mischievously to Part III, where another rat peeks out again, like a further outbreak of the verbal plague:

> White bodies naked on the low damp ground
> And bones cast in a little low dry garret,
> Rattled by the rat's foot only, year to year.

---

1. Freud, *Complete Works*, Vol. 13, p. 61. For the other quotations in this paragraph, see pp. 20–22, 41, and 27 in the same volume.
2. Freud, *Complete Works*, Vol. 13, p. 33. For the other quotations in this paragraph, see pp. 27 and 28.

However, Eliot seems to have forgotten one rodential apparition in between:

> But at my back in a cold blast I hear
> The *rattle* of the bones, and chuckle spread from ear to ear.
>
> A *rat* crept softly through the vegetation
> Dragging its slimy belly on the bank
> While I was fishing in the dull canal
> On a winter evening round behind the gashouse
> Musing upon the king my brother's wreck
> And on the king my father's death before him.
> White bodies naked on the low damp ground
> And bones cast in a little low dry garret,
> *Rattled* by the *rat's* foot only, year to year.
>
> (185–95: my emphases)

It is the sound, here, which connects the rattle to the rat, as opposed to a semantic link between them. And it is the rattle of the words, rather than their meaning, that propels the poem forward. Indeed, the sound preempts the sense and spreads like an infection.

Notice that the text associates the rattle of the rats with "the king my brother's wreck" and "the king my father's death before him." For the contiguity suggests that it is these calamities that taint these signs, causing them to fester and grow verminous. Wrenched from their context in *The Tempest,* these deaths suggest the downfall of the father, as do the oblique allusions to the Fisher King, a figure Eliot derives from Jessie Weston's study of the Grail romance.[3] According to this legend, the King has lost his manhood, and his impotence has brought a blight over his lands. Eliot connects the Fisher King to "the man with three staves" in the Tarot pack, as if to hint that both have failed to fecundate the waste land, to fish the sense out of its floating signifiers. Their emasculation corresponds to other injuries, particularly to the mutilation of the voice: as if the phallus were complicit with the Logos. Lacking both, language has become a "waste of breath", a barren dissemination: "Sighs, short and infrequent, were exhaled . . .".

In the *Waste Land* manuscript, this anxiety about the Logos remains explicit. For here the pilgrim is searching for the "one essential word that frees", entrammelled in his own "concatenated words from which the sense seemed gone."[4] In the finished poem, all that

---

3. See Jessie Weston, *From Ritual to Romance* (1920; rpt. Garden City, New York: Doubleday, 1957), Ch. 9, pp. 113–36. [For a selection from this chapter, see "The Fisher King," p. 78 above—*Editor.*]
4. *Facsimile*, pp. 109, 113. The following quotation from the *Waste Land* manuscript is also from p. 109.

remains of the lightning of the Word is the belated *rattle* of the sign, the "dry sterile thunder" of the desert (342). And this is why the poem is for ever grieving its belatedness: for not only does it come too late to establish an originary voice, but after the nymphs, after the messiah, after the tradition:

> After the torchlight red on sweaty faces
> After the frosty silence in the gardens
> After the agony in stony places. . . .
>
> (322–4)

The manuscript goes on at this point to lament the lateness of its own inditing: "After the ending of this inspiration." For writing, in the waste land, is the "wake" of voice—at once the after-image of the author and his obsequies.

If writing is in league with death, however, it is also in cahoots with femininity. In *The Waste Land,* the "hearty female stench" converges with the odour of mortality—and both exude from *writing,* from the violated and putrescent corpse of speech. To use the text's sexology, writing and the stink of femininity have overpowered the priapic realm of voice. Eliot to some extent repressed this hearty female stench when he excised it from the manuscript: but it survives in the strange synthetic perfumes of the lady in "A Game of Chess", which "troubled, confused / And drowned the sense in odours". ("Sense", here, may be understood as both semantic and olfactory: as if, under the power of the feminine, the sense of words becomes as "unguent . . . or liquid" as her scents.) Now, the strange thing about smell, as opposed to vision for example, is that the subject smelling actually imbibes the object smelt, endangering their separation and integrity. And it is the fear of such *displacements* that Eliot's misogyny reveals, a terror deeper even than the dread of incest, which is merely the most scandalous offence to place. In *The Waste Land,* the fall of the father unleashes infinite displacements, be they sexual, linguistic or territorial. Even personal identity dissolves into the babble of miscegenated tongues.[5] As effluvia, the feminine dissolves the limits of the private body, and the boundaries of the self subside into pneumatic anarchy. It is as if the father's impotence entailed the dissolution of identity, imaged as asphyxiation in the body of the feminine.

---

5. Lacan claims that the paternal law is "identical to an order of Language. For without kinship nominations, no power is capable of instituting the order of preferences and taboos which bind and weave the yarn of lineage down through succeeding generations." ("The Function of Language in Psychoanalysis", in *The Language of the Self,* ed. Anthony Wilden [New York: Dell, 1968], p. 40). In *The Waste Land,* the phallus stands for these discriminations, but all three staves have detumesced, and the father has been shipwrecked on the ruins of his own distinctions.

At the end of the poem, Eliot demolishes the discourse of the West, petitioning the East for solace and recovery.

> London Bridge is falling down falling down falling down
> *Poi s'ascose nel foco che gli affina*
> *Quando fiam uti chelidon*—O swallow swallow
> *Le Prince d' Aquitaine à la tour abolie*
> These fragments I have shored against my ruins
> Why then Ile fit you. Hieronymo's mad againe.
> Datta. Dayadhvam. Damyata.
> Shantih shantih shantih

$$(426-33)$$

Here at last the poem silences its Western noise with Eastern blessings. But ironically, the effort to defeat its own "concatenated words" has only made the text more polyglot, stammering its orisons in Babel. It is as if the speaking subject had been "ruined" by the very fragments he had shored. "'Words, words, words' might be his motto", one of Eliot's earliest reviewers once exclaimed, "'for in his verse he seems to hate them and to be always expressing his hatred of them, in words.'"[6] Because the poem can only abject writing with more writing, it catches the infection that it tries to purge, and implodes like an obsessive ceremonial under the pressure of its own contradictions.

The Violet Hour

It is in another ceremonial that Freud discovers the compulsion to repeat, in the child's game he analyses in *Beyond the Pleasure Principle*. Here, his grandchild flings a cotton-reel into the abyss beyond his cot, and retrieves it with an "aaaa" of satisfaction, only to cast it out again, uttering a forlorn "oooo." Freud interprets these two syllables as primitive versions of the German words "fort" (gone) and "da" (here), and he argues that the child is mastering his mother's absences by "staging" them in the manipulation of a sign.[7] Indeed, Freud compares this theatre of abjection to the catharses of Greek tragedy, and he sees the child's pantomime renunciation as his first "great cultural achievement."

It is important, however, that the *drama* fascinates the child rather than the toy itself, for the bobbin belongs to a series of objects which

---

6. Anon., review of *Ara Vos Prec*, *TLS*, no. 948 (1920), 184. See also Graham Pearson, "Eliot: An American Use of Symbolism", in Martin, ed., *Eliot in Perspective*, pp. 83–7, for an illuminating discussion of "the social as well as verbal logic" of "the conversion of words into the Word."
7. Freud, *Complete Works*, Vol. 18, p. 28.

he substitutes indifferently for one another.[8] While the cotton-reel stands for the mother, rehearsing her intermittencies, it also represents the child himself, who sends it forth like an ambassador. As if to emphasise this point, he tops his first act by staging his own disappearance. Crouching underneath a mirror, he lisps, "Baby o-o-o-o!" [Baby gone!], in a kind of abject inversion of Narcissus. By casting *himself* out, the child founds his subjectivity in a game that can only end in death. As Kristeva writes: "I expel *myself*, I spit *myself* out, I *abject* myself within the same motion through which 'I' claim to establish *myself*."[9] By attempting to control his world with signs, the subject has himself become a function of the sign, *subjected to* its own demonic repetition.

In this scenario, Freud intervenes between the mother and the child, bearing the law of language. For it is he who transforms the oscillation of the child's vowels into intelligible speech. But he neglects the vengeful pleasure that the infant takes in their vibratory suspense and in the *rattle* of their sounds. It is significant, moreover, that the little boy never changed his "o-o-o-o" into the neutral "fort" when he acquired the command of language. Instead, he sent his bobbin to the trenches. "A year later", Freud writes:

> the same boy whom I had observed at his first game used to take a toy, if he was angry with it, and throw it on the floor, exclaiming: "Go to the fwont!" He had heard at that time that his absent father was "at the front," and was far from regretting his absence. . . .[1]

Like this child, *The Waste Land* is confronting the specific absence that succeeded World War I, and it evinces both the dread and the desire to hear the voices at the "fwont" again. In fact, the poem can be read as a seance, and its speaker as the medium who tries to raise the dead by quoting them. Its ruling logic is "prosopopeia", as Paul De Man defines the trope:

> the fiction of an apostrophe to an absent, deceased, or voiceless entity, which posits the possibility of the latter's reply and confers upon it the power of speech. Voice assumes mouth, eye and finally face, a chain that is manifest in the etymology of the trope's name, *prosopon poien*, to confer a mask or face (*prosopon*).[2]

---

8. In the same way, Ricoeur argues that defilement is acted out through "partial, substitutive and abbreviated signs" which "mutually symbolise one another": *Symbolism of Evil*, p. 35.
9. Kristeva, *Powers of Horror*, p. 3.
1. Freud, *Complete Works*, Vol. 18, p. 16.
2. Paul De Man, "Autobiography as De-facement", *Modern Language Notes*, 94 (1979), 926; repr. as Ch. 4 in *The Rhetoric of Romanticism* (New York: Columbia University Press, 1984).

With the dead souls flowing over London Bridge, the corpses in the garden and the hooded hordes, *The Waste Land* strives to give a face to death. But it is significant that these figures have no faces, or else that they are hidden and unrecognisable:

> Who is the third who walks always beside you?
> When I count, there are only you and I together
> But when I look ahead up the white road
> There is always another one walking beside you
> Gliding wrapt in a brown mantle, hooded
> I do not know whether a man or a woman
> —But who is that on the other side of you?
>
> (359–65)

Here, these nervous efforts to reconstitute the face only drive it to its disappearance. Neither absent nor present, this nameless third bodies forth a rhetoric of disembodiment, and figures the "continual extinction" of the self. For the speaker rehearses his own death as he conjures up the writings of the dead, sacrificing voice and personality to their ventriloquy. Freud compares his grandchild to victims of shell-shock, who hallucinate their traumas in their dreams, repeating death as if it were desire. This is the game *The Waste Land* plays, and the nightmare that it cannot lay to rest, for it stages the ritual of its own destruction.

TIM ARMSTRONG

[Eliot's Waste Paper]†

In *The Waste Land,* the discourses of economic and bodily waste * * * merge. It is a Veblenian[1] poem in the broad sense of describing a place in which social waste is apparent both in the sterility and luxury of the rich and the indigence and eugenic incontinence of the poor. But it is also a poem which takes pleasure in the production of waste; as Maud Ellmann comments, 'one of the most abject texts in English literature'.[2] The materials of abjection include bodily parts (dirty ears, hands, feet; teeth, parted knees, bones, hair),

---

† From *Modernism, Technology, and the Body: A Cultural Study* (Cambridge, Eng.: Cambridge University Press, 1998), pp. 69–74. Copyright © 1998 by Cambridge University Press. Reprinted by permission of the licensor through PLSclear. Unless otherwise indicated, notes are by the author. Some notes have been edited.
1. Reference to Thorstein Veblen's *Theory of the Leisure Class* (1899), in which he argues that "conspicuous consumption" and "conspicuous waste" are necessary by-products of capitalism [*Editor*].
2. Maud Ellmann, *The Poetics of Impersonality: Eliot and Pound* (Brighton: Harvester, 1987), p. 93. [See also p. 265 above—*Editor*.]

clothing (underwear), places (dead land, desert), animals (scorpions, bats), acts (rape, abortion, copulation), and actors. The draft is particularly productive of dirt, though Pound and Eliot's editing intrudes here: in 'The Fire Sermon' the 'dirty camisoles' of the draft lose their adjective; the young man's hair, 'thick with grease, and thick with scurf' is excised; his urination and spitting are cut.[3]

Recent criticism has linked the recurrent reference to the body in *The Waste Land* to the hystericization of poet, poem, and of Vivien Eliot.[4] The hysteria here is nominally associated with femininity, as in Eliot's 1921 comments on H. D.'s wasteful copiousness: 'many words should be expunged and many phrases amended . . . I find a neurotic carnality which I dislike.'[5] But F. L. Lucas's comment on *The Waste Land* places Eliot in the same camp: 'we have the spectacle of Mr Lawrence, Miss May Sinclair, and Mr Eliot . . . all trying to get children on mandrake roots instead of bearing their natural offspring'.[6] Eliot's 'cure' at Lausanne in late 1921 was designed to alleviate his own distractedness. From there he wrote to his brother on the lack of 'hygiene' endemic to the family: 'The great thing I am trying to learn is how to use all my energy without waste'; adding 'I realize that our family never was taught mental, any more than physical hygiene, and so we are a seedy lot.'[7]

The hygiene which Eliot seeks is visible in Pound's 'surgical' intervention as editor, which excluded much waste material from a poem which Pound saw as fascinatingly excremental ('It also, to yr. horror probably, reads aloud very well. Mouthing out his o o o o o o z e'). Pound tended, as Forrest Read comments, to see poetry as 'phallic' and prose as 'excremental', related to elimination; a distinction which is part of his assessment of Henry James, and which he put to work in editing the more cloachal passages in Joyce's *Ulysses*.[8] Eliot himself figured Pound's editing as purification: 'It will have been three times through the sieve by Pound as well as myself' (sieving is a process applied to sewage).[9] Pound's advice also applied

---

3. *The Waste Land: A Facsimile and Transcript of the Original Drafts Including the Annotations of Ezra Pound*, ed. Valerie Eliot (London: Faber & Faber, 1971), pp. 45–47.
4. See Ellmann and Wayne Koestenbaum, *Double Talk: The Erotics of Male Literary Collaboration* (New York: Routledge, 1989).
5. Eliot to Richard Aldington, 17 November 1921, *The Letters of T. S. Eliot*, vol. 1, 1898–1922, ed. Valerie Eliot (New York: Harcourt Brace Jovanovich, 1988), p. 488. [H. D. is the American poet Hilda Doolittle (1886–1961), to whom Aldington was married at this time—*Editor*.]
6. F. L. Lucas, *New Statesman*, 22 (3 November 1923), 116–118; rep. in T. S. *Eliot: Critical Assessments*, ed. Graham Clarke, 4 vols. (London: Christopher Helm, 1990), 2:118. [The reference is to John Donne's "Song": "Go and catch a falling star, / Get with child a mandrake root . . ."—*Editor*.]
7. Eliot to Henry Eliot, 13 December 1921, *Letters*, p. 493.
8. Pound to Eliot, 24 December 1921, *Letters*, p. 497; Forrest Read, ed. *Pound/Joyce: The Letters of Ezra Pound to James Joyce* (New York: New Directions, 1967), p. 146.
9. Eliot to Scofield Thayer, 20 January 1922, *Letters*, p. 502.

to the bodies of Eliot and his wife. His recuperation at Lausanne was the culmination of years of worry about the health of both. His letters in the late 1910s and early 1920s weave reports on his progress as a man of letters with comments on Vivien's bodily states: teeth, abscesses, neuralgia, nerves, and menstrual problems. In June 1922, Eliot reported to Ottoline Morrell that Vivien had been finally diagnosed as having a dual source for her illnesses: 'glands', and 'poisoning from colitis'. She was to be treated with animal glands (hormones—Eliot adds 'this at present is purely experimental'), and by 'very strong internal disinfection' (fasting).[1] The diagnosis prompted a series of letters to Pound on glands. In July, Eliot replied to Pound on three occasions that he would be glad to meet Louis Berman, twice mentioning the English endocrinologist Thomas Hogben. Both these letters end with a different glandular transaction, however: with invocations of Pound's own virility, one an ideogram-like transcription of the Nagali *Kama-Sutra*, 'grow fat and libidinous' appended; the other a more direct 'good fucking, brother'.[2] Here, as Wayne Koestenbaum suggests, is a circulation of masculine energy conducted around Vivien's body, with the injection of glandular matter from Pound paralleling the treatment Vivien was undergoing.

Yet, for all that the Pound-Eliot team might be seen as acting to 'disinfect' waste coded as 'feminine', *The Waste Land* remains a text with a troubling relation to the waste it describes. Notably, there is an absence of any redeeming vision of social order, or of an internal aesthetic of efficiency. As Cecelia Tichi argues, if 'Ezra Pound cut the "waste" from *The Waste Land* in editorial excision'—a task at best partially achieved—'the poem itself offers no alternative world'.[3] Instead it accumulates detritus. Jean Verdenal—the 'occasion' in part of *The Waste Land*—wrote, on another Christmas day, 1912, that cramming for an examination made his head 'like a department store stocked with anything and everything to hood wink the public'.[4] This is, in fact, the way the poem was seen by many reviewers, particularly in America: as an undergraduate parade of citations. Louis Untermeyer criticized 'a pompous parade of erudition . . . a kaleidoscopic movement in which the bright-coloured pieces fail to atone for the absence of an integrated design'; the poem as window-dressing.[5]

As well as this overproduction of the material of previous culture, reconceived as waste, the poem responds to what it sees as the

1. Eliot to Ottoline Morrell, 15 June 1922, *Letters*, p. 529.
2. Eliot to Pound, 9 and 19 July 1922, *Letters*, pp. 539, 550.
3. Cecelia Tichi, *Shifting Gears: Technology, Literature and Culture in Modernist America* (Chapel Hill: University of North Carolina Press, 1987), p. 71.
4. Verdenal to Eliot, 26 December 1912, *Letters*, p. 36.
5. Louis Untermeyer, "Disillusion vs. Dogma," *Freeman*, 7 January 1923, 453; rep. in *Critical Assessments*, 2:81.

cheapening of mass culture, towards which it is simultaneously fas-
cinated and repelled. The 'human engine' which waits 'like a taxi
throbbing' at the violet hour is a machine not for work, but for lei-
sure—in the seduction scene which follows, and even more clearly
in the draft section from which the lines were incorporated.[6] The
materials of mass culture are crammed in: gramophones, songs,
pubs, convenience foods. The borders of the text are a particularly
rich source of such products—a fact reflected in the list of drinks,
dinners, cigarettes, prostitutes, cabs in the original opening; or the
negative catalogue in 'The Fire Sermon': tonight, 'The river bears
no empty bottles, sandwich papers, / Silk handkerchiefs, cardboard
boxes, cigarette ends.' The excised 'London' section deals with mass
society: 'swarming creatures' driven by social tropisms, 'responsive
to the momentary need', puppet-like in their 'jerky motions'. The
presence of these objects in the text's margins suggests the way in
which Eliot cannot fully incorporate all his materials; his fragments
remain undigested. *The Waste Land* thus bespeaks a simultaneous
fascination with, and revulsion from, waste. The poem seems to
revel in excess, consuming conspicuously in its gratuitous piling of
allusions and eclectic cultural borrowings. Like a potlatch, it par-
ticipates in a paradoxical order, destroying culture in order to rein-
force it. The process of waste-production is knitted into its cultural
moment: it cannot (and Pound cannot) 'edit out' all the waste,
because it *is* waste material; both the abject and a valuable surplus
which enables culture to continue, creating its own moment as it
orders its abjection.[7] There can be no production without waste.

A more extended illustration of this process is provided by one
issue: waste paper.[8] Here Eliot does comment on the 'waste' intrin-
sic in American capitalism. Late in the war, in April 1918, he wrote
to his mother of the limits of frugality across the Atlantic: 'while
America is very conscientiously "conserving foodstuffs" etc. she is
as wasteful of paper as ever. I fear it would take very serious priva-
tion indeed to make Americans realize the wastefulness of such huge
papers filled with nonsense and personalities.'[9] He contrasts Euro-
pean carefulness and adds that 'if less pulp were wasted on news-
papers, good books could perhaps be printed more cheaply'. Eliot
repeatedly links waste paper with the press, from the inhabitants of
Hampstead in the drafts of *The Waste Land*—'They know what they
are to feel and what to think, / They know it with the morning

6. *Facsimile,* p. 31, 43. The quotations following are from p. 37.
7. "I expel *myself,* I spit *myself* out, I abject *myself* within the same motion through which
   'I' claim to establish *myself.*" Julia Kristeva, *Powers of Horror: An Essay on Abjection,*
   trans. Leon S. Roudiez (New York: Columbia University Press, 1982), p. 3.
8. Ellmann comments on waste paper in *Poetics of Impersonality;* my reading pursues a
   more literal line.
9. Eliot to Charlotte Eliot, 28 April 1918, *Letters,* pp. 229–230.

printer's ink'—to the press in section v of 'The Dry Salvages'.[1] Pound agreed: if 'The greatest waste in ang-sax letters at the moment is the waste of Eliot's talent', what threatens him is *journalism*.[2]

The Waste Land is caught up in this debate. At least one reviewer called the poem 'a waste of paper'.[3] It incorporates a great deal of 'pulp', the stuff of scandal-sheets and the popular press: 'personalities' like Madame Sosostris and Mr Eugenides, occultism, royal processions, popular songs, scandal, references to polar explorers. In bodily terms, waste paper is also toilet-paper. The abandoned 'Fresca' section equates faeces with the sexually ambiguous literature disparaged by Modernism as Fresca, 'baptised in a soapy sea / of Symonds—Walter Pater—Vernon Lee', shits while reading Samuel Richardson (more direct, Joyce's Bloom wipes himself on the popular press after reading it—in a passage which Pound cut from the *The Little Review*). We might see the same excremental preoccupations in the fears of a chaos of paper which accompanied the poem's creation. In a letter to Mary Hutchinson written in July 1919, in which Eliot expounds a number of the ideas of order which appear the same year in 'Tradition and the Individual Talent', he writes 'I have a good deal to say which would simply appear as an illegible mass of blottings and scratchings and revisions, on paper.'[4] He distinguishes between 'civilized' and 'cultivated', adding 'I certainly do not mean a mass of chaotic erudition which simply issues in giggling.' *The Waste Land* has its own chaotic erudition in a conscious evocation— 'on paper'—of the decadence described above, so hopelessly clotted that Eliot had to hand it to Pound in order that it might find a shape.

At the same time as it mocks pulp, the poem in its publication as a book also involved Veblenian waste in the sense of the gratuitous consumption of paper. Famously, Eliot claimed to have provided the footnotes in order to flesh out the pages at the end which the printers had to put in to get the sections right, an action which we might see as attempting to cover the 'luxury' of blank pages, producing a text which balances modesty and value, yet which at the same time reverses Pound's hygienic editing, reinflating the text because of the demands of commerce (Horace Liveright, the publisher, was worried about length, and suggested to Pound that Eliot add more).[5] Compare Pound lecturing Margaret Anderson in 1917 on the possibility of expanding *The Little Review*: 'Lady C[unard] says "DONT make it

1. *Facsimile*, p. 105. [*Dry Salvages*, first published in 1941, became the third poem in Eliot's *Four Quartets* (1943)—*Editor*.]
2. Pound to Eliot, 14 March 1922, *Letters*, pp. 511, 514.
3. Humbert Wolfe, "Waste Land and Waste Paper," *Weekly Westminster*, 1 (November 1923), 94; rept. in *Critical Assessments*, 2:120–122.
4. Eliot to Hutchinson, 11 July 1919, *Letters*, p. 317.
5. Lawrence Rainey, "The Price of Modernism: Reconsidering the Publication of *The Waste Land*," *Critical Quarterly*, 31.4 (1989):21–47. [See also this volume, p. 117—*Editor*.]

bigger. DONT make it any bigger, or I won't have time to read it." C'est une egoisme.' He adds, however, that 'ON the other hand "the public" likes a lot of paper for its money. One has to think of it both ways.'[6] Pound was, admittedly, more boosting to Quinn a few months earlier, writing that he wanted to publish Joyce and Ford 'after I have succeeded in enlarging the paper. (That may be nerve, but still one may as well expect to "enlarge")'.[7] Swelling phallically and creatively for Quinn, Pound stresses exclusivity when dealing with an aristocrat. In negotiating to set up the *Criterion* in 1922—a project which became involved with arrangements over *The Waste Land*—Eliot was deeply concerned with economy and not allowing contributors to overrun; he reported to Pound that he had decided on 'quite a good small format and paper, neat but no extravagance and not arty'.[8]

Eliot thus thinks of waste in deeply antithetical ways: as that to be eliminated from the poem; and—less explicitly—as that which is central to its production. The poem is uncertain of its status; producing waste, yet also curtailing it via Pound's editing, with the notes figuring explication as a necessarily wasteful supplement. There is a comparable double-economy in the negotiations over selling the poem. Lawrence Rainey points out that, on the one hand, Eliot discussed a 'fair' price with Scofield Thayer at *The Dial*, noting that George Moore had been paid £100 for a short story; on the other hand negotiations, under Pound's guidance, ballooned to take in book publication and the *Dial* prize, producing an unprecedented total of $2,800 for the package, as if anticipating the hectic financial expansion of the 1920s.[9]

* * * If *The Waste Land* embodies an overproduction which is a necessary part of its richness, Eliot's late poetry, in contrast, seeks solitude, concentration, and pattern, just as it seeks to curb the hysterical voices of the popular press. The abject body is excluded. The 'indigestible portions' of the speaker which 'the leopards reject' in *Ash Wednesday,* particularly the strings of the eyes, suggest something beyond the body and luxury. There is a point of resolution beyond the inside—outside dialectics of the human engine in the evocation of the dance in the heavens and the earth, and in the search for the still or balanced point in the second section of 'Burnt Norton'. The 'trilling wire in the blood' and the

6. Pound to Anderson, 12 November 1917. *Pound/The Little Review: The Letters of Ezra Pound to Margaret Anderson,* ed. Thomas L. Scott and Melvin J. Friedman (London: Faber & Faber, 1989), p. 151.
7. Pound to Quinn, 17 May 1917, *Selected Letters of Ezra Pound to John Quinn 1915–1920,* ed. Timothy Materer (Durham: Duke University Press, 1991), p. 117.
8. Eliot to Pound, 12 March 1922, *Letters,* p. 507.
9. Rainey, "The Price of Modernism."

'dance along the artery' are in the body, yet Eliot's still point is 'Neither flesh nor fleshless':

> The release from action and suffering, release from the inner
> And the outer compulsion, yet surrounded
> By a grace of sense, a white light still and moving,
> *Erhebung*[1] without motion, concentration
> Without elimination . . .

'Elimination' here also means waste; we might even, excrementally, see a pun in 'motion'. Eliot's late poetry, with its fascination with systems, the circulation of messages, feedback, seeks to eliminate the wasteful flows of the early poetry, so that 'dung and death' are subsumed to their proper time. Even where it describes the blood (for example in 'East Coker' IV), it is to evoke the 'wounded surgeon' Christ and his saving sacrifice.[2] * * * Eliot frees himself from the flesh, from the pain-economy, and seeks an aesthetics of purification, as if the problems of production and consumption and their troubling relation to the body had melted away.

---

1. Uplift; elevation (German) [*Editor*].
2. John Gordon has recently argued that "*The Waste Land* and *Four Quartets* enact a classic opposition between head and heart" or between nerves and blood. Certainly nerves dominate the earlier poem, but the blood of "Quartets" seems to me much more sublimated. "T. S. Eliot's Head and Heart," *ELH,* 62.4 (1995): 979–1000.

Reconsiderations and New Readings

HELEN VENDLER

[Inventing Prufrock]†

We have lingered in the chambers of the sea
By sea-girls wreathed with seaweed red and brown
Till human voices wake us, and we drown.

When, after reading the early verse, we return to Eliot's first "perfect" poem, the long-familiar *Love Song of J. Alfred Prufrock* (significantly, it bore as its original title *Prufrock among the Women*), we see it with new eyes, as a cento of almost all the discourses that Eliot had previously attempted. Yes, it takes its form from Browning's dramatic monologues, but the required listener of the Browning genre has here been radically diminished from his usual socially specified self (a wife, some "nephews," an envoy). Prufrock's companion has dwindled to the Cheshire invisibility of ear alone, as the speaker, aridly, truthfully, and lyrically, voices the Eliotic *incipit*[1]— "Let us go then, you and I." The "you" is the Madness of the *Pervigilium,* the mind-moth of *The Burnt Dancer,* the mind-serpent of *Introspection*—now not alienated to a curbstone, a flame, or a cistern, but integrated as an inevitable, even necessary companion. In *Prufrock*, motifs and voices of the early poems reappear—desire, fearful as it enters the social world of "love" and marriage proposals; guilty self-laceration; romantic aspiration; Laforguian[2] irony;

---

† From *Coming of Age as a Poet: Milton, Keats, Eliot, Plath* (Cambridge, MA: Harvard University Press, 2003), pp. 107–13. Copyright © 2003 by the President and Fellows of Harvard College. Reprinted by permission of the publisher. Two parenthetical citations and one footnote have been omitted. Notes are by the editor of this Norton Critical Edition.
1. It begins (Latin); designates the first few words of a text. The three titles in the next sentence refer to early, unpublished poems by Eliot, including thirty lines titled "Prufrock's Pervigilium" that were removed from "The Love Song of J. Alfred Prufrock" in manuscripts.
2. Reference to the French poet Jules Laforgue (1860–1887), an early influence on Eliot. For Baudelaire, see above, p. 83.

Baudelairean urban surroundings; philosophic doubt; literary allusion; lyric pain. But the balance among these motifs has reached an equilibrium not visible in the more derisory or gothic inventions of less successful poems. Eliot has not mastered any new techniques before writing *Prufrock*; rather, he has learned to integrate, in a coherent style, the techniques he already knows, without having them extinguish each other, without himself compulsively resorting, as he once had, to mocking or melodramatic endings that dismiss their precedent speculations. He dares to preface the poem with a serious epigraph from Dante's underworld. He has begun to see the potential aesthetic value of his hatreds and his sufferings: not only will there be time to murder, there will be time to create. He dares to suggest—even if ironically—that his question might disturb the universe (a possibility that his early self-mocking discourses could not have allowed themselves to entertain). He fully enunciates (instead of merely mimicking or parodying) the fatigued repetitiveness of his doubt and his desire ("I have known them all already, known them all") while going forth yet again to the social world, his theater (now fully acknowledged) of lyric action. He is willing to include the rawest physicality of discourse: Prufrock's "wriggling" on a pin had been earlier phrased, equally unflinchingly, as "sprawling" and "squirming."

Instead of representing himself by means of a single image—whether as a clown or a Pierrot or a murderer (or even as a young man on a verandah or in a parlor)—Eliot speculatively becomes (not without irony, but not without seriousness, either) John the Baptist, Hamlet, Lazarus, and a lover of mermaids. Most of all, he has discovered what his poetry—with its insidious rhythms, its hesitations, its etherized evening, its sleeping fog, its effortful confrontation of the moment's "crisis," its satiric sallies—is meant to do. It is to construct the effect "as if a magic lantern threw the nerves in patterns on a screen": that is, to function as an EEG, an image-coded graph of the twitches of the nerves as they respond to life's disorders, above all to the obsessive question of sexual desire. The exacerbated nerves vibrate sometimes towards anesthesia, sometimes towards energy; now towards disgust, now towards ennui; now towards cosmic fear, now towards social agony; now towards romantic longing, now towards a suicidal siren-song. In one superb effort of poetic concentration and polyphonic effect, the gamut of responses and discourses discovered through earlier poems is fluently explored, as a hypnotically alluring voice, sure of its own circuits of stylistic movement, invites us—"Let us go then, you and I."

Although I've mentioned the feelings, and the discourses, gathered up in *Prufrock*, I need to say a few words to show how the formal unity of the poem is attained, why the verse does not fracture along inner fault-lines of incompatible discourses. We have seen the damage done in *Prufrock's Pervigilium* when Eliot reifies and personifies and characterizes his Madness (blind, drunken, with stained boot heels, sitting on a curb). Eliot endangers that fragment, too, by the stutter of self-repeating end-words with feminine endings: *windows, blindness, corners, entries, flickered, papers, together, corner, together, darkness, darkness, fever, darkness, kerbstone, mutters, gutters*—16 such endings in 31 lines. The febrile effect of such end-words is, by contrast, carefully husbanded in the final *Prufrock*, where we find only *table, evening, chimneys, indecisions,* and *revisions*; and then nothing until *windows, fingers,* and *malingers.* Later, in a self-mocking cluster, there are *ices* and *crisis, platter* and *matter, flicker* and *snicker.* The last of such end-words is (fittingly) *question.* After the line in which it appears, where Prufrock imagines rolling the universe "toward some overwhelming question," there are no more lines with feminine end-words: the poem proceeds with solid accents on each end-line monosyllable, accompanied by such emphatic close-placed rhymes as *peach, beach,* and *each*):

I grow old . . . I grow old . . .
I shall wear the bottoms of my trousers rolled.

Shall I part my hair behind? Do I dare to eat a peach?
I shall wear white flannel trousers, and walk upon the beach.
I have heard the mermaids singing, each to each.

Prufrock's Pervigilium suffers damage as well because it situates its speaker among Disneyfied gothic surroundings in which houses point ribald fingers and chuckle, the midnight writhes in fever, and the darkness, octopus-like, stretches out tentacles. *Prufrock* does not abandon the gothic altogether, but it domesticates it into the catlike fog. When it does become high-pitched in its metaphors—as Prufrock is "pinned and wriggling on the wall," his mouth choked with "the butt-ends of [his] days and ways"—it keeps the moments of such outright agony far apart and relatively few. And instead of situating the protagonist in the dubious streets of the *Pervigilium*, where "Women, spilling out of corsets, stood in entries," it situates him in the social world normally inhabited by Eliot: the world of superficially cultivated women, drawing-rooms, and tea.

As we scan the first half of *Prufrock* for the discourses it brings to bear, we see, in sequence, these discourses (which I number for ease of subsequent reference):

1. the urban solitary (the sky, the restless nights, the restaurants, the streets);
2. the gothic descriptive (newly domesticated in fog);
3. the musing propositional ("there will be time . . . for visions and revisions");
4. the upper-class social ("toast and tea . . . talking of Michelangelo");
5. the personally ironic ("With a bald spot in the middle of my hair");
6. the philosophically interrogative ("Do I dare / Disturb the universe?");
7. the ennuyé[3] ("I have known them all already, known them all");
8. the socially terrified ("When I am pinned and wriggling on the wall");
9. the erotic of attraction ("Arms that are braceleted and white and bare");
10. the erotic of revulsion ("But in the lamplight, downed with light brown hair!").

Halfway through the poem there appears Prufrock's first inserted lyric, with its three stanzas and its refrain in "How should I presume." After that lyric ceases, the poem becomes a formal reprise, recapitulating itself, as discourse 1 comes back in the "lonely men in shirt-sleeves, leaning out of windows," 2 in the ragged claws and the tired evening, 4 in the tea and cakes and ices, 5 in the bald head on the platter, 6 in squeezing the universe into a ball, 7 in "Would it have been worth it, after all," 8 in "the nerves in patterns on a screen," 9 in "the skirts that trail along the floor" and so on. During this recapitulation, Prufrock has sung his second lyric, two stanzas linked by their common beginning ("And would it have been worth it, after all") and end ("at all"). The two internal lyrics distinguish *Prufrock* from the Victorian dramatic monologues from which it derives, and assert the affiliation of its dramatic protagonist with its lyric author, who calls his dramatic monologue a "Love Song."

The penultimate part of the poem judges the self with mordant social ennui ("Almost, at times, the Fool"); but the last part sets mocking personal irony ("Do I dare to eat a peach?") against a stubborn romanticism derived from "the chambers of the sea" and the song of the mermaids. The reduplicative semiosis of the close is something new in Eliot:

---

3. Bored (French).

have heard	the mermaids		singing	each to each
	they will		sing	
have seen	them		riding	sea-ward
		on the waves		
the	white hair	of the waves	blown	back
			blows	
	white			black
have lingered		the chambers of the	sea	
			sea-girls	
			seaweed	

This is the discourse of art aspiring to the condition of music, as the overlapping words are reinforced by intense alliteration and assonance. Such a discourse loses its affiliation with any functional social purpose. Its Paterian[4] harmonics, self-referential and self-dissolving, make *Prufrock* end in obliquity—in a vision of mermaids who can be neither possessed nor forgotten.

Prufrock introduces himself with an impulsive anapestic step forward—"Let us *go*"—which immediately lapses into ordinary iambs: "Let us go, then, you and I." This anapestic impulse becomes Prufrock's rhythmic signature—the symbol of his willingness to make his social "visit." The impulse is most frequent at the beginning of the poem:

> Let us *go* then, you and I,
> When the *e*vening is spread out against the sky
> Like a *pa*tient etherised upon a table;
> Let us *go*, through certain half-deserted streets . . .
> Let us *go* and make our visit.

Prufrock's *incipit* is rhythmically mocked by the dismissive woman: "That is *not* what I meant, at all." And by the end of the poem, the courageous little anapestic skip seems to have been trivialized: "Shall I *part* my hair behind? Do I *dare* to eat a peach?" With a renewal of imaginative courage, Prufrock, though a failure with "real" women, regains his skip as he claims a better acquaintance: "I have *heard* the mermaids singing, each to each." This resurgence of romance is followed by a line of sedulously depressed iambs: "I do not think that they will sing to me." Courageous once more, Prufrock insists: "I have *seen* them," and the landscape echoes his skip: "When the *wind* blows the water white and black." Prufrock's last anapest is, surprisingly, voiced in a collective "we" (not the "you and I" or "you and me" of the rest of the poem); it is the same "we" that

4. Reference to the English writer Walter Pater (1839–1894), noted for his mellifluous prose.

we have seen him adopt when a religious or philosophical vision puts him in the suffering company of his fellow human beings: "We have *ling*ered in the chambers of the sea." By this "we" he means, of course, his social self and his artist-self ("Madness"), now companions in better-integrated experience; but he also means other human beings like himself. Although the last two lines let us drown to the music of iambs, the penultimate one is luxurious in reduplicative sound: "By sea-girls wreathed with seaweed red and brown."

Such small matters as anapests and assonance undergird the imaginative effort and the long lines of *The Love Song of J. Alfred Prufrock*. The poem aligns many internal discourses (all of them expressive of some aspect of Eliot's feelings) into one "social" narrative, and encloses within that linear narrative of the disappointing "visit" the more visibly patterned two "lyrics" of ennui. The lyrics are there to show "Madness singing"—and in fact it was after the first "ennui lyric" ("For I have known them all already, known them all") that Eliot left the four-page space in the original *Prufrock* into which he inserted the relatively regular four stanzas of *Prufrock's Pervigilium,* making a second densely-patterned "lyric" follow the first. In the canonical *Prufrock*, Eliot does not split the inner "songs" off from the narrative and ascribe them to his "Madness," an alienated and personified utterer; rather, he has decided to have the same voice uttering both the narrative and its internal lyrics. But in making the lyrics formally visible by means of their stanzaic grouping, Eliot is asserting that even though he has determined on the theater of the social as his lyric venue, he will not thereby be deprived of the intensity of personal song. (He will keep to this resolution, in altered ways, in the more patterned and song-like portions of the *Quartets*.)

The force driving *Prufrock* is Eliot's youthful desire to fuse, in his poetry, his alienated erotic self, his transfixed social self, his intellectual philosophic self, and his introspective artistic self, which we have seen separated out into various incompatible discourses in his early experiments in language. As the social self wanders with the artistic self through the evening streets and the drawing rooms of *Prufrock*, Eliot at last finds a single rich discourse which can absorb, pattern, and express them all. This discourse—Eliot's newly achieved personal style—is the foundation for *The Waste Land*, where he will complicate it by taking it out of the drawing-room and placing it in larger geographical, historical, and literary contexts. But that is another story.

MARJORIE PERLOFF

[Rereading Eliot's "Gerontion"]†

"Gerontion," written in the summer of 1919 and originally intended as the prelude to *The Waste Land*,[1] was first published in T. S. Eliot's 1920 volume *Ara Vos Prec* (London: Ovid Press).[2] It did not have a good press. The anonymous reviewer for the *Times Literary Supplement* complained that the poet's world-weariness was no more than a "habit, an anti-romantic reaction, a new Byronism," while Desmond MacCarthy in the *New Statesman* describes "Gerontion" as follows:

> The whole poem is a description at once of an old man's mind, and of a mood which recurs often in Mr. Eliot's poems, namely, that of one to whom life is largely a process of being stifled, slowly hemmed in and confused. . . . His problem as a poet is the problem of the adjustment of his sense of beauty to these sorry facts.[3]

MacCarthy goes on to say that the symbolism of the first verse of "Gerontion" is "obvious": "When the old man says he has not fought in the salt marshes, etc., we know that means that he has not tasted the violent romance of life. We must not dwell too literally on the phrases by which he builds up the impression of sinister dilapidation and decay." And these reservations about Eliot's language lead MacCarthy to the conclusion that "He belongs to that class of poets whose interest is in making a work of art, not in expressing themselves" (*Critical Heritage* 116).

Imagine criticizing a poet for his desire to make a work of art rather than "expressing" himself! If MacCarthy's distinction sounds naïve, we should bear in mind that the expressivist theory that animates it is still very much with us. Indeed, the assumption that a

† From *Differentials: Poetry, Politics, Pedagogy* (Tuscaloosa: University of Alabama Press, 2004), pp. 20–38. © 2004 The University of Alabama Press. Reprinted by permission of the publisher. Unless otherwise indicated, notes are by the author.
1. See T. S. Eliot, letter to Ezra Pound, 24 January 1922, in *The Letters of T. S. Eliot*, vol. 1:1898–1922, ed. Valerie Eliot (San Diego: Harcourt Brace Jovanovich, 1988), 504. On 27 January, Pound replied to Eliot's query, "I do *not* advise printing G. as preface. One don't miss it AT all as the thing now stands" (*Letters*, 505).
2. The same collection, with minor changes, was published a month later in New York by Alfred A. Knopf under the title *Poems* and has come to be known as *Poems 1920*. The variant texts of the poems in these two volumes [are] reprinted as Appendix C in T. S. Eliot, *Inventions of the March Hare, Poems 1909–1917*, ed. Christopher Ricks (New York: Harvest Books, 1998), 347–84.
3. See Unsigned Review, "A New Byronism," *Times Literary Supplement,* 18 March 1920; rpt. in *T. S. Eliot: The Critical Heritage*, vol. 1, ed. Michael Grant (London: Routledge & Kegan Paul, 1982), 108; Desmond MacCarthy, "New Poets: T. S. Eliot," *New Statesman* 8 (January 1921); rpt. in *T. S. Eliot: The Critical Heritage*, 111–17, 115.

poem's language is no more than a vehicle that points to a reality outside it—in this case, "the description of an old man's mind and mood"—still animates most criticism. In this regard I am particularly intrigued by MacCarthy's "etc." in the sentence "When the old man says he has not fought in the salt marshes, etc., we know that means that he has not tasted the violent romance of life." The phrases "heaving a cutlass" and "Bitten by flies" are presumably part of this etcetera, as if to say that, well, these are just more of the same. "Fought," moreover, despite its chiastic use in the first six lines—

> Nor *fought* in the warm rain
> Nor knee deep in the salt marsh, heaving a cutlass,
> Bitten by flies, *fought*[4]—

doesn't really mean "fought"; the verb must be understood as a metaphor for "lived" or "had intense experiences." "In reading Mr. Eliot," says MacCarthy, "an undue literalness must at all costs be avoided" (*Critical Heritage* 115).

Such reservations about the role played by a poem's actual language stand behind many of the critiques of "Gerontion." The most common charge has been that, brilliant as "Gerontion" is at the local level, it is finally not a coherent poem. "'Gerontion'," writes Bernard Bergonzi, "is Eliot's one poem where the language itself forms a barrier or smoke screen between the reader and the essential experience of the poem. . . . It fails because of the slipperiness of its language: the desire to preserve a maximum openness to verbal suggestiveness makes 'Gerontion' an echo chamber where there is much interesting noise but nothing can be clearly distinguished."[5] And the case is made even more forcefully by Stephen Spender:

> If the second half of "Gerontion" doesn't really convince, either on the level of imagination or of intellectual argument, this is because the attempt to draw a parallel between the poetry of the Jacobean playwrights about political intrigues at small Italian courts with the situation of Europe at the time of the signing of the Treaty of Versailles doesn't work. The modern political theme, which affects the whole world, is being forced through too narrow a channel.

And Spender concludes: "After the strong first part of 'Gerontion,' the poem becomes lost in its own corridors and dark passages. It is not so much obscure as cryptic. . . . The last part of 'Gerontion'

---

4. The text used for "Gerontion" is Eliot's *Collected Poems, 1909–1962* (New York: Harcourt Brace, 1970), 29–31.
5. Bernard Bergonzi, *T. S. Eliot* (New York: Collier, 1972), 55.

hovers ambiguously between tragic statement and black farce, with 'high camp' thrown in at the end."[6]

* * *

In recent years, however, discussion of what "Gerontion" "says" has focused less on the issue of structural coherence than on the poem's purported anti-Semitism, although the two are, as we shall see, not unrelated. The fullest case against Eliot on this score was made by Anthony Julius in his *T. S. Eliot, Anti-Semitism, and Literary Form* (1995). Julius's second chapter, devoted to "Gerontion," makes much of the three lines:

> And the Jew squats on the window sill, the owner,
> Spawned in some estaminet of Antwerp,
> Blistered in Brussels, patched and peeled in London.[7]

This passage, says Julius, "breathes hate, the sibilants hissing scorn" (45). The word "spawned" prompts Julius to expatiate on swamps and slime as breeding ground for the subhuman Jewish race. "Blistered" is a reference to the pustular skin diseases associated with Jews, especially smallpox (46). But the truly offensive word in the passage is "squats." "The squatting Jew," writes Julius, "his posture defecatory, becomes what he expels, just as his own motion enacts what must be done to him." And he reminds us that anti-Semites have commonly referred to the Jew as a form of "social excrement" (134).

That verbs like "spawned" and "squats" are insulting and disparaging—a point taken up in a recent study by Rachel Blau DuPlessis, who calls her methodology in tracing the meanings of these words "social philology"[8]—is obvious enough, the question being what the poem does with this "offensive" material. Julius is forced to admit that the "horror picture" of the passage in question is not carried further in Gerontion's monologue. Why? His own explanation is that "Gerontion resists all consoling visions, including the consolations of anti-Semitism, which is a casualty of its relentless negativity" (59). Since Gerontion believes in nothing—neither God nor History nor Progress of any sort—he rejects all frameworks; and even anti-Semitism, Julius posits, is, after all, a framework. Thus the poem rejects form; it "sets its face against the tradition of the dramatic monologue," which is its chosen genre. And since it refuses even anti-Semitism as an "organizing principle," the poem "lacks coherence" (61).

6. Stephen Spender, *Eliot* (London: Fontana, 1975), 66–67.
7. In all editions prior to the 1962 *Collected Poems,* the word "Jew" was not capitalized.
8. See Rachel Blau DuPlessis, *Genders, Races, and Religious Cultures in Modern American Poetry, 1908–1934* (New York: Cambridge University Press, 2001), 144.

Again, then, the charge against "Gerontion" is that it is incoherent. Coherence, according to this view of poetry, must involve consistency of voice and narrative, of imagery and mythological frame. For Julius, "Gerontion" is not sufficiently Browningesque; it does not carry through the fiction of an individual dramatized subject, whose speech is determined by the control of a silent addressee. Ironically, although Julius's subject is such an important one—Eliot's anti-Semitism and how Eliot's readers have managed to rationalize it away—his reading of "Gerontion" is written under the sign of the New Criticism he ostensibly scorns, for it treats the poem as an autonomous artifact, whose words express certain sentiments about the Jews. But what happens if we look not at genre or external reference but at the poem's actual language, syntax, and rhythm as Eliot's poem took shape in the winter of 1919?

"Language," as Eliot's contemporary Wittgenstein reminds us, "is *not contiguous* to anything else."[9] And further: "to imagine a language means to imagine a form of life."[1] Julius sees "Gerontion" as a "querulous poem" in which "there is no bitterness because there is no loss" (43). To make this assertion, he must take out of context Gerontion's insistence that he is "A dull head among windy spaces" (line 16), and that he has "no ghosts" (line 33), that he has, accordingly, never properly suffered, being no more than an empty vessel.

But does this interpretation really account for the poem? I propose here to look closely at its linguistic and sonic substructure, especially in the first two movements, which comprise lines 1–33. My assumption as we proceed is that there are no "etceteras" here, that every word, and indeed every sound and rhythmic movement, makes a difference. Consider the opening:

> Here I am, an old man in a dry month,
> Being read to by a boy, waiting for rain.
> I was neither at the hot gates
> Nor fought in the warm rain
> Nor knee deep in the salt marsh, heaving a cutlass,
> Bitten by flies, fought.

These lines have received more than their share of explication, beginning with their relationship to the epigraph from *Measure for Measure* and their appropriation of the passage in A. C. Benson's biography of Edward Fitzgerald (1905): "Here he sits, in a dry month,

9. Ludwig Wittgenstein, *Wittgenstein's Lectures, Cambridge, 1930–1932; From the Notes of John King and Desmond Lee*, ed. Desmond Lee (Chicago: University of Chicago Press, 1980), 112.
1. Ludwig Wittgenstein, *Philosophical Investigations*, 3rd edition, trans. G. E. M. Anscombe (New York: Macmillan, 1968), #19.

old and blind, being read to by a country boy, longing for rain." The phrase "hot gates" is a literal translation of the Greek proper name *Thermopylae*—thus a reference to the decisive battle (480 BC) of the Persian Wars, in which the Spartans defeated the Greeks at the narrow pass by that name. Also Greek is the title "Gerontion," meaning "little old man" and signaling (or seeming to signal) that this, like "The Love Song of J. Alfred Prufrock," is a monologue spoken by an invented persona.[2]

But such source study can do little to account for the passage's peculiar power and passion, for the sense that something terribly important, both to the poet and the reader, is at stake here. Indeed, the "little old man" cover recedes almost immediately, and by line 17 ("Signs are taken for wonders") the vocal urgency is clearly the poet's own, even if it is an abstracted version, or "auditory illusion" to use Hugh Kenner's phrase,[3] of that personal presence. The subject may *feel* like an old man because he has not *fought*, because he has made the Dantean "grand refusal" in his rejection of Christ, and because, as we learn later in the poem, his moral and sexual failures have made him lose his "sight, smell, hearing, taste, and touch" (line 60). But physical age has no more to do with the things that count in this poem than it does in "Prufrock," another poem in which the young male speaker feels old. Indeed, as Denis Donoghue points out, the first title Eliot tried out was *Gerousia*, "Greek for a consultative body or council of elders in Sparta" (*Words Alone* 77). Eliot's original intention, it seems from this, was to produce an anatomy of the modern condition by presenting us with a "council," sitting in judgment of those the Tiger devours. Such an anatomy would, of course, accord with *The Waste Land*.

*   *   *

Early readers, not understanding the use of found text, which is now such a common technique in poetic composition, thought the "stealing" of lines from A. C. Benson indicated a lack of originality on Eliot's part. But what is, on the contrary, so remarkable is that Eliot could take a fairly neutral passage like Benson's, delete the words "blind" and "country" as redundant, and change "he sits" to the immediacy of "Here I am." He also transforms the sound structure of Benson's fairly labored prose sentence:

2. For Eliot's sources and allusions in "Gerontion," see B. C. Southam, *A Guide to the Selected Poems of T. S. Eliot* (New York: Harcourt Brace & World, 1968), 43–47. Most Eliot commentaries like Grover Smith's *T. S. Eliot's Poetry and Plays: A Study in Sources and Meaning*, rev. ed. (Chicago: University of Chicago Press, 1960), explain these references. The most recent step-by-step explication of the poem is Denis Donoghue's in *Words Alone: The Poet T. S. Eliot* (New Haven, CT: Yale University Press, 2000), 77–95.

3. Hugh Kenner, *The Invisible Poet: T. S. Eliot* (New York: Harcourt Brace, 1959), 125.

```
        /  /\  /  ||      /   /  |       /      /
      Here I am,    an old man    in a dry month,
        /    /    |  /\  /  ||   /            /
      Being read to   by a boy,   waiting for rain.⁴
```

These lines are so familiar that we sometimes forget just how strange they are. The opening announcement "Here I am," for example, is intentionally misleading, for we never learn where "here" is or indeed who it is that is declaring "I am."[5] Is the voice of line 1 the same who says in line 55, "I would meet you upon this honestly"? And what is the relation of rhythm to the speaker's identity? To note, as have most of the commentaries, that in "Gerontion" Eliot is adapting Jacobean blank verse,[6] doesn't take us very far. In dramas like Thomas Middleton's *Changeling*, the major source for lines 55–61 of "Gerontion," the line, however irregular, has ten syllables and an iambic base, as in

```
        /    /        /        /  /\  /
      But cast it to the ground regardlessly
```

or

```
        /    /      /         /      /
      Was prophet to the rest, but ne'er believed.⁷
```

But although the first line of "Gerontion" has ten syllables, it breaks into three rhythmic units, and its ten monosyllables, all of them basic English words, contain seven stresses broken by a caesura, so that any potential forward thrust the line might have gives way to near-gridlock, in keeping with the "Thoughts of a dry brain in a dry season" of the poem's ending.

The second line, again a pentameter, this time with an extra syllable, again breaks into three groups, but it is more lightly stressed and foregrounds both alliteration and assonance. *Being* and *waiting*: the two present participles stress the suspension of Gerontion's state of consciousness, its activity in a continuous present in which all roles are reversed, boys reading to old men rather than vice versa. The spiritual dryness of Gerontion is stressed throughout the poem,

---

4. Scansion is as follows: primary stress (/), secondary stress (/\), plus juncture or short grammatical pause (|), caesura (||), enjambment (>). Alliterative and assonantal letters are italicized.

5. Julius relates Gerontion's "Here I am" to Abraham's "Behold, here I am," spoken in response to God's call in Genesis. But whereas Abraham's words fix his identity, Gerontion's never do (63).

6. See, for example, Southam, *Guide to the Selected Poems*, 45–47.

7. Thomas Middleton (1580–1627) was a Jacobean playwright and poet. Eliot very freely adapts some lines from *The Changeling* (1622), cowritten with Thomas Rowley, for lines 55–61 of "Gerontion" [*Editor*].

but the reference to "month," rather than "day" or "week" or "year," is by no means arbitrary. Like "depraved May" in line 21 or "April is the cruelest month" in *The Waste Land*, the time reference *** is to the lunar cycle, the repeat in history. In its tension between linear and cyclical time, between the linear life span and the possibility of cyclical renewal, "Gerontion" also looks ahead to the *Four Quartets*.

In lines 3–6, even the ghost of pentameter gives way to a heavily stressed free verse:

>   /   /   /
> I was neither at the ho*t* ga*t*es
>   /   /   /
> Nor fought in the warm rain
>   /   /   /   / | /   /
> Nor kn*ee* d*ee*p in the *sal*t m*a*rsh,   heaving a cutlass, >
>   /   / || /
> *Bitten by* flies,   fough*t*.

Lines 3 and 4, with their matched stresses on "hot gates" and "warm rain," are curiously resonant. "Hot gates" (*Thermopylae*) is an allusion to the battlefields of World War I, where Eliot longed to serve, especially after the United States entered the war in 1917.*** Nor has the speaker come to terms with sexual maturity: "I was neither at the hot gates" refers not only to war but also to the disaster of Eliot's marriage to Vivien, in which no "heat" was ever generated.

But what is perceived in life as a painful failure becomes the occasion for a poetic, especially a rhythmic, triumph. The impact of the word "fought," put forward rather quietly in line 4—"Nor fought in the warm rain"—is held in suspension in the progress of the long irregular alexandrine of line 5—"Nor knee deep in the salt marsh, heaving a cutlass," a line enjambed so that the reader pushes on for another four strongly accented syllables—"Bitten by flies"—only to come to the caesura, followed by the reappearance of the isolated verb *fought*. The alliterative "*f*lies || *f*ought" is something of a tongue twister; the verb, moreover, is now intransitive: it's not just that Gerontion refused to "fight" at one time or that he refused to fight someone specific; rather, *refusal* seems to be his general condition. The self-reproach is intensified by the harsh fricative and voiceless stop that frame the long dipthong of *fought*: the word is almost spit out.

*   *   *

It is in the context of Gerontion's extreme agitation—an agitation contained in sound and rhythm of the passage rather than in the words themselves—that we must consider the lines that follow:

> My house is a decayed house,
> And the Jew squats on the window sill, the owner,
> Spawned in some estaminet of Antwerp,
> Blistered in Brussels, patched and peeled in London.
> The goat coughs at night in the field overhead;
> Rocks, moss, stonecrop, iron, merds.
> The woman keeps the kitchen, makes tea,
> Sneezes at evening, poking the peevish gutter.
>
> I an old man,
> A dull head among windy spaces.

Those who defend this passage against the charges Julius and others have made usually do so on the grounds that "Gerontion" is, after all, not Eliot's own meditation but the monologue of a diseased mind. "Gerontion's mind," writes Jewel Spears Brooker, "is a metaphor for the mind of Europe, a collapsing mind with which Eliot had little sympathy. . . . [The poem's] characters—whether Greek, Christian, or Jewish—exist in Gerontion's demented mind, and all, including himself, are represented as withered and repulsive remnants."[8] And Christopher Ricks remarks, "The consciousness in 'Gerontion,' is not offered as healthy, sane and wise; who would wish to be he, and what endorsement then is being asked for the thoughts of his dry brain in its dry season?" And Ricks adds, "Some of the queasy resentful feelings are bent upon a different Jew who may indeed be the owner, Christ."[9]

The argument for Gerontion as fictional persona is never quite convincing. For one thing, as in the case of "Prufrock," Gerontion is too perceptive, too aphoristic and definitive in his judgments to be dismissed as some sort of mental case. In the course of the poem, moreover, Gerontion asks questions—"After such knowledge, what forgiveness?" "What will the spider do, / Suspend its operations . . . ?"—or makes revelatory statements—"I that was near your heart was removed therefrom," "I have lost my passion"—that look straight ahead to related passages in The Waste Land, a poem of multiple, often contradictory voices.

But if the portrait of the squatting Jew is not just a projection of Gerontion's diseased mind, how then *are* we to take it? Perhaps a

---

8. Jewel Spears Brooker, "Eliot in the Dock: A Review Essay," *South Atlantic Review* 62, no. 4 (Fall 1996): 107–14, 112.

9. Christopher Ricks, *T. S. Eliot and Prejudice* (Berkeley: University of California Press, 1988), 29. Hugh Kenner (129) similarly notes that "the Jew who was spawned in some estaminet of Antwerp cannot but prolong into the present the reputation of another who was born in a different inn," and Brooker notes that the etymology of *estaminet* (little café) is *barn* or *cowhouse* (310), so that the reference is indeed to Christ in the Bethlehem manger.

brief biographical excursus will be helpful here. After the war Eliot knew that he would not be returning to the United States to live. In England his poetry had at least found some acclaim, he had a foothold in the literary press, and he could eke out a living and take care of Vivien, with the help of her family and their friends. Yet he was by no means reconciled to British life. On 2 July 1919 he wrote to his brother Henry:

> Don't think that I find it easy to live over here. It is damned hard work to live with a foreign nation and cope with them—one is always coming up against differences of feeling that make one feel humiliated and lonely. *One remains always a foreigner.* . . . It is like being always on dress parade—one can never relax. It is a *great strain.* . . . People are more aware of you, more critical, and they have no pity for one's mistakes or stupidities. . . . They seek your company because they expect something particular from you, and if they don't get it, they drop you. They are always intriguing and caballing; one must be very alert. . . . *London is something one has to fight very hard in, in order to survive.*[1]

This was written just a week before Eliot wrote John Rodker[2] that he had completed "the new poem I spoke of—about seventy-five lines" (*Letters* 312), which was "Gerontion." And a day or two later he remarked to Mary Hutchinson:[3] "But remember that I am a *metic*—a foreigner" (318).

Remaining "always a foreigner" was especially painful in view of Eliot's circumstances in 1919. In May 1915 he had lost the man he may have loved more than any other—Jean Verdenal—who had been the friend of his youth in Paris and was killed in action in the Dardanelles. Eliot's impulsive marriage to Vivien Haigh-Wood, a month later—perhaps on the rebound from the sorrow of Verdenal's death—had revealed itself as a nightmare, even as Bertrand Russell, once Eliot's mentor, was having an affair with Vivien right under Eliot's nose and partly with his collusion.[4] And then, having failed to get a military commission or to reconcile with his parents, who had disapproved strongly of his marriage, he received the news of

---

1. *Letters*, 310–11, emphasis mine. ° ° °
2. Writer and publisher (1894–1955), whose Ovid Press published Eliot's *Ara Vos Prec* [*Editor*].
3. Short-story writer (1889–1977), a close friend of the Eliots in the early years of their marriage [*Editor*].
4. For the sordid story of Vivien Haigh-Wood's affair with Russell, which went on intermittently from 1915 to 1918, see Ray Monk, *Bertrand Russell: The Spirit of Solitude, 1872–1921* (New York: Free Press, 1996), 432–50, 487–91; Carole Seymour-Jones, *Painted Shadow: The Life of Vivienne Eliot, First Wife of T. S. Eliot, and the Long-Suppressed Truth about Her Influence on His Genius* (New York: Nan A. Talese, Doubleday, 2001), 93–106 and *passim*. Seymour-Jones, whose sympathies are always with Vivien, may be exaggerating Russell's treachery, but her basic story accords entirely with Monk's.

his father's sudden death. Clearly, the poet's personal troubles—his almost visceral revulsion from both Vivien and Russell as well as his alienation from the Bloomsbury of the Stephens sisters, Vanessa and Virginia, and the Garsington circle of Lady Ottoline Morrell—demanded an outlet in his writing.[5]

Ironically, none of the above had even the slightest amount of Jewish or foreign blood; they were, on the contrary, of pure English stock, and Lord Russell was a member of the high English aristocracy. In this context the venom directed against the Jew "spawned in some estaminet in Antwerp," like the venom displayed vis-à-vis women, especially in *The Waste Land*, must be understood as a psychic displacement: all of Eliot's hatred and resentment for Russell and Vivien, like his guilt feelings toward his parents, were displaced onto nightmare figures with labels like "the Jew," or, later in the poem, "Mr. Silvero / With caressing hands" and "De Bailhache, Fresca, [and] Mrs. Cammel." Reluctant to write openly about evils he could not quite put his finger on, he invented an elaborate objective correlative based on stereotypes of Jewish or "Oriental" or female behavior. The closest Eliot came to "direct treatment of the thing"[6] was in *The Waste Land*, where the twenty-eight-line passage in "The Game of Chess" that begins with line 111—"'My nerves are bad to-night. Yes, bad. Stay with me. / 'Speak to me. Why do you never speak. Speak'"—and culminates in the "Shakespeherian Rag," with its assertion that "'I shall rush out as I am, and walk the street / With my hair down, so'"—has been shown to be closely modeled on Vivien's own speech habits; indeed, it was she who added the devastating line "What you get married for if you don't want children?" found in the pub sequence.[7] In "Gerontion," however, the hostility is deflected onto "acceptable" targets like the Jews.

But isn't this precisely what anti-Semitism is? Isn't it inherently *ressentiment* or displacement of hostility and self-hatred onto a scapegoat? Of course, if we add the proviso that the self-disgust and suffering displayed in Eliot's "objective correlative" is what makes "Gerontion" such a powerful and, quite literally, memorable poem. We see the speaker threatened by a "Jew" who, far from being a successful grasping landlord, squeezing money out of poor old Gerontion, is himself a squatter, a victim of poverty, misery, and disease, a figure who, in Julius's words, "becomes what he expels." Squatting on the window sill, he neither belongs inside the

---

5. Virginia Woolf (1882–1941), née Stephen, was already married to Leonard Woolf when she met Eliot in 1917. Her sister, Vanessa (1879–1961), a painter, had married Clive Bell in 1907. Lady Ottoline Morrell (1873–1938) held a well-known literary salon at Garsington Manor, near Oxford [*Editor*].
6. One of the basic rules of imagist poetry, as laid down by Ezra Pound [*Editor*].
7. See *Collected Poems*, 57–59, and cf. Seymour-Jones, *Painted Shadow*, 308–10.

"decayed house," nor can he escape its precincts. In a similar vein, Eliot's misogyny, which will be more openly declared in *The Waste Land*, is here displaced onto a nameless, faceless, generic old woman, who "Sneezes at evening, poking the peevish gutter" (note the remarkable use of the long *e* phoneme)—a sexless figure who is no more of a threat than the goat that "coughs at night in the field overhead." Note that there is no flock of goats in this field but only "the" goat, on the analogy of "the" Jew and "the" woman. And this goat, a far cry from Pan the goat god or the satyr of Greek mythology, does nothing but "cough," even as the woman does nothing but sneeze and poke. As the *scapegoat* of Jewish mythology,[8] it is a fitting companion for Gerontion.

The key to this proto-surreal nightmare landscape, peopled by characters devoid of humanity, is found in line 12—

$$\overset{/}{\text{Rocks,}} \quad \| \quad \overset{/}{\text{moss,}} \quad \| \quad \overset{/}{\text{stonecrop,}} \quad \overset{\wedge}{\text{iron,}} \quad \| \quad \overset{/\wedge}{\text{merds}} \quad \| \quad \overset{/}{}$$

where each noun in the poet's catalogue is separate and emphatically sounded, as in a roll call. The first four nouns, moreover, are phonemic variations on the same *o*, *r*, and *s* sounds: *stonecrop* echoes *rocks* and *moss*, as does the second syllable of *iron*.[9] But then comes a new vowel sound (*e*) and an even nastier reference, this time to the shit (*merds*, from the French *merde*, here rhyming with *turds*) that dominates the scene. By the time we come to the refrain, "I an old man / A dull head among windy spaces,"[1] the various occupants of this arid stonecrop seem no more than a projection of the poet's own self-hatred and despair: Gerontion, the goat, the Jew, the woman who "keeps the kitchen" and "sneezes at evening," even the gutter, described in a transferred epithet as "peevish"—all are interchangeable. The woman "makes tea," the Jew "squats," but the poet himself does nothing at all; he merely exists, verbless, "a dull head among windy spaces." Eliot's winds have been read as allusions to Dante's ceaseless and aimless winds, to the biblical wind that bloweth where

8. According to the *OED*: "*Scapegoat* (1530). 'Goat sent into the wilderness on the Day of Atonement, symbolic bearer of the sins of the people,' coined by Tyndale from scape (M.E. aphetic form of escape)+goat, to translate L. caper emissarius, mistranslation in Vulgate of Heb. azazel (Lev. xvi.8, 10, 26), which was read as 'ez ozel 'goat that departs,' but is actually the proper name of a devil or demon in Jewish mythology (sometimes identified with Canaanite deity Aziz). Meaning 'one who is blamed or punished for the mistakes or sins of others,' first recorded 1824."

9. In *Eliot in Perspective, A Symposium*, ed. Graham Martin (New York: Humanities Press, 1972), 83–101, Gabriel Pearson points out that the plural ending of *rocks* "is disturbed by being echoed by the singular 'moss' to be pluralled in its own turn by the initial *s* of 'stonecrop.' . . . Though one gets images, a landscape of sorts, one hardly reads past and through the words to a world without" (85).

1. In the typescript and in *Ara Vos Prec*, these two lines were set off from the rest; see Ricks, *March Hare*, 349.

it listeth and even, by Genesius Jones,[2] to the Holy Spirit, but I want to note here that contrary to Desmond MacCarthy's caution that we mustn't take Eliot too literally, these windy spaces really *are*, first and foremost, just that—the winds blowing in the empty spaces of the infinite sky over the "Rocks, moss, stonecrop, iron, merds" of Gerontion's—more accurately, the poet's—mental landscape.

If the poem continued in this despairing vein, the scene might become too oppressive. But Eliot, a master of vocal registers, now suddenly shifts tone:

> Signs are taken for wonders. "We would see a sign!"
> The word within a word unable to speak a word,
> Swaddled with darkness. In the juvescence of the year
> Came Christ the tiger

The shift to the cry of the unbelieving Pharisees (who are, of course, Jews), calling upon Christ to prove his divinity by performing a sign (Matthew 12:38), modulates, in turn, into the words of Lancelot Andrewes's Christmas sermon, adapting the Gospel of St. John ("The word without a word; the eternal Word not able to speak a word"), a phrase that is given an Eliotic twist in the substitution of "within" for "without" to refer to the difficulty of receiving the Logos. The springtime ritual looks ahead to "April is the cruelest month": "juvescence" is not, I think, an incorrect version of "juvenescence," as is often suggested, but a neologism, based on its opposite—"senescence." The tiger is of course Blake's tiger, but John Crowe Ransom, in one of the first and most detailed explications of "Gerontion," is right to note that "the lamb who came to be devoured turns into the tiger when Gerontion has forgotten the lamb."[3]

But beyond its allusive texture, this is a highly complex passage. Take the opening alexandrine:

> /   /   /   ‖   /   /   /
> Signs are taken for wonders.   "We would see a sign!"

The first sentence, with its trochaic/dactylic rhythm, is a summarizing commentary, no doubt spoken by the poet whose voice now merges wholly with Gerontion's, whereas the second sentence, a direct citation from Matthew, is iambic. Eliot's Imagist contemporaries would no doubt have given each sentence its own line:

---

2. Author of *Approach to the Purpose: A Study of the Poetry of T. S. Eliot* (London: Hodder and Stoughton, 1964) [*Editor*].
3. John Crowe Ransom, "Gerontion," in Allen Tate, ed., *T. S. Eliot: The Man and His Work; A Critical Evaluation by Twenty-six Distinguished Writers* (New York: Delacorte, 1966), 151.

Signs are taken for wonders.
"We would see a sign!"

In joining both sentences in one line, Eliot obscures the distinction between commentary and citation, the voice of the narrator and the voice of the Pharisee addressing Christ. And this is obviously intentional: for the "dull head among windy spaces" that has been our guide thus far, there is no real distinction between these voices. Indeed, the poet himself is a Pharisee, whose passivity and inability to act or even think ("Think now" will become a major motif in this poem) causes "Signs" to become so essential. Meanwhile "the word within a word, unable to speak a word" remains unheard, "Swaddled in darkness." The long thirteen-syllable line, run over into the next foreshortened one, creates the explosion of

/   /   /
Came Christ the tiger

where the alliteration of the *k* sound yields to the assonance of "Christ" and "tiger"—the two becoming immediately seen as one.

And now, without transition, the poem shifts from the image of Gerontion's general condition and the Christian admonition that follows to a particular surreal scene:

In depraved May, dogwood and chestnut, flowering judas,
To be eaten, to be divided, to be drunk
Among whispers; by Mr. Silvero
With caressing hands, at Limoges
Who walked all night in the next room;
By Hakagawa, bowing among the Titians;
By Madame de Tornquist, in the dark room
Shifting the candles; Fräulein von Kulp
Who turned in the hall, one hand on the door.
      Vacant shuttles
Weave the wind. I have no ghosts,
An old man in a draughty house
Under a windy knob.

In the passage from *The Education of Henry Adams*[4] to which the first line alludes (see Southam 44), "dogwood and chestnut, flowering judas" represent the lush, sensual vegetation of the Washington-area landscape so unfamiliar to a New Englander. Eliot, it is generally assumed, parodied Adams's ecstatic description so as to set the scene for the ghostly parody of the sacrament in the modern world—a kind of Black Mass. The "dry month" of line 1 is now a

4. Essayistic autobiography by the American historian Henry Adams (1838–1918) [*Editor*].

"depraved May," and the reference to "judas" points back, of course, to the betrayal of Christ.

Yet this obvious contrast between contemporary debasement and the Christian Word is hardly the whole story. Indeed, when we read Adams's own account, it seems to point elsewhere. "No European spring," writes Adams, "had shown him the same intermixture of delicate grace and passionate depravity that marked the Maryland May. He loved it too much as if it were Greek and half human" (see Southam 44). It is the Greek connection and the "lov[ing] it too much" that makes the reader of "Gerontion" pause; for like Adams, Eliot longed for the "delicate grace and passionate depravity" associated with things "Greek and half human." Gerontion, after all, is himself Greek, and the denizens of the poem are certainly presented as only "half human." In this context, the memory of "depraved May, dogwood and chestnut, flowering judas" may not be primarily negative after all. On the contrary, the suggestion is that "depraved May" was the "month" in which Gerontion flourished—as lush and wet as that other month has been "dry." One thinks of the Hyacinth Girl in *The Waste Land*, "Your arms full, and your hair wet" * * *. When Adams says he associates "passionate depravity" with the Greeks, he is thinking not of the actual Greek landscape, which is dry and rocky ("Rocks, moss, stonecrop, iron, merds"), but of the Greek deities, half-human, half-animal, sporting in the shade. "Judas," however much an emblem of betrayal, is, after all, depicted as "flowering." So, the poem implies, the pagan sacrament ("To be eaten, to be divided, to be drunk") was seductive enough to attract Gerontion and his friends until it was received "Among whispers" by a particular arty coterie. The nymphs and satyrs have departed, and instead we get sophisticated city dwellers like Mr. Silvero, Hakagawa, Madame de Tornquist, Fräulein von Kulp.

Like "the Jew [who] squats on the window sill," these participants in what seems to be a sinister rite are less characters than caricatures, their mongrelized names testifying to their dubious pedigrees. *Silvero* (a silver alloy of some sort, a silver cover for *vero*, true),[5] *Hakagawa* (whose affix, as Pound remarked when Eliot sent him the poem, means "river" in Japanese), the Blavatsky-clone *Madame de Tornquist* ("turncoat"?), who is soon to metamorphose into the Madame Sosostris of *The Waste Land*, and Madame de Tornquist's German accomplice Fräulein von Kulp (*culpa*). In the cartoon metropolis where these figures operate, there are no actions, merely gestures. What objects (or is it people?) have come under the touch of Mr. Silvero's "caressing hands"? And if he "walked all night in the next room," next to what was it? Or is the room in question next in

---

5. Latin, as is *culpa* (fault or failing) at the end of this sentence [*Editor*].

line? Silvero is "caressing," Hakagawa—an inveterate art groupie, no doubt, or a gallery owner or art collector—is "bowing among the Titians," and Madame de Tornquist "shifting the candles," not, as one might expect, at the church altar, but in "the dark room." Is it a séance? And who is to be raised from the dead instead of Christ? Fräulein von Kulp's movements are especially mysterious: she only "turned in the hall, one hand on the door." Will she run into Mr. Silvero in this "cunning passage"? Is she leaving the séance or about to participate in one? We never find out, for now Eliot gives us the biblical statement: "Vacant shuttles / Weave the wind" (an allusion to Job's "My days are swifter than a weaver's shuttle, and are spent without hope. Oh remember that my life is wind" [Job 7:6–7]), followed by the curious confession that "I have no ghosts," and then the refrain "An old man in a draughty house / Under a windy knob."

The passage leads up to the dramatic question that has since taken on a life of its own: "After such knowledge, what forgiveness?" Ironically, the immediate question these words evoke is not about forgiveness but about knowledge. For what can the knowledge be that has produced such a conundrum? What is it Gerontion *knows* that demands forgiveness? I believe that the "Depraved May" passage contains many hints, buried in the very fabric of the language. "Depraved," for starters, contains the paragram *pray*. It is the refusal to pray, the absence of prayer in this remembered scene, that has made the poet's May so "depraved." "Judas" contains the syllable "jew," which is to say that the eating, dividing, and drinking going on here might have been the real sacrament rather than its debasement into "flowering judas." The "whispers" in line 23 are literally enacted in the sequence "*whispers*" / "*Mister*" / "*Silvero*," and the hissing *s* is carried over into "caressing." Because Gerontion's story has never been inscribed on the loom of history, because the shuttles remain vacant, there is little to go by. The poet, moreover, doesn't want exposure, and so he avoids all lessons the past might provide. And the "draughty" house is also the house of "drought."

But of course Gerontion does have his ghosts. Consider this passage:

> After such knowledge, what forgiveness? Think now
> History has many cunning passages, contrived corridors
> And issues, deceives with whispering ambitions,
> Guides us by vanities. Think now

> (ll. 34–37)

Again, let us ask: what does Gerontion *know* that makes it so difficult for him to forgive himself? To begin with, he had a chance to know Christ, to partake of His body and blood, to take Communion, but somehow he refused. Accordingly, "The tiger springs in the new year. Us he devours." But there are other forms of knowledge the poet refused. "Gerontion" was supposed to be the prelude to *The Waste Land*, and there we read:

> *Datta*: what have we given?
> My friend, blood shaking my heart
> The awful daring of a moment's surrender
> Which an age of prudence can never retract
> By this, and this only, we have existed
>
> (ll. 401–05)

This passage is nicely glossed by the lines in "Gerontion," "Gives too soon / Into weak hands, what's thought can be dispensed with / Till the refusal propagates a fear." And again, the admonition is "Think."

After such knowledge, what forgiveness? After having known what "blood shaking my heart" could be, how could the poet have rejected love in the interest of prudence? How could he have been so weak as to think he could dispense with love, only to find himself a potential "old man" whose "refusal propagates a fear"? Thinking, unfortunately, won't change anything.

These are the "ghosts" that haunt the Gerontion who tries to tell himself that he has no ghosts:

> I that was near your heart was removed therefrom
> To lose beauty in terror, terror in inquisition.
> I have lost my passion: why should I need to keep it
> Since what is kept must be adulterated?
> I have lost my sight, smell, hearing, taste and touch:
> How should I use them for your closer contact?
>
> (ll. 55–61)

These "Jacobean" lines make sense only if we take them to be both about secular and spiritual love. What a poem says, as Jacques Roubaud[6] puts it, cannot be said any other way. The loss of the five senses in line 50 takes us back to that earlier catalogue, "Rocks, moss, stonecrop, iron, merds"—items threatening to the touch, to smell, taste, sight, and hearing—that constitute the landscape when all that matters has been lost.

What is left is no more than a "wilderness of mirrors," in which some further humanoids—De Bailhache, Fresca, Mrs. Cammel— are "whirled / Beyond the circuit of the shuddering Bear / in fractured atoms." In this ghostly frozen landscape, the little white gull cannot fight the wind and collapses in a mass of "white feathers" in the snow. All that is finally left, as the poem's speaker knows, is

---

6. French mathematician and poet (b. 1932) [*Editor*].

$$\text{/} \qquad\qquad \text{/}$$
Tenants of the house,
$$\text{/} \qquad \text{/} \cdot \text{/} \qquad \text{/} \quad \text{/}$$
Thoughts of a dry brain in a dry season.

What is striking here is that the stress clusters, reminiscent of the poem's opening, are now unbroken by midline caesurae. The rhythm merely *flows*, weakly alluding to the agitated pace of "Here I am, ‖ an old man | in a dry month." The game, Eliot suggests, is over.

Is "Gerontion" incoherent? Certainly not at the level of language and rhythm, where every word and phrase has its echo in the "wilderness of mirrors" of earlier or later strophes. Eliot moves easily between the concrete of "Hakagawa, bowing among the Titians" and the abstract of "Gives too late / What's not believed in." The tension between the two, which has bothered numerous critics, seems quite intentional: only by exploring the tension between abstract/concrete, conceptual/perceptual, general/particular, can the Voice of the poem come to terms with the reality of its situation.

What is that situation? At one pole, the poet who might have known the mercy and grace of God, the Christian dispensation, has rejected it and must hence live in a secular realm in which redemption is precluded. At the other, more personal pole, Eliot presents himself as one who, having neither been "at the hot gates / Nor fought in the warm rain," turned to the literary life of London and country houses, the life of English upper-class society, which, as I remarked earlier, was hardly the society of "the Jew," "Patched and peeled in London"; or the society of Mr. Silvero with his cult of Limoges, or Fräulein von Kulp, "one hand on the door"; or certainly not the oddly named Fresca, who seems to have no family name at all and keeps company with Mrs. Cammel, whose name sounds suspiciously Jewish. No, the society Eliot frequented during the war years and their aftermath was the best "literary" society England had to offer. It was the bisexual "enlightened" society of Bloomsbury, perhaps, that sullied the memory of the poet's own private savior, the romantic young Frenchman named Jean Verdenal and all he stood for. And it was further a society that all too off handedly rejected the Christ of the Gospels. Bertrand Russell, for example, was a confirmed atheist, and Bloomsbury generally made fun of Christian faith as hopelessly childish and antiquated. In this religious void, only "vacant shuttles weave the wind." And since Eliot can never reveal his real secret about Verdenal, he can only turn to Christ, who will forgive all sins.

One of the wonders of "Gerontion" is thus how a deeply personal situation finds its objective correlative so that the poem appears to be, in its later passages, a disquisition about larger, impersonal issues, questions of history and memory, sin and redemption. It is a matter of charging language with meaning so that "depraved May" will readily reveal the power of what it means to *pray*. Is "Gerontion" an anti-Semitic poem? No one could deny that the three lines in question have a nasty, anti-Semitic cast. But does this mean that the thrust of Eliot's complex monologue is a slur on the Jews? Hardly. For it is finally a meditation in which critique is pointed inward. There is no forgiveness, only the knowledge of how one has come to such a pass.

Like all good poems, "Gerontion" cannot be paraphrased; it cannot be described as "about" an old man's confused mind or "about" the refusal to take Communion, or about the decay of religion in a secular world. All these motifs enter in, but the force of the poem depends on its extraordinary language. Take the name De Bailhache in the last section, De Bailhache being one of those "whirled / Beyond the circuit of the shuddering Bear / In fractured atoms." De Bailhache is not a "proper" French surname; its parts don't cohere. But literally the name gives us the first syllable of *bailler* (to yawn) plus *hache* (axe). An *hache de guerre* is a battle-axe or tomahawk; *haché* means "minced" or "crushed," as in *bifteck haché,* which is hamburger.

Bailhache as yawner looks ahead to the "sleepy corner" to which this person and his friends will soon be driven. Bailhache as "battle-axe" or "tomahawk" is a variant on the cutlass the poet wishes he had heaved in the salt marsh. Bailhache represents the hamburger one becomes when one's proper names seem to be at odds. And finally the "De" is the most common of affectations: the prefix designating an aristocratic connection.

All of these connotations obtain. But in line 68, De Bailhache is also an anagram on the word *delay* that precedes it. And that is perhaps the most intriguing suggestion of the proper name. Would that there were a delay for De Bailhache, Fresca, and Mrs. Cammell, "whirled beyond the circuit of the shuddering Bear / In fractured atoms"! Gerontion may tell us he has no ghosts, but the poem knows better. In Eliot's great phantasmagoria, the ghosts are everywhere.

DAVID TROTTER

From T. S. Eliot and Cinema†

The aim of this essay is to establish that our understanding of Eliot's "poetics of impersonality" will be enhanced by a definition of its informing will-to-automatism which takes full account, for the first time, of his commentary on cinema. The parallel histories in play, here, are those of the development of Eliot's poetry up to and including *The Waste Land* (1922), and of the emergence during the same period of a fully narrative cinema (that is, of character-driven story films capable of absorbing a diverse mass audience into a self-sufficient world unified across space and time). In my view, the only way to establish the relation between those histories is through an examination of Eliot's evolving commentary, in poems, essays, and letters, on cinema. Eliot did not write cinematically. But there is a history to his changing view of the medium which can usefully be compared to the history of the ways in which the medium itself changed, during the silent era, as well as to the history of his own attempts to change literature.

※　※　※

Cinema appears first in the poems, rather than in letters or essays; and it appears by way of a shared terminology of the screen, and of images that flicker on the screen. The view these poems propose is of consciousness as a space, or event, or drama, of projection. Thoughts or feelings can only be known as they hang in the distance between an internal source of illumination and a configured surface belonging to the world outside. They can only be known technologically.

Or so "The Love Song of J. Alfred Prufrock," Eliot's hall-mark early poem, completed in the summer of 1911, would have us believe. As the poem begins, a question arises, or might arise, during the course of an urban expedition the speaker means to undertake (has already undertaken?) with a nameless (probably male) companion. To pose the question directly would be to be overwhelmed by it.

> Oh, do not ask, "What is it?"
> Let us go and make our visit.

Prufrock's prim rhyme nips curiosity in the bud. The visit, coming quick and tart upon the companion's (possible) question about a

† From *Modernism/modernity* 13 (2006): 241–47. © 2006 Johns Hopkins University Press. Reprinted with permission of Johns Hopkins University Press. Unless otherwise indicated, notes are by the author. The author's parenthetical citations have been omitted.

question, meets it, in sound if not in sense, before it has fully arisen; and so prevents, or postpones, the damage its arising might do. The visit, of a kind Eliot himself had made often enough as an undergraduate at Harvard, is (or would be) to a room where women come and go, where there is music, and tea, and cakes and ices.[1] Prufrock, it has often been said, behaves, or imagines himself behaving, as though he were in a story by Henry James: "Crapy Cornelia," whose protagonist strikingly fails, under comparable circumstances, to propose to the woman of his dreams.[2] The purpose of the visit is to relieve him, through ordeal by embarrassment, of any remaining thought of an overwhelming question. For the one person who cannot be admitted, who will never make his presence felt there, is the person Prufrock would have to be if he were to pose the question: a prophet, Lazarus come from the dead.

The space Prufrock at once anticipates and remembers entering is a space of pure specularity. "Prufrock," Ellmann notes, "sees himself *being seen*." He sees the bald spot on his head as it might appear from the point of view of the women who have gathered at the top of the stair to observe an ungracious departure. He has been estranged, Ellmann adds, by the eyes which "fix" him in a "formulated phrase," to the exteriorities of language and space.[3] Does he even show up? "He is not there yet when we hear him speaking," Hugh Kenner observes: "he will never be there, or will perpetually return there—it does not matter." He will never be there as the person he would like to be, Lazarus come from the dead; but he will always be there, in his own absence, through memory and anticipation. He may consider defying whatever "automatism" propels him repeatedly, in memory or in anticipation, "through these streets, through that door, up those stairs."[4] But he needs it more than it needs him.

The trouble is that the automatism does not work; or does not work as Prufrock would like it to work, for all the embarrassment it causes him, as a shield against overwhelming questions. For this visit undertaken automatically poses a question even more overwhelming, in its sheer immediacy, than anything that might have arisen on an expedition through argumentative streets. The question is sexual arousal, and the sense of self it generates, on the spot, at the time (*which* time no longer matters). Prufrock has been, or will be,

1. Conrad Aiken, "King Bolo and Others," in Tambimuttu and March, eds., *T. S. Eliot: A Symposium* (London: Frank Cass, 1948), 20–3; 21–2.
2. Lyndall Gordon, *Eliot's Early Years* (Oxford: Oxford University Press, 1977), 47.
3. Maud Ellmann, *The Poetics of Impersonality: T. S. Eliot and Ezra Pound* (Cambridge, MA: Harvard University Press, 1987), 69 [*Editor*].
4. Hugh Kenner, *The Invisible Poet: T. S. Eliot* (London: Methuen, 1959), 21.

or let us risk saying is, aroused by the arms of the women who come and go:

> Arms that are braceleted and white and bare
> (But in the lamplight, downed with light brown hair!) . . .

What finally puts him at the scene, in the picture, is his attention to bodily texture: the film of light brown hair on a white arm. In describing the body, Victorian writers had for the most part confined themselves to that which was most expressive about it: its overall shape; or its most characterful component, the face; or a particular feature (eyes, nose, mouth). Edwardian writers chose instead to describe the flesh between features. The focus of the new eroticism in literature was on the body as body, rather than as an expression of soul. The down on a woman's body looms large as a provocation to and emblem of male desire in novels by Arnold Bennett, D. H. Lawrence, May Sinclair and others.[5] The story Prufrock now finds himself in is a story by Bennett or Lawrence, rather than by Henry James. Eliot had brought himself bang up to date.

The intensity of Prufrock's arousal produces or is produced by an intensification in the verse. By comparison with its sparse and evenly paced predecessor ("and white and bare"), the line describing the hair on the women's arms seems positively swollen: the echo of "lamplight" in "light brown hair" and the internal rhyme on "downed" and "brown" fill it from within with sameness of sound, with emphasis. In this moment of absolute fixation, the poem dwells on the inexpressive body, and also on that in its own formal procedures which foreshadows and outlasts expression: on technique, on poetic matter. It is characteristic of Eliot, however, that he should have embedded the moment of absolute fixation in a parenthesis. The ear hears the conjoining rhyme, the eye sees the disjoining brackets. So Prufrock's arousal is at once overwhelming and ghostly. He must be reckoned most fully present only when absent. The automatism propelling him, in memory or in anticipation, through that door, up those stairs, observes as he would not actually have observed, had he been there himself, in his own person, with an overwhelming question to hand. The couplet describing what the prosthesis or automatism has seen or will see in his place exemplifies the disembodiment of perception by technique.

The circle of illumination within which the light brown hair on a white arm appears in alluring close-up might make us think of the cinema. Such close-ups of the body's less expressive stretches played an important part in some of the earliest narrative films.

---

5. David Trotter, *The English Novel in History 1895–1920* (London: Routledge, 1993), 201–2.

G. A. Smith's *As Seen through a Telescope* (1900) begins with a long shot of an elderly man brandishing a telescope, while a woman and a younger man wheeling a bicycle advance up the street towards him. As the telescope settles on the pair, Smith cuts to a medium close-up of the woman's foot resting on a pedal, isolated within a circular vignette. The young man has knelt down to tie her shoelace. She gradually raises her skirt, revealing an expanse of stockinged ankle and leg, which her companion proceeds to caress. As the long shot resumes, the elderly voyeur seats himself contentedly, at the peep-show's conclusion, only to receive a punitive cuff from the young man, who has caught him looking, as the couple pass. By severing foreground from background, the close-up induces a change of medium rather than scale, a metamorphosis. The expanse of ankle and leg on display is an object as much of touch as of sight. Like Prufrock, the elderly man has been made present (has been presented to desire, has shown up) in and through his absence, in and through a prosthesis. The erotic effect of Smith's film lies in what visual technologies see that the human eye cannot; that of Eliot's poem in what poetic technique renders that other forms of representation cannot.

"The Love Song of J. Alfred Prufrock" is indeed a love song; the love song of a voyeur equipped with a telescope, or a movie camera, or a page or two in a modern novel. Once body-hair has posed its overwhelming question, there is no way back, for Prufrock. He cannot undo the knowledge his automatism has given him. What remains is to make sense of experience: whether the experience has been of sunsets, and sprinkled streets, or of novels, teacups, and trailing skirts. After all this, Prufrock laments, and so much more,

> It is impossible to say just what I mean!
> But as if a magic lantern threw the nerves in patterns
>   on a screen: . . .

There is technique, here, and technology. The odd swerve of *"But as if . . ."* at the beginning of the line gets the figure of the magic lantern going. A colon at its end keeps that figure oddly in suspension, at once the product of and contained by a shift or warp in the stanza's rhetorical development. A rhyme conjoining lines of unequal length into a couplet holds it all together, in some fashion: technique exposed as technique, as mechanism. Rhyme itself is the configured surface, the screen, on which a pattern appears which might or might not "say" just what one means.

Walter Benjamin was to seize eagerly on Baudelaire's description of the person routinely suffering the shocks and strains of modern urban experience as a *"kaleidoscope* equipped with consciousness." Light pours into a kaleidoscope pressed up against the eye from outside, from the world beyond. Benjamin took from Baudelaire's figure its preoccupation with passivity. He imagines a pedestrian forever on the alert for traffic signals, for the cautionary light shone at him or her through pieces of colored glass. "Thus technology," he concludes, "has subjected the human sensorium to a complex kind of training." Cinema, in which "perception in the form of shocks" has been established as a "formal principle," would complete the training.[6] One could say that Eliot's figure presents the modern man or woman as a magic lantern equipped with consciousness. His interest in technology does not, however, entail a comparable techno-determinism.

The magic lantern's light source is internal rather than external. A beam of light, shone through hand-painted or photographic glass slides, takes shape on the screen positioned in front of and at a certain distance from the projector. Two aspects of Eliot's development of the magic lantern as a figure for the way the mind works are worth noting. First, he stresses the force of projection: the image *thrown* onto or against the screen. There can be no doubting the power of the mind's internal light source. Eliot's magic lantern has been equipped with a rather more active consciousness than Baudelaire's kaleidoscope. Secondly, the nerves thrown violently onto the screen have at least been thrown onto it in a pattern. The shape the beam of light has taken is intelligible. The patterned image solicits interpretation. It might even amount to what Eliot was to call in his 1919 essay on *Hamlet* the "objective correlative" or "formula" for a particular emotion.[7]

In this respect, the history of the magic lantern, a mainstay of the Victorian entertainment industry, and one of cinema's most significant precursors, can help to explain Eliot's emphasis. Some features of lantern showmanship, such as musical accompaniment, and the commentary provided by a narrator or lecturer, carried over into early film presentation.[8] It seems likely that, given the presence of a narrator or lecturer, the relationship the magic lantern spectator maintained with the images on the screen was, as Noël Burch puts it, "an *exploratory* one"; a relationship also characteristic of the first

6. Walter Benjamin, "On Some Motifs in Baudelaire," in *Illuminations*, transl. Harry Zohn (London: Fontana, 1973), 157–202; 177. Benjamin's essay, first published in 1939, begins where the first section of *The Waste Land* ends, with Baudelaire's salutation of the "*hypocrite lecteur.*"
7. T. S. Eliot, "Hamlet," in *Selected Prose*, ed. Frank Kermode (London: Faber and Faber, 1975), 45–9, 48; see above, p. 157 [*Editor*].
8. Ian Christie, *The Last Machine: Early Cinema and the Birth of the Modern World* (London: BBC Educational Developments, 1994), 90. See also Laurent Mannoni, *The Great Art of Light and Shadow: Archaeology of the Cinema*, transl. Richard Crangle (Exeter: University of Exeter Press, 2000), ch. 11.

film shows.[9] The magic lantern co-existed with the moving pictures
for a decade or more after 1895. So Eliot's reference to it, in 1911,
was slightly archaic; and no doubt with intent. Prufrock finds
himself in the predicament Eliot was to describe in "The Dry Sal-
vages" * * *.[1] He has had the experience (of sunsets and sprinkled
streets, of novels, teacups, and trailing skirts), but missed the mean-
ing. The magic lantern—the kind of technology, genteel and old-
fashioned, with which Prufrock feels at home—intervenes. It cannot
restore meaning to experience. But its automatism has created a pat-
tern, there, on the screen, for exploration, which Prufrock alone
would have been incapable of creating.

It is possible that Prufrock is rather too much at home with his
old-fashioned technology. His vision of mermaids riding the waves,
or lolling in sea-weed drapes in chambers beneath it, has something
of the magic-lantern show about it. Perhaps Prufrock had been to
see (Eliot himself could not possibly have done) the dances presented
at the Palace Theater by a lady calling herself La Pia. The perfor-
mance, we learn from a report in the Times, is "considerably
heightened by a shimmering background of glistening tinsel ribbons
and the artful aid of many-coloured lights in combination with clever
cinematograph and magic lantern illusions." Two of La Pia's dances
apparently brought the "opposing elements" of fire and water into
play with "quite extraordinary realism." In the fire dance, drapery
and streaming hair sucked by a "furious draught" coalesce into
flame. In the water dance, a cinematograph turns the whole of the
back of the stage into a tossing sea. The waves submerge La Pia, but
each time she comes up again unharmed.[2]

The third of the "Preludes," dated July 1911, describes a woman
who, dozing, watches the night reveal the sordid images of which
her soul is constituted "flicker" against the ceiling. When Prufrock
wistfully remarks that he has seen the moment of his greatness
"flicker," the flickering is that of a candle, or lamp. Here, by con-
trast, it is the images which flicker, not a light source; the flickering
is mechanical. The OED's first citation for "flicker" in its cinematic
sense—a succession of changes in a picture occurring when the
number of frames per second is too small to produce reliable persis-
tence of vision—is from H. V. Hopwood's Living Pictures (1899).
"There is little doubt but that a continual rattle impinging on the
ear," Hopwood complained of early projection systems,

9. Noël Burch, Life to Those Shadows, transl. Ben Brewster (London: BFI Publishing,
1990), 87.
1. "We had the experience but missed the meaning" (T. S. Eliot, Complete Poems and
Plays [London: Faber and Faber, 1969]), 186 [Editor].
2. "Variety Entertainments," [London] Times, 15 February 1910, 11.

tends to intensify irritation caused to the eye by flicker on the screen, and it is towards the minimising or concealment of this same flicker that attention is at the present time most strenuously directed. This objectionable phenomenon is traceable to the fact that the picture is periodically cut-off from view, a state of affairs which, of course, does not obtain in natural vision. It must be remembered that though persistence of vision ensures the continuance of one image until such time as another is received, yet the impression does not continue in its full strength, and the general result is therefore a perpetual increase and decrease in the brilliancy of the picture as perceived by the eye. Furthermore, the decrease of light is progressive, but every fresh view is presented in full brilliancy.[3]

The flicker, or perpetual increase and decrease in the brilliancy of the picture projected, is one mark of cinema's automatism: a "state of affairs" which "does not obtain in natural vision." It is unlikely that such an effect would allow for an "exploratory" relationship between viewer and projected picture. There does not seem to be a great deal of pattern, in Eliot's poem, to the sordid images thrown violently onto or against the ceiling. In this case, projection offers little relief from, and indeed exacerbates, the woman's irritability. One thinks of Leopold Bloom, in *Ulysses,* desperate, like the elderly man in *As Seen through a Telescope,* for a glimpse of a woman climbing into a carriage ("Watch! Watch! Silk flash rich stockings white. Watch!"), and thwarted when a tramcar slews between. Again, the perpetual increase and decrease in brilliancy engenders (and expresses) irritation. "Flicker, flicker: the laceflare of her hat in the sun: flicker, flick."[4]

References to visual technology, in the early poems, enabled Eliot to define the "exteriorities of language and space" (in Ellmann's phrase) which constitute social subjectivity. Indeed, to imagine consciousness as an event or drama of projection was to grasp the implication of one exteriority in the other: to find space in language. Spatial prepositions (across, against, along, among, behind, by, under, upon) play an important part in these poems. The most interesting spatial preposition of all is "across," which Eliot uses to indicate both the distance between viewer and scene, and the distance from one side of the scene to the other. "Interlude in London" was based on a visit Eliot made to London, from Paris, in April 1911. In the hotel, he told Eleanor Hinkley, "one looked through the

3. H. V. Hopwood, *Living Pictures: Their History, Photo-Production, and Practical Working* (London: Optician and Photographic Trades Review, 1899), 208.
4. James Joyce, *Ulysses,* ed. Jeri Johnson (Oxford: Oxford University Press, 1993), 71.

windows, and the waiter brought in eggs and coffee. . . ."⁵ The speaker of the poem rather more complicatedly laments that he must live "across the window panes." He looks out through a window into the world beyond; but that world might also seem to have spread itself out, as it quite often does in Eliot's early poems, from one side of the frame to the other. The panes are transparent; and they form a screen. So it is, too, after a fashion, in "Interlude: in a Bar," of February 1911, which also concerns a space of projection. Across—on the other side of—the room, shifting smoke settles around "forms" which pass through or clog the brain. Yet that other side also functions as a flat surface, a kind of screen. The walls "fling back" the scattered streams of a life which appears "Visionary, and yet hard": at once "immediate" and "far," like a projected image. How very few people there are, observes the speaker of the fourth and last poem in the "Mandarins" sequence of August 1910, who see their "outlines" on the "screen." Christopher Ricks glosses "on the screen" by reference to the *OED*'s first cinematic citation, from a 1910 issue of *Moving Picture World*: "People . . . like to see on the screen what they read about".⁶

✻   ✻   ✻

JUAN A. SUÁREZ

[The Gramophone in *The Waste Land*]†

Here's a well-kept secret about modernism: during the composition of *The Waste Land*, throughout 1921 and early 1922, T. S. Eliot was attached to his gramophone much in the same way as Andy Warhol was later "married" to his movie camera, Polaroid, and tape recorder. Both artists, representatives of very different cultural moments and vastly separate in ideology, social and cultural positioning, self-understanding, and public personae, were nonetheless equally dependent on the technological continuum for the production of their work. While Warhol flaunted this dependence and a sense of kinship with the machine ("I've always wanted to be a

---

5. T. S. Eliot, *Letters*, vol. 1, ed. Valerie Eliot (London: Faber and Faber, 1988), 18. "Interlude in London," "Interlude: in a Bar," and "Mandarins" are early, unpublished poems, quoted here from T. S. Eliot, *Inventions of the March Hare: Poems 1909–1917*, ed. Christopher Ricks (London: Faber and Faber, 1996) [*Editor*].

6. *Inventions of the March Hare*, 139 [*Editor*].

† From *Pop Modernism: Noise and the Reinvention of the Everyday* (Champaign, Illinois: University of Illinois Press, 2007), pp. 121–25, 132–34. Used with permission of University of Illinois Press. Unless otherwise indicated, notes are by the author. The author's parenthetical page references and some of his notes have been omitted.

machine"),[1] Eliot concealed it, recoiling into interiority, religion, myth, and tradition. But for a brief moment, Eliot's writing, like Warhol's multimedia projects, was uneasily entangled in gadgets, circuits, media networks, and technologies of textual production and reproduction. If Warhol mimed the workings of his gadgets, so did Eliot; if Warhol was a recorder-camera-xerox machine, Eliot was a gramophone. But the point here is not to pursue the (certainly contrived) parallel between these two wildly divergent figures. It is to rescue the technological dependency of one of the gray eminences of modernism and to resituate *The Waste Land*, an "apotheosis of modernity"[2] and mainstay of the twentieth-century canon, within the discourse networks of its time.

*   *   *

The gramophone is heard in a prominent, if squalid, segment of *The Waste Land*. It appears in part 3 ("The Fire Sermon"), in one of the emblematic moments of modern degradation that the poem seeks at once to portray and to overcome. This is the sexual encounter between a jaded typist and a "young man carbuncular"—"A small house agent's clerk . . . on whom assurance sits / As a silk hat on a Bradford millionaire." Their tryst is prefaced by elliptical views of the city (the polluted Thames and its banks; the bustle of traffic), invocations of death and decay, and by a brief passage, "under the brown fog of a winter noon," in which the ever-mutating first-person narrator receives an ambiguous invitation from a Mr. Eugenides, "the Smyrna merchant": "Asked me in demotic French / to luncheon at the Canon Street Hotel."[3] These contemporary scenes are haunted by gadgets, mass-produced objects, and industrial landscapes that render the present mechanical, jarring, lifeless, and disenchanted. Take, for example, "the sound of horns and motors" in city streets; the "empty bottles, sandwich papers, / silk handkerchiefs, cardboard boxes, cigarette ends / or other testimony of summer nights" on the river banks; the "gashouse" by "the dull canal," where the rats scurry over moldy bones; or the customs forms that fill Mr. Eugenides's pockets.

As one more vignette of present-day decadence, the exhausted rendezvous between the typist and her suitor also unfolds under

---

1. Andy Warhol, "What Is Pop Art?" interview by G. R. Swenson, *Artnews* (62) 1963: 24–60. Warhol's actual words are: "The reason I'm painting this way is because I want to be a machine. Whatever I do, and do machine-like, is because it is what I want to do."
2. John Crowe Ransom, "Waste Lands," in *T. S. Eliot: The Critical Heritage*, vol. 1, ed. Michael Grant (London: Routledge and Kegan Paul, 1981), 176.
3. It seems to me that the reader is invited to cringe at the invitation ("in demotic *French*" no less!), whose placement reveals that, for Eliot, this kind of homoerotic possibility sounds the depths of contemporary decadence. For another example of Eliot's homophobic anxieties, see Peter Ackroyd, *T. S. Eliot: A Life* (London: Hamish Hamilton, 1984), 243–44.

emblems of industrial modernity. It takes place in the early evening, after work, when "the human engine waits / Like a taxi throbbing, waiting." Home from the office, the typist lights up her stove, tidies up, and "lays out food in tins." Her guest arrives "with one bold stare." Once dinner is over, he makes his advance, which meets with neither resistance nor encouragement. The encounter is unspirited; the insistently mechanical rhythm of the lines underlines its somnambulistic quality. After he leaves, she remains prey to automatism and machine conditioning:

> She turns and looks a moment in the glass,
> Hardly aware of her departed lover
> Her brain allows one half-formed thought to pass . . .
> Paces about her room again, alone,
> She smoothes her hair with automatic hand,
> And puts a record on the gramophone.

The music of the gramophone highlights the squalor of the scene and comes to stand for the vulgarity and disenchantment of contemporary existence. Similar connotations accrue around this device in other parts of Eliot's corpus. In the short story "Eeldrop and Appleplex," for example, gramophones provide a soundtrack for the dismal suburban setting: "[T]he gardens of the small houses to left and right were rank with ivy and tall grass and lilac bushes; the tropical South London verdure was dusty above and mouldy below; the tepid air swarmed with flies. Eeldrop, at the window, welcomed the smoky smell of lilac, the gramaphones [sic], the choir of the Baptist chapel, and the sight of three small girls playing cards on the steps of the police station."[4] In a very different piece, Eliot's homage to the British music-hall artist Mary Lloyd, the gramophone, along with the cinema and the radio, are blamed for replacing the "organic" participatory popular arts with the standardized, lifeless output of the culture industry.[5] And in "Portrait of a Lady," the stale pretentiousness of the lady's manners and quarters (which have "[a]n atmosphere of Juliet's tomb") is underlined by the music streaming from—where else?—a gramophone: "And so the conversation slips / Among velleities and carefully caught regrets / Through attenuated tones of violins / Mingled with remote cornets / And begins." Later on in the poem, canned music is aligned once more with lackluster existence; its sound unnerves the hypersensitive first-person "narrator," the lady's interlocutor:

---

4. T. S. Eliot, "Eeldrop and Appleplex, II," *Little Review* (September 1917): 16. Part I had appeared in the May 1917 issue.
5. T. S. Eliot, "Marie Lloyd," in *Selected Prose of T. S. Eliot,* ed. Frank Kermode (London: Faber, 1975), 174.

I remain self-possessed
Except when a street piano, mechanical and tired
Reiterates some worn-out common song
With the smell of hyacinths across the garden
Recalling things that other people have desired.

But to return to *The Waste Land,* the gramophone's sound closes the poem's bleak, necromantic first half. Shortly afterward begin the intimations of rebirth and redemption. The next stanza evokes "the pleasant whining of a mandolin," heard in a pub on Lower Thames Street, and the neoclassical splendor of the Church of Magnus Martyr, by Christopher Wren. The folk performance and the "Ionian white and gold" of the monument offset debased modern existence and its accoutrements. The following section, "Death by Water," contains a poignant memento mori; and in the closing fragment, "What the Thunder Said," the scorched, rocky earth breaks into new life. The oppressive present is obscurely redeemed. Modern city scenes are replaced by timeless landscapes, while the shrill sounds of contemporary life are displaced by the rumble of thunder, mythic invocations drawn from the *Upanishads,* and literary allusions ranging from antiquity to the Renaissance. In the end, the choral voice of tradition drowns the artificial sounds of modernity—among them, the mechanical grinding of the gramophone—and restores to life a hard-won, new organicity. And yet if one listens closely, it becomes apparent that the sounds of tradition are played back by a gramophone. The organic, mystic unity with which, it is generally agreed, the poem ends, is entirely dependent on it. Its prerecorded sound is the condition of possibility for the entire work. In his attempt to modernize the idiom of modern poetry, Eliot was shaping an old medium in the image of a new one.[6]

*   *   *

* * * We have already pointed out how the voice media fragment the organic wholeness of oral and written communication. We may add that these media, particularly the gramophone, worked as data banks. They were information-storage devices—mechanical memories detached from self and psychology. They made all the speech and music of the world instantly retrievable. The gramophone made possible the existence of sound and music archives, like the *Musée*

6. This inverts somewhat Marshall McLuhan's idea that the content of a new medium is always an older one: the content of the radio is the written word; of cinema, the theater; of television, both the cinema and the radio, and so on. Marshall McLuhan, *Understanding Media: The Extensions of Man* (New York: Vintage, 1964).

glossophonographique, created in 1900 by the Anthropology Society of Paris, or the phonographic collection of the Vienna Academy of Science, founded the same year.[7] Such aural memory banks were, in turn, the basis for the sound collages that would later be broadcast on the radio.

In the late 1920s, following up on the success of his film *Berlin, Simphonie der Großstadt,*[8] the experimental German director Walter Ruttmann [1887–1941] created several sound montages. He recorded them on the magnetic sound band of an unexposed film strip using the recently developed Tri-Ergon process, one of the most sophisticated at the time. The resulting pieces were *Wochenende,* a sound picture of leisure activities, and *Tönende Welle,* a simulation of radio zapping. Simultaneously, the Soviet avant-garde filmmaker Dziga Vertov [1896–1954] was experimenting with similar ideas for his "Radio-Pravda" montages.[9] These were the radio equivalents of his "Kino-Pravda" film newsreels: sounds and voices spliced together to depict, or comment on, contemporary events.

It is not difficult to see a kinship between these experiments and *The Waste Land.* Eliot's poem zaps through a sort of prerecorded literary archive that seems to be kept on the air at different frequencies.[1] As it runs through the length of the spectrum, the dial picks up some voices and frequencies while it skips others; the resulting collage is transcribed onto the page. It is small wonder that the messages transcribed are fragmentary. Mechanized communication does not respect the organic boundaries of grammar and sense. One may tune in and out in midsentence; the connection may be interrupted by leakage, power failure, or sudden malfunctioning. Or one may simply remove the record, turn the dial, or hang up the telephone whether the message has been completed or not.

> London Bridge is falling down, falling down, falling down
> *Poi s'ascose nel foco che gli affina*
> *Quando fiam uti chelidon*—O swallow swallow
> *Le Prince d'Aquitaine à la tour abolie*
> These fragments I have shored against my ruins
> Why then Ile fit you. Hieronymo's mad againe.

7. Stephen Kern, *The Culture of Time and Space, 1880–1918* (Cambridge, Mass.: Harvard University Press, 1983), 38.
8. First shown in 1927 and usually presented in English as *Berlin: Symphony of a Metropolis* or, more literally, *Berlin: Symphony of a Great City. Wochenende (Weekend),* first shown in 1930, and *Tönende Welle (Sounding Wave),* first shown in 1928, are short "films" with sound but no images [*Editor*].
9. Vertov believed that new media should transcribe truth (*pravda*) directly and with as little intervention as possible from the artist. Thus "Radio-Pravda" is a series of sound montages, and "Kino-Pravda" a series of film montages [*Editor*].
1. Daniel Albright has applied this image to Ezra Pound's *Cantos.* See Daniel Albright, "Early Cantos, I-XLI," in *The Cambridge Companion to Ezra Pound,* ed. Ira B. Nadel (Cambridge: Cambridge University Press, 1999), 60–61.

Datta. Dayadhvam. Damyata.
Shantih shantih shantih.

The poet himself is the tuning dial here, or else a disc jockey that delights in creating such mosaics of sound and language. The idea appears elsewhere in Eliot's work. In his famous essay "Tradition and the Individual Talent," written three years before *The Waste Land*, he repeatedly characterizes the mature poet as an impersonal "medium" for the storage and transmission of information: "The mind of the mature poet differs from that of the immature poet not precisely in any valuation of 'personality,' not by being necessarily more interesting or having 'more to say,' but rather by being *a more finely perfected medium* in which special, or very varied, feelings are at liberty to enter into new combinations."[2] He continues, "The poet's mind is in fact a receptacle for seizing and storing up numberless feelings, phrases, images, which remain there until all the particles which can unite to form a new compound are present together." This kind of writing is no longer based on *inventio* (imagination) or the rephrasing of experience. In the discourse network of 1900, writing means something akin to receiving, channeling, or playing back existing files. It is fashioned after the automatic receptivity of the electronic media; at its origin one finds the babble (the Babel) of machines, not the intimate pouring of the soul—that "infinitely gentle, infinitely suffering thing." This was clearly perceived by Eliot's reviewers, who often criticized his writing for its excessive bookishness and apparent lack of "lived experience." Clive Bell's words are symptomatic in this respect: "He cannot write in the great manner out of the heart of his subject: birdlike he must pile up wisps and straws of recollection round the tenuous twig of a central idea. And for these wisps and straws he must go generally to books."[3] What Bell and others fail to point out, however, is that the book is no longer the ultimate receptacle of discourse; wisps and straws of language and refracted experience also circulate through a variety of technological devices. The modern poet, whom Pound defined as "antenna of the race," is one of these.

Together with the voices of tradition, automatic receivers pick up noise as well: the communication channels often hiss with static, the sound may be garbled, and the gramophone needle may skip. This random, nonsignifying noise is faithfully transcribed. Noise travels through modernist literature as it does through the media. In part, the solipsism of the moderns may be attributed to the presence in their writing of obstreperous matter that does not

2. T. S. Eliot, "Tradition and the Individual Talent," in *The Sacred Wood* (London: Faber and Faber, 1972), 53–54, 55. [See above, p. 150—*Editor.*]
3. Grant, *Critical Heritage*, 188.

yield meaning. The abrupt, seemingly haphazard transitions of *The Waste Land* are a way to encode the noise in the circuits, as are the occasional forms of glossolalia that punctuate the text:

> The barges wash
> Drifting logs
> Down Greenwich reach
> Past the Isle of Dogs
>   Weialala leia
>   Wallala leialala
>
> And further,
>   la la
> To Carthage then I came
>   Burning burning burning burning
> O Lord thou pluckest me out
> O Lord thou pluckest
> burning.

* * *

At moments like these, literary discourse incorporates noise and momentarily sidesteps reason and understanding. It becomes a matter of pure externality, not a pathway to interiority, meaning, or a postulated "spirit." The media, in a way, displace all these and bring on the nonsignifying pleasures of pure sound—the grain of the voice, the whirrs, clicks, and grinds that always accompany communication relayed through circuits. * * * Touch and noise, traditionally on the outside of meaning, are now its harbingers. Woven with them, meaning itself becomes an intermittence. Discourse is at once message and massage—content *and* tactile stimulus that seems to skip sense and logic and caresses the ear and the skin.

It might be objected that the noise signals in *The Waste Land* are unduly amplified in this essay, that the poem's randomness *does* mean, and that even the least articulate, glossolalic moments respond to plan. However, the connections between fragments are so recondite and the meanings so far-fetched that, as *The Waste Land* first broke into print, it seemed to hover between attitudinizing and illegibility. Until the first efforts at explanation, led by Eliot's footnotes, the poem was consumed in the dark, noise and all. But the notes throw scarce light on the text and do little to filter out meaninglessness. Eliot himself dismissed them as "a remarkable exposition of bogus scholarship";[4] they have primarily aesthetic rather than explanatory value. They prolong and amplify the moods

4. See above, p. 136 [*Editor*].

and atmospheres of the poem by piling on further allusions and images and by suggesting further poetic and narrative departures. Where Eliot was aesthetic, others have tried to be didactic, yet after decades of hermeneutic exertions, scholarly glosses on sources and structure still fall short of explaining the work's fascination.

SARAH COLE

[Violence in *The Waste Land*]†

The Waste Land disperses and disseminates a complex language of aestheticized violence, but the pattern is quietly condensed in one interlude, "Death by Water":

> Phlebas the Phoenician, a fortnight dead,
> Forgot the cry of gulls, and the deep sea swell
> And the profit and loss.
> > A current under sea
> Picked his bones in whispers. As he rose and fell
> He passed the stages of his age and youth
> Entering the whirlpool.
> > Gentile or Jew
> O you who turn the wheel and look to westward,
> Consider Phlebas, who was once handsome and tall
> > as you. (lines 312–21)

Despite its truncated status among the poem's five acts, "Death by Water" has unique features. The powerful, unbroken brevity of these lines (Eliot appended no notes to this section) creates a sense of completeness, which the image of the whirlpool also highlights, a drawing inward, as an antidote to the wild outward spiraling that characterizes so much in the poem's diffuse atmosphere.[1] It is the most meditative section in the poem, a rumination on death, something like a reflective, later stage in the mourning process set in motion by the poem's opening, "The Burial of the Dead." Moreover, even if Phlebas enters a deep forgetfulness—metaphor for death, of course—the water and whirlpool have the effect of reconstituting and recalling, as many of the poem's motifs return here in a softened manner, their edges blunted. The whirlpool acts *in* the poem

---

† From "Enchantment, Disenchantment, War, Literature," *PMLA* 124.5: 1640–47. Reprinted by permission of the Modern Language Association; permission conveyed through Copyright Clearance Center, Inc. Unless otherwise indicated, notes are by the author. Some of the author's notes and parenthetical citations have been omitted, and some notes have been edited.

1. These lines were written, in only slightly different form, in the 1918 poem "Dans le Restaurant" (in French). It was "Death by Water" that Pound most ruthlessly sheared, its nine lines a mere snippet of Eliot's original ninety.

the way it acts *on* Phlebas, transforming and suggesting, in a calm and gestural way, a paradigm for poetic consolation. To enchant, in this sense, is to imagine the body not in its physical agonies or material decomposition—bones have replaced Phlebas's flesh—but as an agent of the creative faculty. The seas generate a self-perpetuating fantasy of immortality and imagination, a site for the churning of images into aesthetic wonders.[2] That drowned bodies should present an especially grim spectacle, moreover, or that drowning might be seen as an especially horrific form of death, only increases the sense of the poem's flex and magic, its sealike ability to effect transformation.

The sea holds many associations in *The Waste Land*. Not only is it a site of death and longing, and a metaphor for purifying change, but it also represents a set of commercial routes and passages, as suggested by one of its representatives in the poem, the Smyrna merchant [l. 209]. A place of trade, Smyrna was a great port city in the early twentieth century, as it had been for centuries. In the period when Eliot was composing *The Waste Land,* it also housed intense internal violence. As anyone reading the papers from 1919 until the time of the poem's publication would have known, the fierce fighting between Greeks and Turks, which enveloped the region, reached a peak in the city of Smyrna. Not only was there a Greek occupation and combat in the streets, but Smyrna also became a locus for the policy of forced migration of Greeks and Turks into separate nations. Eliot himself took a keen interest in these events, writing a letter to the *Daily Mail* in 1923 in which he praised the paper's coverage of the war in Turkey. Here, then, was a location that dramatized the chaos and spiraling violence still being unleashed by the First World War, as the old imperial order disintegrated.

And one more thing: Smyrna is the reputed birthplace of Homer, as Eliot certainly knew.[3] For Homer, the presiding genius of Western literature in general and of the poetry of war and the sea in particular, to underpin the fraught city of Smyrna is to hint at what *The Waste Land* wants to promise, that aesthetic potency will develop directly out of real-world agony. In the years immediately following the war, Homer's connection to Smyrna and to Troy must have provided a powerful association, because the notion, widely held among classicists, that the real first world war was the Trojan War suggested an ongoing cycle of violence, in which war was increasingly intertwined with global commerce—but also, for Eliot, with artistic

---

2. Eliot refers extensively to Shakespeare's *The Tempest* as well as to Wagner's *Tristan and Isolde*. Both works highlight ache and loss with respect to the sea, but also trickery and magic spells—other forms of enchantment.

3. For centuries there has been debate about Homer's birthplace: Smyrna versus the island of Chios. When *The Waste Land* was written, the dominant theory was that Homer most likely came from Smyrna or composed *The Iliad* there. See Denton J. Snider, *The Biographical Outline of Homer* (Saint Louis: Miner, 1922).

payoff. The Smyrna merchant, holding in his person the explosive and terrible history of modern nations, simultaneously brings the complex legacy of modern war into view and obscures the picture, as the poem pursues its own goal of erecting new monuments on the site of still-smoldering ruins. Thus the merchant's mutation into Phlebas in the following section, himself soon to be metamorphosed by watery transformation into something rich and strange, seems a willful relief, an aesthetic forgetting of modern calamity. Or perhaps it is a signal that even such intransigent conflicts as those left in the wake of the Ottoman Empire can be amalgamated into the imaginative project of enchantment.

The whirlpool may create an inward spiral, a vast embrace and ingathering vortex, but *The Waste Land* opens with burial in the ground, and it is the problem of the corpse that requires Eliot to invoke the sea as a contrastive death fantasy. In the poem's celebrated opening, Eliot sets the stage for a rumination on the land and the dead. The lines, so different in spirit from the drunken brothel scene that inaugurated the draft version, convey multiple valences on the way death and land conjure each other, including the vegetative structure of resurrection and life worship referenced in Eliot's opening note, in which he invokes Frazer and Weston. Of course, it will not be long before the metaphor of death leading to new flowers takes comic shape:

> There I saw one I knew, and stopped him, crying,
>   "Stetson!
> "You who were with me in the ships at Mylae!
> "That corpse you planted last year in your garden,
> "Has it begun to sprout? Will it bloom this
>   year? . . ."   (ll. 69–72)

* * *

In addition to drowning and burial, several other images in the poem reach out in the direction of enchantment. Most central is color, a riveting site of intensity. There are many colors in the poem—white, brown, ivory, gold, green, orange, black, and red (this last particularly pronounced)—and they are part of the dense sensory pattern that characterizes *The Waste Land* at every stage. But there is something special and unique about one color, and that is violet. The word *violet* is used four times in the poem, twice in quick succession, and each time it describes something ethereal or amorphous in the atmosphere:

> At the violet hour, when the eyes and back
> Turn upward from the desk, when the human engine waits
> Like a taxi throbbing waiting, . . .   (ll. 215–17)

> At the violet hour, the evening hour that strives
> Homeward, and brings the sailor home from
>   the sea,
> The typist home at teatime, . . .   (ll. 220–22)

> What is the city over the mountains
> Cracks and reforms and bursts in the violet
>   air . . .   (ll. 370–71)

> And bats with baby faces in the violet light
> Whistled, and beat their wings . . . (ll. 379–80)

The hour, air, and light—each iteration attempts to capture something both precise and uncertain in the moment. In the first two examples, the violet hour is twilight, a time of transitions and transformations, literally as day turns to night, figuratively as a hovering between one mode of existence and the next, a thick and tense anticipatory pause, as indicated by the image of the human engine throbbing. Even in the context of the depleted and degraded sexual interaction between the typist and the "young man carbuncular" (l. 231), the violet hour is a time of enchantment, the word "violet" adding luster and shine to the sordid occasion. Its use is partly mock-heroic and ironic, but it is also real; its beauty and resonance transform the lines, enhancing the sense of anticipation and tragedy in the scene. When air and light and the hour are violet—the color of sorcery in *The Odyssey,* of Mary's poignant humility in Christian iconography, and of both mourning and royalty in the modern world—they seem piercing, aesthetic, saturated, deepened.

Perhaps most importantly, the word *violet* is so close to *violent* as nearly to become it, and certainly suggests it. This metonymic affinity is further tightened when we consider that each time "violet" is used, it is at a place in the poem when violence impends. The violet air tolls with the apocalyptic sound of bells and the explosions of warfare; the violet light is the light of terror, after and before such reverberations, of burning cities, also of bats and hysterical strains; the violet hour is a time of compressed urban rage, the human energy beastlike in its containment, and of impending sexual assault. For *The Waste Land,* the nature of violet is to usher in violence, to herald or represent it; but it is also to soften and beautify it. Indeed, violetness is an emblem of enchantment at its most enriching. Its transforming energy is all in the direction of the aesthetic; it forges an exceptionally sensitive kind of perception.

Such transformation would seem especially welcome in the case of the swallow and Philomela, two interlocked figures that are deeply embedded in the poem's language of violence. The Philomela narrative first arises in "A Game of Chess," where it forms part of a painting to adorn the lady's room:

> Above the antique mantel was displayed
> As though a window gave upon the sylvan scene
> The change of Philomel, by the barbarous king
> So rudely forced; yet there the nightingale
> Filled all the desert with inviolable voice
> And still she cried, and still the world pursues,
> "Jug Jug" to dirty ears.
> And other withered stumps of time
> Were told upon the walls; staring forms
> Leaned out, leaning, hushing the room
>   enclosed.   (ll. 97–106)

Philomela's is a terrible tale: lured to the woods by her sister Procne's husband, King Tereus, she is isolated, raped, and then silenced by having her tongue cut out. That she is ultimately able to communicate her tale by a clever ruse, spinning her story into a loom, and that she and her sister, having taken grisly revenge on the king, are transformed, along with Tereus, into birds—such artistic outcomes seem only mildly reparative after the extremity of her violation and suffering. Indeed, in Ovid's canonical telling of the myth in *Metamorphoses*, there is no sense of recompense (no "yet") in the "inviolable voice" of the nightingale.[4] It is Eliot's proclivity to stress the compensatory nature of song, "the change of Philomel." The poem emphasizes how art becomes a lingering record and a sensory trace for the violence that cannot be spoken directly—as Philomela cannot speak her own story and must create a form of pictorial art to convey the events.

Although Eliot shows how the rape and mutilation are, in effect, enchanted into art, the text is not exactly complacent about such an outcome. For one, the transliteration of "Jug Jug," even before we get to "dirty ears," is an ugly sound, far from the "ecstatic sound" or "full-throated ease" of Keats's or Hardy's nightingale.[5] And, too, "other withered stumps of time / Were told upon the walls": these stumps suggest a later literary iteration, Shakespeare's Lavinia from *Titus Andronicus*, who not only had her tongue chopped off but also her hands (to prevent her from taking Philomela's route of writing her way to explication and revenge). More generally, the phrase suggests a weariness with the subject matter of art in its most

4. See above, pp. 48–51 [*Editor*].
5. Thomas Hardy (1840–1928), "The Darkling Thrush" (l. 26); John Keats (1795–1821), "Ode to a Nightingale" (l. 10) [*Editor*].

time-weathered manifestations. Those staring forms seem less exalted than traumatized, a painted version of contemporary shell shock.

The stumps can also be read more literally: they evoke amputated arms, bringing the visual spectacle of war's injuries into view. If Eliot's contemporary culture often worked to avert its collective glance from the war's lasting attack on the flesh, here the disenchanting imperative to see those amputated limbs is enfolded into Eliot's larger plot line.[6] The stumps have withered; they point to a long future, well beyond the immediate blast of injuring. Art, it seems, continually tells the longest stories of brutality. Its narratives cannot erase, perhaps cannot even fully beautify, the horrors that human beings inflict on one another. On one hand, then, the poem relies on the chain of powerful associations that the history of literature has bequeathed, including the history of ghastly violence; it makes its music from these. The poem is like Philomela herself, another creature of the violet hour, who wove her loom out of the color we might have intuited, purple. On the other hand, the poem hates these stumps, and their repeated appearances have the effect of a sputter or involuntary cough, irruptions that simply cannot be avoided.

The withered stumps of Philomela's rape return on several occasions, always in disruptive, broken phrases, suggesting the kind of abrasive and uncomfortable role in the poem that actual stumps played in postwar civilian culture. These passages (there are only a few in the poem) read like chunks of linguistic jetsam in the midst of the poem's larger sea:

> Twit twit twit
> Jug jug jug jug jug jug
> So rudely forc'd
> Tereu   (ll. 202–06)

These strange sounds hold in their tight, nearly nonrepresentational packages a sense of what the world does not want to be its oldest stories. As such, they cannot be excluded from Eliot's larger poetic project. They are withered stumps of time, but these half-erased traces of old stories are also resonant little bits of song in their own right, an interesting and important complement to such melodies as the nymphs' chorus ("Wiealala leia / Wallala leialala"), the Augustinian chant ("Burning burning burning burning") and the cry of the desert ("Drip drop drip drop drop drop drop"), which Eliot thought

---

6. For discussion of this phenomenon of looking and not looking at the injuries of returned soldiers after the war, see Joanna Bourke, *Dismembering the Male: Men's Bodies, Britain, and the Great War* (Chicago: U of Chicago P, 1996); Sarah Cole, *Modernism, Male Friendship, and the First World War* (Cambridge: Cambridge UP, 2003).

one of the most beautiful parts of *The Waste Land* (ll. 277–78, 309, 357).[7] There is power in those repetitions, as there is in the poem's final benediction, the thrice-repeated *shantih*. At the same time, these bursts of language can also be read in the opposite way, as broken echoes of disenchantment, as symptoms of an anti-aesthetic spirit that emerges, side by side with enchantment, from the violent events at the base of the poem. The narratives bound to those repeated words are dense, elaborate, and terrible; what they offer is, in their own way, thick with history and experience.

In *The Waste Land's* final burst of stuttered lines, Philomela's story reappears in the image of the swallow, solidifying its place at the endpoint of the poem's violent trajectory and returning us to the poem's other primary locus for the aestheticizing of violence, the whirlpool. The swallow represents the way art filters and keeps alive the most detestable crimes. Its language is that of tortured remembering, which forces a withered history into the present. Yet the swallow also represents that burst of song that rises even from the pits of human experience. The whirlpool, too, makes art out of destruction, with its transformative, magical properties. If the swallow combats silence, the whirlpool creates it, its whispering currents a kind of speaking silence. For both, in *The Waste Land*, the central idea is to utilize imagery of change, rebirth, resurrection, and metamorphosis as part of a reflection on the troubling relation between art, with its core commitment to beautiful forms, and the violence that has wrecked human life throughout history, most recently, for Eliot, in the First World War.

The Waste Land can come to no conclusion about this basic contradiction. To recognize that art neither flees violence, nor transcends it, nor merely represents it, but rather that it trades on its power, at times appropriating its force and creating something especially brilliant, at other times succumbing to the sheer waste that violence leaves in its wake: such an insight represents, in poetic form, one of the signal achievements of Eliot's poem. *The Waste Land* offers a way to understand literature as a self-conscious artifact produced out of and within a history of violence, recognizing its origins in a frightful set of half-forgotten tales.[8] It is precisely this willingness to offer a poetic of enchantment that at the same

7. For reference to Eliot's praise of the water-dripping lines (in a letter to Ford Madox Ford), see B. C. Southam, *A Guide to the Selected Poems of T. S. Eliot* [San Diego: Harcourt, 1984].

8. Impacted in the poem's last eight lines are not only the swallow but also the London Bridge rhyme (of which one verse is "Take the key and lock her up"), Hieronymo's murder spree in *The Spanish Tragedy* (a tale of wild, theatrical violence), and the kind of ruined architecture often associated with war ("these fragments," "la tour abolie"). To reach the Eastern peace encoded in the three *shantihs*, we must pass through a corridor of Western violence.

time ruthlessly disenchants its own origins, that sets Eliot's work off from many other engagements with violence in the period—especially those that grew out of the war, with its dichotomizing energy. It is one of the poem's accomplishments that it can see in violence the genesis of beauty and form—as Yeats wrote in relation to his own moment of enchanted violence, "A terrible beauty is born"—and can also vivify the human tragedies that are swept into that old, innocuous phrase, "the waste of war."[9]

9. W. B. Yeats (1865–1939), "Easter 1916." "Waste of war" does not appear in that poem but is proverbial [Editor].

T. S. Eliot: A Chronology

1888   Born on September 26 in St. Louis, Missouri.

1898   Attends Smith Academy, St. Louis.

1904   Attends St. Louis World's Fair.

1905   Graduates from Smith. Spends the academic year 1905–06 at Milton Academy, Milton, Massachusetts.

1906   Matriculates at Harvard.

1907   Publishes several poems in *The Harvard Advocate*. Meets Conrad Aiken.

1909   Joins the editorial board of the *Advocate*, having published several more poems there. Receives his B.A. and begins graduate work in literature and philosophy.

1910   Delivers Class Ode at graduation. Receives his M.A., having studied with Irving Babbitt and George Santayana. Travels to Paris to attend the Sorbonne. Attends lectures of Henri Bergson at the Collège de France. Meets Alain-Fournier and Jean Verdenal.

1911   Visits London for the first time. Returns to the United States and to Harvard Graduate School to pursue a Ph.D. in philosophy. Completes "Prufrock," "Portrait of a Lady," and "Preludes."

1913   Reads F. H. Bradley's *Appearance and Reality*. Studies with Josiah Royce.

1914   Meets Bertrand Russell, who is visiting at Harvard. Receives a Sheldon Travelling Fellowship to study philosophy at Merton College, Oxford. In London, meets Ezra Pound, who sends "Prufrock" to *Poetry*. Earliest fragments of *The Waste Land* (later incorporated into the poem as lines 377–84) composed.

1915   Marries Vivien Haigh-Wood on June 26. "Prufrock," "Preludes," and "Portrait of a Lady" published. After a visit to his parents in the United States, returns to England and makes his permanent home there. Teaches at High Wycombe Grammar School.

1916   Teaches at Highgate Junior School. Thesis accepted at Harvard. Through Russell, gains acquaintance with Bloomsbury Group, including Virginia Woolf.

1917   Takes a job in the Colonial and Foreign department of Lloyds Bank. *Prufrock and Other Observations* published.

1919   "Tradition and the Individual Talent" published in *The Egoist*. *Poems* published by Leonard and Virginia Woolf at Hogarth Press.

1920   *Ara Vos Prec* published in England, *Poems* by Knopf in the United States. Meets James Joyce in Paris. *The Sacred Wood*, Eliot's first collection of essays, published. First explicit mention of *The Waste Land*, in letter to his mother, September 20.

1921   After mental and physical collapse, given three months leave from Lloyds. Spends time at Margate in October, then goes to Lausanne for treatment in November, during which time the *Waste Land* drafts are completed.

1922   Pound and Eliot revise *The Waste Land*, which appears in the first issue of *The Criterion*, a new magazine edited by Eliot, and then in *The Dial*. Published in book form in December by Boni & Liveright.

1923   *The Waste Land* published in England by Leonard and Virginia Woolf at Hogarth Press.

1924   *Homage to John Dryden*, a second collection of essays, published.

1925   Leaves Lloyds to join Faber & Gwyer (later Faber & Faber) as editor and publisher. *Poems 1909–1925* (including "The Hollow Men") published by Faber.

1926   Delivers the Clark Lectures at Cambridge. *Sweeney Agonistes* published in *The Criterion*.

1927   Joins the Church of England and becomes a British citizen.

1928   Publishes *For Lancelot Andrewes: Essays on Style and Order* and in the preface delivers his famous self-description: "classicist in literature, royalist in politics, and anglo-catholic in religion."

1930   *Ash-Wednesday* published.

1932   Begins academic term as Charles Eliot Norton Professor of Poetry at Harvard.

1933   Harvard lectures published as *The Use of Poetry and the Use of Criticism*. Delivers lectures at University of Virginia later published as *After Strange Gods*. Separates from Vivien Eliot.

1935   *Murder in the Cathedral* first performed.

1936   *Burnt Norton* published in *Collected Poems 1909–1935*.

1938   Vivien Eliot certified insane and committed to an asylum for the rest of her life.

1939   *The Criterion* ceases publication. *The Family Reunion* first performed. *Old Possum's Book of Practical Cats* published.
1943   Complete version of *Four Quartets* published.
1947   Vivien Eliot dies.
1948   Awarded the Order of Merit and the Nobel Prize for Literature. *Notes towards the Definition of Culture* published.
1949   *The Cocktail Party* first performed.
1953   *The Confidential Clerk* first performed.
1957   Marries Valerie Fletcher on January 10. *On Poetry and Poets* published.
1958   *The Elder Statesman* first performed.
1964   Awarded U.S. Medal of Freedom.
1965   Dies on January 4. Ashes deposited at East Coker.

Selected Bibliography

• indicates works included or excerpted in this Norton Critical Edition.

BIBLIOGRAPHIES

Blalock, Susan E. *Guide to the Secular Poetry of T. S. Eliot*. New York: G. K. Hall, 1996.

Frank, Mechthild, Armin Paul Frank, and J. P. S. Jochum. T. S. *Eliot Criticism in English, 1916–1965: A Supplementary Bibliography*. Edmonton: Yeats Eliot Review, 1978.

Gallup, Donald. *T. S. Eliot: A Bibliography*. New York: Harcourt, Brace & World, 1969.

Knowles, Sebastian D. G. and Scott A. Leonard. *An Annotated Bibliography of a Decade of T. S. Eliot Criticism: 1977–1986*. Orono, ME: National Poetry Foundation, 1992.

Martin, Mildred. *A Half-Century of Eliot Criticism: An Annotated Bibliography of Books and Articles in English, 1916–1965*. Lewisburg, PA: Bucknell UP, 1972.

Ricks, Beatrice. *T. S. Eliot: A Bibliography of Secondary Works*. Metuchen, NJ, and London: Scarecrow P, 1980.

BIOGRAPHIES

Ackroyd, Peter. *T. S. Eliot: A Life*. New York: Simon and Schuster, 1984.

Behr, Caroline. *T. S. Eliot: A Chronology of His Life and Works*. London: Macmillan, 1983.

Crawford, Robert. *Young Eliot: From St. Louis to* The Waste Land. New York, Farrar, Straus and Giroux, 2015.

• Gordon, Lyndall. *The Imperfect Life of T. S. Eliot*. London: Virago, 2012.

Kirk, Russell. *T. S. Eliot and His Age*. New York: Random House, 1971.

Seymour-Jones, Caroline. *Painted Shadow: A Life of Vivienne Eliot*. London: Constable, 2001.

WORKS AND EDITIONS

• *Prufrock and Other Observations*. London: Egoist P, 1917.

Poems. London: Hogarth P, 1919.

Ara Vos Prec. London: Ovid P, 1920.

• *Poems*. New York: Knopf, 1920.

The Sacred Wood. London: Methuen, 1920.

• *The Waste Land*. New York: Boni & Liveright, 1922.

Homage to John Dryden. London: Hogarth P, 1924.

Poems 1909–1925. London: Faber & Gwyer, 1925.

For Lancelot Andrewes: Essays on Style and Order. London: Faber & Gwyer, 1928.

Ash-Wednesday. London: Faber & Faber; New York: Putnam's, 1930.

Selected Essays, 1917–1932. London: Faber & Faber; New York: Harcourt, Brace, 1932.

Sweeney Agonistes. London: Faber & Faber, 1932.

The Use of Poetry and the Use of Criticism. London: Faber & Faber; Cambridge, MA: Harvard UP, 1933.

After Strange Gods. London: Faber & Faber; New York: Harcourt, Brace, 1934.

Murder in the Cathedral. London: Faber & Faber; New York: Harcourt, Brace, 1935.

Collected Poems: 1909–1935. London: Faber & Faber; New York: Harcourt, Brace, 1936.

Essays Ancient and Modern. London: Faber & Faber; New York: Harcourt, Brace, 1936.

The Family Reunion. London: Faber & Faber; New York: Harcourt, Brace, 1939.

The Idea of a Christian Society. London: Faber & Faber, 1939.

Old Possum's Book of Practical Cats. London: Faber & Faber; New York: Harcourt, Brace, 1939.

Four Quartets. London: Faber & Faber; New York: Harcourt, Brace, 1943.

Notes towards a Definition of Culture. London: Faber & Faber, 1948.

The Cocktail Party. London: Faber & Faber; New York: Harcourt, Brace, 1950.

The Confidential Clerk. London: Faber & Faber; New York: Harcourt, Brace, 1954.

On Poetry and Poets. London: Faber & Faber; New York: Farrar, Straus, 1957.

The Elder Statesman. London: Faber & Faber; New York: Farrar, Straus, 1959.

Collected Poems 1909–1962. London: Faber & Faber; New York: Harcourt, Brace & World, 1963.

Knowledge and Experience in the Philosophy of F. H. Bradley. London: Faber & Faber; New York: Farrar, Straus, 1964.

To Criticize the Critic. London: Faber & Faber; New York: Farrar, Straus, 1965.

Complete Plays. New York: Harcourt, Brace, 1967.

Poems Written in Early Youth. London: Faber & Faber; New York: Farrar, Straus, 1967.

Complete Poems and Plays. London: Faber & Faber, 1969.

The Waste Land: A Facsimile and Transcript of the Original Drafts Including the Annotations of Ezra Pound. Ed. Valerie Eliot. London: Faber & Faber; New York: Harcourt Brace Jovanovich, 1971.

The Varieties of Metaphysical Poetry: The Clark Lectures at Trinity College, Cambridge, 1926, and the Turnbull Lectures at the Johns Hopkins University, 1933. Ed. Ronald Schuchard. London: Faber & Faber, 1993.

Inventions of the March Hare: Poems 1909–1917. Ed. Christopher Ricks. London: Faber & Faber; New York: Harcourt Brace, 1996.

The Letters of T. S. Eliot. Ed. Valerie Eliot and Hugh Haughton. New Haven: Yale UP, 2011–16.

The Poems of T. S. Eliot: Collected and Uncollected Poems. Ed. Christopher Ricks and Jim McCue. New York: Farrar, Straus and Giroux, 2015.

CRITICISM

• Aiken, Conrad. "An Anatomy of Melancholy." *The New Republic* (7 February 1922): 294–95.

Albright, Daniel. *Quantum Poetics: Yeats, Pound, Eliot, and the Science of Modernism.* Cambridge, Eng.: Cambridge UP, 1997.

• Armstrong, Tim. *Modernism, Technology, and the Body.* Cambridge, Eng.: Cambridge UP, 1998.

Bedient, Calvin. *He Do the Police in Different Voices:* The Waste Land *and Its Protagonist.* Chicago: U of Chicago P, 1986.

Bergonzi, Bernard. *T. S. Eliot.* New York: Macmillan, 1972.

Blackmur, R. P. "T. S. Eliot." *Hound and Horn* 1 (1928): 187–210.

———. *Anni Mirabiles, 1921–1925*. Washington: Library of Congress, 1956.

Bolgan, Anne C. *What the Thunder Really Said: A Retrospective Essay on the Making of* The Waste Land. Montreal: McGill-Queen's UP, 1973.

Booth, Allyson. *Reading* The Waste Land *from the Bottom Up*. New York: Palgrave Macmillan, 2015.

Brooker, Jewel Spears. *Mastery and Escape: T. S. Eliot and the Dialectic of Modernism*. Amherst: U of Massachusetts P, 1994.

Brooker, Jewel Spears and Joseph Bentley. *Reading* The Waste Land: *Modernism and the Limits of Interpretation*. Amherst: U of Massachusetts P, 1990.

• Brooks, Jr., Cleanth. *Modern Poetry and the Tradition*. Chapel Hill: U of North Carolina P, 1939.

Bush, Ronald. *T. S. Eliot: A Study in Character and Style*. New York: Oxford UP, 1983.

———, ed. *T. S. Eliot: The Modernist in History*. Cambridge: Cambridge UP, 1991.

Calder, Angus. *T. S. Eliot*. Brighton, Eng.: Harvester P, 1987.

Chinitz, David. *T. S. Eliot and the Cultural Divide*. Chicago: U of Chicago P, 2003.

Clarke, Graham, ed. *T. S. Eliot: Critical Assessments*. London: Christopher Helm, 1990.

Cole, Sarah. *At the Violet Hour: Modernism and Violence in England and Ireland*. New York: Oxford UP, 2014.

• Cowley, Malcolm. *Exile's Return: A Literary Odyssey of the 1920's* (New York: Viking, 1951).

Craig, David. "The Defeatism of *The Waste Land*." *Critical Quarterly* 2 (1960): 241–52.

Crawford, Robert. *The Savage and the City in the Work of T. S. Eliot*. Oxford, Eng.: Clarendon P, 1987.

Cuddy, Lois A. and David Hirsch, eds. *Critical Essays on T. S. Eliot's* The Waste Land. Boston: G. K. Hall, 1991.

Davidson, Harriet. *T. S. Eliot and Hermeneutics: Absence and Interpretation in* The Waste Land. Baton Rouge: Louisiana State UP, 1985.

Drew, Elizabeth. *T. S. Eliot: The Design of His Poetry*. New York: Scribner's, 1949.

• Ellison, Ralph. *Shadow and Act* (New York: Random House, 1964).

• Ellmann, Maud. *The Poetics of Impersonality: T. S. Eliot and Ezra Pound*. Cambridge, MA: Harvard UP, 1987.

Froula, Christine. "Eliot's Grail Quest: Or, the Lover, the Police, and *The Waste Land*." *Yale Review* 78.2 (Winter 1989): 235–53.

———. "Corpse, Monument, *Hypocrite Lecteur*." *Text* 9 (1996): 297–314.

Frye, Northrop. *T. S. Eliot*. Chicago: U of Chicago P, 1963.

Gardner, Helen. *The Art of T. S. Eliot*. New York: Dutton, 1959.

Grant, Michael, ed. *T. S. Eliot: The Critical Heritage*. London: Routledge and Kegan Paul, 1982.

Gray, Piers. *T. S. Eliot's Intellectual and Poetic Development 1909–1922*. Brighton, Eng.: Harvester, 1982.

Hay, Eloise Knapp. *T. S. Eliot's Negative Way*. Cambridge, MA: Harvard UP, 1982.

Jay, Gregory. *T. S. Eliot and the Poetics of Literary History*. Baton Rouge: Louisiana State UP, 1983.

Julius, Anthony. *T. S. Eliot: Anti-Semitism and Literary Form*. London: Thames & Hudson, 2003.

Kearns, Cleo McNelly. *T. S. Eliot and Indic Traditions: A Study in Poetry and Belief*. Cambridge, MA: Cambridge UP, 1987.

• Kenner, Hugh. "Prufrock of St. Louis." *Prairie Schooner* 31.1 (Spring 1957): 24–30.

———. *The Invisible Poet: T. S. Eliot*. New York: Harcourt, Brace & World, 1959.

Koestenbaum, Wayne. *Double Talk: The Erotics of Male Literary Collaboration*. New York: Routledge, 1989.

Langbaum, Robert. *The Mysteries of Identity: A Theme in Modern Literature.* New York: Oxford UP, 1977.

• Leavis, F. R. *New Bearings in English Poetry.* London: Chatto & Windus, 1932.

Lentricchia, Frank. *Modernist Quartet.* Cambridge, Eng.: Cambridge UP, 1994.

Levenson, Michael. *A Genealogy of Modernism: A Study of English Literary Doctrine, 1908–1922.* Cambridge, Eng.: Cambridge UP, 1984.

Litz, A. Walton, ed. *Eliot in His Time.* Princeton: Princeton UP, 1973.

Longenbach, James. *Modernist Poetics of History: Pound, Eliot, and the Sense of the Past.* Princeton: Princeton UP, 1987.

MacCabe, Colin. *T. S. Eliot.* Tavistock: Northcote House, 2006.

Manganaro, Marc. "Dissociation in 'Dead Land': The Primitive Mind in the Early Poetry of T. S. Eliot." *Journal of Modern Literature* 13.1 (1986): 97–110.

Martin, Graham, ed. *Eliot in Perspective.* London: Macmillan, 1970.

Materer, Timothy. *Vortex: Pound, Eliot, and Lewis.* Ithaca: Cornell UP, 1979.

Matthiessen, F. O. *The Achievement of T. S. Eliot.* Boston: Houghton Mifflin, 1935.

McIntire, Gabrielle. *Modernism, Memory, and Desire: T. S. Eliot and Virginia Woolf.* Cambridge, Eng.: Cambridge UP, 2008.

Menand, Louis. *Discovering Modernism: T. S. Eliot and His Context.* New York: Oxford UP, 1987.

Moody, A. D., ed. The Waste Land *in Different Voices.* London: Edward Arnold, 1974.

———. *Thomas Stearns Eliot: Poet.* Cambridge, Eng.: Cambridge UP, 1979.

———, ed. *The Cambridge Companion to T. S. Eliot.* Cambridge, Eng.: Cambridge UP, 1994.

Moretti, Franco. *Signs Taken for Wonders: Essays in the Sociology of Literary Forms.* Tr. Susan Fischer, David Forgacs, and David Miller. London: Verso, 1983.

North, Michael. *The Political Aesthetic of Yeats, Eliot, and Pound.* Cambridge, Eng.: Cambridge UP, 1991.

———. *The Dialect of Modernism: Race, Language, and Twentieth Century Literature.* Oxford, Eng.: Oxford UP, 1994.

———. "T. S. Eliot." In *The Cambridge Companion to English Poets.* Ed. Claude Rawson. Cambridge, Eng.: Cambridge UP, 2011, pp. 491–507.

Pearce, Roy Harvey. *The Continuity of American Poetry.* Princeton: Princeton UP, 1961.

Perl, Jeffery M. *Skepticism and Modern Enmity: Before and After Eliot.* Baltimore: Johns Hopkins UP, 1989.

• Perloff, Marjorie. *Differentials: Poetry, Politics, Pedagogy.* Tuscaloosa: U of Alabama P, 2004.

• Pound, Ezra. "T. S. Eliot." *Poetry* 10 (August 1917): 265–71.

Raine, Craig. *T. S. Eliot.* Oxford, Eng.: Oxford University Press, 2006.

Rainey, Lawrence. *Institutions of Modernism: Literary Elites and Public Culture.* New Haven: Yale UP; 1998.

• ———. *Revisiting* The Waste Land. New Haven: Yale UP, 2005.

• Richards, I. A. *Principles of Literary Criticism.* New York: Harcourt, Brace, 1926.

Ricks, Christopher. *T. S. Eliot and Prejudice.* Berkeley: U of California P, 1988.

———. *Decisions and Revisions in T. S. Eliot.* London: British Library; Faber & Faber, 2003.

• Riding, Laura and Robert Graves. *A Survey of Modern Poetry* (Garden City, NY: Doubleday, Doran, 1928).

Riquelme, John Paul. "'Withered Stumps of Time': Allusion, Reading and Writing in *The Waste Land.*" *Denver Quarterly* 15 (1981): 90–110.

Rosenthal M. L. *Sailing into the Unknown: Yeats, Pound, and Eliot.* New York: Oxford UP, 1978.

Ross, Andrew. *The Failure of Modernism: Symptoms of American Poetry*. New York: Columbia UP, 1986.

• Schwartz, Delmore. "T. S. Eliot as International Hero." *Partisan Review* 12 (Spring 1995): 199–206.

Schwartz, Sanford. *The Matrix of Modernism: Pound, Eliot, and Early Twentieth Century Thought*. Princeton: Princeton UP, 1985.

Scofield, Martin. *T. S. Eliot: The Poems*. Cambridge, Eng.: Cambridge UP, 1988.

Seldes, Gilbert. "T. S. Eliot." *The Nation* (6 December 1922): 614–16.

Sherry, Vincent. *Modernism and the Reinvention of Decadence*. Cambridge, Eng.: Cambridge UP, 2015.

Shusterman, Richard. *T. S. Eliot and the Philosophy of Criticism*. New York: Columbia UP, 1988.

• Sinclair, May. "*Prufrock and Other Observations*: A Criticism." *The Little Review* 4 (December 1917): 8–14.

Smith, Grover. *T. S. Eliot's Poetry and Plays*. Chicago: U of Chicago P, 1974.

———. *The Waste Land*. London: Allen and Unwin, 1983.

Spanos, William. "Repetition in *The Waste Land*: A Phenomenological De-Struction." *Boundary* 27 (1979): 225–85.

Spender, Stephen. *T. S. Eliot*. New York: Viking, 1975.

Spurr, David. *Conflicts in Consciousness: T. S. Eliot's Poetry and Criticism*. Urbana: U of Illinois P, 1984.

Stead, C. K. *Pound, Yeats, Eliot and the Modernist Movement*. Basingstoke, Eng.: Macmillan, 1986.

• Suárez, Juan. *Pop Modernism: Noise and the Reinvention of the Everyday*. Champaign: U of Illinois P, 2007.

Tate, Allen, ed. *T. S. Eliot: The Man and His Work*. New York: Delacorte, 1966.

Thormählen, Marianne. *The Waste Land: A Fragmentary Wholeness*. Lund, Sweden: Gleerup, 1978.

• Trotter, David. "Modernism and Empire: Reading *The Waste Land*." *Critical Quarterly* 28.1–2 (1986): 143–53.

• Vendler, Helen. *Coming of Age as a Poet: Milton, Keats, Eliot, Plath*. Cambridge, MA: Harvard UP, 2003.

• Waugh, Arthur. "The New Poetry." *Quarterly Review* (October 1916): 384–86.

• Wilson, Edmund. "The Poetry of Drouth." *The Dial* 73 (December 1922): 611–16.

———. *Axel's Castle*. New York: Scribner's, 1931.

• Woolf, Virginia. "Is This Poetry?" *The Athanaeum* (June 20, 1919): 491.

• Wylie, Elinor. "Mr. Eliot's Slug-Horn." *New York Evening Post Literary Review* (20 January 1923): 396.